ASTROGEOGRAPHIA

Siderial Babylonian System.

Books by Robert Powell

Christian Hermetic Astrology
The Star of the Magi and the Life of Christ

Chronicle of the Living Christ
The Life and Ministry of Jesus Christ
Foundations of Cosmic Christianity

Cultivating Inner Radiance and the Body of Immortality
Awakening the Soul through Modern Etheric Movement

Elijah Come Again
A Prophet for Our Time
A Scientific Approach to Reincarnation

The Most Holy Trinosophia
The New Revelation of the Divine Feminine

The Mystery, Biography & Destiny of Mary Magdalene
Sister of Lazarus John & Spiritual Sister of Jesus

Prophecy - Phenomena - Hope
The Real Meaning of 2012

The Sophia Teachings
The Emergence of the Divine Feminine in Our Time

Books Coauthored with Kevin Dann

The Astrological Revolution
Unveiling the Science of the Stars
as a Science of Reincarnation and Karma

Christ & the Maya Calendar
2012 & the Coming of the Antichrist

Edited by Robert Powell

Journal for Star Wisdom (annual)

The Clockwise House System
A True Foundation for Sidereal and Tropical Astrology
by Jacques Dorsan (edited with Wain Farrants)

ASTROGEOGRAPHIA

Correspondences between the Stars and Earthly Locations

A Bible of Astrology and Earth Chakras

ROBERT POWELL
DAVID BOWDEN

Lindisfarne Books
2012

Lindisfarne Books
An imprint of SteinerBooks / Anthroposophic Press, Inc.
610 Main St., Great Barrington, MA 01230
www.steinerbooks.org

Design: William Jens Jensen

Library of Congress Control Number: 2012954590

Print edition: ISBN 978-1-58420-133-5

eBook edition: ISBN 978-1-58420-134-2

Contents

Introduction

For many years a widespread awakening not only to the beauty and majesty but also to the sacredness of our Earth has been taking place, and many books have been written on this theme—The Sacred Earth (1991) being just one example.[1] Other more recent works that take the Earth's sacredness as their starting point and then go a step further to consider the spirituality of the Earth are Shambhala[2] and Sacred Geography.[3] These three works are mentioned as examples, for there are many other books on the sacredness and the spirituality of the Earth. Few books, however, deal with the relationship between the Earth and the cosmos. This, however, is the central theme for the research presented in this book, which takes as its point of departure that there is a one-to-one correspondence between the encircling round of the starry heavens, the celestial sphere, and the sphere of the Earth's globe. My coauthor, David Bowden, has not only worked out the mathematics of this one-to-one correspondence but has also written a computer program that applies it in practice.[4] Thus a new science has been born—*Astrogeographia*—concerning the one-to-one correspondence between the earthly sphere and the celestial sphere.

While working on the manuscript of this book, there was worldwide uproar over the cartoon depictions of the Prophet Muhammad, originally printed in a Danish newspaper and then reprinted across Europe. Arab ambassadors in Copenhagen thrust the affair into the international arena by calling upon the Danish government to punish

1 Milne, *The Sacred Earth.*

2 LePage, *Shambhala.*

3 Pogacnik, *Sacred Geography.*

4 See chapter 8, appendix 1 (available at astrogeographia.org), and chapter 10 concerning Earth chakras.

the publisher. From Palestine to Pakistan the Danish flag was burnt to protest the newspaper caricatures of the Prophet Muhammad. Fleming Rose, the editor of the liberal Danish newspaper *Jyllands-Posten*, with a relatively small circulation (150,000) in a country of only five million people, saw no reason to apologize for having published the cartoons, especially considering that Danish prosecutors had determined that the cartoons were not blasphemous. In the opinion of Fleming Rose: "I think it would be unfortunate if people in Saudi Arabia or some other parts of the world influenced what we speak about in Denmark."[5] Nevertheless the response, with Muslims across the globe taking to the streets in protest, was sometimes militant and violent, embassies and other buildings were attacked and several deaths occurred as a consequence of the violence.

Just around the time of these violent demonstrations Mars entered Taurus (February 7, 2006)[6] and the red planet was visible in the evening sky approaching the star cluster of the Pleiades, located at 5° Taurus, marking the neck of the Bull. As described in this book, there is a one-to-one correspondence between the starry heavens and the terrestrial globe such that every star is mirrored at a unique place on the Earth's surface. For example, the star Alnitak in the belt of Orion is aligned with the Great Pyramid at Giza, and the star Alnilam (also in the belt of Orion) is projected onto the globe in the region of the city of Alexandria in Egypt. I had made the discovery of the one-to-one correspondence between the celestial and terrestrial globes in October 2005, naming this new science Astrogeographia. Already at that time I saw that the Pleiades, marking the neck of the Bull in Taurus, are mirrored on the Earth just off the west coast of Denmark. Imagine my consternation upon perceiving in the night sky Mars, identified in ancient times as "the planet of war," approaching the Pleiades and simultaneously seeing in the media Denmark at the center of a violent controversy, very Mars-like in character. The connection of Mars to war and aggression is indicated in the word *martial*.

5 *Newsweek* (Feb. 13, 2006), p. 64.

6 Powell and Treadgold, *Christian Star Calendar 2006*, monthly ephemeris for February, p. 45. The yearly *Christian Star Calendar* now appears annually as the *Journal for Star Wisdom*.

This stellar correlation relating to Denmark is just one example of Astrogeographia serving as a body of wisdom toward the understanding of world events. In addition to world events, appendix 2 (available online at astrogeographia.org) describes how Astrogeographia is helpful in understanding weather-related events, earthquakes, etc. Moreover, the science of Astrogeographia can be applied as well toward the understanding of individual human lives and destinies. Why is one person drawn to live at one location and another to live somewhere else?[7] It is with such questions that the new science of Astrogeographia can be illuminating, often providing astonishingly accurate answers. In order to arrive at an understanding of the basis of Astrogeographia, this book employs an easy-to-follow, step-by-step approach to describing the new science.

Interwoven within the main theme, Astrogeographia, is a consideration of the "Bible" of astrology, the *Tetrabiblos,* written by the Greek astronomer Ptolemy around AD 150. In the following pages, this important work is revealed in a new way. This subsidiary theme sheds completely new light upon the *Tetrabiblos.* The consequences thereof, if properly understood, have ramifications for the whole history and practice of astrology.[8]

This book is both scientific and spiritual in perspective. For those who do not feel inclined to read the scientific material, there remains a large content that can be read, elucidating the principles and application of Astrogeographia.

---

7 This aspect of Astrogeographia is not addressed in this volume, but will be the subject of a second book.

8 See also Powell and Dann, *The Astrological Revolution.*

Acknowledgments

First and foremost, I would like to express my heartfelt appreciation to my friend and colleague, Brian Gray, who first drew my attention to the correspondence between the starry heavens and the Earth. Brian communicated to me that he had been working on this correspondence for many years and had come to an approximate solution but that he had been unable to determine precisely how this correspondence is specified. Brian, who teaches at the Rudolf Steiner College in Fair Oaks, California, had also discussed his approximate solution with his colleague and fellow teacher at Rudolf Steiner College, Dennis Klocek. Dennis took this up from Brian and applied this correspondence in a slightly modified way in his pioneering work of predicting weather conditions from the movements of the planets against the background of the starry heavens. Dennis' approach is discussed in chapter 5 of this book and, as can be seen from this discussion, the solution that Dennis arrived at is actually very close to the solution that I have arrived at, the difference being a matter of just a few degrees.

It is clear, therefore, that there are different approaches to the question of the correspondence between the celestial globe and the terrestrial globe—two being those of Brian Gray and Dennis Klocek. Other approaches are also mentioned in chapter 5 of this book. Here I would like to acknowledge that I would never have found the solution that I am proposing without the indication that I received from Brian Gray to consider the book *The Orion Mystery*. Again my profound gratitude to Brian for this, and also to the authors of *The Orion Mystery*, Robert Bauval and Adrian Gilbert, who provided the key to what I believe to be the solution to the problem of the one-to-one correspondence between the starry globe and the earthly globe.

It was a fortunate chain of circumstances which led me to meet mathematician David Bowden in Melbourne, Australia, in 2009. When I mentioned the need for Astrogeographia to be placed on a firm mathematical basis, David indicated that he would be willing to take this on. The resulting collaboration has been a wonderful enrichment. Thanks to David, Astrogeographia now has a solid scientific foundation. Those who are interested to learn from the outset about the mathematical basis of Astrogeographia are invited to read appendix 1 first (contributed by David and available online at astrogeographia.org), and then chapter 8, also contributed by David. Chapter 10, which brings in the Earth chakras in relation to the planets, is the result of our joint authorship. Apart from chapter 10, the other chapters of this book are concerned specifically with the relationship of the earthly globe to the celestial sphere, that of the fixed stars. Chapter 10, however, looks at the continents of the Earth *in relation to the planets*. Here, too, thanks to David, a mathematical formulation of the pathways of the two major energy lines connecting the Earth's main planetary centers has been found and brought to graphical expression.

Isaac Newton, quoting Bernhard of Chartres, remarked in a letter of February 5, 1676: "If I have seen further it is by standing on the shoulders of Giants."[1] Newton said this in relation to his discoveries in the realm of astronomy made on the basis of the discoveries of earlier astronomers, for example the discovery by Johannes Kepler of the laws of planetary motion. In turn, Kepler's discoveries were made possible through the extensive astronomical observations collected by Tycho Brahe. This exemplifies the principle of scientific endeavor, where the results of one scientist are extended and expanded upon by another. Generally discoveries do not come entirely on their own. They usually have inspiring precedents which serve as a starting point for further inquiry. To this the scientist then brings through his own resources a particular lens of observation which is either empirical or else has something of a revelatory nature—for example, Kepler describes how the third law of planetary motion one day just "turned up in my head."[2]

1 Cohen, "Isaac Newton," *Dictionary of Scientific Biography* 10, p. 55.

2 Koestler, *The Sleepwalkers* (Penguin Books: London, 1973), p. 400.

With regard to the research presented in this book, after taking as a starting point the alignment of the Great Pyramid at Giza with the star Alnitak in the belt of Orion, the relationship of the entire stellar sphere to the whole sphere of the Earth came into view. Having this starting point, combined with the application of mathematical astronomy, one revelation after another revealed itself—in particular, that certain special places on the Earth are aligned with prominent stars (Vienna with Aldebaran, Salt Lake City with Altair, Alexandria with Alnilam, Ephesus with Bellatrix, etc.). It became clear that from this archetypal perspective there indeed exists a correspondence between the celestial sphere and the earthly globe. There is evidence that in the past the stars have provided—and perhaps continue to provide—a shaping impulse upon the culture and civilization of the Earth. Whether this is the "final truth" regarding the question of this correspondence, time will tell. At any rate, I hope that the contents presented in this book offer the reader inspiration as to how the "stars above" are related to the "Earth below" in the sense of the ancient saying, "As above, so below," and I express my gratitude to all who have contributed to this research in one way or another, a research which opened up for me as I was preparing to lead a group of the Sophia Foundation to Egypt in March 2006.

Upon completion of this book, I was given a remarkable book written by an Egyptian, Dr. Ibrahim Karim, entitled *BioGeometry: Back to a Future for Mankind*. Dr. Karim brings to modern awareness something of the knowledge of the Ancient Egyptians who built the pyramids:

> After identifying a location on Earth that had a very strong sacred energy quality, the ancient builders also took into consideration the building's astronomical orientation. So, not only did the Ancient Egyptians consider the location of sacred energy on Earth, but they also strove to detect and map the locations of similar ones in the sky. The connection with the sacred places in the sky was used to empower the sacred energy of the power spot on Earth. These connections created a three-dimensional grid of sacred energy quality.[3]

3 Karim, *BioGeometry*, p. 81.

Here is revealed that there are two sides to be considered: the earthly and the cosmic. This work focuses primarily on the cosmic perspective, whereas Dr. Karim in his book focuses mainly on the earthly. These two complement one another, as is brought to expression in the above quote, which puts the interweaving between the earthly and the cosmic in a clear and concise way. And not only Ibrahim Karim but also all other researchers who have dedicated their time and energy to investigating sacred sites and power spots and thus increased our awareness of the sacred organism of the Earth, I would like to gratefully acknowledge here.[4]

In conclusion, I would like to express gratitude to publishers Chris Bamford and Gene Gollogly of Lindisfarne Books for enabling this book to become available, and to the able assistance of William Jens Jensen for his meticulous work in shepherding this book into print.

4 See, for example, Pogacnik, *Sacred Geography*, as one of the most prominent authors on this theme.

Chapter 1

Alnitak and the Great Pyramid at Giza

"Also there radiates into the Earth soul an image of the sense perceptible zodiac and of the whole firmament as a bond of sympathy between heaven and Earth.... This imprint into the Earth soul through the sense perceptible zodiac and the entire sphere of fixed stars is also confirmed through observation."[1]

"All fixed land swims and the stars hold it in position.... The continents swim and do not sit upon anything. They [the continents] upon the Earth are held in place from without by the starry constellations. When the constellations change, the continents change, also. On the old maps and atlases these relationships between starry constellations and configurations on the Earth's surface were correctly shown, including also the constellations of the zodiac."[2]

"We are led to the center of the Earth as the polar opposite [of the sphere of the starry heavens].... The counterpart to this star is here, the counterpart to that star is there, and so on. We arrive at a complete counter image in the Earth itself to that which is outside [in the sphere of the starry heavens].... In other words, we can conceive of the active heavenly sphere mirrored in the Earth. We can think of the Earth's mineral realm as a result of this mirroring."[3]

---

1 Kepler, *Weltharmonik IV, 7,* "Harmonies of the World." book IV, chap. 7, pp. 262–263 (tr. by RP).

2 Steiner, *Faculty Meetings with Rudolf Steiner,* vol. 2 (1922–1924), "Questions and Answers," April 25, 1923. (English translation amended by RP after comparing with the German original.)

3 Steiner, *Das Verhältnis der verschiedenen naturwissenschatlichen Gebiete zur Astronomie,* lecture, Jan. 10, 1921 (tr. by RP).

The question has long occupied me: in what sense can the words quoted above be understood—i.e., how "can [we] conceive of the active heavenly sphere mirrored in the Earth" such that "the counterpart to this star is here, the counterpart to that star is there, and so on"? Does this imply a new science, which might be called Astrogeographia, concerning the correspondence between stars in the heavens and earthly geographical locations such that each star is mirrored at a specific location on the Earth?

With regard to research into this question a breakthrough came in 2005. Already sometime previously my attention had been drawn to the book *The Orion Mystery* by Robert Bauval and Adrian Gilbert, which concludes that the three pyramids at Giza mirror the three stars (Alnitak, Alnilam, Mintaka) in the belt of Orion.[4] *The Orion Mystery* was first published in the United Kingdom in 1994. In this book Bauval and Gilbert cite the work of the Egyptologist A. Badawy and astronomer V. Trimble published thirty years earlier (in 1964) in volume 10 of the *Mitteilungen des Instituts für Orientforschung der Akademie der Wissenschaften zu Berlin.* Virginia Trimble's article "Astronomical Investigation Concerning the So-Called Air Shafts of Cheops's Pyramid" is reproduced as appendix 1 in *The Orion Mystery.* She concludes that, "These three stars [Alnitak, Alnilam, Mintaka]...passed once each day, at culmination, directly over the southern shaft of the Great Pyramid at the time it was built."[5] Following on this original finding, Bauval states that he found further stellar alignments for the other three shafts in the Great Pyramid. He came to this conclusion:

> The pyramids exhibit stellar alignments: the bases are aligned meridionally (north to south) with the stars. The Great Pyramid has four shafts pointing meridionally toward important stars relating to the rebirth cult. One points directly to Orion's Belt—more specifically to Al Nitak, the lower star in Orion's Belt. Correlating this star to the Great Pyramid, we can see the same

4 Bauval and Gilbert, *The Orion Mystery.*

5 Ibid. p. 255.

> pattern of layout between the three pyramids of Giza with the three stars of Orion's Belt.[6]

Summarizing these alignments as computed by Bauval, which hold for the period from 2475 to 2425 BC (mean date: 2450 BC) when the Great Pyramid (according to Bauval) was being constructed:

- the southern shaft from the King's Chamber pointed to Alnitak in Orion;
- the southern shaft from the Queen's Chamber pointed to Sirius in Canis Major;
- the northern shaft from the King's Chamber pointed to Thuban in Draco;
- the northern shaft from the Queen's Chamber pointed to Kochab in Ursa Minor.[7]

Here it should be pointed out that for his computations Bauval utilized the data provided by Rudolf Gantenbrink who in 1993 used robots to investigate the small shafts, which turned out to be not more than about 8 by 8 inches (20 by 20 cm). Gantenbrink, in response to the question as to whether the shafts were aligned to the stars, says:

> No! All the shafts bend, often several times. In addition, all the shafts begin, at their lower ends, with horizontal sections about two meters in length. So there is no way light from any source could ever have penetrated from the outside into either of the chambers. In several parts of the shafts, with the exception of the lower southern one, we even found extreme angle fluctuations. It is therefore ridiculous for anyone to claim that the shafts could ever have pointed precisely to certain stars. Given the many angle fluctuations, the shafts could be construed to be pointing at some 100 different stars, especially if construction of the pyramid is gratuitously redated to match specific stellar constellations.[8]

---

6 Ibid. p. 302.

7 See the diagram representing these four stellar alignments in *The Orion Mystery*, p. 182.

8 From http://www.cheops.org.

Gantenbrink's criticism of Bauval's findings cannot be dismissed lightly. Nevertheless Gantenbrink does postulate a reason for the existence of the shafts which is not very different from Bauval's perspective, if the consciousness of the ancient Egyptians is taken into account, as I shall discuss below, hopefully reconciling the diverging standpoints of Bauval and Gantenbrink. Here is the reason postulated by Gantenbrink for the shafts:

> They are spirit or soul shafts. This is the most probable explanation, based on the solid data we have available to us. At least it corresponds to the system of religious beliefs of the ancient Egyptians. But this brings us to a truly great mystery. If they were designed as soul escape routes, why were such shafts built only during one single generation? Why were none constructed before or after Cheops?[9]

The answer to this last question—in light of Astrogeographia—is that the Great Pyramid was built at a unique point in time to align with the star Alnitak and that the upper southern shaft from the King's Chamber recalls precisely this alignment. This star alignment was indeed a "spirit or soul shaft" in line with the belief of the ancient Egyptians that at death the soul of the pharaoh becomes identified with Osiris and ascends to this god's constellation, which is Orion. Why this particular star—Alnitak—within the constellation of Orion? This will become clear in the further course of this work, where—through Astrogeographia—it emerges that various great architectural structures of antiquity were associated with different stars. Thus the Great Pyramid is associated with the star Alnitak—the very meaning and purpose of the Great Pyramid having been inspired by the influence proceeding from this star—as will become apparent later.

A careful study of Gantenbrink's findings, which he has published at his website www.cheops.org, indicates that it is possible to utilize the shaft angle that he has determined for the southern shaft from the King's Chamber. He says:

> The initial horizontal shaft segment . . . [then] the shaft inclines at an angle of 39.20° . . . [then] the shaft inclines more sharply, reaching

9 Ibid.

> an angle of 50.54°.... From this point, all the way to the outlet on the pyramid's flank...the shaft maintains an angle of 45°.[10]

It is this constant angle of 45° maintained for the larger part of the shaft that is crucial for the alignment with the star Alnitak. Based on this angle, using Peter Treadgold's *Astrofire* program,[11] which includes a star catalog based on the Hipparcos catalog,[12] I checked Bauval's computations and found that the exact alignment of Alnitak with the southern shaft from the King's Chamber was in 2495 BC, a little earlier than the date 2475 BC found by Bauval. While the earlier part of this shaft—first being horizontal, then inclined at 39.20°, then at 50.54°—is irregular, this could be seen as a "search and find" technique on the part of those engaged in constructing the shafts. It has to be borne in mind that the construction of the shafts was extraordinarily difficult and time-consuming. Their very existence is nothing short of miraculous as an architectural achievement. That the entire latter part of the southern shaft from the King's Chamber maintains an angle of 45° is a remarkable achievement—as if the constructors of this shaft at first were engaged in a search and then having found what they were looking for managed to keep firmly to their orientation. One hypothesis is that it was the star Alnitak that they were searching for, not using the physical senses but rather a soul or spiritual sensing of this star. Once they found the star on an inner level, they were able to steer a course toward it, and this was the angle of 45°—fitting exactly for the building of the pyramid around 2495 BC.

Admittedly this hypothesis is difficult for modern consciousness to comprehend, since for the modern human being everything is based upon the physical senses. However, Egyptian reliefs attest to a different mode of consciousness and perception—i.e., that the Egyptians saw and experienced a level of existence which modern human

---

10 Ibid.

11 *Astrofire* contains a star catalog of more than 4,000 stars and is available from the Sophia Foundation, www.sophiafoundation.org.

12 The Hipparcos catalog derives from the stellar observations made by the Hipparcos satellite from 1989–1993 during which time Hipparcos collected remarkably accurate data on 117,955 stars, giving positions, magnitudes, parallaxes, and proper motions.

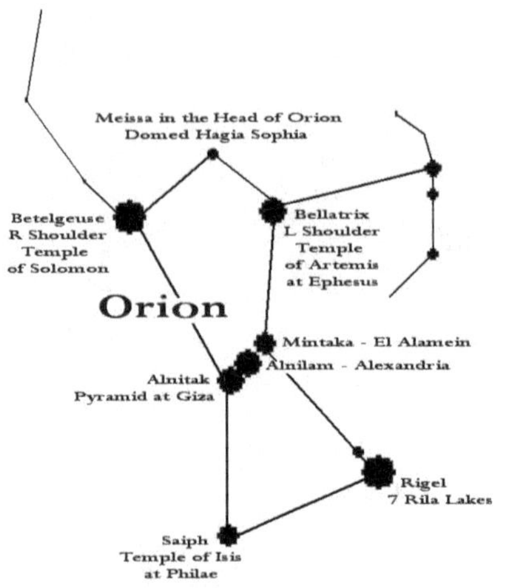

beings generally do not perceive. Could this have been by way of "spiritual/soul sensing"? At least one scholar, Frances Rolleston, has identified a figure on the famous zodiac of Denderah *"pointing to a star, Al Nitak, the wounded, as his."*[13] Anyone who sees the zodiac of Denderah, now in the Louvre Museum, will see that it depicts numerous gods and animal-headed beings (i.e., not what is perceptible to the physical senses). Of course, a person depicted pointing toward Alnitak could naturally be thought of as physically pointing up to this star. Yet within the context of the whole depiction, where there are clearly non-physical levels (gods) portrayed, could it not be that one is oriented toward the star on a soul/spiritual level and that this is how the orientation of the shaft in the Great Pyramid toward Alnitak in (and around) 2495 BC was achieved?

Along the lines of this hypothesis it would follow that in the construction of the Great Pyramid a "spiritual/soul sensing" was used in aligning the southern shaft from the King's Chamber with the star Alnitak. This still leaves open the question of the other shafts, and it is quite possible that these too were made in the same way by virtue of a "spiritual/soul sensing" of alignment with certain stars.

However, following up the alignments proposed by Bauval (based on Gantenbrink's data), around the date 2450 BC there was not anywhere near an alignment of the northern shaft from the King's Chamber with Thuban in Draco nor was there anything close to an alignment of the northern shaft from the Queen's Chamber with Kochab in Ursa Minor. This leaves only the southern shaft from the Queen's Chamber, which according to Gantenbrink, "Inclines at an average angle of 39.6078°."[14] That is, while there are relatively small

13 Rolleston, *Mazzaroth*, part 4, p. 13.

14 From http://www.cheops.org.

fluctuations and deviations, nevertheless an angle does emerge. Based on this angle, again using Peter Treadgold's *Astrofire* program, it transpires that the date of alignment of the southern shaft from the Queen's Chamber with Sirius was not until 2360 BC, which is too late—considering that the whole pyramid was probably completed in a space of about twenty years, and moreover its construction has to be seen in relation to the life of Pharaoh Cheops, who was certainly no longer alive at this date but could well have been alive in 2495 BC. This does not disprove Bauval's idea of alignment of this shaft with Sirius, since the average angular incline is not necessarily the angle that should be taken for such a computation, but rather another slightly differing value, which could easily change the computation and set it back to an alignment some 130 years earlier.

Summarizing, therefore, a careful investigation of Bauval's research reveals that it is really only the alignment of the southern shaft from the King's Chamber that can be relied upon, but this is the decisive one, as it shows—as we shall see later—the fundamental correspondence between the Great Pyramid and the star Alnitak that is foundational for Astrogeographia.

Bauval's research, however, goes further than this discovery of stellar alignments relating to the shafts in the Great Pyramid. In addition, as indicated above, he maintains that the three pyramids at Giza mirror the three stars in the belt of Orion. How, precisely, does he conceive of this correspondence?

Having made an aerial photograph of the Giza pyramids, which he showed to various people, he writes concerning their response to seeing the photo:

> The three pyramids were each set along their own meridian (north–south) axes and everyone noticed the southwest diagonal along which the two larger pyramids are set. They agreed that this indicated a unified plan. Then came the confusion I had anticipated: they wondered why the third pyramid was so much smaller than the other two, and, even more puzzling, why it was slightly offset east of the southwest diagonal line which linked the two larger pyramids. All agreed that the size and offset of the Menkaura

> pyramid had been a deliberate choice by the architect. The question was why?[15]

Bauval then gave the picture to another group of friends:

> This time, however, I traced in black ink the southwest diagonal line which linked the two larger pyramids, and extended the line to the Menkaura pyramid to show the curious offset. I also provided them with the assumed sequence of building: Khufu (Cheops with the Great Pyramid), then Khafra (Chephren with the second pyramid) and Menkaura (Mycerinos with the smaller third pyramid)....Why did the master plan specify two large pyramids and one smaller? Why offset the smallest to the east? Now the answer became obvious: these "anomalies" were not anomalies at all but constraints imposed in the planning, design and layout of a master plan which were reflected in the third pyramid.[16]

In November 1983 while camping in Saudi Arabia and stargazing one night, a friend of Bauval's, pointing to the belt of Orion, said:

> The three stars of Orion's Belt are not perfectly aligned. If you look carefully you will see that the smallest of them, the one at the top, is slightly offset to the east and they are slanted in a southwesterly direction.[17]

At this moment, Bauval realized that here—visible in the heavens in the belt of Orion—was the master plan underlining the layout of the three pyramids at Giza. The layout signifies that "as above" in the heavens (the three stars in the belt of Orion) "so below" on Earth (the three pyramids) such that the Cheops' pyramid mirrors Alnitak, the Chephren pyramid mirrors Alnilam, and the Mycerinos (Menkaura) pyramid mirrors Mintaka—Alnitak being the lower (southeast) star in Orion's belt, Alnilam the middle star, and Mintaka the upper (northwest) star. (This description holds for Northern Hemisphere stargazers; for viewers in the Southern Hemisphere the correspondence still applies, but there Alnitak is the upper star and Mintaka

15 Bauval and Gilbert, *The Orion Mystery*, p. 112.

16 Ibid. pp. 113–115.

17 Ibid. p. 120.

is the lower star—i.e., the three stars are seen "upside down" for the Northern Hemisphere.)

The layout of the three pyramids—if we accept Bauval's research that their layout indicates the intention for them to symbolically mirror the three stars in Orion's belt—is such that the alignment of the Great Pyramid *with the star Alnitak* was pivotal for the whole architectural plan of the three pyramids at Giza. That is, the alignment of the Great Pyramid with Alnitak was crucial to the whole enterprise of the construction of the three pyramids at Giza. As we shall see, this is a starting point for a new science: Astrogeographia.

The alignment of the Cheops' pyramid at the time of its construction with Alnitak is proven, if the date of construction does indeed fall around 2500 BC. It is not possible to speak *in the same way* of an alignment of the Chephren (Khafra) pyramid with Alnilam or of an alignment of the Mycerinos (Menkaura) pyramid with Mintaka. In the first place, there are no shafts in these latter two pyramids which would indicate their alignment with any particular stars at the time they were constructed. Second, if Alnitak is projected from the stellar globe onto the Earth at Giza, then the projection of Alnilam from the stellar globe onto the Earth would be at a distance of about 100 miles (161 km) from Giza, and the projection of Mintaka from the stellar globe onto the Earth would be a further (approximately) 100 miles (161 km) distant from the earthly location of the projection of Alnilam. It is clear, therefore, that the layout of the three pyramids at Giza mirrors the three stars of Orion's belt on Earth *symbolically* rather than actually. Nevertheless, the alignment of the Great Pyramid with Alnitak at the time of its construction (assuming this to have been around 2500 BC) was *actual* rather than symbolical. This alignment is pivotal for Astrogeographia, as we shall see.

There is, moreover, a striking anomaly regarding this correspondence between the layout of the three pyramids at Giza and the three stars in Orion's belt—an anomaly which highlights the symbolic nature of the architectural plan. There are two ways of grasping this anomaly—one requiring the participation of our active imagination, and the other entailing a logical appraisal. First the logical approach:

when we look up at Orion's belt, we see that Alnilam (the central star of the three) is northwest of Alnitak (the lowest star), and Mintaka (the highest star) is northwest of Alnilam. Yet the Chephren pyramid (corresponding to Alnilam) is *southwest* of the Cheops pyramid (corresponding to Alnitak) and the Mycerinos pyramid (corresponding to Mintaka) is *southwest* of the Chephren pyramid. In other words, the projection of the three stars of the belt of Orion onto the Earth not only does not work in terms of the distances entailed by this projection, as referred to in the preceding paragraph, but also it does not work in terms of geographical direction. With the help of our active imagination, we can "see" that this is so and that therefore the layout of the three pyramids at Giza mirrors the three stars in Orion's belt *symbolically* and not actually. Let us imaginatively step beyond the sphere of the starry heavens to a place where we could look down to the Earth *from beyond the stars in Orion's belt*—from a place far, far beyond these three stars. If we were to look down from this far-distant place—holding the stars of Orion's belt in our gaze and seeing the Earth in the background—at such an angle that the star Alnitak could be seen aligned with Giza (directly projected onto Giza), we would then see Alnilam projected onto a place about 100 miles (162 km) northwest of Giza, coinciding more or less exactly with the city of Alexandria! In turn, we would see Mintaka projected onto a place about 100 miles (162 km) further northwest of Alexandria, over the Mediterranean Sea. The point is that the actual stellar projection of the three stars of Orion's belt in the sequence Alnitak-Alnilam-Mintaka follows a diagonal line to the *northwest* and not to the southwest as is the case with the layout of the three pyramids at Giza.

If one studies the diagrams (in the 1994 edition, pages 148, 203, and 232) of the projection of the constellation of Orion onto Egypt with the three stars in Orion's belt coinciding with the three pyramids at Giza, the anomaly referred to in the preceding paragraph emerges from the fact that in these diagrams Orion's head appears projected in the south of Egypt and his feet appear projected in the north. That which we see in these diagrams is an inversion (in the north–south axis) of what we actually see in the heavens when we look up to Orion. Having said this, it is nevertheless clear that there was an actual alignment of the Great Pyramid with Alnitak at the time of its construction and, moreover, that the layout of the three pyramids at Giza *symbolically* mirrors the three stars in the belt of Orion. Therefore, a starting point for Astrogeographia is to begin with the alignment of Giza with Alnitak and to consider what results from an *actual projection* of the stars upon the Earth. Then one sees, for example, that the city of Alexandria is aligned with Alnilam. Is this something *real*? Is this the solution of the question posed at the beginning, arising from the quoted statement: "Can [we] conceive of the active heavenly sphere mirrored in the Earth" such that "the counterpart to this star is here, the counterpart to that star is there, and so on?"

Once having pinpointed the alignment of Giza with Alnitak, the question arises as to what this means exactly? One way of approaching this question is in terms of the coordinates of earthly geography in relation to the coordinates of celestial geography. However, whereas there is only one coordinate system of earthly geography, in which places are located by latitude and longitude, there are several systems (three principal ones) of celestial geography. It is in the book *Geography* by the Greek astronomer Ptolemy (second century AD) that we find the first systematic use of the geographical coordinates of latitude and longitude, although his meridian of zero longitude ran through the "Fortunate Islands"—the Canary Islands—which was chosen as the reference meridian because these islands were the western-most location of the known world (at that time). The modern meridian of zero longitude is known as the *Greenwich meridian* since it runs through the Royal Greenwich Observatory in London. Any place located on the Greenwich meridian has 0° longitude. The point where the Greenwich meridian intersects the Earth's equator has 0° latitude as well as 0° longitude. For the Earth's equator is defined as the axis of 0° latitude. The latitude of a place is the distance in degrees and minutes (and seconds, if great accuracy is required) *north or south of the equator*, whereas the longitude is the distance in degrees and minutes (and seconds in the case of highly accurate measurements) *east or west of the Greenwich meridian.* In terms of this coordinate system, Giza is located at a longitude of 31°08' east of Greenwich (written 31E08) and at a latitude of 29°59' north of the equator (written 29N59).[18] Now it is a matter of specifying how these earthly geographical coordinates relate to those of celestial geography.

As mentioned above, there are three principal methods of specifying the location of a star in the heavens. These are:

1. horizon coordinates;
2. celestial equatorial coordinates;
3. ecliptic coordinates.

Let us consider these one by one.

Horizon coordinates: these coordinates are called *altitude* and *azimuth*. The *altitude* is the angular distance of a star above the horizon, and the *azimuth* is the angular distance from the north point, measured clockwise around the horizon (although sometimes *azimuth* is measured clockwise around the horizon not from the north point but from the south point). The use of horizon coordinates is limited in scope, since its application is specific to the given location on Earth. Although it is applicable anywhere around the globe, it is not a global method with universal validity all around the globe, since each observer uses his own personal horizon as his plane of reference. Nevertheless, as a practical method for astronomical observation of the night sky, it is of great practical significance.

Celestial equatorial coordinates: these coordinates are known as *declination* and *right ascension*. The *declination* is the angular distance of a star above or below the celestial equator, which is simply the projection of the Earth's equator onto the celestial sphere. *Declination* is exactly the same coordinate in celestial geography as *latitude* is in earthly geography—i.e., *declination* and *latitude* are

18 *The Times Atlas of the World* gives the longitude and latitude of Giza as 31E07 and 29N59. However, according to Google, the longitude and latitude of the Great Pyramid are 31°08'03" east and 29°58'4" north. This latitude rounded to the nearest minute agrees with the value given in The Times Atlas of the World and the rounded longitude is one minute of arc different, which amounts to a little over one mile or a little less than two kilometers in distance. This small difference is probably due to the specification of the Great Pyramid as place rather than Giza. The values of longitude and latitude of the Great Pyramid that have been adopted in this book are 31E08 and 29N59.

equivalent to one another, the one being applied to stars in the heavens and the other to places on the Earth. Both *declination* and *latitude* are measured in degrees and minutes north (+) or south (-) of the celestial or terrestrial equator. Similarly, the other celestial equatorial coordinate, *right ascension*, is the counterpart in celestial geography to *longitude* in earthly geography. However, whereas *longitude* is measured in degrees east or west of the Greenwich meridian, *right ascension* is measured in hours and minutes eastward of the vernal point. One hour of *right ascension* is equal to 15° *longitude*, since 24 x 15° = 360°. It is easy, therefore, to convert from the units for *right ascension* of hours and minutes to degrees and minutes of *longitude*.

Ecliptic coordinates: the *ecliptic* is the apparent path of the Sun against the background of the zodiacal constellations. It is the central line running through the zodiacal belt, and it is inclined to the celestial equator at an angle of about 23½°. In terms of observing the movements of the planets through the constellations of the zodiac, the zodiac itself is the natural frame of reference. Since the days of Ptolemy (second century AD), it has been customary in astronomy to refer to the locations of planets and stars in terms of their *latitude*, which is their angular distance above or below the ecliptic, and their *longitude*, which—since Ptolemy—is measured as angular distance eastward of the vernal point, defining the vernal point as the zero point of the zodiac. This definition unfortunately led to a misunderstanding which has served to veil the science of the stars, and it is the task of this book to unveil the mystery surrounding Ptolemy's definition which created the misunderstanding in the first place. Before embarking upon this undertaking, it should be noted that the use of *latitude* and *longitude* in celestial geography (as *ecliptic* coordinates) is different from the use of these terms in earthly geography, where it is the *equator* which is the frame of reference. Further, whereas modern astronomy measures ecliptic longitude in degrees and minutes from the vernal point, it was customary (until fairly recently) to divide the ecliptic circle into twelve zodiacal signs, each 30° long, beginning with the sign of Aries (the first of the twelve signs) at the vernal point. This system used by Ptolemy, based on the vernal point, supplanted the earlier Babylonian system using *sidereal longitude*, in which the signs of the zodiac were defined by certain fixed stars belonging to the zodiacal belt, whose location was defined in relation to the two first magnitude stars Aldebaran in the middle of the constellation of Taurus (15° Taurus) and Antares in the middle of the constellation of Scorpio (15° Scorpio), as specified by the Babylonians, and as will be discussed in the next chapter.[19] In order to unravel the mystery surrounding this substitution of one zodiac in place of the original zodiac of the Babylonians, it is necessary to turn our attention to Ptolemy's book the *Tetrabiblos*, which we shall do in chapter 2. Before proceeding to chapter 2, however, it is important to reflect briefly on the following, which maps the two key concepts underlying the method of Astrogeographia as a way of projecting stars onto the earthly globe.

As we shall see in the course of this book, the different methods of celestial geography described above are of key significance when it comes to understanding the projection of stars upon the Earth. The primal intuition underlying the basis for Astrogeographia, which subsequently proved to be correct, emerged from the correspondence

19 The complex history of the zodiac is the subject matter of my Ph.D. thesis: *History of the Zodiac*. See also *The Zodiac: A Historical Survey* and the *The Sidereal Zodiac* (coauthor Peter Treadgold). The stars Aldebaran and Antares were central in the definition of the Babylonian zodiac. These two first magnitude stars both belong to the zodiacal belt, with Aldebaran (15° Taurus) at the center of the constellation of Taurus and Antares (15° Scorpio) at the center of the constellation of Scorpio. 15° Taurus and 15° Scorpio are the *sidereal longitudes* of Aldebaran and Antares, which remain fairly constant over long periods of time. Every star has a sidereal longitude, and this defines a star's stellar meridian, discussed in chapter 6 as of key significance for Astrogeographia. See also the Fiorenza Star Map (celestial atlas) at the end of this book (pages 296–297), which shows the entirety of the starry heavens mapped out in terms of sidereal longitudes and latitudes. From this map, the idea of a correspondence between the heavens (celestial atlas) and the Earth (geographical atlas) can be seen. From the Fiorenza Star Map the stellar meridians of stars are specified by the vertical axis running north-south through the star, determined by the sidereal longitude at which this vertical axis intersects the ecliptic, the central line running through the map that traces the Sun's path against the background of the starry heavens, divided into twelve equal 30° zodiacal signs, coinciding more or less with the zodiacal constellations of the same names as the signs. The sidereal longitudes of stars are usually given in degrees and minutes within the zodiacal sign, and the latitude is the number of degrees and minutes that the star is positioned north or south of the ecliptic.

between the method of earthly latitudes and longitudes and the method of equatorial coordinates, as described above in the section on celestial equatorial coordinates—in particular, that *declination* is exactly the same coordinate in celestial geography as *latitude* is in earthly geography. The motion of a star in declination, as viewed from the Earth over the precession cycle of 25,920 years, is mirrored, when the star is projected onto the Earth, in a corresponding motion in geographical latitude. This is one important concept, which comes to expression later in this book as the "equation of declination." The other important concept, described in chapter 6, is *stellar meridians* and how, when a star is projected onto the Earth, that star's meridian, which is expressed in terms of its sidereal longitude, is projected onto a particular longitudinal line running between the Earth's north and south poles. This can best be understood once the concept of stellar meridian is grasped more fully, as discussed in chapters 6 and 9 (see also footnote 19).

Chapter 2
The Bible of Astrology

It is well known that Ptolemy's *Tetrabiblos* enjoyed the status of being the Bible of astrology.[1] The message of the *Tetrabiblos*, however, has not been understood in its profundity until now—and no doubt it will continue to bear fruit in future times. Only after having completed my Ph.D. on the history of the zodiac and then returning to Ptolemy's work did I come to realize that, when correctly interpreted, it contains the seeds of the science of Astrogeographia. Astrogeographia is an exact science that completely transforms astrology, and it is the purpose of this book to set forth this new (and yet ancient) science. Before embarking upon an exposition of Astrogeographia, it is necessary first of all to elaborate upon the misunderstanding surrounding the Bible of astrology, which has unfortunately succeeded in veiling the true nature of astrology. This book is directed toward penetrating through to this veiled wisdom, to arrive at a powerful and sophisticated science of the stars. For Astrogeographia sheds new light upon every horoscope ever cast!

Ptolemy was a Greek astronomer living in Alexandria, the principal city of Greco-Roman Egypt, in the second century AD. His great astronomical work, the *Almagest*,[2] was considered the "Bible" of astronomy until the publication of Copernicus' *On the Revolutions*[3] in 1543. Claudius Ptolemaeus (ca. AD 100–178)[4] had access to the library in

1 Ptolemy, *Tetrabiblos* is the standard edition of this classical work, comprising Greek text with English translation and commentary by F. E. Robbins.

2 *Ptolemy's Almagest.*

3 Copernicus, *On the Revolutions.*

4 Robbins, op. cit., p. viii.

Alexandria, which was the best library in the ancient world, and it was probably here that he compiled the *Tetrabiblos*, making use of the available astrological literature. Even though it is clear that he was drawing upon earlier sources—for example, he refers to "Those who have written on these things"—nowhere does he mention them by name! Further, Ptolemy himself was not a practising astrologer. He was an astronomer and scholar who applied his academic skills to researching the astrological literature at his disposal. The *Tetrabiblos* does not contain much in the way of original research, and it does not contain a single horoscope. It represents primarily a *synthesis of ideas* prevailing in the astrological literature of that time. Ptolemy's gift was that of bringing his great mind to bear upon the intricate variety of astrological doctrines and to order them clearly and systematically. The result, the *Tetrabiblos* (written around AD 150), is an excellent compendium of the state of the art of astrology in the second century AD.

The sheer number of commentaries upon the *Tetrabiblos* is an indicator of its enormous influence. One of the commentators, Hephaestian of Thebes (fifth century AD), wrote of "the divine Ptolemy," expressing unusually lofty esteem for the great astronomer.[5] "The Tetrabiblos enjoyed almost the authority of a Bible among the astrological writers for a thousand years or more."[6] This millennium of authority of the Bible of astrology extended from the middle of the second century to the middle of the twelfth century AD. It is by examining this period of time that it is possible to identify the great misunderstanding that has affected astrology through a misreading of the *Tetrabiblos*. To help elucidate the nature of this misunderstanding, I shall summarize the main findings of my thesis on the history of the zodiac.[7]

From the time of the first scientific definition of the zodiac by Babylonian astronomers around 500 BC, the term *zodiac* used throughout Babylonia, Egypt, Greece, and Rome, meant the circle of twelve zodiacal constellations *divided into twelve equal-length signs* (each 30° long) by way of reference to certain bright stars: Aldebaran

5 Ibid. p. vii.

6 Ibid. p. xii.

7 For a summary of the main findings presented in this thesis, see *The Zodiac: A Historical Survey* and *The Sidereal Zodiac*.

("the Bull's eye") at 15° Taurus, Regulus ("the Lion's heart") at 5° Leo, Spica ("the spike of the sheath of wheat held by the Virgin") at 29° Virgo, Antares ("the Scorpion's heart") at 15° Scorpio, etc. In antiquity this was THE zodiac and there was no other scientific definition of the zodiac as an astronomical coordinate system. The positions of the planets were observed in relation to the background of zodiacal fixed stars and their positions were determined accordingly. For example, if Jupiter was seen in conjunction with Aldebaran, its longitude was recorded as 15° Taurus. In other words, the fixed stars of the zodiac provided the frame of reference for the movements of the *planets* (meaning in Greek, "wandering stars"). This relationship of wandering stars to fixed stars was not only the essence of ancient astrology but is also the foundation for the science of Astrogeographia. According to this science, as will be seen later, the star Aldebaran is reflected on Earth at the location of a large European city, so knowledge of a conjunction of Jupiter or any other planet with Aldebaran is a portent of particular significance for the people of that city.

The Greek word *zodiac* means "animal circle" and describes the great circle of animals (Bull, Lion, Scorpion, Goat, etc.) visible in the twelve zodiacal constellations in the heavens. These twelve constellations were singled out from the other constellations by virtue of the fact that they provide the background framework of reference for the movements of the planets. In antiquity the Sun ("light of the day") and the Moon ("light of the night") were counted as planets together with Mercury, Venus, Mars, Jupiter, Saturn to make up the seven *classical* planets visible to the naked eye.[8] The zodiac was thus the visible "way" traveled by the seven planets on their journey around the starry heavens.

It was owing to the genius of the Babylonians, perhaps under the inspiration of the great teacher Zoroaster (sixth century BC, called by the Babylonians Zaratas), that the zodiac of twelve constellations became divided into twelve equal signs, each 30° in length.[9] From

8 The newly discovered planets Uranus (1781), Neptune (1846), and Pluto (1930) were found with the aid of telescopes.

9 The evidence that Zoroaster, who was (according to various sources) in Babylon at precisely the time when the zodiac was introduced into

this time onward (ca. 500 BC) the zodiac serves as an astronomical coordinate system for the planets—both in astronomy and astrology. The earliest known horoscopes found to date were cast in terms of the ancient zodiac,[10] now known as the *sidereal zodiac* in order to distinguish it from the *tropical zodiac* introduced into astrology (unwittingly) by Ptolemy in the *Tetrabiblos*. It was the introduction of the astronomical coordinate system of the zodiac in Babylon that enabled the development of astronomical theories leading to the ability to *calculate and predict* future planetary movements.

The records of positions of the planets written down by the Babylonians in relation to the zodiacal fixed stars *based on observation* are called *astronomical diaries*. The positions of the planets derived by the Babylonians *by way of computation* are known as *astronomical ephemerides*. The Babylonians also identified the location of the *vernal point* in the signs of the zodiac. For them the vernal point was located at 10° Aries in approximately 500 BC.[11]

Once having grasped the astronomical phenomenon of the *precession of the equinoxes*—the slow retrograde movement of the vernal point through the signs of the zodiac, shifting back 1° every 72 years—it is possible to grasp the misunderstanding unwittingly created by Ptolemy in the *Tetrabiblos*. Before examining this in detail, however, let us consider the *zodiacal ages* arising through precession. These ages are directly related to the location of the vernal point. Now, at the present time, the vernal point is placed at 5° Pisces, and therefore we are in the Age of Pisces. In 500 BC, when the vernal point was located at 10° Aries, it was the Age of Aries. Since the movement of the vernal point through the signs of the zodiac can be calculated, correspondingly the zodiacal ages are determined as follows, each age lasting 2,160 years, the length of time for the vernal point to shift

Babylonian astronomy, is circumstantial and too complex to go into here. See Powell, *Christian Hermetic Astrology: The Star of the Magi and the Life of Christ*, pp. 19–24.

10 Rochberg, *Babylonian Horoscopes*.

11 Van der Waerden, *Science Awakening* (vol. 2): *The Birth of Astronomy*, p. 266. The vernal point is the location of the Sun in the zodiac on the day of the vernal equinox—at the present time around March 20.

back through the 30° comprising a zodiacal sign (1° in seventy-two years, i.e., 30° in 2,160 years)[12]:

from	-8425	to -6265	Age of Cancer
from	-6265	to -4105	Age of Gemini
from	-4105	to -1945	Age of Taurus
from	-1945	to +215	Age of Aries
from	+215	to +2375	Age of Pisces
from	+2375	to +4535	Age of Aquarius

The fact of the arising of such historical periods each 2,160 years long is *in itself* proof that the zodiacal constellations, spiritually understood, are *equal* in length, each 30° long, and are not *unequal constellations* as designated in modern astronomy. Evidently the Babylonians defined the twelve equal-length, 30° signs according to their spiritual perception, whereas the unequal constellations of modern astronomy stem from Ptolemy's *Almagest*.[13] Ptolemy drew up his star catalog, from which the constellations are defined, purely on the basis of physical observation. The succession of zodiacal ages, however, is a *spiritual reality* giving rise to equal-length cultural epochs, each 2,160 years long, as indicated in the following quotation:

> When the Sun entered the sign of Cancer at the vernal equinox the first...civilization [ancient India] began. We can actually call it the "Cancer civilization"—if the expression is not misunderstood. If we grasp things in their true light, then we can say: When the Sun rose in the spring it stood in the sign of Cancer....

12 Powell, *Hermetic Astrology, vol. I: Astrology and Reincarnation*, p. 63. The dates of the zodiacal ages are "average dates" based on the assumption that the vernal point moves at a uniform rate of 1° in 72 years. In practice, however, the dates can shift by a few years because the rate of motion of the vernal point is not uniform but is sometimes slightly faster and sometimes a little slower than 1° in 72 years. The notation used here for these dates is astronomical, in which BC dates are written - and AD dates are written +. Note that in this astronomical notation the year 1 BC = 0, the year 2 BC = -1, the year 3 BC = -2, and so on.

13 *Ptolemy's Almagest*, op. cit., Books VII and VIII.

> Macrocosmically one can characterize this first, ancient Indian culture by saying that it took its course while the vernal equinox was in Cancer.... Then the Sun entered the sign of Gemini, the Twins, at the vernal equinox. And then as long as the vernal equinox continued to be in Gemini, we have to do with the second...cultural epoch, the ancient Persian.[14]

Here our attention is drawn to cultural epochs (ancient Indian, ancient Persian, etc.), each of which are 2,160 years long.[15] It is important to note that in this quotation the zodiac referred to is the sidereal zodiac with twelve equal length signs, each 30° long, since this is the length of time taken by the vernal point, moving retrograde at a rate of 1° in 72 years, to regress through 30° comprising a zodiacal sign. In other words in the above quotation the use of the term "*signs of the zodiac*" is the same as that of the Babylonians, Egyptians, Greeks, and Romans—i.e., the twelve constellations of the zodiac are equal in length, each 30° long, rather than unequal, as in modern astronomy.

It is interesting to note, further, that this original conception of the zodiac was transmitted (probably from Alexandria, which was the main center of astrology in the two centuries before and after Christ) to India in the middle of the second century AD,[16] around the time that Ptolemy wrote the *Tetrabiblos*. To the present day, astrologers in India continue to use the sidereal zodiac, albeit with a different definition than that of the original Babylonian sidereal zodiac defined with Aldebaran at 15° Taurus and Antares at 15° Scorpio. For, according to the Babylonian definition, the star Spica is located at 29° Virgo, whereas the official Indian zodiac is defined with Spica at 30° Virgo, leading to a 1° difference from the original zodiac.

Without going into detail concerning this difference, it is evident that astronomers and astrologers in India remained true to the original principal established by the Babylonians of the signs of the zodiac

---

14 Steiner, *Ancient Myths*, pp. 51–53 (words in [ ] added by R.P).

15 Steiner, *Man: Hieroglyph of the Universe*, p. 162, indicates that the cultural epochs are each 2,160 years in length.

16 Pingree, "*Astronomy and Astrology in India and Iran*," *Isis* 54, pp. 229–246, discusses details of this transmission.

as equal-division constellations. How does Ptolemy fit into this discussion of the zodiac? Why did the *Tetrabiblos* come to be known as the "Bible" of astrology?

The important point to note is that in AD 150, when Ptolemy wrote the *Tetrabiblos*, the vernal point—identified by the Sun's position in the zodiac at the time of the vernal equinox—was located at 1° Aries. It is this fact that underlies the following words from the *Tetrabiblos*:

> Two signs are called equinoctial, the one which is first from the spring equinox, Aries, and the one which begins with the autumnal equinox, Libra.... There are two solstitial signs, the first interval of 30° from the summer solstice, the sign of Cancer, and the first from the winter solstice, Capricorn.[17]

It is this passage—and six other similar passages[18]—in the *Tetrabiblos* that led to the misunderstanding that has affected astrology since the time of Ptolemy. This misunderstanding resulted in the consequence that from that time onward the zodiac in astrology in the western world was considered to be defined with the vernal point *permanently* at 0° Aries. This newly defined zodiac introduced into astrology by Ptolemy is called the *tropical* zodiac to distinguish it from the earlier zodiac of the Babylonians which it replaced, and the Babylonian zodiac, in turn, is called the *sidereal* zodiac in order to distinguish it from the tropical zodiac. At that time, when Ptolemy wrote the *Tetrabiblos*, it was justifiable to define the sign of Aries as the 30° arc extending eastward from the vernal point, since the vernal point was very close to 0° Aries in the Babylonian sidereal zodiac. However, this definition adopted by Ptolemy does imply a 1° error, since in AD 150, at the time of writing the *Tetrabiblos*, the vernal point was actually located at 1° Aries, not at 0° Aries. In this connection it is interesting to note that Ptolemy, lacking the powerful instruments at the disposal of modern astronomers, in compiling his catalog of stars for the *Almagest*

17 Ptolemy, *Tetrabiblos* I,11 (tr. Robbins, p. 67).

18 Ptolemy, *Tetrabiblos* I,10 (tr. pp. 59–61); I,12 (tr. p. 69); I,15 (tr. p. 77); I,18 (tr. pp. 83–87); I,19 (tr. p. 89); II,10 (tr. pp. 195–199).

made an error of 1°15' in his specification of the location of the vernal point.[19]

As we shall see, it was definitely not Ptolemy's intention to create a new zodiac to replace the existing one. However, the impression given in Ptolemy's *Tetrabiblos* is that the zodiac is defined by fixing the vernal point permanently at 0° Aries. This new definition of the zodiac was adopted by default, because hardly anyone knew of any other definition of the zodiac. This was not so much the case with Greek astrologers who lived in the centuries after Ptolemy, although some of them did (e.g., Rhetorius, one of the last Hellenistic astrologers, who flourished in the early sixth century AD, did adopt the tropical zodiac). However, it was the case above all with Arabic astrologers, for whom Ptolemy's *Tetrabiblos* was their primary source. It is primarily in the Arab culture that the *Tetrabiblos* became the "Bible" of astrology.

Initially Greek astrologers paid little attention to Ptolemy's new astrological creation of the tropical zodiac.[20] This has been demonstrated in studies of Greek horoscopes spanning the first to the fifth centuries AD, compiled by Neugebauer and van Hoesen in the publication *Greek Horoscopes*. From Neugebauer's analysis it is evident that most of the Greek horoscopes were sidereal, using the same (or similar) frame of reference as the Babylonian sidereal zodiac.[21] Neugebauer distinguishes between the horoscopes found in literary sources and other horoscopes ("original documents") mainly written on papyrus, and concludes that the later literary horoscopes, almost all from the fifth century AD, were in terms of the tropical zodiac.[22] The "original documents" extend over the period from 62 BC to AD 478, and the

19 Neugebauer, *A History of Ancient Mathematical Astronomy*, vol. 1, p. 284. It has to be borne in mind that Ptolemy did not have accurate modern astronomical instruments at his disposal.

20 Here a distinction is being drawn between the use of the tropical zodiac as an astronomical coordinate system introduced by Hipparchus and the astrological use of the tropical zodiac in which it is considered, over and above its function as a coordinate system, to possess astrological qualities or influences expressed in its twelve signs.

21 Neugebauer and van Hoesen, *Greek Horoscopes*, p. 172.

22 Ibid. pp. 171–172.

literary horoscopes from 72 BC to AD 621. The bulk of these approximately 180 Greek horoscopes are thus distributed over the first to the fifth centuries.

An example of a literary horoscope is one cast for October 28, AD 497 in which all the planetary longitudes are between 2° and 4° less than those computed by Neugebauer using the tropical zodiac. Even allowing for computational errors on the part of the astrologer who cast the horoscope, it is evident that a sidereal frame of reference was used.[23] The literary horoscope from AD 516 is too incomplete to enable an assessment concerning whether it was cast in the sidereal or tropical zodiac. The last literary horoscope is for the birth of the new religion of Islam, cast for September 1, AD 621, the beginning of the Byzantine year preceding the Hijra. Here again the values computed by Neugebauer in the tropical zodiac are greater than those given in the horoscope, again pointing to a sidereal frame of reference.[24] This horoscope was cast by the astrologer Stephanus, and his comments attached to the horoscope reveal a knowledge of events up to AD 775, thus indicating that this horoscope for AD 621 was cast over one and a half centuries later than this date.[25]

23 If this horoscope were cast in the framework of the Babylonian sidereal zodiac, the amount in 497 that sidereal longitudes would be less in value than the tropical longitudes would be 3°51', since this is the amount of precession between 220 and 497. The year AD 220 is the "zero year" when the vernal point was located at 0° Aries in the Babylonian sidereal zodiac. It should be noted that 220 is the *actual* zero year, whereas 215 (given in the above tabulation of the zodiacal ages) is the *average* year—i.e., the year computed assuming that the vernal point moves uniformly at 1° in 72 years without any fluctuation in this value for the rate of precession.

24 If this horoscope were cast in the framework of the Babylonian sidereal zodiac, the amount in 621 that sidereal longitudes would be less in value than the tropical longitudes would be 5°41', since this is the amount of precession between 220 and 621. However, the planetary longitudes in this horoscope (excluding Venus' and Mercury's longitudes which are grossly inaccurate) are between only 1° and 4° less than the computed value, and in the case of the Moon the longitude given on the horoscope is 2° *more* than the computed value. Thus it seems unlikely that this astrologer was using the Babylonian norm for the sidereal zodiac, and perhaps he was using another sidereal norm. However, it is also conceivable that he was using tropical longitudes but made a consistent error in his computations so that they all (apart from the Moon) turned out to be less than they should have been.

25 Neugebauer and van Hoesen, *Greek Horoscopes*, op. cit., p. 190.

An independent analysis by Kollerstrom of the computations upon which nineteen Greek horoscopes were based (together with five Babylonian horoscopes included in the analysis) leads to this conclusion:

> A single frame of reference for the sidereal zodiac was used by both Babylonian and Greek astrologers, enduring over eight centuries, before being forgotten in the Dark Ages.... These horoscopes show that even in the centuries after Ptolemy, the astrologers writing in Greek continued to use a sidereal reference. The horoscopes are mainly from Alexandria, indicating that even in Ptolemy's native city the sidereal tradition endured.[26]

With the expansion of Christianity in the West, the practice of astrology in the Christian world declined, effectively disappearing by the sixth century AD, except for isolated examples such as the horoscope from AD 621 for the birth of Islam. The last definitely sidereal horoscope from *Greek Horoscopes* is the one referred to above dated to the year AD 497.[27] Soon after this astrology—as the practice of casting horoscopes—was taken up in the Arabic-speaking world with the first Arabic horoscope dating to the year 531.[28] While some Arab astrologers continued to use the sidereal zodiac, the available

26 Kollerstrom, "The Star Zodiac of Antiquity," *Culture and Cosmos*, vol. 1, p. 15. Kollerstrom used 19 horoscopes from Neugebauer and van Hoesen, *Greek Horoscopes*, and an additional 5 Babylonian horoscopes later published by Rochberg, *Babylonian Horoscopes*, spanning the years 235 to 69 BC He analyzed the longitudes of planets (excluding Mercury for which the values are less reliable) from each horoscope. Leaving out obviously incorrect values, his analysis is based on 96 longitudes from which he concludes that the sidereal zodiac was the sole frame of reference used by Babylonian and Greek astrologers. Kollerstrom's analysis shows a best fit for a zodiacal framework in which the star Spica is located at 30° Virgo as in the Indian zodiac. See also Nicholas Kollerstrom, "On the Measurement of Celestial Longitude in Antiquity," *Optics and Astronomy*, ed. G. Simon and S. Débarbat (Bruxelles, 2001), pp. 145-159.

27 As discussed in footnote 31, although the likelihood is that the horoscope of AD 621 was sidereal, using a different norm than the Babylonian one, it is also possible that it was an inaccurately cast tropical horoscope, so this example is not really conclusive.

28 Neugebauer and van Hoesen, *Greek Horoscopes*, op. cit., p. 161: "*The earliest Arabic horoscope, as far as known to us, is cast for the coronation of the Sasanian King Khosro Anōsharwān (*AD *531 August 18).*"

evidence, as far as one can tell,[29] shows that many Arabic astrologers used the tropical zodiac in casting horoscopes.[30]

When Ptolemy's *Tetrabiblos* was translated from Greek into Arabic, it became a standard reference work on astrology for many Arab astrologers, who adopted Ptolemy's introduction of the tropical zodiac into astrology. It is hard to know if these astrologers were even aware that there had ever been an astrology based on the sidereal zodiac prior to Ptolemy. By and large the sidereal zodiac was forgotten.

Thus, as astrology based on the sidereal zodiac disappeared from the Christian world, at the same time a new kind of astrology based on the tropical zodiac and the work of Ptolemy began to grow and flourish in the Arabic-speaking world. This new astrology was then introduced into Christian Europe from about AD 1140 onward through translations from Arabic into Latin.[31] At this stage, evidently the very existence of the sidereal zodiac was unknown to European astrologers. In this way the tropical astrology of the Arab astrologers became established in Europe in place of the ancient sidereal astrology that had flourished for at least nine hundred years: from 410 BC, the date of the world's oldest horoscopes found so far,[32] to AD 497, the date of one of the last Greek horoscopes that is known definitely to be sidereal, as discussed above. The extraordinary thing is that apparently no one in Europe knew that there had been any other kind of astrology than that of Ptolemy based on the tropical zodiac.[33] And it

29 It is not always easy, as can be seen from the discussion of the horoscope of the birth of Islam (cast for AD 621 September 1) discussed above, to assess whether a horoscope is using tropical coordinates or a sidereal frame of reference.

30 Neugebauer and van Hoesen, *Greek Horoscopes*, op. cit., p. 172; cf. also Pingree, *The Thousands of Abū Ma'shar*; and Kennedy and Pingree, *The Astrological History of Māshā'allāh.*

31 Tester, *A History of Western Astrology*, p. 147.

32 Rochberg, *Babylonian Horoscopes.*

33 Evidently Ptolemy did not consciously intend to introduce a new zodiac, the tropical zodiac, into astrology through the *Tetrabiblos*, since—as will be discussed in chapter 3—his own references in this work indicate a sidereal frame of reference. Rather, his introduction of the tropical zodiac into astrology was a historical accident occasioned by the fact that at the time

was not until the twentieth century that knowledge of the existence of the Babylonian sidereal zodiac reemerged in the West through the excavation and decipherment of cuneiform texts.

---

he wrote the *Tetrabiblos* (ca. AD 150) the vernal point was at 1° Aries in the Babylonian sidereal zodiac, and so Ptolemy's placing of the vernal point at 0° Aries was fairly accurate. The historical accident consisted in this placing of the vernal point at 0° Aries becoming later interpreted as something permanent and unchanging.

Chapter 3

Ptolemy's *Tetrabiblos*: A Manual of Sidereal Astrology

The thesis developed in this book, based on a careful study of the "Bible" of astrology, is that not only did Ptolemy not intend to introduce a new zodiac into astrology but, further, that the astrology he expounds upon in the *Tetrabiblos* is *sidereal*. This conclusion, which is a shocking one for the astrological world, is based on Ptolemy's own statements, which we shall now consider in detail. Before doing so, however, let us recall that the purpose of this book is to reveal the new science of Astrogeographia contained in seed form in the *Tetrabiblos*, if it is read correctly. To read the *Tetrabiblos* correctly, it is necessary to grasp that whenever Ptolemy refers to the zodiac, he means the *sidereal* zodiac. Once this is grasped—and it is abundantly clear that this is so from a consideration of Ptolemy's statements—the way is open to understand Astrogeographia and its extraordinary scope for deepening one's knowledge of horoscopes. Then we shall return in the next chapter to further develop the theme outlined in the first chapter concerning the relationship between the Great Pyramid and the star Alnitak, between the city of Alexandria and the star Alnilam, between a large European city and the star Aldebaran, and many other remarkable relationships existing between geographical locations and fixed stars.

Let us recall that the signs of the sidereal zodiac, as originally defined by the Babylonians, are defined by the fixed stars comprising that sign. As an example, the most prominent star in the constellation of Taurus, Aldebaran ("the Bull's eye") is located in the center of this sign at 15° Taurus. In the image of the constellation of Taurus (see below) Aldebaran is located in the vicinity of the left eye of the Bull (all references to right and left are from the perspective of the viewer; note, further, that the perspective adopted here in relation to the stellar sphere is that of a viewer in the Northern Hemisphere).The star Aldebaran marks the left tip of the V-shaped star cluster known as the Hyades (in the region of the face of the Bull). The vertex of the V is marked by the star Hyadum I ("the first of the Hyades"), located at 11° Taurus.[1] And the right tip of the V of the Hyades is marked by the star Ain ("the [second] eye of the Bull") at 13¾° Taurus, which coincides with the right eye of the Bull. For the Babylonians the Hyades were an intrinsic part of the sign of Taurus, just as were the Pleiades (5° Taurus) in the neck of the Bull and El Nath (28° Taurus) and Alhecka (30° Taurus) marking the tips of the upper and lower horns of the Bull. The visual appearance of the constellation of Taurus as delineated by these stars is:

Urania's Mirror, Taurus (1823)[2]

1 All longitudes of stars given in the sidereal zodiac are from the reconstructed star catalog underlying the Babylonian sidereal zodiac in my Ph.D. thesis *History of the Zodiac*, appendix 1. See also Powell and Treadgold, *The Sidereal Zodiac*, pp. 34–37.

2 *Urania's Mirror, or a View of the Heavens* is a collection of thirty-two hand-colored engravings of the constellations. A boxed set of 32

Astrologers in antiquity, who were all siderealists, connected up the stars in a constellation and in this way derived the sign or astrological glyph—♉ in the case of Taurus.[3] Each zodiacal sign is embedded within the corresponding constellation of the zodiac—at least, this was the view of all astrologers in antiquity: from Babylon to Egypt, Greece, and Rome. It was also the view of Ptolemy, who wrote in the *Tetrabiblos*:

> The sign of Taurus as a whole is indicative of both temperatures and is somewhat hot; but taken part by part, its leading portion, particularly near the Pleiades, is marked by earthquakes, winds, and mists; its middle moist and cold, and its following portion, near the Hyades, fiery and productive of thunder and lightning.[4]

Here Ptolemy is speaking as a *sidereal astrologer*, acknowledging that the Pleiades and the Hyades—with its bright star Aldebaran at 15° Taurus—belong to the sign of Taurus. In contrast, modern tropical astrologers—disagreeing with Ptolemy—locate Aldebaran ("the Bull's eye") in the sign of Gemini, currently at 10° Gemini (tropical). Seventy-two years ago Aldebaran was at 9° Gemini (tropical); 144 years ago Aldebaran was at 8° Gemini (tropical); and 216 years ago Aldebaran was at 7° Gemini (tropical). This slow shift of the fixed star Aldebaran (fixed at 15° Taurus in the sidereal zodiac) through the tropical sign of Gemini takes place on account of the precession of the equinoxes at a rate of 1° in 72 years.

In the same chapter of the *Tetrabiblos* Ptolemy writes:

> The sign of Cancer as a whole is one of fair, warm weather; but, part by part, its leading portion and the region of Praesepe is stifling, productive of earthquakes, and mists.[5]

---

constellation cards of the engravings was published by Samuel Leigh. The engravings by Sidney Hall were based on artwork that is attributed to Rev. Richard Rouse Bloxam.

3 Powell, *Hermetic Astrology*, vol. I, pp. 233–237 shows how each of the astrological glyphs for the twelve signs of the zodiac is derived by connecting up the (more prominent) stars comprising that sign. See also Paul and Powell, *Cosmic Dances of the Zodiac*.

4 Ptolemy, *Tetrabiblos* I,11 (tr. Robbins), pp. 201–203.

5 Ibid.

Here again Ptolemy is speaking as a sidereal astrologer, like the Babylonians, for whom Praesepe ("the Beehive") was located at 12½° Cancer. At the present time, on account of precession, tropical astrologers locate Praesepe at 7½° Leo, totally disagreeing with Ptolemy! In his day, just as today, one clearly sees the star cluster Praesepe in Cancer, whereas 7½° Leo is in the vicinity of the star Regulus marking the heart of the Lion. For the Babylonians, Egyptians, Greeks, Romans, and Ptolemy, Praesepe belonged to the sign of Cancer. And as we shall see below, in the light of Astrogeographia, Ptolemy's indication that Praesepe is productive of earthquakes turns out to be very true.

There is yet another interesting point to notice in connection with the star cluster of the Pleiades in Taurus and the star cluster Praesepe in Cancer. This has to do with the astrological teaching of *exaltations* deriving from a very early phase of development of astrology in Babylon, where they were called "*qaqqar nisirti*." The Babylonian *qaqqar nisirti* are precisely the *hypsomata* or exaltations of Greek astrology. There is a Babylonian text listing the "*qaqqar nisirti*" of the planets.[6] In the Babylonian text each planet's exaltation (*hypsoma*) is in a sign of the zodiac, e.g., for Jupiter it is in the sign of Cancer, or between the sign of Cancer and the sign of Leo. In the three *hypsomata* depictions published by Weidner in 1919, Plate V, the engraved drawings each depict a planet in relation to a sign of the zodiac and to stars within that sign, e.g., the Moon is drawn in Taurus adjacent to a cluster of seven stars.[7] The identification of these seven stars as the Pleiades cluster is certain, since the name "MUL.MUL" is engraved on the drawing and from other texts it is known that MUL.MUL means the Pleiades. Hermann Hunger and David Pingree transcribe *ašar nisirti* or *bīt nisirti* for *hypsoma* (exaltation) instead of *qaqqar nisirti*, and concerning exaltations Pingree remarks that, "The earliest attestation of this concept is found in the inscriptions of Esarhaddon of Assyria" (680–668 BC).[8] So the astrological teaching of exaltations

6 Kugler, *Sternkunde und Sterndienst in Babel*, vol. i, p. 40.

7 Weidner, "*Babylonische Hypsomatabilder*," *Orientalistische Literatur-Zeitung* 22, cols. 10–16.

8 Hunger and Pingree, *Astral Sciences in Mesopotamia*, p. 28.

stems from the first half of the seventh century BC, long before the tropical zodiac was defined,[9] and so it is possible to grasp the meaning of the exaltations only in relation to the ancient sidereal zodiac of the Babylonians.

The signs of exaltation are well known in Greek astrology, although they are not mentioned by Ptolemy. They are referred to by Vettius Valens, Firmicus Maternus, Dorotheus Sidonius and Sextus Empiricus. The Greek tradition of *hypsomata* refers to specific positions of the planetary exaltations, generally given as:[10]

Sun 19°	Aries
Moon 3°	Taurus
Saturn 21°	Libra
Jupiter 15°	Cancer
Mars 28°	Capricorn
Venus 27°	Pisces
Mercury 15°	Virgo

Moreover, exactly the same positions are recorded by Muslim astrologers, who add to the list exaltations for the lunar nodes:[11]

Ascending Node 3°	Gemini
Descending Node 3°	Sagittarius

As handed down in the astrological tradition, the exaltations of the planets are specific locations (degrees) in the zodiac, where the planets are most powerful and influential. A study of these degrees reveals that they refer to the positions of certain stars or star clusters in the sidereal zodiac, and it was this mode of specification of the

9 The tropical zodiac, as it is defined in relation to the vernal point, presupposes a certain level of astronomical ability in order to be able to accurately determine the location of the vernal point, and this level was attained only in Greek astronomy—apparently by Hipparchus (second century BC) and certainly by Ptolemy (second century AD).

10 MacKenzie, "Zoroastrian Astrology in the *Bundahišn*," *Bulletin of the School of Oriental and African Studies* 27 (1964), p. 524.

11 Pingree, *The Thousands of Abū Ma'shar*, p. 61.

planetary exaltations which existed from the first half of the seventh century BC (when the exaltations were first specified) until the sidereal zodiac was introduced around 500 BC. Recalling that the teaching of exaltations is very ancient (first half of the seventh century BC)—preceding the introduction of the zodiac in Babylon in the early fifth century BC—it is not surprising to find that the degrees of exaltations given are not very accurate. Take, for example, the Moon, whose exaltation is given as 3° Taurus and is depicted in conjunction with the Pleiades. Here there is a 2° error, since the Pleiades are located at 5° Taurus.[12] The important point, however, is that it is the conjunction of the Moon with the Pleiades which signified that the Moon was at its exaltation. This was the ancient form of reference to the exaltation of the Moon and not the degree in the zodiac. It was only after the introduction of the sidereal zodiac in Babylon around 500 BC that the exaltations were assigned zodiacal degrees. This assigning of degrees was only approximate. For example, in the case of the Pleiades (the exaltation of the Moon) the longitude assigned to the Pleiades in the sidereal zodiac was given as 3° Taurus whereas, more accurately, it should have been 5° Taurus.

If a modern tropical astrologer calculates that the Moon is at 3° Taurus in the tropical zodiac, and if he knows about the astrological teaching of exaltations, in accordance with this astrological tradition he will say that "the Moon is at exaltation." Yet, in actual fact, at the present time this statement of tropical astrology ("Moon at 3° Taurus") means that the Moon would be at about 8° Aries in the sidereal zodiac, near the stars marking the horns of the Ram (Aries), a long way from the Pleiades in the neck of the Bull. This one could verify by looking up into the night sky and seeing the actual Moon near the stars marking the horns of the Ram, even while a tropical ephemeris would list the Moon's position as 3° Taurus.

As a second example, the exaltations of the lunar nodes refer to the place of intersection of the great circle of the Milky Way with the circle of the sidereal zodiac. The Milky Way—as a visible phenomenon—is a band of stars, and so is the zodiac. In antiquity it

12 According to the reconstructed Babylonian zodiac in appendix 1 of my Ph.D. thesis. See also Powell and Treadgold, *The Sidereal Zodiac*, p. 34.

was difficult to be precise in terms of giving an exact degree of the intersection of these two bands of stars in the heavens. However, it appears that their intersection was identified as the place where the lunar nodes are most powerful—i.e., the place of exaltation of the lunar nodes. Now, through modern astronomy, the central band of the Milky Way (galactic equator) and the central band of the zodiac (ecliptic) are well defined, and the zodiacal locations of the intersection of these two great circles—the ecliptic and the galactic equator—have been identified as 5° Gemini and 5° Sagittarius. In light of the foregoing, it is possible, therefore, that the true exaltations of the lunar nodes are to be considered as 5° Gemini and 5° Sagittarius, in which case there is a 2° discrepancy from the values of 3° Gemini and 3° Sagittarius given by astrological tradition for the exaltations of the Northern and Southern lunar nodes.[13]

In the case of the exaltation of Saturn at 21° Libra, the Babylonians saw that Saturn was exalted when it appeared in conjunction with the star Zubenelgenubi, the brightest star in Libra, marking the southwestern end of the beam of the Balance. The exact degree of this star is 20½° Libra, so the exaltation should be corrected from 21° to 20½° Libra. In this case the original specification of the exaltation of Saturn—the star Zubenelgenubi—was (after the introduction of the zodiac) equated with the zodiacal longitude of 21° Libra. This was fairly accurate, in contrast to the 2° error in the case of the Moon's exaltation, the Pleiades.

The exaltation of the Sun is more or less opposite in the zodiac to that of Saturn. In the case of the Sun it is not possible to see the actual position of the Sun against the background of the stars, except at the rare event of a total solar eclipse.[14] Because the Sun and Saturn were felt to be opposite in nature—Saturn was called "the Sun of the

13 Based on the location of the galactic center at 2° Sagittarius in the Babylonian sidereal zodiac, another possibility would be to define the exaltations of the lunar nodes as 2° Gemini and 2° Sagittarius, respectively, with just a one-degree discrepancy from the traditional values of 3° Gemini and 3° Sagittarius.

14 The term *ecliptic*, the path of the Sun through the middle of the zodiacal belt, is the locus of points at which solar eclipses can take place, hence the term *ecliptic*.

night"[15]—it is quite conceivable that the Sun's exaltation was therefore located opposite that of Saturn in the zodiac (with a 2° shift from exact opposition). Another plausible explanation for the Sun's exaltation at 19° Aries has to do with the Babylonian practice of watching for the first appearance of the thin sickle crescent of the New Moon on the western horizon after sunset, which for them signified the beginning of the month. For the New Moon to be visible in this way, it has to be a certain number of degrees advanced from the Sun (say 14° to ensure clear visibility). If the thin crescent of the New Moon were to have been seen in conjunction with the Pleiades after sunset on the western horizon—i.e., with the Moon at exaltation, the Babylonians might have deduced that the Sun had to be located 14° behind the Moon at 19° Aries and concluded that, with the Moon at exaltation, the visible appearance of the "birth" of the Moon out of the setting Sun indicated that the Sun, too, was at exaltation. Since there is no star cluster or prominent star in this region of Aries to refer to as the clearly identifiable place of exaltation, then—in contrast to the other planets (except for Venus, see below)—it is not possible to identify the exact degree of the Sun's exaltation.

The place of exaltation of Jupiter is given in the astrological tradition as 15° Cancer (handed down since the phase of Babylonian astrology *after* the introduction of the zodiac around 500 BC). As in the case of the Moon's exaltation (3° Taurus), when the Moon is in conjunction with the star cluster of the Pleiades (5° Taurus), where there is a 2° discrepancy, so in the case of Jupiter's exaltation (15° Cancer), when Jupiter is in conjunction with Praesepe ("the Beehive" at 12½° Cancer), there is a 2½° discrepancy. Prior to the intoduction of the zodiac, the exaltation of Jupiter was originally seen by the Babylonians as Jupiter's conjunction with Praesepe. After the introduction of the zodiac around 500 BC, the exaltation of Jupiter (Praesepe) was assigned 15° Cancer in the sidereal zodiac whereas, more accurately, it should have been 12½° Cancer, coinciding with Praesepe. Therefore Jupiter's exaltation should be corrected to 12½° Cancer. In terms of Astrogeographia the devastating earthquake that hit Pakistan's mountainous Kashmir region on October 8, 2005,

15 Powell, *History of the Planets*, p. 11.

killing some 90,000 people and leaving more than 3½ million homeless, is connected with Praesepe which, as indicated by Ptolemy, "is productive of earthquakes."

The location of Mars' exaltation, given as 28° Capricorn, coincides with Deneb Algiedi ("the tail of the Goat") at 28¾° Capricorn—this being the exact place of the exaltation of Mars in the sidereal zodiac. As in the case of Saturn's exaltation, the assigning of a degree in the sidereal zodiac (after its introduction around 500 BC) to the exaltation (Deneb Algiedi) of Mars, is a fairly accurate degree assignment.

With respect to the exaltation of Mercury (15° Virgo), this location coincides with the vertical line in Virgo between Vindemiatrix (15¼° Virgo) and Porrima (15½° Virgo). The exact location of Mercury's exaltation is thus 15¼° Virgo, taking Vindemiatrix as the stellar indicator of Mercury's place of exaltation.[16] As in the case of Mars' and Saturn's exaltation, the assigning of a degree in the sidereal zodiac (after its introduction around 500 BC) to the exaltation (Vindemiatrix) of Mercury, is a fairly accurate degree assignment.

Lastly, the exaltation of Venus (27° Pisces) is in a region of the zodiac where there are no star clusters or bright stars. To grasp the significance of this zodiacal location of Venus' exaltation it is necessary to consider the shape of the constellation of Pisces. The figure comprising this constellation is made up of two fishes connected by a band of stars: the eastern fish, swimming up toward the north, and the western fish swimming horizontally, parallel to the ecliptic, in the direction of Aquarius, whereas the band of stars connects their tails.[17] According to ancient mythology, the goddess Venus and her son Cupid were one day at the banks of the Euphrates when a giant

16 It is possible that Porrima (rather than Vindemiatrix) was the original exaltation of Mercury in the pre-zodiac period of the exaltations, when the planetary exaltations were identified solely by stars or star clusters. Now, over 2,600 years later (since the original exaltations stem from the first half of the 7th century BC), it is not possible to conclude one way or the other whether Mercury was seen to be exalted when in conjunction with Vindemiatrix or with Porrima. It could well have been the line *between* Vindemiatrix and Porrima that was the visible location of Mercury's exaltation.

17 The astrological glyph ♓ based on the figure of the constellation of Pisces simplifies the depiction by showing both fishes in the vertical connected by a horizontal band.

monster, Typhon, suddenly appeared. To save themselves from the monster, they plunged into the river and escaped by changing themselves into fishes. To commemorate this event the two fishes were placed among the stars. The exaltation of Venus (27° Pisces) is in the region of the ecliptic that is directly beneath the eastern fish of Pisces, the fish that is swimming up toward the north, which can be seen in connection with the goddess Venus (vertical figure), whereas the other fish can be seen in connection with her child Cupid (horizontal figure). The exaltation of the planet Venus, therefore, is in precisely the zodiacal region with which the goddess Venus is associated in mythology. However, as there is not a star cluster or prominent star located here in the vicinity of 27° Pisces, it is not possible—in contrast to the other planets (with the exception of the Sun)—to specify the exact location of the exaltation of Venus.

To summarize the locations of the exaltations of the planets:

Sun	19°00'	Aries
Moon	5°15'	Taurus (Pleiades–Alcyone)
Saturn	20°17'	Libra (Zubenelgenubi)
Jupiter	12°39'	Cancer (Praesepe)
Mars	28°48'	Capricorn (Deneb Algiedi)
Venus	27°00'	Pisces
Mercury	15°12'	Virgo (Vindemiatrix)
Ascending Node	5°16'	Gemini (intersection of galactic equator and ecliptic)
Descending Node	5°16'	Sagittarius (intersection of galactic equator and ecliptic)

The above sidereal longitudes are computed for the epoch 2000.0 in relation to the Synetic Vernal Point defined in *The American Sidereal Ephemeris*, based on the definition found by Cyril Fagan and Donald Bradley in 1957 and used since then by sidereal astrologers in the west.[18] At the root of this definition is the discovery by

18 Michelsen, *The American Sidereal Ephemeris, 1976–2000*, introduction. See also Michelsen, *The American Sidereal Ephemeris, 2001–2025*, introduction.

Babylonian astronomers that the axis between the two first magnitude stars Aldebaran and Antares, each in the center of their respective signs (Taurus and Scorpio), divides the zodiac exactly in two, with Aldebaran defined to be at 15° Taurus and Antares at 15° Scorpio. However, since the fixed stars are subject to proper motion, they display small changes in relation to one another over thousands of years, and so no single star or pair of stars can be chosen to define the entire zodiac. It was this insight that led Donald Bradley to search for an objective basis for a modern definition of the sidereal zodiac, which he believed he had found in 1956 and which he called the *Synetic Vernal Point* (SVP). He used statistical methods (applied to astrology) to find the SVP, which is defined in relation to the vernal point for the epoch 1950.0.[19] It is indeed an anomaly that the sidereal zodiac ("zodiac of the stars") is defined in relation to the vernal point, yet this—in terms of modern astronomy—is a secure definition, because the vernal point is the one point which modern astronomy is able to determine with complete accuracy and thus uses as the basis for all astronomical calculations. Once having determined the location of the SVP in the sidereal zodiac for any moment in time (allowing for precession before or after the epoch 1950.0), it is then a simple matter to transform modern astronomical calculations into sidereal coordinates. The SVP is obviously a compromise solution for defining the sidereal zodiac, but in lieu of finding something better, it is the best definition of the sidereal zodiac in terms of modern astronomy that exists at the present point in time. Moreover, it is in harmony with the original Babylonian definition, as can be seen from the following consideration. Using the SVP definition of the sidereal zodiac and computing the sidereal longitude of Aldebaran (taking account of its proper motion) going back in time, it emerges that Aldebaran was located at 15°00' Taurus from 477 BC to AD 213—the time during which the astronomy of the Babylonians, based on their definition of the zodiac (with Aldebaran at 15° Taurus) flourished. The

19 Ibid. The Synetic Vernal Point is determined for the epoch 1950.0 in such a way that the vernal point at that date was located at 5°57'28.64" in the sign of Pisces in the sidereal zodiac.

following table indicates the shift in Aldebaran's sidereal longitude, owing to its proper motion, since that time, using the SVP definition of the sidereal zodiac:

Prior to 477 BC	14°59'	Taurus
477 BC–AD 213	15°00'	Taurus
AD 214–923	15°01'	Taurus
AD 924–1655	15°02'	Taurus
AD 1655–2413	15°03'	Taurus

Further, the longitude of Antares, taking account of its proper motion, based on the SVP definition of the sidereal zodiac, has been 15°01' Scorpio during the entire period from 7494 BC and will remain at 15°01' Scorpio until AD 2671—i.e., its sidereal longitude remains unchanged for a period of more than 10,000 years.[20] Thus, during the time when the Babylonian zodiac was introduced and utilized, Aldebaran was at 15°00' Taurus and Antares at 15°01' Scorpio, agreeing exactly with the definition of Babylonian astronomers, who were unable to measure stellar longitude with the precision we are able to now, and for whom, therefore, the fact that Antares was located at 15°01' Scorpio rather than 15°00' Scorpio could not have been detected. The earliest recorded use of the sidereal zodiac found thus far is that of a cuneiform text which presents calculated (and observed?) data for thirty-eight possibilities of solar eclipses in the period from December 5, 475 to July 21, 457 BC.[21] With the decline of Babylonian culture, Babylonian astronomy died out during the first century AD. As can be seen from the above table, during the period when Babylonian astronomy—based on the sidereal zodiac with Aldebaran at 15° Taurus—flourished, this was precisely during the period when Aldebaran was *exactly* at 15° Taurus in terms of the sidereal zodiac defined by the SVP. In this sense the SVP definition of the sidereal zodiac—as a "modern solution" as to how to define the zodiac accurately—is in perfect agree-

20 However, during this 10,000-year period the latitude of Antares shifts just over 1° from 3S34 in 7494 BC to 4S39 in AD 2671.

21 Aaboe and Sachs, "Two Lunar Texts of the Achaemenid Period from Babylon," *Centaurus* 14 (1969), pp. 1–22.

ment with the original definition of the sidereal zodiac by Babylonian astronomers. Therefore, while the procedure by which Donald Bradley arrived at the definition of the SVP in 1957 is not completely transparent—i.e., it is not specified in an objectively verifiable way (except for Donald Bradley himself, who was convinced of the objective basis of his specification of the SVP), it is evident that the SVP does fulfil two important criteria:

1. it is in exact agreement with the original Babylonian zodiac specified by Aldebaran 15° Taurus and Antares at 15° Scorpio[22];
2. and it is completely identifiable in terms of modern astronomy and thus provides an astronomically reliable basis for all computations.

In conclusion, therefore, the SVP is something that—fortuitously—allows the sidereal zodiac to be defined within the framework of modern astronomy, even if the method by which it was derived is not wholly objective and transparently clear. It does take care, however, of the problem that other definitions of the sidereal zodiac have—at least, those definitions which are specified in relation to one or other fixed star[23]—namely, that of the movement of fixed stars on account of proper motion.

To round off this digression on the modern scientific specification of the sidereal zodiac: It was around 300 BC that the teachings of Babylonian astrology were in the process of being transmitted to

22 As shown in my Ph.D. thesis *History of the Zodiac*, the location of Aldebaran at 15° Taurus and Antares at 15° Scorpio provides the *intrinsic definition* of the Babylonian zodiac.

23 As an example, let us consider the modern Indian sidereal zodiac with Spica as the primary marking star, which was given official recognition by the Council of Scientific and Industrial Research, on behalf of the Indian government, where Spica is defined to be at 0° Libra, dividing the zodiac exactly in two—see "Report of the Calendar Reform Committee" (New Delhi, 1955). As this "official" Indian zodiac is defined in relation to Spica, the whole zodiac shifts with the proper motion of Spica. Nevertheless, the proper motion of Spica is very small. In terms of the sidereal zodiac defined by the SVP, Spica was located at 29°07' Virgo for over two thousand years, from 945 BC to AD 1120. Since AD 1121 Spica's sidereal longitude in the sidereal zodiac defined by the SVP is 29°06' Virgo.

Greece and Alexandria by figures such as the Chaldean astrologer Berossus, who founded an astrological school on the Greek island of Cos early in the third century BC. It was through figures such as Berossus that the Babylonian zodiac, defined by Aldebaran at 15° Taurus and Antares at 15° Scorpio, was transmitted to Greece, Egypt, and Rome.[24] Now, in our time, there is a modern definition of the sidereal zodiac which—as shown above—is in complete accordance with the original Babylonian definition. In terms of the modern definition of the sidereal zodiac based on the Synetic Vernal Point, here below is the table of exaltations computed for 300 BC, at the height of the practice of Babylonian astronomy and astrology, shortly after the start of the Seleucid Era in 311 BC.

Sun	19°00' Aries
Moon	5°14' Taurus (Pleiades–Alcyone)
Saturn	20°20' Libra (Zubenelgenubi)
Jupiter	12°39' Cancer (Praesepe)
Mars	28°33' Capricorn (Deneb Algiedi)
Venus	27°00' Pisces
Mercury	15°16' Virgo (Vindemiatrix)
Ascending Node	5°16' Gemini (intersection of galactic equator and ecliptic)
Descending Node	5°16' Sagittarius (intersection of galactic equator and ecliptic)

Comparing this table for the year 300 BC with the earlier one above for the year AD 2000, it can be seen that the exaltations of the planets have hardly changed, the largest shift being that of Mars (Deneb Algiedi), which shifted from 28°33' Capricorn in 300 BC to

24 Neugebauer, *A History of Ancient Mathematical Astronomy*, volume II, p. 960: "Cleomedes states that there exist two bright stars such that the rising of one coincides with the setting *of the other:* Aldebaran (*α Tauri*) and Antares (*α Scorpii*), both being located at the 15th degree of their respective sign." The Greek author Cleomedes quoted heavily from the Stoic philosopher and astrologer Posidonius (died around 50 BC), who taught on the island of Rhodes, a neighbouring island to the island of Cos. Here a line of transmission of knowledge of the definition of the Babylonian zodiac emerges: from Berossus to Posidonius to Cleomedes.

28°48' Capricorn in AD 2000, a shift of 0°15', the other shifts being all less than 0°05'.

After this digression let us return to consider the "Bible" of astrology, the *Tetrabiblos*, which reveals that Ptolemy was a sidereal astrologer, for whom the signs of the zodiac were more or less the same as the constellations of the same name. Thus he uses the words "sign" and "constellation" interchangeably, and so it would be wholly in accordance with Ptolemy to write "zodiacal sign/constellation." For example, he writes: "Constellations of the human form, both in the zodiac and among the fixed stars, cause the event to concern the human race."[25]

The zodiacal signs/constellations of human form are: Gemini, Virgo, Libra,[26] Aquarius, and (in part) Sagittarius. In the *Almagest* Ptolemy lists in his star catalog thirty-six extra-zodiacal constellations. These thirty-six constellations are above or below the zodiacal signs/constellations. Among these thirty-six constellations, those with human form are Cepheus (the Crowned King), Boötes (the Ploughman), Hercules (the Kneeling Man), Cassiopeia (the Enthroned Queen), Perseus (the Hero), Ophiucus (the Serpent Holder), Andromeda (the Chained Woman), Orion (the Hunter), and (in part) Centaurus (the Centaur). All the designations listed here stem from Ptolemy's star

25 Ptolemy, *Tetrabiblos* II,7, pp. 171–173. There is a similar passage in Tetrabiblos III,11 (tr. p. 315), concerning "The constellations both within and outside of the zodiac which are of human shape produce bodies which are harmonious of movement and well-proportioned."

26 In antiquity the figure of the Balance Holder was sometimes depicted holding the Scales. See, for example, Neugebauer and Parker, *Egyptian Astronomical Texts, vol. 3: Decans, Planets, Constellations and Zodiacs*, plate 40 (Daressy zodiac), plate 43 (Esna [B] zodiac), and plate 52 (Salamuni zodiac). These Egyptian zodiacs show a human figure holding the Scales—in the case of the Esna [B] zodiac, this figure is clearly a woman. These depictions solve a curious anomaly regarding the signs/constellations of the zodiac. For all the zodiacal constellations are either human or animal figures, with the exception of the Scales, which is an inanimate object. Since the word zodiac means "circle of the zoa," and zoa means "living creature," it is a strange anomaly that one of the circle should be an inanimate object. The depiction of this sign as a pair of scales held by a human figure—taking this to be the original depiction of Libra—restores this constellation to the circle of the zoa. The story as to how the Balance Holder was "banished" from the zodiac is an interesting one, too complex to relate in the space of a footnote.

catalog in the *Almagest*. It is clear from Ptolemy's statement quoted above that he attributed astrological influence not only to the twelve zodiacal signs/constellations but also to the thirty-six extra-zodiacal constellations.

Here the question arises: What sort of astrological event would involve an extra-zodiacal constellation? Such as Perseus, for example? Normally an astrologer would not have any reason to consider Perseus in terms of astrological events. For the astrologer is generally focused solely upon the movements of the Sun, Moon, and planets through the signs of the zodiac or—what is the same thing for sidereal astrologers—against the background of the constellations of the zodiac. However, when a comet appears, its movement is not restricted to the constellations of the zodiac. It traces its path across the heavens through the zodiacal and extra-zodiacal constellations alike. Two recent comets did move through the constellation of Perseus: the highly visible comet Hyakutake (1996) and the giant comet Hale-Bopp (1997), both of which passed through the constellation of Perseus, whose paths crossed at the star Algol exactly one year apart (on April 11).[27] Algol is the star marking the "evil eye" of Medusa, whose head was severed by Perseus wielding his sword and who—having taken the head of Medusa as a trophy—is depicted flying through the heavens holding the head of Medusa (whose primary marking star is Algol) in one hand. After passing by Algol in Perseus, Hale-Bopp re-entered the zodiacal belt in the region of Gemini. "The last sightings of Hale-Bopp in 1997 occurred while it passed through the constellation of the Twins (Gemini)."[28]

Comets have always been considered portents—astrologically speaking—usually of disasters and calamities, as indicated by the Roman astrologer Manilius (first century AD): "Such are the disasters which the glowing comets oft proclaim. Death comes with these celestial torches.... Wars, too, the fires portend, and sudden insurrection.... Comets also presage civil discord and strife between

27 Starfire Three (Bento, Schiappacasse, and Tresemer), *Signs in the Heavens*, explore the significance of the extraordinary coincidence of the two comets' paths crossing at Algol, exactly one year apart.

28 Ibid. p. 20.

kin."[29] And according to Ptolemy: "They show, through the parts of the zodiac in which their heads appear and through the directions in which the shapes of their tails point, the regions upon which misfortunes impend."[30]

With these words in the "Bible" of astrology, Ptolemy clearly indicates that comets are astrologically significant, agreeing with his predecessor Manilius that they portend misfortune. The fact that comets roam freely through the entire starry heavens means—(astro-)logically—that the *entire celestial sphere* provides the background for the movements of comets, just as the circle of the twelve zodiacal signs/constellations provides the background for the movements of the Sun, Moon, and planets. It is particularly in relation to comets that Ptolemy's words quoted earlier are relevant to astrology: "Constellations of the human form, both in the zodiac and among the fixed stars, cause the event to concern the human race." This statement from *Tetrabiblos* II,7 is just one of many in which the thirty-six extra-zodiacal constellations are treated equally with the twelve zodiacal signs/constellations.[31] For example, another statement by Ptolemy indicates: "In the constellations pertaining to rivers, such as Aquarius and Pisces, they concern the creatures of rivers and springs, and in Argo they affect both classes alike."[32]

The constellation of Argo the Ship, associated in antiquity with the ship in which Jason and the Argonauts set sail in search of the Golden

29 Manilius, *Astronomica* I.895-909 (tr. G. P. Goold; Loeb Classical Library/ Harvard University: Cambridge, MA, 1977), pp. 75–77.

30 Ptolemy, *Tetrabiblos* II,9, pp. 194–195.

31 The star catalog in Books VII and VIII of Ptolemy's *Almagest* lists twelve zodiacal constellations and thirty-six extra-zodiacal constellations, where the latter may be seen in relation to the *decans*, which are 10° divisions of the zodiacal signs/constellations—each 30° sign/constellation being subdivided into three 10° decans. See Paul and Powell, *Cosmic Dances of the Zodiac*, where the relationship of the thirty-six extra-zodiacal constellations to the thirty-six decans is described in detail. In modern astronomy an additional forty extra-zodiacal constellations have been specified since Ptolemy's days, most of them belonging to the southern celestial sphere, making a total of seventy-six extra-zodiacal constellations that, together with the twelve zodiacal constellations, makes up the eighty-eight constellations of modern astronomy.

32 Ptolemy, *Tetrabiblos* II,7, p. 175.

Fleece, is now—in modern astronomy—divided into three constellations: Vela (the Sail), Puppis (the Stern), and Carina (the Keel). The important point is that Ptolemy is definitely speaking as a sidereal astrologer when he mentions the constellations of Aquarius, Pisces, and Argo in the same breath. Moreover, he opens up a completely new perspective (new for modern astrology, but ancient in terms of the astrology of antiquity): that the astrologer's domain is the *entire celestial sphere*, embracing the constellations above and below the twelve zodiacal signs/constellations.[33] It is this breathtaking perspective that is of significance for Astrogeographia, where a one-to-one correspondence emerges between the whole celestial sphere and the globe of the Earth. Once one grasps that there is a one-to-one correspondence such that every star on the celestial globe is mirrored at a unique location of the earthly globe, it is clear that this correspondence has to be expressed in terms of the sidereal zodiac, where there is a continuity between the twelve zodiacal signs/constellations and the constellations above or below them. What is meant here by continuity?

Continuity in this context refers to the *continuity* between perception and thought (or conception). This can best be grasped by way of an example. Let us consider again the path of the comet Hale-Bopp which, after crossing through the constellation of Perseus, re-entered the zodiac in the region of the constellation of Gemini. Those who watched the Hale-Bopp trajectory saw it leave the constellation of Perseus and then enter the constellation of Gemini. Thus for the astronomer or sidereal astrologer watching the comet leave the constellation of Perseus and enter the constellation of Gemini, the thought or conception is the same as the perception. However, according to tropical astrology the comet left the constellation of Perseus and entered the sign of *Cancer*. In this latter case there is a lack of continuity in terms of visual perception and the thinking

33 Powell and Dann, *The Astrological Revolution*, chapter 5, show that true astrology embraces the entire celestial sphere—for example, the star Deneb, located 60° above the ecliptic, whose sidereal longitude is 10½° Aquarius, is active along the entire stellar meridian running through 10½° Aquarius. Every star in the entire celestial sphere, regardless of latitude north or south of the ecliptic, is significant. Thus, the research presented in *The Astrological Revolution* confirms Ptolemy's inclusion of the 36 extra-zodiacal constellations above and below the twelve zodiacal constellations.

process, since the comet was *seen* in Perseus, then *seen* in Gemini but simultaneously *thought to be in Cancer* in the tropical zodiac. For the astronomer and the sidereal astrologer alike, there is no such discontinuity in terms of perception and thought. For both, the comet was seen to leave Perseus and then enter Gemini—the difference between the astronomer and the sidereal astrologer being that for the former Gemini is a constellation some 28° long, whereas for the latter Gemini is a stellar constellation (or sign) extending 30° in length and which is utilized as a coordinate system (in this case to record the exact location of the comet—or of any planets in this sign/constellation—in degrees in the sidereal sign of Gemini).

That Ptolemy also thought in terms of a continuity between the extra-zodiacal constellations and the zodiac is evident from remarks such as, "Whether they be fixed stars or signs of the zodiac"[34] or "the constellations both within and outside of the zodiac"[35] as is also clear from the following statement:

> Those who live under the more northern parallels, those, I mean, who have the Bears over their heads, since they are far removed from the zodiac and the heat of the Sun, are therefore cooled.[36]

By the "Bears" Ptolemy means the two northern constellations—the Great Bear (Ursa Major) and the Little Bear (Ursa Minor). Ptolemy's words imply that there is such a thing as Astrogeographia in the sense that the Bears, which are northern constellations, are influential in "the more northern parallels," implicitly drawing a correspondence between the celestial sphere and the earthly globe. The central question is: How does the correspondence or projection of the starry heavens onto the earthly globe work?

If we consider one particular star—for example, Benatnasch or Benetnasch (also known as Alkaid), marking the tip of the tail of the Great Bear[37]—this star's current declination is 49°16' north of

34 *Tetrabiblos* II,8, p.179.

35 *Tetrabiblos* III,11, p.315.

36 *Tetrabiblos* II,2, p. 123.

37 Benetnasch is the end star of the group of seven bright stars in the Great Bear—these seven stars being referred to as the Plough or the Dipper—and

the celestial equator. Thus once every twenty-four hours it passes directly over all cities whose geographical latitude is around 49N16. It passes directly over Vancouver (latitude 49N16), British Columbia, on the west coast of Canada, and then crosses the Pacific Ocean on its passage from east to west. After traversing the Pacific it passes over Poronaysk (49N13) on the Sakhalin Island off the east coast of Russia, then Kukan (49N12) in the far east of mainland Russia, then Hailar (49N12) in China, Bayandun (49N12) in Mongolia, Katon-Karagaj (49N11) in Kazakhstan, Star'obelsk (49N16) in the Ukraine, Brno (49N12) in the Czech Republic, Saarbrücken (49N14) in Germany, Reims (49N15) in France. Then it traverses the Atlantic Ocean and crosses over Canada (not the United States, with the exception of Alaska and the Northwest Angle, since the 49th parallel is the main divide between Canada and the U.S.).[38] It passes directly over Lewisporte (49N15) on Newfoundland, then Hornepayne (49N13) in Ontario, Morris (49N21) in Manitoba, Warner (49N17) in Alberta, returning to cross directly over Vancouver (49N16) in British Columbia, completing its apparent daily circuit of the Earth.[39]

Ptolemy's statement quoted above could be interpreted to mean that all the more northern parallels come under the influence of Ursa Major and Ursa Minor by virtue of their daily rotation as described in the above example in relation to the star Benetnasch. This is a logical conclusion. However, it is clearly not this simple relationship of

---

is used as a pointer star (together with the other stars in the tail of the Great Bear) toward Arcturus, which is the second brightest star visible in the northern heavens (after Sirius).

38 The term *49th parallel* is used as a popular term for the entire Canada–United States border. However, many of Canada's most populated regions are well south of the 49th parallel, including the two largest cities: Toronto (43N39) and Montreal (45N31) and the capital Ottawa (45N25)—as are the three Maritime provinces and parts of Vancouver Island. Similarly parts of the United States—Alaska and the Northwest Angle—are located north of the 49th parallel. Nevertheless, it is accurate to say that the 49th parallel of north latitude forms *part* of the international boundary between Canada and the United States from Manitoba to British Columbia on the Canadian side and from Minnesota to Washington on the U.S. side.

39 In reality, of course, it is the Earth's rotation once every twenty-four hours which gives the appearance that the stars move overhead from east to west making a circuit of the Earth during this period of time.

directly equating a star's declination with the corresponding earthly latitude that the Egyptians had in mind when they aligned the Great Pyramid with the star Alnitak. For the latitude of Giza, where the Great Pyramid is located, is 29N59 and Alnitak's declination was 15° South of the celestial equator in 2495 BC around the time when the Great Pyramid was built. Now, owing to precession, Alnitak's declination is 2° South. In other words Alnitak passes directly overhead above all places approximately 2° south of the equator and certainly does not pass directly over the Great Pyramid, which is almost 30° north of the equator, nor did it do so at the time when the Great Pyramid was under construction, since at that time Alnitak passed directly overhead above all places 15° south of the equator. This raises the question as to the nature of the Great Pyramid's alignment with Alnitak. How may this be understood?

In the next chapter we shall return to ponder this question further. First, though, in order to round off this chapter, let us return to consider some further remarks by Ptolemy—from the *Tetrabiblos*, the "Bible" of astrology—clearly indicating that he was a sidereal astrologer.

> *Of Bodily Form and Temperament*.... We must, then, in general observe the eastern horizon...for it is...through the forms of the fixed stars that are rising at the same time that the formation of the body is ascertained.[40]

> For blindness in one eye is brought about when the Moon...applies to one of the star clusters in the zodiac, as for example to the cluster in Cancer [Praesepe], and to the Pleiades of Taurus, to the arrow point of Sagittarius, to the sting of Scorpio, to the parts of Leo around the Coma Berenices, or to the pitcher of Aquarius.[41]

In another astrological context concerning indicators of depravity, Ptolemy refers to, "the forward and hinder parts of Aries, the Hyades [V-shaped star formation in Taurus], and the Pitcher [held by Aquarius], and the hind parts of Leo, and the face of Capricorn."[42]

40 *Tetrabiblos* III,11, pp. 307–309.

41 *Tetrabiblos* III,12, pp. 32), word in [ ] inserted by RP.

42 *Tetrabiblos* IV,5, pp. 403, words in [ ] inserted by RP.

Finally, in a rather gruesome context—astrologically speaking—Ptolemy indicates, "in the mutilated and imperfect signs,[43] or in the Gorgon of Perseus, death by decapitation or mutilation; in Scorpio and Taurus, death through cautery...and particularly in Cepheus and Andromeda, by being set up on stakes."[44]

The above selection of quotations from the *Tetrabiblos* suffices to show that for Ptolemy, when he was referring to the signs of the zodiac, he was looking at the actual star formations of the constellations and that there was a continuity for him between the constellations of the zodiac and the constellations above or below the zodiac. The fact that he referred to the sign of Aries beginning at the vernal point[45] was simply an indication that *at the time he was writing the vernal point was in conjunction with 0° Aries*—or, more precisely, it was located at 1° Aries in the Babylonian sidereal zodiac (and thus, as referred to already, Ptolemy was 1° in error). With the confirmation that Ptolemy was a sidereal astrologer, clearly the movement of the vernal point backward through the signs of the sidereal zodiac since his day (around AD 150, when he wrote the *Tetrabiblos*) has to be taken into consideration. Expressed in terms of the SVP, the vernal point is approaching 5° Pisces and will be located at exactly 5° Pisces in the year 2018 and will then enter the sign of Aquarius in AD 2375, signifying the start of the Age of Aquarius.

If any reader is still in doubt about the sidereal nature of Ptolemy's *Tetrabiblos*, the entire section 9 in Book I is entitled "Of the Power of the Fixed Stars" and deals with the signs/constellations of the zodiac (Aries, Taurus, Gemini, etc.) as *constellations of stars*.[46] For example, in describing the influence of the fixed stars in Scorpio, he writes:

43 *Tetrabiblos* IV,9, pp. 435, footnote 2: "*such as Taurus, the blind Cancer, Scorpio, Sagittarius.*"

44 Ibid. footnote 4: "crucifixion."

45 It is this statement by Ptolemy which gave birth to tropical astrology, in that it was subsequently interpreted that the vernal point is *fixed* at 0° Aries. Ptolemy's statement—apart from the 1° error—was accurate *for that time*, but with the precession of the equinoxes the vernal point has in the meantime shifted back from the beginning of Aries, through most of Pisces, to 5° Pisces.

46 *Tetrabiblos* I,9, pp. 47–59.

> Of the stars in the body of Scorpio, the bright stars on the forehead act in the same way as does Mars and in some degree as does Saturn; the three in the body, the middle one of which is tawny and rather bright and is called Antares, the same as Mars and, in some degree, Jupiter; those in the joints, the same as Saturn and, in some degree, Venus; those in the sting, the same as Mercury and Mars; and the so-called cloud-like cluster, the same as Mars and the Moon.[47]

After describing the nature of the fixed stars in the twelve signs/constellations of the zodiac, Ptolemy then goes on to describe the nature of the fixed stars in the extra-zodiacal constellations:

> Of the stars in the configurations north of the zodiac, the bright stars in Ursa Major have a similar quality to that of Saturn and, to a lesser degree, to that of Venus; those in Ursa Major, to that of Mars.[48]

It is clear that Ptolemy here considers the *entire celestial sphere* with all the fixed stars and constellations of stars as the domain of astrology, and there is a continuity in his description in passing from the zodiacal signs/constellations to the extra-zodiacal constellations. Reading his description, it is for him clearly a whole. Later in this book, in setting forward the principles of Astrogeographia, it emerges that this is a basic and fundamental premise—i.e., *the celestial sphere is a whole and is to be considered astrologically in its entirety.* Before coming to this, however, let us summarize the main conclusions of this chapter.

To summarize: the introduction of the tropical zodiac into astrology through Ptolemy's *Tetrabiblos* was not intended by Ptolemy himself, who was clearly a sidereal astrologer. It was a "historical accident" based on a misunderstanding. This misunderstanding led to the creation of a new zodiac (the tropical zodiac) that was substituted in place of the original zodiac (the Babylonian sidereal zodiac). The invention of the tropical zodiac as an *astronomical coordinate system*, as it was used by the Greek astronomers Hipparchus and

47 Ibid. p. 51.

48 Ibid. p. 55.

Ptolemy,[49] and as it is used to the present day in modern astronomy, was an achievement of *Greek astronomy*. However, anyone interested in astrology who wishes to remain faithful to the *ancient astrology* of the Babylonians, Egyptians, Romans, and Greeks (including Ptolemy) needs to take the highly accurate computations of modern astronomy using the tropical coordinate system and *transform them back into sidereal coordinates*, which is exactly what the Synetic Vernal Point (SVP) does.

Finally, every astrologer—whether tropicalist or siderealist—recognizes the validity of the location of the vernal point in the sidereal signs/constellations of the zodiac. Since the vernal point is currently located beneath the star Omega Piscium in Pisces, it ought be generally agreed upon that the present astrological age (signified by the location of the vernal point) is the Age of Pisces and that soon the Age of Aquarius will begin.[50] Regardless as to whether a tropical astrologer considers the vernal point still to be in Pisces or already in Aquarius, he or she acknowledges that the location of the vernal point in the zodiacal signs/constellations is astrologically significant as signifying a particular astrological age (Pisces or Aquarius). In this the tropical astrologer is thinking as a siderealist. Here a curious kind of "double think" is revealed, which is highlighted if we consider a specific example that reveals the conflicting points of view of

49 Ptolemy (second century AD) based his astronomical work on that of his predecessor, the astronomer Hipparchus (second century BC), who lived on the island of Rhodes. Who was the astronomer who invented the method of determining the positions of stars according to the tropical ecliptic coordinate system? The answer cannot be given with any degree of certainty, but since Hipparchus—according to Ptolemy's testimony—was the first astronomer who is known to have definitely used this system, even if only for the two stars Regulus and Spica, and since it was adopted also by Ptolemy and continues to be used to the present day, it can be stated that Hipparchus *effectively* introduced the tropical zodiac into astronomy.

50 Many astrologers, ignoring the astronomical reality of the location of the vernal point in Pisces, believe that the Age of Aquarius has already begun. However, according to Michelsen, *The American Sidereal Ephemeris, 1976–2000*, introduction, the Age of Aquarius will start in the year AD 2376, when the SVP will be located at 30° Aquarius—i.e., the Age of Pisces will last until the year AD 2375, in which year the Synetic Vernal Point will be at 0° Pisces. See also Michelsen, *The American Sidereal Ephemeris, 2001–2025*, introduction.

tropical and sidereal astrology. Let us consider the position of Jupiter on January 22, 2011. On this day the SVP is located at 5°6'0.6" or 5°06'01" Pisces, rounded to the nearest second of arc.[51] On this day Jupiter is conjunct with the vernal point at 5:10:51.2 p.m. Universal Time (Greenwich Mean Time), i.e., at 5 hours 10 minutes 51.2 seconds p.m. (GMT). For both the tropical and the sidereal astrologer Jupiter is in Pisces at 5:10:51 p.m. on that day, and likewise for both the vernal point is also in Pisces (close to 5° Pisces, if both agree upon the validity of the SVP). One thirtieth of a second later, the moment that Jupiter is exactly conjunct the vernal point (at 5:10:51.2 p.m.), Jupiter is said to be "in Aries" (at 0° Aries) according to tropical astrology, even though it is in exact conjunction with the vernal point at 5° Pisces! How can this be possible?

If one followed the movements of the planets observationally, on that evening—weather permitting—it was possible to see Jupiter high in the southwest after sunset, visible in the constellation of Pisces, beneath the "Square of Pegasus." At this time for viewers in England, Jupiter has just passed the vernal point by a few minutes of arc, and so is considered to be "in Aries" *tropically*. It is not possible to see the vernal point, but from any star map one can know its location. At the same time one can know that Jupiter is at precisely this location, in conjunction with the vernal point. For the tropical astrologer it is a paradox: the invisible vernal point (known to be in conjunction with Jupiter) is in Pisces, while the visible Jupiter that can be seen in Pisces is supposed to be "in Aries." All the more paradoxical is that the location of Jupiter in conjunction with the vernal point is a *visible indicator* of the location of the vernal point in Pisces—i.e., since the vernal point is invisible, it is with the help of Jupiter that—knowing that Jupiter is in conjunction with the vernal point—one can visualize where the vernal point is located in Pisces. Yet, at the same time, Jupiter is supposed to be "in Aries" according to the tropical ephemerides!

Moreover, at the same time on that day (January 22, 2011) Uranus was located at 2°43' Pisces in the sidereal zodiac based on the SVP.[52] It is clear that there is not only a conjunction of Jupiter with the vernal

51 Michelsen, *The American Sidereal Ephemeris*, 2001–2025.

52 Ibid.

point but also both are in conjunction with Uranus, which is located at a distance of 2°23' from Jupiter and the vernal point. (Heavenly bodies within 3° of one another are generally said to be in conjunction.) For both the tropical and the sidereal astrologer Uranus is in conjunction with the vernal point and both Uranus and the vernal point are in Pisces. For the sidereal astrologer Jupiter is in conjunction with both Uranus and the vernal point and is in Pisces, yet for the tropical astrologer, while acknowledging that Jupiter is in conjunction with the vernal point and Uranus, and also acknowledging that both the latter are in Pisces, he or she maintains that Jupiter itself is "in Aries." This paradox is resolved by returning to the sidereal zodiac of the ancient stargazers: the Babylonians, Egyptians, Romans, and Greeks (including Ptolemy). Only then is the "double thinking" of tropical astrology caused by a misinterpretation of Ptolemy's *Tetrabiblos* brought to a clear resolution. From the standpoint of this book—that of Ptolemy as a sidereal astrologer in the long tradition of sidereal astrology that preceded him—this signifies an unveiling of truth and a true honoring of Ptolemy's achievement in writing the "Bible" of astrology.

Chapter 4

The Foundations of Astrogeographia

As indicated in the preceding chapter, Ptolemy made a statement that is foundational for Astrogeographia—a statement that implies that there is a correspondence between the celestial sphere[1] and the earthly globe:

> Those who live under the more northern parallels, those, I mean, who have the Bears over their heads, since they are far removed from the zodiac and the heat of the Sun, are therefore cooled.[2]

The question is: How is this correspondence between the starry heavens above and the earthly globe below specified? In the last chapter, taking the star Benetnasch marking the tip of the tail of the Great Bear as an example, a straightforward interpretation of Ptolemy's words was considered. In this interpretation the meridian passage of the star directly overhead (over the zenith) was interpreted to be the solution to the mode of correspondence between the stars above and the earthly locations below.[3] In this example the zenith meridian

1 The celestial sphere is the imaginary sphere of the starry heavens. Now it is known that the fixed stars are located at varying distances from our solar system. However, up until the time of Copernicus (1473–1543) and shortly after all the stars were considered to be attached to the celestial sphere and thus at the same distance from our solar system (the latter conceived of as being at the center of the celestial sphere), whereby the Sun and the Earth are so close to one another relative to the vast distance of the nearest stars that practically speaking it does not matter whether one considers the Sun or the Earth to be the center.

2 *Tetrabiblos* II,2, p. 123.

3 See footnote 1 for a definition of the term *celestial sphere*. The *celestial poles* are the projection onto the celestial sphere of the poles of the Earth, just as the *celestial equator* is the projection onto the celestial sphere of the Earth's equator. The *zenith* is the point on the celestial sphere directly

passage of Benetnasch passes directly above cities such as Reims in France and Vancouver in British Columbia, which are on the same latitude (49N16) or "parallel of declination" as Benetnasch, whose declination is currently 49°16' north of the equator. However, as mentioned earlier, in the text this interpretation was evidently not what the Egyptians had in mind when, in constructing the Great Pyramid, there was an intentional alignment with the star Alnitak in the belt of Orion. Here, clearly, a different interpretation is necessary in order to comprehend the "Egyptian mode" of alignment.

Assuming that the alignment of Alnitak with the Great Pyramid is not arbitrary but is an expression of a profound wisdom accessible to the Egyptian(s) who originally conceived the architectural plan of the Great Pyramid, what was the key to this alignment? The key obviously was a different mode of perception than that adopted by modern science.[4] The "observer centered" standpoint of modern science is that of the perspective of looking from the Earth up to the stars. The ancient Egyptians had more of a "*participation mystique*" which could embrace a standpoint of looking down upon the Earth from the vantage point of the stars. For modern consciousness looking up to the stars, the straightforward interpretation described above is an obvious one. However, a "participation mystique" mode of consciousness would include the possibility of looking from the starry realm down upon the globe of the Earth, strange though this may seem to the modern scientific way of looking at things.[5] Consider,

above the observer. The *meridian*, from the point of view of the observer, is the imaginary line that runs from north to south in the sky, passing through both celestial poles and through the zenith. The *meridian passage* takes place when a star (or planet) culminates as it passes across the meridian from east to west, and the *zenith meridian passage* is when it passes directly overhead through the zenith, passing from east to west.

4 One author who describes in a very plausible way the difference in mode of perception of the ancient Egyptians from that of modern science is Jeremy Naydler in his book *Temple of the Cosmos* (Inner Traditions: Rochester/NY, 1996).

5 "Participation mystique" ("mystical participation") was the expression coined by the French anthropologist Lucien Lévy-Bruhl (1857–1939) in his books elaborating his conception of the nature of the primitive, pre-logical mind, which participated with the world rather than being cut off and isolated from the environment as an objective observer.

for example, an astrologer seeking to grasp the nature of a human being: he might consider a person's birth horoscope, viewing the positions of the stars as if gazing down upon the Earth. Similarly, it is conceivable that the ancient Egyptians—at least, the architect(s) who designed the Great Pyramid—looked to the "birth horoscope" of the Earth in order to grasp the Earth from a cosmic perspective. In this case it would be a matter of going back in time to what could be considered a birth moment in the history of the Earth. In order to explore this possibility, it would be reasonable to go back to the time when all the continents of the Earth were together, before they were separated by way of continental drift. When all the continents of the Earth were together, the center of the Earth was considered to be Israel.[6] At that time prior to the effect of continental drift, the Earth was a whole, with all the continents together, and was known as *Pangaia* or *Pangea* ("whole Earth").[7] Furthermore, if we consider the account of the clairvoyant nun, Anne Catherine Emmerich (1774–1824), which indicates Jerusalem as the birth place or place of incarnation of the first human beings, called Adam and Eve in the Biblical tradition, we have an indication of Jerusalem as the center of Pangaia in terms of the Earth's horoscope. She describes the cave on the Mount of Olives where Jesus "sweated blood" on the night of Gethsemane as the same grotto where Adam and Eve lived when they incarnated upon the Earth at the time of the Fall.[8]

> The grotto in which Jesus concealed Himself was about six feet deep.... There He prayed. I saw the awful visions following Him into the grotto, and becoming ever more and more distinct. Ah!

6 Suchantke, et al., *Israel: Mitte der Erde* ("*Israel: Midpoint of the Earth*"), p. 298. See also chapters 9 and 10 of this book for further elucitation concerning the centrality of Israel—more specifically of Jerusalem.

7 Prior to the effect of continental drift, the Earth was a whole, with all the continents together, and was known as *Pangaia* or *Pangea* ("whole Earth"). Israel—more specifically Jerusalem (see next footnote)—was the center of Pangaia. This was at a very early stage in the history of the Earth's formation, long before the event of the Fall, by which time the continents had drifted apart.

8 The fact that the death and resurrection of Christ (the "new Adam") took place at Jerusalem is also an indicator of this location as the centerpoint of the Earth's surface from a spiritual perspective.

> It was as if that narrow cave encompassed the horrible, agonizing vision of all the sins...committed from the Fall of our first parents till the end of the world. For it was here on the Mount of Olives that Adam and Eve, driven from Paradise, had first descended upon the inhospitable Earth.[9]

The perspective of Jerusalem as the centerpoint for the Earth's horoscope is strengthened when we consider that the moment of the birth of Adam and Eve is referred to in another context—in the teachings of Zarathustra, the founder of the Zoroastrian religion—as the birth horoscope of the Earth, designated in Latin by the expression *thema mundi* ("the horoscope of the world"). In the *Bundahišn*, the Zoroastrian book of creation, equivalent to the book of Genesis in the Bible, the first man (corresponding to Adam) is called Gayomart. "The *thema mundi* [in the *Bundahišn*] is treated as the 'nativity' of Gayomart, the First Man."[10] The birth horoscope of the Earth, according to this ancient Persian tradition, coincided with the birth of the first human being on the Earth, corresponding to the Fall in the Biblical tradition, when Adam and Eve descended into incarnation. It is this moment that we are interested in—the horoscope of the Earth—in finding the archetypal correspondence between the starry heavens above and the earthly globe below as the basis for Astrogeographia. What is of special interest in the account of the *thema mundi* in the *Bundahišn* is that the actual horoscope of this moment is given as a point in time when all the planets were in their place of exaltation[11] (tabulated in the previous chapter). Against this background the significance of the planetary exaltations may be understood—these being the positions of the planets in the birth horoscope of the world—this being, simultaneously, the birth horoscope of Adam or Gayomart. In the case of the Moon, for example—whose place of exaltation is the Pleiades in

9 Emmerich, *The Life of Jesus Christ*, p. 80.

10 MacKenzie, "Zoroastrian Astrology," in the *Bundahišn*," *Bulletin of the School of Oriental and African Studies* 27 (1964), p. 522; words in [ ] added by RP.

11 Ibid. p. 523: "The *thema mundi* of the *Greater Bundahišn* is basically that known as Chaldean or Babylonian, according to which the planets were all in their astrological *hypsomata* or exaltations—i.e., their positions of greatest power."

the neck of the Bull—this is where, according to old Babylonian tradition referred to in the previous chapter and supported by the ancient Persian tradition recorded in the *Bundahišn*, the Moon was located in the *thema mundi*, the horoscope of the world. Every time that the Moon returns to the Pleiades, located at 5° Taurus in the sidereal zodiac of the Babylonians, it returns to the place where it was located in the nativity of the Earth and of the first human being. This is why it is "exalted," where its influence is most powerful. In terms of modern astrology, every time the Moon returns to the Pleiades it "transits" its position in the birth horoscope of the world.

The *thema mundi* or nativity of the world, when all the planets were at exaltation, was not only part of the ancient Persian and Babylonian traditions. It is also recorded in ancient Egypt. Two zodiacs found at Esna in Egypt—Esna A (around 200 BC) and Esna B (around AD 75)—both show the planets in the zodiacal signs of their exaltation. "In Esna A and Esna B they are found to be associated with the zodiac in signs of special power known as exaltations so that Jupiter is in Cancer, Mercury in Virgo, Saturn in Libra, Mars in Capricorn, and Venus in Pisces."[12] Here the exaltations of the Sun (in Aries) and the Moon (in Taurus) are not mentioned. On account of its existence in the Persian, Babylonian, and Egyptian traditions, the *thema mundi* was evidently something of powerful symbolic significance that was a widespread astrological doctrine in antiquity, even though it is obvious that it cannot refer to an actual horoscope—at least, not a geocentric horoscope—since from the geocentric perspective Mercury can never be more than 28° from the Sun, and so it would be impossible for the Sun to be in Aries and, simultaneously, for Mercury to be in Virgo.

For Astrogeographia it is not so much the planetary configuration (real or symbolic) of the *thema mundi* itself, but rather the imprinting of the entire starry heavens into the Earth at the moment of the nativity of the world that is of key significance. Crucial to these considerations is that Jerusalem is the central focus of the nativity of the world and therefore, from the perspective of cosmic consciousness, the parallel

12 Neugebauer and Parker, *Egyptian Astronomical Texts, vol. 3: Decans, Planets, Constellations and Zodiacs*, pp. 176–177.

of 0° declination runs through Jerusalem rather than around the equator. This means that the latitude of Jerusalem—31N47—equates with 0° declination in Astrogeographia.[13]

Upon this foundation, let us return to consider Alnitak's alignment with the Great Pyramid. The location of the Great Pyramid at Giza has a latitude of 29N59, which is 1°48' south of the 0° latitude represented by the parallel of declination running through Jerusalem. This figure of -1°48' is close to the present-day declination of Alnitak, which is 1°56' South, computed for the year AD 2000. Yet as Alnitak's declination in 2495 BC, when (according to the research presented in chapter 1 of this book) the Great Pyramid was under construction, was 15° South, obviously declination cannot be utilized with regard to determining the alignment of stars with geographical locations in a general sense—although, of course, it can be used in a specific sense—i.e., for a given historical date, as indicated in *The Orion Mystery*.[14] The reason for the shift in a star's declination in the course of time—for example, in the case of Alnitak, from 15° South in 2495 BC to 2° South in AD 2000—has to do with the phenomenon of the precession of the equinoxes, whereby there is a gradual shift taking place continuously in the relationship between the Earth's alignment and the celestial sphere. One way this comes to expression is the shift in the location of the vernal point, which was at 7°22' Taurus (close to the Pleiades at 5° Taurus) in 2495 BC and is now at 5° Pisces (it will be at exactly 5° Pisces in AD 2018). This is what is meant by the term "precession of the equinoxes."

It is not only by means of the precession of the equinoxes that the gradual change in the Earth's alignment relative to the celestial sphere comes to expression. It is also expressed in the shift in the axis

13 *The Times Atlas of the World* gives the latitude and longitude of Jerusalem as 31N47 and 35E13. According to www.onhiatus.com/journal/journal.cgi, the latitude and longitude of Jerusalem are 31°46'53" north and 35°13'52" east. This latitude rounded to the nearest minute agrees with the value given in *The Times Atlas of the World* and the rounded longitude is one minute of arc different, which amounts to just over one mile or a little less than two kilometers in distance. Thus, it is reasonable to adopt the values from *The Times Atlas of the World*, which are well known and have become standard.

14 Bauval and Gilbert, *The Orion Mystery*, p. 255.

of the Earth's poles in relation to the stars—what could be called the "shifting of the polar axis" or simply "polar shift." There are two pole stars—the north pole star, toward which the Earth's north pole is oriented, and the south pole star, toward which the Earth's south pole is oriented—and to simplify the discussion we shall focus solely upon the north pole star. At the present time the axis running from the Earth's south pole to the Earth's north pole, projected onto the northern half of the celestial sphere, is oriented toward the star Polaris, the brightest star in the constellation of the Little Bear (Ursa Minor). This alignment of the polar axis with Polaris is not exact, but is very close. Just as the projection of the Earth's equator upon the celestial sphere is called the celestial equator, so the projection of the Earth's north pole onto the celestial sphere is called the north celestial pole. At the present time the north celestial pole is about ¾° distant from the star Polaris, and this distance is getting less. In the year AD 2102 the distance will be at a minimum—it will be less than ½°. Thereafter it will start to increase again. Here and in the following, in referring to the pole star, what is meant is the relatively bright star (clearly visible to the naked eye) closest to the north celestial pole, which is Polaris at the present time.

Going back to the time when the Great Pyramid was built, the star Thuban in the constellation of Draco (the Dragon) was the pole star. At the time (2765 BC) of the closest approach of the north celestial pole to Thuban, the brightest star in Draco, was at a distance of less than 0°10' from the celestial pole, and it was still very close (only about 1° away) when the Great Pyramid was under construction in 2495 BC. As shown in *The Orion Mystery* and confirmed in this book the southern shaft from the king's chamber of the Great Pyramid was oriented toward Alnitak—the orientation being exact around 2495 BC.[15]

The gradual shifting of the polar axis means that since 2765 BC the north celestial pole has shifted further and further away from Thuban and is now drawing close to Polaris. After AD 2102 it will

15 Ibid., p. 180; it gives the orientation as precise for 2450 BC. However, as referred to in chap. 1, more exact research shows the precise date to be 2495 BC.

The path of the north celestial pole among the stars due to the precession (assuming constant precessional speed and obliquity of epoch JED 2000)

gradually start to shift away from Polaris, and in AD 10373 it will be closest to the star Deneb marking the tail of the Swan (or the head of the Northern Cross, depending upon whether one sees this constellation as a Swan, as the Greeks did, or as a Cross, as some Christian astronomers have done). After AD 10373 the north celestial pole will gradually shift away from Deneb and will draw closest to Vega, the brightest star in the constellation of the Lyre, in AD 13895, although it will still be about 12° distant from Vega at its closest approach.

The rotation axis of the Earth describes, over a period of 25,920 years, a small circle among the stars, centered on the ecliptic north pole (see figure above). It should be noted that in the figure the brighter a star is in terms of its apparent magnitude, the larger it appears. In this figure, the largest (and brightest) star is Vega in the constellation of the Lyre (see below). The upper bright star resting on (just above) this circle in the figure is Polaris in the constellation of the Lesser Bear, which is the current pole star (closest approach in +2102 = AD 2102). Proceeding clockwise around the circle to -2764 (2765 BC), the faint star Thuban in the constellation of Draco, the previous pole star, can be seen located *exactly* on the circle. More or less directly across the circle from Thuban, at +10373, a very bright star can be seen just a little outside the circle—this is Deneb in the constellation of the Swan, which will be pole star at that time (AD 10373), more than 8,000 years in the future.[16] Proceeding from Deneb further around the circle in a counterclockwise direction to +13895, an exceedingly bright star can be seen located just a little outside the circle—this is Vega in the constellation of the Lyre, which is the brightest of all the stars serving as markers for the shift of the north celestial pole and is actually the fifth brightest star in the heavens in terms of apparent magnitude. Vega will be pole star some 3,500 years after Deneb will have served as a marker.

Through the shifting of the polar axis, the north celestial pole traces out a circle in the starry heavens in the space of 25,920 years. This corresponds exactly with the precession of the equinoxes, which signifies that during a period of 25,920 years the vernal point moves retrograde (clockwise from the perspective of the Northern Hemisphere) through the twelve signs/constellations of the sidereal zodiac. The rate of motion of the vernal point is 1° in 72 years—this being the average rate of motion during the whole cycle. At times it can be slightly faster and at other times it can be slightly slower than 1° in 72 years, but on average it is exactly 1° in 72 years. Thus it takes 2,160 years to precess through one sign/constellation (30° long) of the zodiac, since 30 x 72 = 2,160, and it takes 25,920 years to move retrograde through all twelve zodiacal signs/constellations, since 12 x 2,160 = 25,920. Correspondingly, during this period of time the north celestial pole traces out a circle among the stars, signifying that

16 The direction in which the Earth's rotation axis is moving in time—Thuban, Polaris, Deneb, Vega—is counterclockwise. In the description in our text, however, the order begins with Polaris and goes backward in time—i.e., clockwise, to Thuban, and then jumps forward across half the cycle of precession to Deneb, and only then proceeds in linear time forward—and hence counterclockwise—from Deneb to Vega.

gradually over time the pole star changes. The center of this circle is called the *ecliptic north pole* and it is located in the middle of the coiled neck of Draco, the Dragon. The head of the Dragon is under the left foot of Hercules, and the first bend in the neck of the Dragon is in the region of the right foot of Cepheus, the Crowned King. The neck of the Dragon coils back beneath the feet of Ursa Minor, the Little Bear, and then there is a second bend. It is in the middle of this coil traced out from the head of Draco round the first bend and back to the second bend that the ecliptic north pole is located.

Vega and Polaris lie approximately across from one another on opposite sides of the north pole of the ecliptic, as can be deduced from the fact that it will take the north celestial pole 11,793 years to move from conjunction with Polaris in AD 2102 to conjunction with Vega in AD 13895. This period of 11,973 years is close, relatively speaking, to the half-period of 25,920 years, which is 12,960 years. If this period of 11,973 years was *exactly* the same as the half-period, Vega and Polaris would lie *exactly* opposite one another on the great circle traced out by the north celestial pole in the space of 25,920 years. Since the Earth's axis is inclined at approximately 23½° to the pole of the ecliptic, the radius of the circle traced out on the celestial sphere has a radius of around 23½°. This angle, which is the same as the *obliquity of the ecliptic*, varies slightly in the course of time—the obliquity being the angle at which the celestial equator is tilted with respect to the ecliptic—and this variation has to be taken into account in Astrogeographia.

On January 1, 2000, the obliquity of the ecliptic was 23°26'21" and on January 1, 2495 BC, when the Great Pyramid was under construction, the obliquity was 23°58'26". This is the value that needs to be included in the equation of latitude—for example, in considering the alignment of Alnitak with the Great Pyramid. If the Earth's axis were not tilted at this angle, it would not be necessary to include it, as the earthly coordinates (latitude and longitude) would then coincide with the ecliptic coordinates (latitude and longitude) of the stars. This is best illustrated by way of an example. Let us consider the star Alnitak again.

The present sidereal coordinates of Alnitak, based on the SVP, are:

latitude 25S18 — longitude 29°56' Taurus

Owing to proper motion, however, the sidereal coordinates of Alnitak in 2495 BC were:

latitude 25S53 — longitude 29°51' Taurus

These were the sidereal coordinates of Alnitak at the time when the Great Pyramid was built.

Above it was indicated that for a consciousness looking from the starry realm down upon the globe of the Earth, things appear differently, and that just as an astrologer, in order to grasp the nature of a human being, looks at that person's birth horoscope, so it is possible to imagine a perspective of consciousness gazing down to the Earth looking to the "birth horoscope" of the Earth in order to grasp the Earth from a cosmic perspective, which would be a matter of going back in history to a crucial time in the Earth's formation, to the time of the Fall and the incarnation of the first human being (Adam or Gayomart) on the Earth. From the considerations above what has emerged is that from such a perspective Jerusalem lies on the 0° parallel, signifying that Jerusalem's latitude (31N47) equates cosmically with 0° latitude. How does the tilt of the Earth's axis figure in this? In order to find the alignment of stars with places on the globe of the Earth, the angle of the Earth's tilt (obliquity of the ecliptic) has to be included. For example, in the case of the alignment of the Great Pyramid with the star Alnitak, the equation of latitude is as follows:

> Great Pyramid (Giza)—latitude: 29N59—is 1°48' south of the 0° latitude of Jerusalem.
>
> Including the obliquity of the ecliptic (23°58' in 2495 BC) means that the "cosmic latitude" of the Great Pyramid is 23°58' further to the south than 1°48' = 25°46' south, which is very close to the actual latitude of Alnitak (25S53) in 2495 BC, indicating a close alignment—the difference in latitude being 0°07'.

The next step is to find the "equation of longitude," which is very simple, since from a cosmic perspective the lines of longitude correspond exactly with the sidereal longitudes of the stars. In the case of Alnitak, the equation of longitude is:

Great Pyramid (Giza)—longitude: 31E08—
equates with the longitude of Alnitak in 2495 BC = 29°51' Taurus.

Once having determined this equation of longitude, the corresponding sidereal longitude of any place on the globe can be specified and, vice versa, the sidereal longitude of any star can be equated with any geographical longitude. Let us take the city of Alexandria as an example. As we shall see, there is a relationship of Alexandria to the star Alnilam. Alexandria was founded by Alexander the Great in 332 BC. At that time Alnilam's sidereal longitude was 28°41' Taurus. The geographical longitude of Alexandria is 29E55, which is 1°13' west of Giza (31E08-29E55 = 1°13'). This signifies that the corresponding sidereal longitude is 29°51'-1°13' = 28°38' Taurus, coinciding almost exactly with the sidereal longitude of Alnilam—the difference in longitude being 0°03'.

How is this correspondence in terms of latitude? The latitude of Alexandria is 31N13, which is just 0°34' south of Jerusalem (31N47-31N13 = 0°34'). However, the obliquity of the ecliptic in 332 BC was 23°44' which has to be included in order to find Alexandria's "cosmic latitude." 23°44' further south than 0°34' yields 24°18' south. In 332 BC Alnilam's latitude was 24S49, close to the "cosmic latitude" of Alexandria—the difference in latitude being 0°31'. While the alignment of Alexandria with Alnilam (latitudinal difference: 0°31') is not as close as that of the Great Pyramid with Alnitak (latitudinal difference: 0°07'), it is nevertheless close enough to conclude that Alexandria is in the "sphere of influence" of the star Alnilam projected onto the globe of the Earth, if we postulate that each star has a 1° sphere of influence. Alnilam's projection onto the Earth coincides closely with Alexandria in terms of longitude (longitudinal difference: 0°03') but in terms of latitude a place 35½ miles (57½ km) south of Alexandria would fit the projection more precisely,[17] which would be close to Abu Mina, the old monastery and city located at the site of an oasis in the Egyptian desert, which became a place of pilgrimage by AD 600 on account of the miracle-working martyr St. Mina. In founding the city of Alexandria, there was the practical reason for choosing a location

17 1° corresponds to 69.055055 miles (111.13333 km).

on the Mediterranean coast as a sea port, rather than building a city in the desert to the south of the coast. As we shall see, the longitude is more important than considerations of latitude, and thus the association of Alexandria with Alnilam is given through its longitude coinciding with the celestial longitude of Alnilam, even though there is not a precise coincidence in terms of latitude.

Reflections on latitude and longitude in relation to stellar projections

In the above examples of the projections of the stars Alnitak and Alnilam, whereas the projected longitudes in both cases coincide closely with the geographical longitudes of Giza and Alexandria, the projected latitudes are not so precise. Nevertheless, it is the longitudinal projection that is most important. At this point it needs to be understood that the projection of a star onto the Earth, according to Astrogeographia, is not fixed for all time. As shown by David Bowden in chapter 8, while the projected longitude of a star remains close to constant, the projected latitude, because of the tilting of the Earth's axis during the precession cycle of 25,920 years, shifts a total of 47° in its north/south movement during the 12,960-year half-cycle of precession—47° being twice 23½°, which is the tilt of the Earth's axis. Each star moves alternately 23½° north and 23½° south on its longitude meridian, corresponding to its movement north and south in declination occasioned by the tilting of the Earth during the cycle of precession. In Astrogeographia the primary influence of a star is its meridian influence, acting upon all the places along its geographic longitude meridian. For example, in the case of Betelgeuse this is the meridian that runs through Jerusalem (35E13). Thus, from the perspective of Astrogeographia all places along or close to the geographical meridian 35E13 are subject to the influence of Betelgeuse. As David Bowden points out in chapter 8, a star exerts an influence along its entire meridian all the time. However, its meridian influence is especially heightened when it is also in simultaneous latitude alignment with a location along its meridian, something that can occur at certain points in time during the cycle of precession. This location is called the *historical projection* and can be easily determined for any given year with the help of David Bowden's SINEWAVE program.[18]

An example given in chapter 8 of an historical projection is that of Betelgeuse. The historical projection of Betelgeuse, the main star (a red supergiant) in the constellation of Orion, was aligned in 1371 BC with the site in Jerusalem where some four hundred years later the Temple of Solomon was built. There is generally a time-lag between the sowing of a seed of a new spiritual impulse and the cultural flourishing that results from the sowing of the seed. Moreover, at the time of the building of Solomon's Temple, shortly after 1000 BC, the historical projection of Betelgeuse was still very close to the site where the temple was built. Another example is the historical projection of Aldebaran, the primary star in the constellation of Taurus, with Vienna in the middle of the eighteenth century, when this city rose to prominence as a great cultural center for the arts, sciences, and music, and in chapter 7 the historical projections of other prominent stars in Orion—not just Betelgeuse—are indicated.

Here is not the place to go into the changing historical projection in detail, which has to do with the continual slow change in latitude of a star's projection onto the Earth, which in turn is correlated directly with the star's changing declination during the 25,920-year cycle of precession. Rather, the primary focus in this and subsequent chapters is upon the longitudinal projection of a star onto the globe—the star's meridian mirrored on Earth—whereby, as already indicated, the influence of the star extends all the way along its meridian. The changing historical projection—the changing latitude of a star's projection, correlated with the star's changing declination—is considered in detail in chapter 8. The perspective opened up there is extremely helpful for understanding the overall significance of the projection of stars upon the globe according to Astrogeographia.

Continuing with the Foundations of Astrogeographia

Having located the projection of two of the stars from Orion's belt onto the Earth's globe, the question arises: Where does the projection

18 The SINEWAVE program, together with the basic ASTROGEO program, is available from the Sophia Foundation (see page 309).

of the third star, Mintaka, fall on the surface of the Earth? In order to answer this question, let us transform Mintaka's sidereal coordinates into earthly ones, again taking the date of the founding of Alexandria as our starting date. In 332 BC Mintaka's sidereal coordinates were: latitude–23S52; longitude–27°35' Taurus. Since 27°35' Taurus is 2°16' less than Alnitak's longitude of 29°51' in 2495 BC, this means that the projection of Mintaka has a geographical longitude 2°16' less than the longitude of the Great Pyramid (31E08-2°16' = 28E52).

Now let us consider—from the standpoint of Astrogeographia—the "equation of latitude" for Mintaka. Since the obliquity of the ecliptic in 332 BC was 23°44', this differs from 23S52 by only 0°08'. This is the value which has to be subtracted from Jerusalem's latitude (31N47-0°08' = 31N39) to yield the corresponding earthly latitude of 31N39.

To summarize: Mintaka's projection onto the Earth's globe around 332 BC coincided with a location that has the following geographical coordinates: latitude–31N39; longitude–28E52. This location is in the Mediterranean Sea, a little less than 1° north of El Alamein (30N49; 28E57). It was here where the great artillery and tank engagement of the British Army under General Montgomery broke through the lines of the Italians and the German Africa Corps, commanded by General Rommel, in the autumn of 1942. In one of the greatest tank battles of World War II the Germans were forced to retreat into Libya, losing some 90,000 men who were killed or taken prisoner.

The latitudinal difference between the projected location of Mintaka in the Mediterranean Sea and the town of El Alamein amounts to 0°50', equating with a distance of 57½ miles (92½ km), whereas the longitudinal difference is only 0°05', amounting to 5¾ miles (9¼ km).[19] As remarked upon above, in connection with the latitudinal displacement of the projection of Alnilam in relation to the city of Alexandria, it is the *alignment in longitude* which is most important. Clearly, in the case of the location of the stellar projection of Mintaka into the Mediterranean Sea, it was not possible to build a city there, and the nearest possibility was directly south of this location, on the coast, at El Alamein. In this respect El Alamein can be

19 Ibid.

thought of as the city mirroring the star Mintaka, the third star in the belt of Orion, just as Alexandria mirrors Alnilam, the middle star, and the Great Pyramid mirrors Alnitak.

In the next chapter we shall consider why the alignment in longitude is more important than that in latitude. Also, the deeper question as to the implication of this one-to-one correspondence between the celestial sphere and the earthly globe will be considered, and the basic assumptions underlying this correspondence will be examined. Before proceeding to these more fundamental questions, however, let us consider the implications of the above discovery of the three locations mirroring the stellar projection of Alnitak, Alnilam, and Mintaka upon the globe. Given that each of these three places—the Great Pyramid at Giza, the city of Alexandria, and the town of El Alamein—is unique in quality, is it possible to come to some insights regarding the nature of the influence of the three stars?

Concerning the unique quality of the three places under consideration, the Great Pyramid was a *mystery place* where the sacred rites of death and resurrection of the soul were enacted; Alexandria, from its founding, was a very cosmopolitan city, where *many different traditions met* and fructified one another—Babylonian and Greek influences met there with the local Egyptian tradition; El Alamein is remembered above all on account of the *great military battles* that took place there during World War II. It is very clear that these three qualities, when brought into correspondence with the planets, express the nature of Saturn, Jupiter, and Mars—the three "upper planets" of the seven classical planets. It is reasonable to hypothesize, therefore, that the stars Alnitak, Alnilam, and Mintaka express on a stellar level something of the qualities associated with Saturn, Jupiter, and Mars.

Saturn has always been the planet of profound interiority, having to do with the mysteries of death and rebirth, and the Great Pyramid was constructed as a sanctuary for the guidance of the soul of the pharaoh in the life after death. The very purpose of the Great Pyramid speaks of the quality of Saturn as the "lord of death." The area where the pyramids of Giza stand is called the *Memphis necropolis*—a cemetery. The relationship with Saturn comes out especially clearly when we read the *Pyramid Texts*, recalling that the Egyptians referred to Saturn as "Horus, Bull of the sky."[20]

> O Horus, this King is Osiris, this pyramid of the King is Osiris, this construction of his is Osiris; betake yourself to it.... May a stairway to the Netherworld[21] be set up for you to the place where Orion is, may the Bull of the sky take your hand.... The door of the sky at the horizon opens to you, the gods are glad at meeting you.[22]

The central finding of *The Orion Mystery* is that the Egyptians saw Orion as the dwelling place of the soul of Osiris, who appeared in the south, and the orientation of the southern shaft from the king's chamber in the Great Pyramid pointed directly to the star Alnitak at its meridian passage around the time of the pyramid's construction in 2495 BC.[23]

> The ancient Egyptians quite literally saw Osiris appear in the southern sky in the constellation of Orion, in the period immediately preceding the flood. But the flood itself was directly heralded by the appearance of Isis in the iridescent star Sirius, some time after the first reemergence of Orion from below the southern horizon. The Nile's inundation was said to be caused by the tears of Isis for her stricken lord, tears that, as it were, came streaming from the rainbow hues of this star down into the emaciated river.
>
> If in looking south one gazes toward the Dwat, then behind one are the stars of the north, the pole stars that never set and that for the Egyptians constituted a cosmic image of eternity. It was the uninterrupted circuit of these stars that the most blessed dead would join, the realm beyond the Dwat, the realm of pure spirit.
>
> A person standing and facing south is in the "archetypal" position by which the ancient Egyptians oriented themselves in

20 Neugebauer and Parker, *Egyptian Astronomical Texts, vol. 3: Decans, Planets, Constellations and Zodiacs*, pp. 178.

21 *Dwat*, or *Duat*.

22 Faulkner, *The Ancient Egyptian Pyramid Texts*, pp. 247 and 253.

23 Bauval and Gilbert, *The Orion Mystery*, pp. 100–107 and 180. The date given in *The Orion Mystery* of 2450 BC for the construction of the Great Pyramid is corrected in this book to 2495 BC.

> "the Beloved Land" (*ta-meri*). One of the terms for "south" is also a term for "face," while the word usually used for "north" is related to a word that means "back of the head." The word for "east" is the same as that for "left"; likewise the word for "west" and "right."[24]

Considering this archetypal orientation for the ancient Egyptians: in terms of the construction of the Great Pyramid, its primary orientation is that it faces south toward Orion—more specifically the southern shaft from the king's chamber was oriented to the meridian passage of the star Alnitak in the belt of Orion at the time of construction around 2495 BC. Then there is the space "behind"—at the "back of the head"—facing north to the realm of the circumpolar stars,[25] the "realm of pure spirit," in the direction of the star Thuban, which was the pole star at that time (ca. 2495 BC), whose place in the heavens was approximately due north.

> The Pyramid Texts frequently allude to the king's association in his afterlife with the stars and, in particular, with the circumpolar stars and with Orion and Sothis [Sirius]. Scientific study has shown that...the three stars in Orion's belt passed each day at culmination directly over the southern channel (shaft), whose slope is 44½°.[26]

All of this supports the idea of the Saturnine quality of the Great Pyramid, associated with the mysteries of death and rebirth. Given the correlation with Alnitak, it is reasonable to conclude that Alnitak's influence is also Saturnine in nature, having to do with the central theme of death and rebirth.

---

24 Naydler, *Temple of the Cosmos*, p. 9.

25 Circumpolar stars are stars that never set as seen from a given location.

26 Edwards, "The Air Channels of Cheops' Pyramid," *Studies in Honor of Dows Dunham* (1981), pp. 55–57, quoted in *The Orion Mystery*, p. 107 (words in [ ] added by RP). As indicated in chapter 1, the measurements made by Rudolf Gantenbrink in 1993 show that the inclination of the shaft is 45°, and that—more specifically—it is the star Alnitak (of the three stars in Orion's belt) which was the star with which the southern shaft from the king's chamber of the Great Pyramid was oriented.

Alnitak, meaning "the girdle," is a triple star. The primary star is itself a close binary star. It is a hot blue supergiant at a distance of some 800 light-years and with a luminosity around 11,000 times that of our Sun. Its luminosity would be measured at around 100,000 times that of the Sun if the ultraviolet light radiating from Alnitak's surface were to be taken into account. Alnitak is estimated to be about twenty-eight times the mass of our Sun, with a diameter approximately twenty times wider. Its faint companion star, a blue dwarf, is reckoned to be about twenty-three times heavier than our Sun. Alnitak is a young star, probably not more than about seven million years old, which will eventually become a red supergiant. The region around Alnitak contains numerous clouds of interstellar dust and gas, including the famous dark nebula known as the *Horsehead Nebula*.

Let us now consider the city of Alexandria. Its quality is Jupiterian (Jupiter as the planet of wisdom[27]) in view of the great library there, which unfortunately was destroyed, signifying the loss of a vast collection of treasures of ancient wisdom. Alexandria was also the location of the Pharos Lighthouse which, like the Great Pyramid, was one of the seven wonders of the ancient world. Just as the very nature of the Great Pyramid speaks of the mystery of Saturn, so the Pharos Lighthouse communicates, as a symbol, the mystery of Jupiter, which is to spread the light of wisdom. Alexander the Great founded the city in 332 BC, and upon his death in 323 BC his widespread empire was divided among several rulers. Ptolemy, one of his generals, chose Egypt and started a new royal house. Alexandria became the capital of the state, and by the year 200 BC, it grew into the largest metropolis in the world, and became the world's scientific and intellectual Mecca.

The legacy of the rule of the Ptolemies was highlighted by major achievements, notably its university, the great library, the Pharos Lighthouse that was considered among the seven wonders of the world, as well as the "Temple of Serapis" and the "Heptastadion" that connected the Island of Pharos with Alexandria. The library of Alexandria was the largest in all antiquity. It was also a part of a research institute,

27 Powell, *History of the Planets*, p. 9 for the Babylonians Marduk, the god of Jupiter, was known as "*the lord of wisdom.*"

known as the "Alexandrian Museum" or "Mouseion"—a word related to the shrine of the "Muses" which was a customary feature of the Greek schools that attributed philosophic and artistic inspiration to the Muses and science. The chief librarian of Alexandria was chosen from the most prominent scholars in science or literature, and was appointed by the king himself. He was described as "the one in charge of the king's library," "president of the library" or "bibliophylax" (keeper of archives). Demetrius of Phaleron was the first to hold this elite post. The emphasis on Jupiter's wisdom denoted the signature or stamp of the quality of the city of Alexandria. Given the correspondence with Alnilam, it is evident that this star's influence is one that promotes wisdom and learning, spreading the light of knowledge, for which the Pharos Lighthouse served as a symbol.

Alnilam, meaning "the string of pearls," is the central and brightest of the three stars marking the belt of Orion. It is a large blue-white supergiant around 1,300 light-years away, and is surrounded by the Orion molecular cloud, which is partly illuminated as a reflection nebula by Alnilam's intense radiation. Alnilam's luminosity is over 30,000 times that of our Sun. If the ultraviolet light radiating from Alnilam is taken into account, its luminosity is estimated to be about 275,000 times that of the Sun. Its mass is reckoned to be about 40 times that of the Sun. Thought to be about four million years old, Alnilam will one day evolve into a red supergiant.

Turning now to the town of El Alamein: this Egyptian desert railway halt, situated about 59 miles (95 km) west of Alexandria, gave its name to two different encounters between Allied and Axis forces during the Western Desert campaigns of World War II. The first was a defensive battle fought by the British and the Commonwealth Eighth Army from July 1-4, 1942 to halt Rommel's bid to conquer Egypt and seize the Suez Canal. Before this battle between the two armies, Germany had conquered most of Western Europe and had strong allies in Italy and Japan. The United States had just entered the fray after Japan bombed Pearl Harbor. The war was threatening to enter into a world-wide crisis involving at least one country on every continent in the world. In the second El Alamein battle, the Eighth Army, now commanded by General Montgomery, fought successfully between October 23 and November 4, 1942, to pierce Rommel's defenses, forcing him to retreat into Tunisia. Rommel was outgunned and outmanned by the British. Montgomery's armored divisions first took up defensive positions against any German attack and did not go on to the offensive until the infantry battle—the "crumbling process" as Montgomery called it—had been won. Rommel launched fierce counter-attacks but these were contained and constant Allied air attacks and concentrated artillery bombardments aided the infantry's "crumbling" of Rommel's forces. Then Montgomery launched what was called the "supercharge." This was launched on the night of November 1/2 by the New Zealand Division and other infantry units. Rommel warned Hitler on November 2 that his army was without fuel and faced annihilation. Hitler ordered him to stand fast. Rommel tried to do so but, once started, the process could not be reversed. At midday on November 4 Rommel's defenses caved in and that evening Hitler gave him permission to withdraw. But by then Rommel's defeated army had started its headlong retreat across Libya during which Montgomery netted 30,000 prisoners of war. Allied casualties during the battle had amounted to 13,560. El Alamein was the climax of the Western Desert campaigns and one of the turning-points of the war.

This, essentially, is what El Alamein is remembered for, although nowadays it has developed into a popular tourist resort on account of its remarkable beaches and extraordinary climate, as well as the attraction of the war memorials. The quality of Mars—known in antiquity as the god of war—is palpably associated with El Alamein. Mars does not have to do solely with war. It is also associated with will power, courageous deeds, and moral strength—and it is these qualities that can be related to the star Mintaka, with which El Alamein is connected.

Mintaka is the faintest of the three stars marking the belt of Orion. The name Mintaka is derived from the Arabic word *manṭaqah*, which means "area" or "region." Mintaka is a multiple star, classified as an eclipsing binary variable. The primary component is a double star consisting of a class B (blue-white) giant and a hot class O (blue) star. Mintaka is approximately 900 light-years distant. Its luminosity is more than 8600 times that of our Sun. Taking account of its ultraviolet light radiation, the class B and the class O stars are both roughly 90,000 times more luminous than our Sun, and each has a mass approximately 20 times that of our Sun.

To summarize: in the light of Astrogeographia the three stars in the belt of Orion—Alnitak, Alnilam, and Mintaka—are characterized in terms of their qualities in relation to the planets Saturn, Jupiter, and Mars. These three stars—sometimes also referred to as the "*three kings*"[28]—are aligned in such a way that they point directly toward the star Sirius. As a celestial image of the three kings, these stars in the heavens are mirrored historically on Earth with the journey of the three kings to the birth of Jesus. The latter corresponds to Sirius in the heavens—in the words of Rudolf Steiner, "Sirius is the heart of Jesus-Zarathustra."[29] By way of analogy, since the three stars in the belt of Orion are oriented toward Sirius, and since Jesus corresponds to Sirius, the three stars in the belt of Orion can be thought of as the three kings following Jesus—the parallel here is that Alnitak-Alnilam-Mintaka appear in the heavens always to be following Sirius, just as the three kings followed a route leading to Jesus. These three stars are also mirrored geographically on Earth by the locations of the Great Pyramid at Giza, the city of Alexandria, and the town of El Alamein. The astrological qualities of these three stars are to be discovered at these locations on the Earth, helping us to understand the nature of these places and also providing us with insight into the astrological nature of the stars to which these locations correspond. In the next chapter we shall consider further examples of Astrogeographia.

28 *Meyers Grosse Sternenatlas*, p. 76.

29 Rudolf Steiner's words, recorded in *The Birth of a New Agriculture*, p. 89.

Chapter 5

The Prime Meridian and the Zero Parallel in Astrogeographia

In geographical parlance it is customary to speak of "parallels of latitude"—for example, the 49th parallel of northern latitude that divides much of Canada from the United States.[1] It is not so common to speak of "meridians of longitude" except in the case of the 0° meridian, the Greenwich meridian, also known as the *prime meridian*, which was decided upon in October 1884. The prime meridian is the meridian (line of longitude) that passes through the Royal Greenwich Observatory, London, England, and it is defined to be the meridian with 0° longitude.

Just as all latitudes can be called "parallels," so all longitudes can be called "meridians." The same holds true for celestial longitudes, and there is a good reason for referring to sidereal longitudes in this way, as will be discussed in the following. First, though, let us consider how the sidereal longitude of a star is specified.[2] The primary reference is the ecliptic, which is the (apparent) path that the Sun traces against the background of the celestial sphere—passing through the middle of the zodiacal belt comprising the twelve signs/constellations of the zodiac. In terms of the sidereal zodiac defined in relation to the SVP, the ecliptic is divided into twelve equal sectors which are the sidereal signs coinciding more or less with the zodiacal constellations bearing the same names. The sidereal sign of Taurus, for example, coincides

1 See discussion of the 49th parallel in footnote 38, chapter 3.

2 As discussed in chapter 3, the specification of the sidereal zodiac used throughout this book is that based on the Synetic Vernal Point (SVP) defined in Michelsen, *The American Sidereal Ephemeris*, 1976–2000, introduction. See also Michelsen, *The American Sidereal Ephemeris*, 2001–2025, introduction.

more or less with the constellation of Taurus—in such a way that the center of the sidereal sign (15° Taurus) coincides with the central star in the constellation of Taurus, which is Aldebaran. As mentioned in chapter 3, the position (in terms of the sidereal zodiac based on the SVP) of Aldebaran in the sidereal zodiac when it was introduced and used by the Babylonians was exactly 15° Taurus, and its current position is 15°03' Taurus. This shift in longitude has to do with the proper motion of the star Aldebaran. There is also a small shift—owing to proper motion—in the latitude of most stars over a long period of time. For example, in the case of Aldebaran, in the same period of time that its longitude shifted by 0°03', its latitude shifted by 0°10'—from 5S38 in the fourth century BC to its current latitude of 5S28. These small shifts do not make much difference in terms of the projection of the stars onto the globe of the Earth. However, these shifts are taken into account in the computations presented in this book. Also, it is necessary to take account of another shift that also plays a role in terms of this projection, and that is the gradual change in the obliquity of the ecliptic.

Since the obliquity of the ecliptic changes slowly in the course of time, it is helpful to have a grasp of this movement. The obliquity of the ecliptic is the angle between the Earth's equator and the ecliptic plane in which the Earth orbits around the Sun—or, what is entirely equivalent, in which the Sun *appears* to rotate around the Earth. As discussed in chapter 4, the obliquity is the same angle as the angle of inclination of the Earth's polar axis to the axis running from the north pole of the ecliptic to the south pole of the ecliptic. At the present time this angle is about 23½°, and this is therefore the radius of the circle that the polar axis traces out on the celestial sphere around the pole of the ecliptic as center. This angle changes, however, for the same reason as the *precession of the equinoxes*, which is because there is a slow *gyration* of the Earth's axis caused by the gravitational pull of the Sun, Moon, and planets upon the Earth's equatorial bulge. The Sun and Moon—and also the planets (to a much lesser extent)—pull harder on the nearest part of the Earth's equatorial bulge than the farthest part, and this causes a torque which imparts a gyration to the Earth's rotational axis. This gravitational pull causes the gyration of the Earth's axis which is visible in the gradual shifting of the polar axis projected onto the celestial sphere, and simultaneously it causes the vernal point to move backward in relation to the celestial equator (the precession of the equinoxes) at a rate of about 50" per year or 1° in 72 years. The entire period of precession of the vernal point through 360° of the zodiac lasts for 25,920 years, which is the same period taken by the polar axis to trace out its circle around the pole of the ecliptic. For example, Thuban was the pole star when the Great Pyramid was under construction (2495 BC), at which time the vernal point was at 7°22' Taurus. Adding 25,920 years to 2495 BC, we arrive at AD 23426, at which time Thuban will again be pole star and the vernal point will again be at 7°22' Taurus.

A new computer-simulated study of the change in the obliquity of the ecliptic reveals that the Earth's axis tilts between 24°14' and 22°37' during a period of approximately 19,560 years, having attained a maximum inclination (24°14'07") in about 7530 BC and attaining a minimum inclination (22°36'41") in about AD 12030.[3] According to this new study, during this period of some 19,560 years the obliquity of the ecliptic varies by 1°37', the average value being 23°26', so that the present value of the obliquity (23°26'21" for the year 2000) is close to the midpoint of the cycle of angular variation (the midpoint will be reached in approximately AD 2250).

In order to draw a comparison between coordinates of geographical location and the celestial coordinates of stars, the obliquity of the ecliptic—and the gradual shift in the value of this angle of inclination—has to be taken into account. If the obliquity were to be 0°, then the Earth's polar axis would coincide with the axis between the north and south poles of the ecliptic. The pole star would then be permanently fixed and would be identical with the location of the north pole of the ecliptic. In the case of the north ecliptic pole, as mentioned in

3 Giessen, *Obliquity Applet* (2004)—http://www.jgiesen.de/obliquity; see also Akcam, *Precession and the Obliquity of the Ecliptic* (2004)—http://www.tenspheres.com/researches/precession.htm, who concludes that the cycle between the maximum (24°36') and minimum (22°00') inclination of the obliquity of the ecliptic *and back again* lasts for approximately 41,000 years. See also Keller, "Kippt die Erdachse?" *Kosmos Himmelsjahr* 2000, p. 83, who indicates that obliquity changes over a period of approximately 21,000 years between 24°18' and 21°55'—this being the half-period of the value arrived at by Haluk Akcam (who investigated the whole cycle).

chapter 4, this lies within the coil of the neck of Draco (the Dragon), and this is where the north pole star would be located. There would then also be no precession of the equinoxes, since the vernal point, which is defined by the intersection of the equator with the ecliptic, would disappear (since there would be no intersection), and there would be no changing seasons during the cycle of the year as for a given location the Sun would always be at the same altitude at midday every day of the year. If at some future point in time there were to be a pole shift in which the Earth's inclination would change from its present 23½° to be 0° in the future, the relationship of the stars (celestial sphere) to the Earth's globe would then be very simple and direct, with no angular inclination (obliquity) to take into account.

Recent research shows that climatic changes in prehistoric times were influenced by changes in the inclination of the Earth's axis. It has now been estimated that the inclination of the Earth's axis around 750 to 550 million years ago amounted to 54°.[4] This meant that on average the poles at that time received more sun during the course of the year than the equatorial regions, which correspondingly were colder than polar regions. Therefore the polar regions had a more tropical climate while there was large-scale icing over our present tropical regions during the time paleontologists refer to as the Neoproterozoical period. Geologically speaking, this was the time of transition from the Pre-Cambrian to the Cambrian period. This recent research pointing to a pole shift at that time confirms Rudolf Steiner's indications, albeit Steiner's dating of this event is different:

> The Earth's axis shifted gradually. In earlier times there was a tropical climate at the North Pole; later, through a pole shift, the tropical climate came to the middle. This transition proceeded relatively quickly, but it lasted perhaps four million years. The Lemurian Age was twenty-two million years ago. The Lunar Pitris took four million years to shift the axis.[5]

Here Steiner indicates that the change that occurred to the Earth's axis took place during the Lemurian Age some 22 million years ago,

4 Keller, "*Kippt die Erdachse?*" *Kosmos Himmelsjahr 2000*, p. 83.

5 Steiner, *Grundelemente der Esoterik*, p. 185 (lecture, Oct. 25, 1905).

whereas modern research places it more than 500 million years ago. However, it is possible that the planetary periods, rate of precession, etc., were different in those times, and the scientific method of counting years can be inaccurate when not taking these differences into account. Apart from the difference in the dating of the pole shift, there is also an astonishing agreement—that Rudolf Steiner also spoke of a tropical climate in the polar regions prior to the pole shift. For our considerations the important point is the scientific estimate that the pole was previously inclined at approximately 54° whereas now its inclination is about 23½°. For there are good reasons to suppose that this last pole shift occurred at the time of the Fall and that in fact it was an aspect of the Fall, which is said to have taken place during the Lemurian Age. In this case, evidently the pole shift coincided with the event of the Fall and was even a cosmic expression of this catastrophic event.

Whether or not it was the event of the Fall that led to the present angle of inclination (obliquity of the ecliptic) of approximately 23½°, for Astrogeographia this angle has to be factored into considerations of the correspondence between the celestial sphere and the globe of the Earth. Since the Fall also coincided with the incarnation of the first human beings on the Earth—in the region of Jerusalem, considered (from the perspective of looking down from the cosmos) to be the middle of the whole Earth[6]—it is the "parallel of Jerusalem" (31N47) which can be considered astro-geographically as the 0° parallel of the whole Earth. As handed down in the ancient Persian myth concerning the birth of the first human being (Gayomart), the birth horoscope of the Earth took place when all the planets were at their place of exaltation. As discussed in chapter 4, the birth of Gayomart in the Persian tradition equates with the incarnation of Adam (depicted in the Bible as the Fall)—the first human being to incarnate upon the Earth. At that moment in time there took place the *thema mundi* ("nativity

6 As indicated in the previous chapter, prior to the effect of continental drift, the Earth was a whole, with all the continents together, and was known as *Pangaia* or *Pangea* ("whole Earth"). Israel—more specifically Jerusalem—was the center of Pangaia. This was at a very early stage in the history of the Earth's formation, long before the event of the Fall, by which time the continents had drifted somewhat apart.

of the world") and evidently there also took place an imprint of the entire celestial sphere upon the earthly globe.

The Persian tradition brings this imprint to expression in an interesting way in the ancient Zoroastrian rites of initiation. The candidate for initiation wore a sacred girdle, since it was believed that Ahura Mazdao, the great Creator Spirit, made the original sacred girdle of the starry heavens and wrapped it around the Earth. The candidate wrapped the sacred girdle (*kusti*) around the waist in imitation of Ahura Mazdao's imprint of the stars upon the Earth.

Returning now to consider the main coordinates of Astrogeographia, the zero parallel and the prime meridian: If the "parallel of Jerusalem" constituted the 0° parallel with respect to this imprint of the starry heavens upon the Earth, where was the 0° meridian (prime meridian)—not the humanly chosen Greenwich meridian but the 0° meridian viewed cosmically from the perspective of the starry heavens?

In his *Geography* Ptolemy's reference meridian was the meridian running through the "Fortunate Islands"—the Canary Islands—which he chose because these islands were the westernmost part of the world as it was known at his time.[7] The Canary Islands are located some 14° west of the Greenwich meridian and, as can be readily seen, do not constitute a prime meridian for the Earth from the perspective of the starry heavens. The consideration that applies here is the following:

- Longitude of the Great Pyramid (31E08) equates with the sidereal longitude of Alnitak in 2495 BC (29°51' Taurus).
- Subtract 29°51' from 31E08 = 1E17.
- It follows that the longitude of 1E17 equates with the sidereal longitude of 0° Taurus—
- coinciding with the towns of Norwich (1E18) and Dover (1E19) in the east of England.
- Subtract 30° from 1E17 = 28W43.
- It follows that the longitude of 28W43 equates with the sidereal longitude of 0° Aries—
- coinciding with the archipelago of the Azores in the middle of the North Atlantic Ocean.

7 Ptolemy, *Geography* (tr. Stevenson), p. 34; see also Evans, *The History and Practice of Ancient Astronomy*, p. 102.

From a cosmic perspective, therefore, the prime meridian is located at 28W43, which equates with 0° Aries, acknowledged as the starting point of the zodiac.[8] This "cosmic meridian" equated with 0° Aries runs through the middle of the Azores—a group of nine volcanic islands at the westernmost border of the European Economic Union, atop some of the tallest mountains on the planet, as measured from their base at the bottom of the ocean. The islands were discovered in 1427 by one of the Portuguese captains sailing for Henry the Navigator and were then colonized by the Portuguese and settlers from other European countries, becoming an autonomous region within the European Economic Union in 1976.

Considering the globe as a whole, the zodiacal signs are projected onto the globe beginning with the Azores (28W43) as the point of departure. Thus the sign of Aries is projected onto an area extending from 28W43 to 1E17, including most of Britain except for the easternmost part of England (the axis between Norwich and Dover and eastward thereof). This finding of Astrogeographia is confirmed by Ptolemy:

> Aries: Britain...each of the fixed stars has familiarity with the countries with which the parts of the zodiac, which have the same inclinations as the fixed stars upon the circle drawn through its poles, appear to exert sympathy.[9]

This statement by Ptolemy provides a foundation for Astrogeographia and it will be explored in depth in the next chapter. Before embarking upon this in-depth exploration, it is important to consider research work which is related to the field of Astrogeographia and which helps to shed light on the basic principles of Astrogeographia. Therefore I would like to draw attention to the research of my esteemed colleague, Dennis Klocek, who utilizes a projection of the sidereal zodiac around the globe in

---

8 As will be explained later, because of Alnitak's proper motion, the current sidereal longitude is 29°56' Taurus. This means that currently 28W48 equates with the sidereal longitude of 0° Aries. Thus, 28W48 replaces 28W43, a shift of 0°05' that is almost negligible.

9 *Tetrabiblos* II,3, pp. 157–161.

order to predict the weather.[10] In his paper "Projective Fields in Astroclimatology" he presents a case study:

> This study is an attempt to unite three different fields under one technique. The first field is the climate record. Case studies made from recent years by observing a 500 mb map of the northern hemisphere will be presented. Second, this climate data will be placed into a field of planetary motion in arc data from Neil Michelsen's *Sidereal Ephemeris 1976–2000.* Third, using projective geometric techniques observations of motion in arc events have proven to exert a predictable and significant influence upon the onset and decay of unusual climatic scenarios. This is the fundamental thesis of this study.
>
> To establish the context for this work the map of the northern hemisphere was divided using the longitudinal coordinates from the geodetic equivalency technique of Chris McRae (*The Geodetic World Map,* American Federation of Astrologers, 1988).... The system described in this paper is the result of a phenomenon driven protocol with very little reference to planetary convention except for geodetic projection and the accurate ephemeris data concerning motion in arc in sidereal longitudes. I have also taken the liberty of displacing the McRae placement 23° to the west in order to allow for precession of the equinoxes.[11]

The whole paper "Projective Fields in Astroclimatology" is of great interest, written by Dennis Klocek, one of the leading pioneers of astroclimatology. He arrived at his method of weather prediction by way of empirical study and found that the sidereal zodiac (based

---

10 Dennis Klocek is known to the readers of the *Urban Almanac* as *Doc Weather* and is the source of the yearly weather predictions and outlooks in that magazine. He also has a website at docweather.com that contains articles based on his twenty-five years of research on the influences that planetary motions have upon the weather. Dennis has a new book published called *The Seer's Handbook: A Guide to Higher Perception.* He devotes most of his year to work in the *Consciousness Studies Program* at Rudolf Steiner College in Fair Oaks, California, and he also travels frequently to give workshops on various themes. His latest and most comprehensive book about his research is *Climate: Soul of the Earth.*

11 From http://www.weather-week.com/papers_projective.shtml, introduction (page 1).

on the SVP)[12] is foundational for his work, and that the prime meridian for astroclimatology is located 23W00 of the Greenwich meridian. I greatly respect and admire Dennis Klocek's work, and yet there is some research, presented in appendix 2, indicating that if instead of locating the prime meridian 23W00 he were to place it 28W43 of the Greenwich meridian, he would obtain still better results in predicting the weather. It would be a small but significant refinement to the methods of astroclimatology that he has developed.

It is of interest to know the basic premises underlying astroclimatology, since this also helps in the process of gaining a deeper understanding of Astrogeographia. The following is a specific example discussed by Dennis in his paper "Projective Fields in Astroclimatology":

> In many instances a 135° line between outer planets is a factor in the most unusual climate shifts. A particularly vivid case study arose around the time of the lunar eclipse on January 21, 2000. Jupiter had been transiting Africa during the fall and early winter. In mid-January it had reached a position where it stood at 134° of arc to Pluto in the longitude of Hawaii. Jupiter was then poised over Africa to move in arc on the same day as the lunar eclipse. Over the years it has been a consistent feature of astroclimatics that a planet moving in arc into the angle of 135° to another planet is significant in the production of storms and tempests arising out of the polar jet.

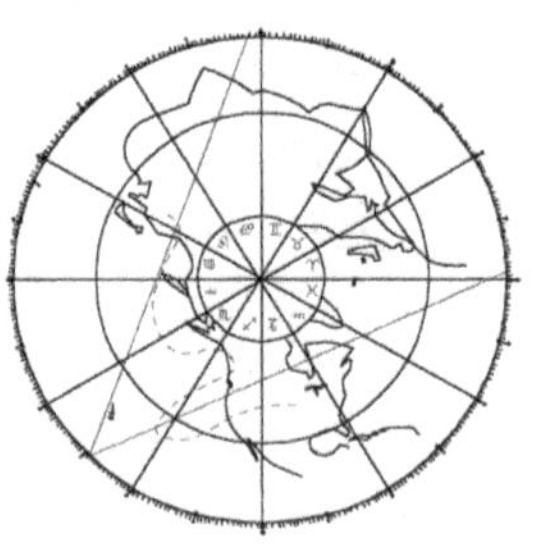

> The storm pattern in this sequence began on January 21 2000 (see figure) as the Moon went into eclipse at 5° Cancer. A few hours after that event the Moon moved in arc into a 135° aspect to Pluto. The next day the jet stream from Japan tracked the 135 line like an arrow directly at Hawaii from the dateline area. Also on the next day (January 22) Jupiter, over Africa, moved in arc to a 135° aspect to Pluto. As a result, Pluto formed the point of the intersection of two 135 lines in a very small time window. The weather in the eastern Pacific had been in a drought pattern for almost four months.

12 The Synetic Vernal Point (SVP) is defined in Michelsen, *The American Sidereal Ephemeris*, 1976–2000, Introduction. See also Michelsen, *The American Sidereal Ephemeris*, 2001–2025, introduction.

> Precipitation in California was about 20 percent of normal. This is the background of the eclipse and the Jupiter / Pluto aspect.
>
> On the 23rd, 24th, and 25th, more rain fell in the central valley than had fallen in the whole winter up to that point. The situation was a total reversal. The storm jet during this sequence dropped into the eastern Pacific and tracked the line between Pluto and Jupiter. The unusual path of the storm jet can be seen in the chart. The storm jet flowed out of the Sea of Ohotsk along the 135 line from the lunar eclipse point, then wove north into the Gulf of Alaska. Once there it followed the Pluto / Jupiter 135 line south toward Hawaii then the jet reversed to the northeast and dumped large amounts of rain on regions which were just beginning to face impending drought. The axis for the storm trough was the projection line of the 135° aspect between Jupiter and Pluto. The ultimate significance of this is that all other climatic parameters stayed the same during this remarkable transition as they were during the drought sequence. As far as standard climatology is concerned there is no good explanation for so sudden and vigorous a reversal. The effects of 135° lines are not always as dramatic as this case but they are reliable indicators of sudden switching of long held climatic scenarios.[13]

To grasp the methods of astroclimatology developed by Dennis Klocek, let us consider the above quotation in detail. It begins by referring to an angle of 135° between two planets. Angular relationships between planets are known as *aspects*, although 135° is not one of the classical aspects mentioned by Ptolemy. In the *Tetrabiblos* he refers to four aspects: opposition (180°), trine (120°), square (90°), and sextile (60°).[14] He does not class conjunction (0°) as an aspect, although it is treated as an aspect throughout the *Tetrabiblos*. These five aspects are the "classical" ones, now generally called the "major aspects" to distinguish them from the new aspects called "minor aspects."

The classical or major aspects were expanded to include minor aspects by Kepler in his work *Harmonice Mundi* ("The Harmony of

13 Page 12, http://www.weather-week.com/papers_projective.shtml.

14 *Tetrabiblos* I,13, p. 73.

the World"), written in 1619. In this work he refers to a range of minor aspects, including the aspect of 135° mentioned by Dennis Klocek.

180°	opposition....
90°	square....
120°	trigon, and 60° sextile....
45°	semi-square, and 135° sesquiquadrate....
30°	semi-sextile, and 150° quincunx....
72°	quintile, and 36° semi-quintile....
144°	biquintile, and 108° tri-semi-quintile....

Effective configurations are those that cut the above arcs through the zodiac[15]*:*

Klocek's research shows that in addition to the powerful influences of major aspects such as opposition (180°) and square (90°), certain minor aspects—for example, sesquiquadrate (135°) and biquintile (144°)—show up again and again as significant in influencing weather patterns, especially in producing storms and tempests. As indicated in Dennis' article, it is especially the angular relationships between planets at the time of solar or lunar eclipses that are of key significance with regard to weather patterns.

Then there is the figure in Klocek's article. It can be seen in the figure that the prime meridian (coinciding with 0° Aries in the sidereal zodiac) runs through the Atlantic Ocean, crossing this ocean along a meridian displaced by 23° from the Greenwich meridian. The twelve signs of the zodiac are thus mapped out around the globe, with sidereal Aries extending from 23° west to 7° east, sidereal Taurus from 7° east to 37° east, sidereal Gemini from 37° east to 67° east, etc. The figure shows only the northern hemisphere of the globe. In order to have a fuller picture one has to imagine an actual three-dimensional globe divided into twelve segments, with the meridians defining the twelve segments (corresponding to the twelve signs) departing from the Earth's north pole and proceeding around the globe to the south pole. The figure shows the globe from above (flattened) with the north pole at the center of the circle. As

15 Kepler, *Harmonice Mundi* IV,11: tr., Caspar; *Weltharmonik*, p. 242.

will emerge in the following, for Astrogeographia it is the *entire celestial globe* that is imprinted onto the Earth, not just the twelve signs/constellations of the zodiac.

Let us now consider the planetary configuration for January 22, 2000, that is mentioned in the article on astroclimatology. In this article the position of the Moon at the eclipse on January 21 is referred to as decisive for the shaping of the subsequent weather conditions. The Moon was at 5°44' Cancer in the sidereal zodiac at the middle of the eclipse and the Moon's declination was 19°39' north. The sidereal longitude of the 5°44' Cancer equates (in astroclimatology) with a geographical longitude of 72°44' east, since 72°44' + 23° = 95°44' = 5°44' Cancer. The projection of the Moon onto the surface of the Earth (in terms of Dennis' astroclimatology) coincides with a geographical location 72°44' east and 19°39' north—i.e., it coincides with Mahim (72E46; 19N40) on the west coast of India, north of Bombay. It is not so much this particular location that Dennis—in his weather analysis presented in the article on astroclimatology—is interested in, but rather the *connecting line* (projected onto the globe) between the Moon and Pluto. In particular, a few hours before the eclipse, the Moon, when it was at 2°24' Cancer, had formed an angle of 135° with Pluto at 17°24' Scorpio, since 2°24' Cancer + 135° = 17°24' Scorpio. In Dennis' research the angle of 135° is very active in promoting stormy weather. Dennis considered the *connecting line* (projected onto the Earth) between the Moon and Pluto and saw that this connecting line crossed just south of Japan across the Pacific Ocean in the direction of Hawaii, and that through it the jet stream from the area of Japan across the Pacific was activated.

In addition to the angle of 135° between the Moon and Pluto, there was also an aspect of 135° (sesquiquadrate) between Jupiter and Pluto on January 22. On that day Jupiter was at 2°02' Aries and Pluto at 17°24' Scorpio in the sidereal zodiac, signifying that the angular distance between them was 134°38' (almost exactly 135°). In the article on astroclimatology it is mentioned that Jupiter "had been transiting Africa during the fall and early winter" and that Pluto was "in the longitude of Hawaii." How may this be understood?

On January 22, 2000, Jupiter was at 2°02' Aries with a declination 9°14' north.[16] Since 0° Aries equates with 23° west in Dennis Klocek's astroclimatology, then 2°02' Aries equated with 20°58' west. Jupiter was thus positioned in a projection relationship to the Earth over latitude 9°14' north and longitude 20°58' west—i.e., in a position over the Atlantic Ocean off the west coast of Africa, some 7½° west of Point Sallatouk (9N05; 13W22) on the west coast of Africa where Guinea meets Sierra Leone. Jupiter's projection (in terms of astroclimatology) was therefore off the west coast of Africa and had been over Africa during the fall of 1999. Thus, at the beginning of September 1999, Jupiter was at 10° Aries, declination 11°48' north—equating with a longitude of 13° west (13° west + 10° = 23° west = 0° Aries)—more or less over the town of Touba (11N36; 13W00) in Guinea.

Now let us consider Pluto's projection onto the Earth on that day, in terms of astroclimatology. On January 22, 2000, Pluto was at 17°24' Scorpio, declination 11°26' south. 17°24' Scorpio is 132°36' from 0° Aries (17°24' Scorpio + 132°36' = 360° = 0° Aries). Since 0° Aries in astroclimatology coincides with 23° west, this implies that Pluto's projection onto the Earth's surface was located 155°36' west and 11°26' south. The Mauna Loa volcano on the Big Island of Hawaii is 155°36' west, coinciding exactly with the projected longitude. However, Mauna Loa is 19°28' north of the equator. On the other hand, Flint Island in the South Pacific is 11°26' south and 151°48' west. Thus Pluto's projection on that day (in the sense of astroclimatology) lay about 4° west of Flint Island, 31° due south of the Mauna Loa volcano and was thus "in the longitude of Hawaii" as referred to by Dennis Klocek.

Here it is simply a matter of clarifying how the principle of projecting the planets onto the surface of the Earth applies in astroclimatology as developed by Dennis Klocek. How does this relate to the

16 Michelsen, *The American Sidereal Ephemeris, 1976–2000* gives not only the positions of the longitude of the planets in the sidereal zodiac but also the declinations of the planets, which are needed in order to be able to find the corresponding latitude of the geographical projection (in terms of astroclimatology), recalling that—as mentioned earlier—declination (in the heavens) corresponds exactly to geographical latitude (on the Earth).

principle of projecting the celestial globe onto the Earth's globe in Astrogeographia?

Before turning to this question, let us contemplate Dennis Klocek's remarks about dividing the globe "using the longitudinal coordinates from the geodetic equivalency technique of Chris McRae (The Geodetic World Map, American Federation of Astrologers, 1988)...displacing the McRae placement 23° to the west in order to allow for precession of the equinoxes." *Geodesy* is Earth measurement on a large scale, allowing for the curvature of the Earth. *Geodetic* is the adjective pertaining to geodesy. The geographical system of a grid of latitudes and longitudes encompassing the surface of the Earth is itself an example of geodesy. The method of projection of planets onto the Earth's surface in astroclimatology is an example of geodetic equivalency—i.e., a system formulated in cosmic terms (e.g., utilizing zodiacal longitudes) equivalent to the earthly geographical system. From the examples in astroclimatology given above it is clear that there are two components to geodetic equivalents:

1. equating zodiacal longitudes with geographical longitudes, and for this it is necessary to know the prime meridian—i.e., which geographical longitude equates with 0° Aries (at the same time it has to be specified whether 0° Aries is in the sidereal or in the tropical zodiac).
2. equating declination with geographical latitudes (or some other way of equating a planet's latitude with geographical latitude).

With regard to (1), the Canadian astrologer Chris McRae has written a comprehensive account of geodetic equivalents in her book *The Geodetic World Map*.[17] In this book she elaborates on the earlier work entitled *Geodetic Equivalents* published by the British astrologer Sepharial (also known as Walter Gorn Old), who wrote during the last part of the nineteenth and the early part of the twentieth century. The starting point for Sepharial, and also for Chris McRae, is that the geodetic equivalent of the Greenwich meridian is 0° Aries *using the tropical zodiac*. Dennis Klocek adapted the system

17 McRae, *The Geodetic World Map*.

of Sepharial and Chris McRae to take the meridian 23° west of Greenwich to be the geodetic equivalent of 0° Aries *using the sidereal zodiac*. The refinement suggested in this book on Astrogeographia is to take the Egyptians seriously who aligned the star Alnitak with the Great Pyramid, signifying—as outlined above—that the meridian 28°43' west of Greenwich is the geodetic equivalent of 0° Aries *using the sidereal zodiac*. Thus the *prime meridian* in Astrogeographia is located 28°43' west of Greenwich and runs through the Azores.

With regard to (2), as indicated earlier, in Astrogeographia the second component of projection (in addition to the longitude component) is not simply a matter of a straightforward identification of declination with geographical latitude, as in the case of astroclimatology. Rather, instead of the Earth's equator, the latitude of Jerusalem (31N47) is taken to be the *zero parallel*. This brings us back to the question of the influence upon (2) of changes in the obliquity of the ecliptic that was touched upon at the start of this chapter and which will be explored more fully in the next chapter.

Before embarking upon this exploration, let us summarize the essential points relating to geodetic equivalents:

1. The global system of longitudes and latitudes was inaugurated on November 18, 1883, in which the Greenwich meridian was specified as the prime meridian.
2. Shortly thereafter the British astrologer Sepharial identified the Greenwich meridian with 0° Aries (tropical zodiac), thus establishing the principle of geodetic equivalents in which the 360° of the zodiac are mapped onto the 360° grid of geographical longitudes enveloping the globe.
3. In 1988 the Canadian astrologer Chris McRae resurrected Sepharial's system of geodetic equivalents with the publication of her book *The Geodetic World Map* published by the American Federation of Astrologers.
4. Shortly thereafter the American researcher Dennis Klocek discovered that the system of geodetic equivalents—if transposed to the sidereal zodiac—offers a key to predicting the weather, whereby he identified the prime meridian (equated with 0° Aries in the sidereal zodiac) with the geographical longitude of 23° west (23W00).

5. While acknowledging Dennis Klocek's discovery of the true principle of geodetic equivalents—i.e., that it has to be applied in relation to the sidereal zodiac, in October 2005 the discovery was made that the key to geodetic equivalents is to be found in the alignment of the star Alnitak with the Great Pyramid at the time of its construction in 2495 BC, which places the prime meridian—equated with 0° Aries in the sidereal zodiac (SVP)—at 28W43, signifying a small westward shift of 5°43' from the prime meridian (23W00) utilized by Dennis Klocek; this shift is supported by empirical findings obtained by applying both the system of Astrogeographia and Dennis Klocek's system to earthquakes and extreme weather conditions, as discussed in appendix 2, "Earth's Weather and Earthquakes in Relation to the Planets and Stars" (posted on the website www.astrogeographia.org > Astrogeographia-Book).

Chapter 6

Meridians in Astrogeographia

As mentioned in the previous chapter, the following quote by Ptolemy provides a foundation for Astrogeographia:

> Each of the fixed stars has familiarity with the countries with which the parts of the zodiac, which have the same inclinations as the fixed stars upon the circle drawn through its poles, appear to exert sympathy.[1]

While this statement brings to expression that there is a correspondence between the celestial sphere—that of the fixed stars—and the globe of the Earth, the *mode* of this correspondence is ambiguous, leading one to question further. On the one hand Ptolemy is obviously referring to the circle drawn through the poles of the ecliptic, through the star in question, and intersecting the zodiac. In the case of Alnitak, the lower of the three stars in the belt of Orion, the circle passing through the poles of the ecliptic and Alnitak intersects the sidereal zodiac at 29°56' Taurus currently, and at the time of the construction of the Great Pyramid (2495 BC) it intersected the zodiac at 29°51' Taurus. On the other hand Ptolemy is indicating that each fixed star exerts an influence upon a corresponding place upon the Earth, and since he refers to the "parts of the zodiac," he can only mean that the key to this influence is the geodetic equivalent (however that may be determined). To illustrate by way of an example, the fixed star Alnitak lying on the meridian 29°51' Taurus has "familiarity" with all the locations on the geodetic equivalent to 29°51' Taurus (or 29°56' Taurus, if the current position of Alnitak is taken as the basis for the projection of the celestial sphere onto the globe of the

1 *Tetrabiblos* II,3, pp. 157–161.

Earth). Assuming that the geodetic equivalent to 29°51' Taurus is indicated by the longitude of the Great Pyramid (31E08), Ptolemy's statement implies that every place on the longitude of 31E08 would be influenced by the star Alnitak. In this example, as an application of Astrogeographia, one would consider each of the countries (geodetic equivalent: 31E08) with which this part of the zodiac (29°51' Taurus) is aligned, since the star Alnitak would "appear to exert sympathy" with them. The lack of clarity in Ptolemy's statement arises from his use of the word *inclination,* which is not a precise astronomical expression. If he had used the word longitude, it would have been clearer. Despite the similarity of the word *inclination* and the word *declination* it is clear from the reference to "the circle drawn through its poles" that it is not declination but *longitude* which is meant here.

In Astrogeographia, the word *meridian* is used. There is a quite specific reason for this, which will become clear in the following. The meridian of Alnitak on the celestial sphere is the great circle passing through the ecliptic poles and Alnitak, currently intersecting the zodiac at 29°56' Taurus—taken to be 29°51' Taurus, however, since this was Alnitak's sidereal longitude when the Great Pyramid was built. The geodetic equivalent of this meridian through Alnitak equates with 31°08' east, this being the longitude of the Great Pyramid. This geodetic equivalent could be called the *earthly meridian* corresponding to Alnitak. All geographical locations having a longitude of 31°08' east (or close to this value) are considered to lie on the same earthly meridian as the Great Pyramid, and this earthly meridian corresponds to the celestial meridian of Alnitak. Proceeding north from the Great Pyramid, the earthly meridian passes through (or close to) Yalvaç (38N16; 31E09) in Southern Turkey; then through Düzce (40N51; 31E09) in Northern Turkey; then through Grigor'yevka (46N52; 31E04) in the Ukraine, on the Black Sea, just east of Odessa; then through Novobelitsa (52N24; 31E04) in White Russia; then just west of Novgorod (58N32; 31E16), at one time the spiritual center of Russia; then through Vardø (70N22; 31E06) in Norway on the Island of Vardøya in the Barents Sea, the easternmost tip of the Finnmark in the far north of Norway. Following this earthly meridian south from the Great Pyramid, it passes through Tonya (1N35; 31E05) in Uganda, on Lake Mobuto Sese Seko (formerly Lake Alberta); then through Harare (formerly Salisbury) (17S43; 31E05), the capital of Zimbabwe; then exactly through Tongaat (29S35; 31E07) in South Africa, on the coast of the Indian Ocean, near Durban. All these places lying on the earthly meridian of the Great Pyramid have a "familiarity" with Alnitak, which "appears to exert sympathy" on them.

In order to better understand what is meant in terms of the "familiarity" or "sympathy" exerted by a star upon an entire earthly meridian, it is helpful to consider the use of the word *meridian* in an altogether different context. The word *meridian* is used in Chinese medicine. Its use in Chinese medicine—for example, in acupuncture—helps in the understanding of both the cosmic and the earthly meridians. Chinese medicine recognizes twelve main meridians in the human being and many other secondary meridians. The twelve main meridians are generally connected with inner organs. Thus, there is the heart meridian, the liver meridian, the kidneys meridian, the lungs meridian, and so on. The liver meridian, for example, runs through the region of the liver and extends up to the ribs and beyond, and all the way down to the big toe. In the case of good health, the life energy streams throughout the meridians and there is a sense of wellbeing. If someone has pain on the inside of the knees, this could be indicative of a disturbance to the liver meridian, which runs along the inside of the leg all the way to the big toe. Such a disturbance in the flow of energy through the liver meridian might have its cause in the liver itself, or it could have its origin somewhere else along the liver meridian. In order to re-stimulate the flow of life energy in the liver meridian, an acupuncturist might insert a needle into an acupuncture point on the liver meridian in the region of the big toe in order to exert an influence upon the flow of life energy along the entire meridian, including the liver itself. The implicit understanding here is that every location upon the meridian exerts an influence upon every other location upon the meridian by way of the energy flow along the meridian.

By way of analogy, the influence of the star Alnitak flows along the entire celestial meridian running through it. Likewise the corresponding earthly meridian is receptive, by way of "familiarity" or "sympathy," to Alnitak's influence, which in turn is focused especially upon the Great Pyramid. In this analogy the star Alnitak is like the organ (the liver in the example above) and the celestial meridian running through Alnitak is like the meridian running through the organ (the liver meridian in the above example). The corresponding earthly meridian runs through the towns and cities mentioned above. On this meridian the Great Pyramid, as the "earthly projection" of the star Alnitak, is the "organ" and the rest of the earthly meridian is like the meridian running through the organ. In Chinese medicine the life energy is called *chi* and analogously it is "earthly *chi*" which flows along the earthly meridian and "heavenly *chi*" which flows along the celestial meridian. Apart from the star Alnitak itself, obviously the place of intersection of the "Alnitak meridian" with the zodiac—or rather, with the ecliptic (the central line running through the twelve signs/constellations of the zodiac)—is of key significance, the point of intersection being 29°56' Taurus currently and 29°51' Taurus at the time of construction of the Great Pyramid.

As referred to above, one of the cities located on (or very close to) the earthly meridian running through the Great Pyramid, and thereby partaking of the influence of Alnitak, is Novgorod, the most ancient Slavic city recorded in Russia. Novgorod means "new town." The first chronicled reference to Novgorod is from the year 859. However, it is mentioned in Norse sagas as existing substantially earlier under the name *Holmgard*, the Varangian name of the city. By the middle of the tenth century Novgorod had become a fully developed medieval city. Recalling the Saturnine quality of Alnitak as discussed in chapter 4 in connection with the rites of death and ascension associated with the Great Pyramid, the question is whether it is possible to see anything of this influence in the city of Novgorod. Of all their princes, the people of Novgorod cherished most the memory of Yaroslav the Wise, who lived in the eleventh century. He promulgated Russia's first written code of laws, which could be regarded as something Saturnine, since any code of laws (one of the oldest being "an eye for an eye, a tooth for a tooth"—Exodus 21:24) embodies the principle of justice acting in the realm of destiny or *karma*, under the sway of Saturn. Yaroslav the Wise was also the patron of the construction of the great cathedral of St. Sophia in Novgorod, which could perhaps be seen in the spiritual life of Russia as occupying a similar position to the Great Pyramid in the spiritual life of Egypt. St. Sophia's Cathedral, which was constructed around the middle of the eleventh century (AD 1045 is the usual date given for the laying of the foundation stone), is a vast five-naved, six-domed temple with closed galleries. The impression one receives from its monumental proportions serves to create an unforgettable memory. Like the Great Pyramid, which has been a source of attraction ever since it was built, the cathedral, called the *Sophia Premúdrost Bózhia* ("Sophia the All-Wisdom of God"), has been a place of pilgrimage down through the centuries.

The naming of the cathedral—St. Sophia or Holy Sophia—is interesting. In the Russian Orthodox Church Sophia is regarded as the "Bride of the Lamb" referred to in the last book of the Bible, Revelation. Novgorod is also famous for its tradition of icon painting, one of the most famous icons in the cathedral of St. Sophia being that of Divine Sophia ("Holy Wisdom"—*Sophia* being the Greek word for wisdom). The icon shows a majestic, winged female figure wearing red robes and seated upon a throne appearing against a gold background. To her right stands the Virgin Mary and to her left John the Baptist. Above her, Christ appears in all his glory; and above him appear Angels surrounding the Word of God represented in the form of an open book. The great Russian philosopher and poet, Vladimir Soloviev (1853–1900), frequently visited the cathedral of St. Sophia in order to contemplate this icon. He wrote about this icon of Holy Wisdom in Novgorod's cathedral of St. Sophia:

> Who is it who sits there in royal dignity on the throne, if not Holy Wisdom, the true and pure ideal of humanity itself, the most exalted, all-encompassing form and the living soul of nature and the cosmos, eternally bound to God, who unites everything existing in the temporal world with Her.[2]

2 From Soloviev's lecture about the work of Auguste Comte, quoted in Schipflinger, *Sophia–Maria*, p. 250.

The icon of Holy Wisdom in Novgorod's St. Sophia cathedral was of great significance for Soloviev on account of three visions of Sophia which he had had during the course of his life: the first as a child aged nine attending an Ascension Day service (May 1862) in Moscow's University Chapel; the second at the age of twenty-two (September 1875) in the British Museum Library in London; and the third shortly after in the Egyptian desert near Cairo, where Sophia had instructed him to go, and where he had his greatest vision of her. Here in the life of Vladimir Soloviev a connection emerges between St. Sophia's Cathedral in Novgorod and the Great Pyramid near Cairo. The sense of this connection is heightened in light of Rudolf Steiner's indication that Sophia is the same being whom the Egyptians revered as Isis.[3]

Soloviev says of the poem in which he movingly depicts his three visions of Sophia:

> The experiences that were the most significant in my life up until then are presented in the form of light-hearted verses....
> "O, Eternal Friend...three times you showed yourself to me....
> The first time...my child's soul perceived
> An uneasy dream of love's yearning....
> Ascension Day's high mass. A beautiful morning....
> A blossom of supernatural beauty in your hand,
> With gracious goodness you smiled at me....
> Years passed...the British Museum beckoned....
> Mostly alone in the reading room....
> Then one day...I felt myself surrounded
> By golden light and radiant blue,
> And I saw her again, all full of light,
> Only her countenance, ah!—only her countenance....
> 'On to Egypt!' echoed within me....
> In Cairo I found welcome
> In the lovely hotel Abbat....
> Watching all the while for her sign.
> And lo—in night's stillness,
> She gently wafted through my room:

3 Steiner, *Isis Mary Sophia;* see especially the lectures *The Search for the New Isis, the Divine Sophia.*

'On to the desert! I await you!' ....
The world was glowing with early dawn,
Springtime broke from the morning sky's
Purple glow, and there you were!
A new radiance shining in your eyes,
Like day's light at dawn's creation....
I saw all, and all was one,
The precious image of my Eternal Friend,
A reflection of heaven's radiance
Was all around—my heart was full."[4]

The spiritual connection between Novgorod and the Great Pyramid, both on the same meridian (mirroring the celestial meridian passing through the star Alnitak), is revealed in the life of Vladimir Soloviev, who was guided by Sophia to Egypt, where he had his third, greatest vision of her in the Egyptian desert near Cairo, in the region of the Great Pyramid. This theme could be deepened further. However, to deepen into such connections further would lead away from the essential point. The essential points are:

1. There is a mirroring of the celestial meridians by the corresponding earthly meridians; and
2. The spiritual influence associated with a given celestial meridian (by virtue of it passing through one or more stars) is mirrored in the *entire* corresponding earthly meridian.

It is possible to understand (1) in light of the teaching of Hermes, the great teacher of the Egyptians: "As above, so below."[5] That which is in the heavens above is mirrored on the Earth below—in this case the celestial meridians running through stars are mirrored in the corresponding geographical meridians on Earth. Further, (2) can be grasped against the background of the teaching concerning meridians in Chinese medicine. That is, the influence of a star is active along

4 From Soloviev's poem "Three Meetings" quoted in: Schipflinger, *Sophia–Maria*, p. 256–259.

5 From the famous "Emerald Table" *(Tabula Smaragdina)* ascribed to the great teacher of the Egyptians, Hermes Trismegistus. See "Historical Note Concerning the Emerald Table" in Anonymous, *Meditations on the Tarot*, pp. 21–26.

the entire celestial meridian running through that star, and it is also active by way of "familiarity" or "sympathy" along the entire corresponding earthly meridian.

This explains why—returning to the connections indicated in chapter 4 pertaining to the other two stars in Orion's belt—the star Mintaka is significant with respect to the place El Alamein, since this location is on the earthly meridian corresponding to Mintaka's celestial meridian. It also explains why the city of Alexandria is associated with Alnilam, since Alexandria is located on the earthly meridian corresponding to the celestial meridian passing through Alnilam. In both these cases it was found that the earthly projection of these two stars in Orion's belt, according to Astrogeographia, was in the proximity of the two towns—Alexandria (earthly projection of Alnilam) and El Alamein (earthly projection of Mintaka)—but was not precise in terms of latitude. In the discussion in chapter 4 it was stated that, in any case, it is the longitude which is more important—and the foregoing exposition concerning meridians indicates why this is so.

To elaborate further on this theme of meridians (celestial and terrestrial) in Astrogeographia, it is helpful to consider an important finding relating to stellar meridians. The famous Bayer catalog of stars was compiled in 1603 by Johann Bayer, who assigned *Greek letters* to the brightest stars visible in each constellation, usually in descending order of apparent brightness (although there are inconsistencies). In the early 1700s John Flamsteed assigned *numbers* to the bright stars in each constellation, in order of right ascension. The Flamsteed numbers proved useful, because one eventually runs out of Greek letters, but there is no limit to the number of stars that can be assigned a number. The Flamsteed catalog (which includes the stars in the Bayer catalog) is more or less sufficient in terms of exploring the visible cosmos. Of course, with the development of more and more powerful telescopes, more and more stars in our galaxy have now been catalogued. But for the purpose of exploring the sidereal influences at work in our *cosmos* (defined as our galaxy's *local region* embracing all visible stars), the combined Bayer-Flamsteed catalog is more or less sufficient—"more or less" because there is an interesting group of stars, which can be referred to as *megastars*, that also need to be taken into consideration. The megastars are exceedingly bright stars and, as recent research indicates, they are extraordinarily important.[6]

To illustrate the notion of megastars, let us consider the star Deneb, which marks the tail of the Swan (or the head of the Northern Cross) and which can be seen on high during summer nights in the middle of the Milky Way. Deneb is a first magnitude star (apparent magnitude 1.25), which appears less bright than its neighbor Vega in the constellation of the Lyre. Both the Swan and the Lyre were sacred to Apollo, and both Deneb and Vega are of great significance in relation to our solar system. Deneb and Vega mark two points of the *summer triangle*, whose third point is marked by Altair in the constellation of the Eagle. Whereas Vega is the fifth brightest star that we can see in our cosmos, Deneb is the nineteenth brightest in terms of apparent magnitude. Sirius, of course, is the brightest star we can see. However, neither Vega nor Sirius is a megastar, whereas Deneb is. How may this be understood?

Our grasp of the surrounding cosmos is changed immediately when we consider the *distance* of stars from our solar system. These distances are so vast that a special cosmic unit for measuring them has been devised: *light-years*, where one light-year is the distance travelled by light during the course of one year. To gain an understanding of the enormous distances involved, we need only consider that Sirius—8½ light-years away (amounting to some fifty trillion miles, or about eighty trillion km)—is a *close neighbor*. It is because Sirius is so close, in comparison with other stars, that it appears so bright.

---

6 Powell and Dann, *The Astrological Revolution,* chapter 5. Peter Treadgold's computer program *Astrofire* (distributed by the Sophia Foundation of North America, www.sophiafoundation.org) contains a star catalog of over 4,000 stars based on *The Yale Bright Star Catalog* and *The Hipparcos Catalog*. One definition for megastars is all those stars whose luminosity is at least 10,000 times that of our Sun. Including the red supergiant Betelgeuse from the constellation of Orion, whose luminosity is probably more than 10,000 (but is listed in the *Astrofire* star catalog as having a luminosity of 9,884), there are 140 megastars in our cosmos—i.e., in the local part of our galaxy. Of these 140 stars with a luminosity of 10,000 or more, 56 of them are listed in the Bayer-Flamsteed catalog, and the other 84 stars are listed in the Hipparcos catalog.

We can ask the question: How bright is Sirius objectively? In other words, if we were to place Sirius alongside our Sun, how bright would it appear in comparison with our Sun?

This leads us to the concept of *luminosity*, which measures a star's intrinsic brightness. If the luminosity of our Sun is set at the value one (L=1), then the luminosity of Sirius is 24 (L=24). In other words Sirius, if it were to be placed alongside our Sun, would appear 24 times brighter. From our perspective our Sun is an extremely bright star. However, if the Earth were revolving around Sirius—in other words, if Sirius were our Sun—it would be seen by us to be twenty-four times brighter. If we imagine a second Sun alongside our Sun, then a third Sun, a fourth Sun, a fifth Sun, up to a twenty-third Sun, all bunched together as twenty-four Suns, we gain a conception of the luminosity of Sirius, which would blaze down upon us with the light of twenty-four of our Suns.

Vega, twenty-five light-years away, is *three* times the distance of Sirius. If Vega would appear to us to be just as bright as Sirius then, because the intensity of light decreases proportionately to the *square* of the distance, it would follow that the intrinsic brightness (luminosity) of Vega would be *nine* times (3x3) that of Sirius. However, Vega—as the fifth brightest star—appears a lot *less bright* to us than Sirius. In fact, the luminosity of Vega (L=51) is a little more than *twice* that of Sirius. Vega's luminosity is 51, so that if the Earth were revolving around the star Vega as our Sun, Vega would blaze down upon us with a light over fifty times brighter than that of our Sun.

Having specified luminosity, we are now in a position to understand why Deneb is a megastar. Deneb is some 2,600 light-years distant from our solar system and its luminosity L= 196,000. In other words, Deneb is shining with a light 196,000 times more powerful than our Sun. Thus a megastar is a star that is many thousands of times more luminous than our Sun.

Deneb well illustrates the significance of megastars. Looking up at Deneb, we see that it is 60° north of the zodiac—this is its latitude. If we trace an arc down from the ecliptic pole through Deneb, it intersects the sidereal zodiac at 10½° Aquarius—this is Deneb's sidereal longitude. According to recent research that uncovered the existence of a precise chronology of the life of Christ, at the miracle performed by Christ of the feeding of the 5,000 the Sun was at 10½° Aquarius.[7]

Perhaps it was not mere coincidence that there was a conjunction between the Sun and the megastar Deneb at the feeding of the 5,000? Could it be that the cosmic forces streaming from Deneb were received by our Sun and transmitted to Christ at the time of the miracle of the multiplication of bread and fish? Here the word "conjunction" means a conjunction in *longitude*, where both Deneb and the Sun were at 10½° Aquarius. Even though the Sun and Deneb were 60° apart in terms of latitude, there was still a conjunction in longitude, with the Sun crossing the *Deneb meridian* at the time of the miracle. Here we return again to the concept of *meridian* borrowed from Chinese medicine.

To recapitulate: just as there are meridians—lines of energy flow—in the human being, meridians exist also in the greater cosmos of the macrocosm. As may be understood from the law of correspondences "as above, so below," there are meridians "below" on Earth corresponding to the meridians "above" in the cosmos. We can picture an energy flow streaming from each star and intersecting the zodiac, the place of intersection indicating the point of influx of the energy flow from the cosmos into our solar system. For Deneb this point of influx is 10½° Aquarius, and so whenever the Sun or any planet in our solar system crosses the Deneb meridian at 10½° Aquarius, the Deneb energy flows in to unite with that planet or with our Sun. (Here *energy* is to be understood as the *sustaining energy* radiating from the stars.)

For example, on August 27/28, 2003 Mars was in opposition to the Sun and was at the same time at its perigee, its closest approach to the Earth. The combination of these two factors meant that Mars was physically closer to the Earth than at any time during the last 60,000 years or so. Looking up at the night sky at that time, Mars was exceedingly bright and was visible in Aquarius—at 10½° Aquarius. Mars was crossing the Deneb meridian at the time of its closest approach to

7 Powell, *Chronicle of the Living Christ*, p. 170; see also Powell and Dann, *The Astrological Revolution*, pp. 149–153, 164.

the Earth! At the time of Mars' closest approach to the Earth (perigee), Mars at 10½° Aquarius was simultaneously at the opposition point to the Sun at 10½° Leo. It was not visually obvious that Mars was in conjunction with the megastar Deneb at 10½° Aquarius, since Deneb was 60° above the zodiac. Moreover, Mars was 6½° south of the central line (ecliptic) through the zodiac. Visually, Mars and Deneb were separated by an arc of 66½°. Knowing where the stellar meridian lines flowing down from the pole of the ecliptic intersect the zodiac is the key to grasping the nature of these "conjunctions" in longitude (even if the visual latitudinal separation between these heavenly bodies may amount to many degrees—in this case 66½°). Upon becoming aware of the celestial meridians as streams of heavenly energy, it is possible to grasp the nature of such conjunctions—for example, the "conjunction" of Mars and Deneb on August 27/28, 2003, although they were 66½° spatially apart in terms of latitude. There was a *flowing together* (longitudinal meridian flow) of the quality of Deneb with that of Mars, this becoming united to the primary experience of Mars seen against the background of the stars of Aquarius. This can be summarized as: Mars in Aquarius on the Deneb meridian, or simply: *Mars in Aquarius in conjunction with Deneb.*

While this example—the conjunction of the Sun (and also the conjunction of Mars) with the megastar Deneb at 10½° Aquarius—obviously does not suffice to prove the principle (*) involved here, nevertheless there are numerous other examples which offer support for this principle: (*) *it does not matter how far distant a fixed star is from the zodiac, there is a conjunction between a planet and that fixed star when the planet (including the Sun and Moon as planets) and the fixed star have the same longitude*—i.e., when the planet is crossing that fixed star's meridian. Clearly this principle needs to be tested by further independent research before it can be accepted as proved.[8]

8 My research into the significance of megastars (in particular the conjunction of the Sun with these megastars) during the life of Christ has not yet been published. Two further examples drawn from this research—in addition to the one referred to already of the Sun's conjunction with *Deneb* (L = 196,000) at the feeding of the 5,000—are: (1) the conjunction of the Sun with *Sadr* (L = 24,390) at the healing of the paralyzed man; and (2) the conjunction of the Sun with *Al Jabhah* (L = 15,090) at the raising of Lazarus from the dead. *Sadr* (Gamma Cygni) is at 0°06' Aquarius, latitude 57N07;

For the time being, lacking any further independent research into this principle, if it is assumed that this principle (*) really does hold good, what conclusions can be drawn from this for Astrogeographia?

Returning to the fundamentals of Astrogeographia elaborated in chapters 4 and 5, the zero parallel is that running through Jerusalem (31N47). By way of analogy with the celestial realm, where the ecliptic is the plane of reference for the intersection of the stellar meridians, the earthly parallel running around the globe through 31N47 corresponds to the ecliptic plane on the celestial sphere. It was this that was used in chapter 4 for determining the earthly projections of the three stars in Orion's belt (Alnitak, Alnilam, Mintaka). Let us recall the "equation of latitude" in the case of the earthly projection of Alnitak (remembering that the "equation of longitude" is simply the identification of Alnitak's longitude with the geographical longitude of the Great Pyramid):

> (A) Great Pyramid (Giza)—latitude: 29N59—is 1°48' south of the 0° latitude of Jerusalem. Including the obliquity of the ecliptic (23°58' in 2495 BC) means that the "cosmic latitude" of the Great Pyramid is 23°58' further to the south than 1°48' = 25°46' south, which is very close to the actual latitude of Alnitak (25S53) in 2495 BC, indicating a close alignment—the difference in latitude being 0°07'.

In chapter 4 it was also pointed out:

> (B) The location of the Great Pyramid at Giza has a latitude of 29N59, which is 1°48' south of the 0° latitude represented by the parallel of declination running through Jerusalem (31N47). This figure of -1°48' is close to the present-day declination of Alnitak, which is 1°56' south, computed for the year AD 2000. Yet as Alnitak's declination in 2495 BC, when (according to the research presented in this book) the Great Pyramid was under construction, was 15° south, obviously declination cannot be utilized with regard to determining the alignment of stars with geographical

---

and *Al Jabhah* (Eta Leoni) is at 3°10' Leo, latitude 4N52. These three examples—and there are many more—serve to demonstrate the principle (*) referred to above and, at the same time, point to the significance of megastars.

locations in a general sense—although, of course, it can be used in a specific sense—i.e., for a given historical date. The reason for the shift in a star's declination in the course of time—for example, in the case of Alnitak, from 15° South in 2495 BC to approximately 2° south in AD 2000—has to do with the phenomenon of the precession of the equinoxes, whereby there is a gradual shift taking place continuously in the relationship between the Earth's alignment and the celestial sphere.

Having specified the "equation of longitude" in Astrogeographia according to the system of geodetic equivalents with the prime meridian located at 28W43 (corresponding to 0° Aries in the sidereal zodiac based on the SVP), it remains now to clarify how the latitudinal component of the earthly projection of a star is determined. From consideration of the above example of Alnitak, two approaches are possible:

1. Using the "equation of latitude," which can be expressed as follows:
   a. Find the latitude of the star at the date in question (in this example: the latitude of Alnitak in 2495 BC was 25S53, written -25°53');
   b. Add the value of the obliquity of the ecliptic for the date in question (in this example: the obliquity of the ecliptic in 2495 BC was 23°58');
   c. the resulting value (in this example: 1°55' South, written -1°55', since south values are "-" and north values are "+") is then added to the zero parallel of 31N47;
   d. The result (in this example: 29N52) is the projected geographical latitude of the star. (In this example 29N52 is 0°07' different from the latitude of the Great Pyramid, which is 29N59—i.e., the projected earthly location of Alnitak in 2495 BC was 0°07' south of the actual location of the Great Pyramid, amounting to a difference of about 8 miles (13 km).
2. Let us now apply this "equation of latitude" using the current values for Alnitak, rather than the values for 2495 BC.
   a. the current latitude of Alnitak is 25S18 or -25°18';
   b. add the current value of the obliquity of the ecliptic, which is 23°26';

   c. the result is 1°52' South, written -1°52';
   d. added to 31N47 gives 29N55, which is even closer to the latitude (29N59) of the Great Pyramid—i.e., the current projected earthly location of Alnitak is 0°04' south of the actual location of the Great Pyramid, amounting to a difference of about 4½ miles (7½ km).

3. Let us now apply the "equation of declination" using the current value for Alnitak's declination:
   a. the current declination of Alnitak is 1°56' South, written -1°56';
   b. add this value to the latitude of Jerusalem (31N47);
   c. the resulting value (29N51) is close to the geographical latitude of the Great Pyramid (29N59), the difference amounting to 0°08'—i.e., using method (B) the current projected earthly location of Alnitak is just over 9 miles (a little under 15 km) south of the actual location of the Great Pyramid.

However, as pointed out in chapter 4, if method (B) were to be applied to the declination of Alnitak in 2495 BC—at that time Alnitak's declination was 15° South—the resulting value would indicate a discrepancy of some 13° instead of a mere 0°08' as indicated in above—13° amounting to a distance of 898 miles (1,445 km) on the surface of the Earth. How can this discrepancy be understood?

Here it is helpful to contrast method (A) based on the "equation of latitude" (taking account of the change in the obliquity of the ecliptic with time) and method (B) based on the "equation of declination." First, it is important to grasp these two methods against the background of the above-mentioned principle (*) relating to meridians. In particular, it is clear—whether *meridians* are referred to, or whether one speaks of *geodetic equivalents*—that there is a basic underlying assumption which up until now has not been specified, and this assumption has to do with the question: Why should the system of geodetic equivalents work?

An attempt to approach this question was initiated in chapter 4 and then taken up again briefly in chapter 5, where in connection with the "birth horoscope of the world" mention was made of the incarnation of Adam (depicted in the Bible as the Fall)—the first human being to incarnate upon the Earth. At that moment in time there took place the *thema mundi* ("nativity of the world") and evidently there also took place an imprint of the entire celestial sphere upon the earthly globe.

Let us recall that the *thema mundi* is the birth horoscope of the world, in which all the planets stood at their place of exaltation—in the ancient Zoroastrian tradition related to the birth moment of Gayomart (Adam), the first human being. As remarked upon in chapter 5, it was at this point in time that the Earth's axis acquired its present tilt of about 23½°—this angle being known as the obliquity of the ecliptic. It was also pointed out in chapter 5 that previously the Earth's axis was tilted at about 54°. However, the implicit assumption in the system of geodetic equivalents is that an imprint of the entire celestial globe upon the earthly globe took place at a point in time when the tilt of the Earth's axis (obliquity of the ecliptic) was 0°. *It is only if the tilt is 0° that there is an exact one-to-one correspondence between the celestial meridians running through the fixed stars and the geographical meridians on Earth.* In other words, for the system of geodetic equivalents to hold true, there must have been a time (before the Earth's tilt was around 54°) when the tilt was 0°, implying that there have been two major pole shifts: the first from 0° to approximately 54° and the second from around 54° to about 23½°.[9] If this is accepted, at least as a hypothesis, the above statement quoted from chapter 5 needs to be modified. The first part of the statement can stand as it is—i.e., that the *thema mundi* relates to the Fall (to the incarnation of the first human being or human beings upon the Earth). The second part of the statement should read: "Evidently when the obliquity of the ecliptic was 0° there took place an imprint of the entire celestial sphere upon the earthly globe."

It can be hypothesized that during the first Age of the Earth, known as the *Polarian Age*, the tilt was 0° and it was then that the

9 There could have been other pole shifts, just as the Earth's magnetic field has flipped several times, according to the geologic record—see Roach, "*Why Does Earth's Magnetic Field Flip?*"; http://news.nationalgeographic.com/news/2004/09/0927.

imprint of the celestial sphere upon the globe of the Earth took place; that during the second Age, known as the *Hyperborean Age*, the Earth's axis tilted from 0° to 54°; and that during the third Age, known as the *Lemurian Age*, the Earth's axis tilted again, from 54° to 23½°—the tilt during the Hyperborean Age having been caused by the separation of the Earth from the Sun, and the further tilt during the Lemurian Age having been caused by the separation of the Moon from the Earth (the Moon having separated out from the region of the Pacific Ocean).[10] Whereas the *thema mundi* took place during the Lemurian Age when the first human being(s) incarnated upon the Earth, the imprint of the celestial sphere upon the earthly globe took place already in the Polarian Age at which time the tilt of the Earth's axis was evidently 0°—this is the hypothesis put forward here to account for the system of geodetic equivalents between celestial meridians running through stars and the geographical meridians imprinted from the celestial sphere onto the globe of the Earth. According to this hypothesis there was an actual imprint of the celestial upon the terrestrial in the sense of Rudolf Steiner's words quoted at the beginning of this book:

> The counterpart to this star is here, the counterpart to that star is there, and so on. We arrive at a complete counter image in the Earth itself to that which is outside [in the sphere of the starry heavens] .... In other words, we can conceive of the active heavenly sphere mirrored in the Earth.

As mentioned in chapter 5, when the obliquity of the ecliptic is 0° there is no "tropical zodiac," only the sidereal zodiac, and this consideration alone is sufficient to support Dennis Klocek's astroclimatology based on a *sidereal* system of geodetic equivalents and also to support Astrogeographia based on a sidereal system of geodetic equivalents in which the prime meridian—equated with 0° Aries in

10 Rudolf Steiner describes in various lectures the earlier ages of the Earth: Polaris, Hyperborea, Lemuria, Atlantis, post-Atlantis—this being the present Age following on from the great flood (described in the Bible) that brought an end to the Atlantean Age. He also indicated that the Moon separated out from the Earth during the Lemurian Age, leaving behind the Pacific Ocean where it (the Moon) had been.

the sidereal zodiac (SVP)—is identified with the geographical longitude 28W43 running through the Azores.[11] In light of the above hypothesis, the imprint of the entire celestial sphere upon the Earth's globe during the Polarian Age, when the tilt of the Earth's axis was evidently 0°, gave birth to the sidereal system of geodetic equivalents used in Astrogeographia. Having stated this basic assumption, let us return to consider the contrast between method (A) and method (B)—outlined above—with respect to specifying not only the correspondence between earthly meridians and their celestial counterparts but also the correspondence between stellar latitudes and earthly parallels, with the zero parallel running through Jerusalem (considered as the center point on the Earth's surface).

In the case of the earthly projection of the star Alnitak we have seen that the projection in latitude coincides very closely (to within a few kilometers) with the Great Pyramid, whether method (A) or method (B) is used—except in using method (B) with the declination value for Alnitak at the time when the Great Pyramid was under construction—i.e., provided that method (B) is applied with Alnitak's *current* declination value. In applying method (A) there are two variables:

1. the change in the obliquity of the ecliptic over time; and
2. the change in the star's latitude over time.

Both these variables are relatively small, and usually they are added together, whereby the result of this addition is then given as the star's change in latitude. Considering the period of about 4,500 years that has elapsed since the building of the Great Pyramid (1) amounts to

11 Knowledge concerning the sidereal zodiac was virtually non-existent at the time when Sepharial first proposed the system of geodetic equivalents based on equating the Greenwich meridian with 0° Aries in the tropical zodiac. Sepharial had a profound and far-reaching intuition, but obviously he did not grasp the implicit assumption underlying geodetic equivalents—i.e., that the tilt of the Earth's axis must have been 0° when the original imprint took place, and thus *there was no tropical zodiac at that time.* Sepharial's intuition was therefore incomplete and he missed the essential point. Nevertheless we can be grateful to Sepharial for having taken the step of putting forward a system of geodetic equivalents in the first place. As with other scientific discoveries, this original step—by way of further research and refinement—has now developed a stage further with Astrogeographia, which in turn may be subject in future to further refinement.

0°32' and (2) amounts to 0°35', which is made up of 0°32' owing to the change in the obliquity plus 0°03' *actual shift* in latitude owing to the star's proper motion over this period of time. This value of 0°03' for the actual shift due to proper motion is typical for far-away stars like Alnitak, which is about 800 light-years away. For stars that are much closer the shift due to proper motion can be much greater. For example, in the case of Sirius—8½ light-years away—the shift in latitude between 2495 BC and AD 2000 amounts to 0°58' (*actual shift*, after subtracting the shift owing to the change in the obliquity, amounts to 0°26'). Nevertheless the shift in latitude arising from the combined effect of the change in the obliquity and the star's proper motion is generally not more than 1° over a five thousand year period.[12]

Given that the correspondence between an earthly meridian and a celestial meridian running through a star applies along the whole of the meridian, it might be said that it does not really matter about a small shift in the latitudinal component of the earthly projection of a star. The most important thing is the longitudinal component—i.e., the meridian. However, bearing in mind the analogy referred to earlier—that the star is like the "organ" and the meridian through the star is like the meridian associated with the organ in question—it is certainly of interest to know the exact location of the earthly projection of a star, or at least to know it as closely as possible. Here again there is an implicit assumption—i.e., that there *is* an exact earthly location corresponding to the star. Applying method (A) leads to a range of possibilities for this exact location, whereby the range is relatively small (not more than 1° over a 5,000-year period). Applying method (B) leads to a larger range of possibilities for this exact location, since the shift in a star's declination over time is considerably greater than its shift in latitude. What is the reason for this greater shift in declination?

With regard to a star's shift in declination over the course of time, there is a much more significant changing component to factor into the "equation of declination" than the change in the obliquity of the

12 The change in a star's latitude over time is not usually broken down into these two components but is normally given in such a way that the change in the obliquity of the ecliptic is included implicitly.

ecliptic or the change due to proper motion, and this is the change in the star's relationship to the celestial equator. Declination is the angular distance of a star above or below the celestial equator, and since—owing to the precession of the equinoxes—the relationship of the entire celestial sphere to the celestial equator is continually changing, stellar declinations are also changing continuously—the shift in Alnitak's declination between 2495 BC (15° South) and AD 2000 (about 2° South) amounting to approximately 13°.[13] Nevertheless, it is easier—and more appropriate—to apply method (B), as will be evident in the following example.

Continuing from the examples of Astrogeographia given in chapter 4 in relation to the three stars in the belt of Orion, as a further example let us consider the city of Vienna in relation to the star Aldebaran. Vienna was originally a Celtic settlement and then later a Roman camp. In the early Middle Ages it became the residence first of the Babenberg family and then of the Hapsburg family, through whom Vienna became the capital of the vast Austro-Hungarian empire—essentially the capital of Europe. As no precise date is available for the founding of Vienna, let us—for the sake of simplicity—take the same date as that for the founding of Alexandria, 332 BC. In 332 BC the sidereal coordinates of Aldebaran were: latitude–5S38; longitude–15°00' Taurus.

Aldebaran, "the follower" (following the Pleiades at 5° Taurus), is the brightest star in the constellation of Taurus and is one of the four royal stars of ancient Persia, marking the Bull's eye in the exact center (15° Taurus) of this sign. Aldebaran is on the left-hand end of the V-shaped star cluster called the Hyades who, according to Greek mythology, are the half-sisters (five sisters) of the Pleiades (seven sisters). Aldebaran is an orange giant star whose diameter is about forty times that of the Sun. It is some sixty-five light-years away, with a luminosity over 150 times that of our Sun.

13 The change over ¼ of the cycle of precession—i.e., in 6,480 years (¼ of 25,920 years)—amounts to approximately 23½° (the average value of the obliquity of the ecliptic) and therefore the shift in declination is (on average) approximately 1° in 275¾ years. This is only an average value, since the change caused by obliquity and the change owing to proper motion also needs to be factored in to the calculation.

Applying method (A): According to *The Times Atlas of the World*, Vienna's latitude is 48N13 and Vienna's longitude is 16E20. Vienna is thus 16°26' north of Jerusalem (48N13-31N47 = 16°26') and 14°48' west of the Great Pyramid (31E08-16E20 = 14°48'). Subtracting 14°48' from Alnitak's longitude (in 2495 BC) of 29°51' Taurus, we find that—from a cosmic perspective—Vienna's corresponding sidereal longitude (geodetic equivalent) is 15°03' Taurus, very close to Aldebaran's sidereal longitude of 15°00' Taurus in 332 BC. Since the obliquity of the ecliptic in 332 BC was 23°44', this value has to be subtracted from 16°26' in order to find the "cosmic latitude" of Vienna. Cosmically speaking Vienna's latitude is 7°18' south (16°26'-23°44' = -7°18'), which signifies a difference of 1°40' from Aldebaran's latitude at that time (5S38).

How much does this difference of 1°40' signify in terms of miles on the surface of the Earth? This is a distance of 115 miles (185 km).[14] This is about the distance of the city of Maribor south of Vienna (although Maribor is not exactly due south of Vienna). Maribor, a cathedral city situated on the Drava River, now belongs to Slovenia, but was part of Austria from 1148 to 1918. In terms of latitude, therefore, Maribor lies closer to the method (A) projection of the star Aldebaran onto the Earth. However, Vienna lies more or less exactly on the "Aldebaran meridian" in the sense of the earlier discussion concerning meridians.[15]

As indicated in chapter 3, the current location of Aldebaran in the sidereal zodiac based on the SVP is 15°03' Taurus, and this holds during the period from AD 1655 to 2413. This current location of Aldebaran coincides *exactly* with the corresponding sidereal longitude of Vienna. However, the current latitude of Aldebaran is 5S28, whereas in 332 BC, as indicated above, it was 5S38. This does not coincide exactly with Vienna's "stellar latitude" of 7S18. Here it has to be recalled that the obliquity of the ecliptic was factored into the computation of Vienna's

14 1° corresponds to 69.055055 miles (111.1333 km).

15 See chapter 8 for a description of the shift of Aldebaran's latitude projection from North Africa in 2450 BC to Vienna in the middle of the eighteenth century AD, when this city became a great cultural center for the arts, sciences, and music.

"stellar latitude," and that the value 23°44' was computed for 332 BC. Taking the current value of the obliquity of the ecliptic (23°26') and factoring this in the current "equation of latitude" it is found that Vienna's current "cosmic latitude" is 7°00' south, which signifies a difference of 1°32' from Aldebaran's current latitude of 5S28, amounting to 106 miles (170½ km). There is not a great deal of difference, here, between the values 1°40' in 332 BC and 1°32' currently—these being the values derived by way of applying method (A).

Applying method (B): Taking the current value of Aldebaran's declination (16°32' North) and adding this to Jerusalem's latitude (31N47), the result is a latitude of 48N19, which is very close to Vienna's latitude of 48N13, the difference being 0°06', amounting to just under seven miles (a little more than 11 km). Given that the current sidereal longitude of Aldebaran (15°03' Taurus) coincides *exactly* with the earthly meridian of Vienna (16E20), this signifies an almost precise coincidence—in both latitude and longitude—of the current earthly projection of Aldebaran with the city of Vienna, using method (B). This raises the question—methodologically—as to the significance of the two methods (A) and (B).

Method (A)—applying the "equation of latitude"—determines the projection of a star upon the Earth's globe accurately in terms of longitudinal projection but not in terms of latitudinal projection. On the other hand method (B)—applying the "equation of declination"—is able to determine, for a given point in time (using the star's declination for that time) the projection of a star upon the globe of the Earth both in terms of longitudinal and latitudinal projection. In both cases the earthly projection of the star lies on or very close to the geographical longitude or meridian of the place in question. However, more often than not a divergence will arise with regard to the latitude or parallel of the projected star in relation to the place. In the example of Vienna in connection with the star Aldebaran, the earthly projection in terms of this star coincides exactly with the meridian through the city. Applying method (A) the projection of Aldebaran is specified to lie over 100 miles (over 161 km) south of Vienna, whereas according to method (B) the *current projection* lies under seven miles (just over 11 km) south of the city. How may this be interpreted?

First it needs to be clarified that while method (A) focuses on the projection of a star upon the globe of the Earth, it is not possible to apply it to specify the projection of a star onto the Earth *exactly* (the two variables involved—the star's proper motion and the obliquity of the ecliptic—also need to be taken into consideration). Nevertheless, using method (A) the projection of a star is located upon the surface of the Earth within a relatively narrow range. As pointed out in chapter 5, the range of the obliquity of the ecliptic amounts to 1°37'. This is one of the variables. The other relates to the shift in latitude arising through a star's proper motion. Depending upon the time factor—i.e., which date is chosen for the application of method (A), the shift in latitude can amount to several degrees or it may be just a few minutes of arc.[16] Over a period of five thousand years, for example, the maximum total shift in latitude (including the change in the obliquity of the ecliptic) certainly does not usually exceed 2°—signifying a range of approximately 138 miles (about 222 km) projected onto the Earth's surface. Thus, if the projection of a star using method (A) lies in the middle of this range, then the range could extend for some 69 miles (111 km) to the north and the same distance to the south. This is very small in relation to the total length of a meridian, which is about 12,430 miles (20,004 km) from the North Pole to the South Pole.[17]

In terms of the analogy with meridians in the human being, where it is a matter of an organ and an "energy flow" (meridian) passing through the human being above and below the organ, the location of the projection of a star onto the Earth's surface corresponds to the organ and the geographical meridian running above and below this

16 This shift is usually influenced by the star's distance from our solar system. A far-distant star like Alnitak—817 light-years away—had an actual shift of only 0°03' over a period of about 4,500 years, whereas Sirius, which is very close (relatively speaking) to our solar system, being only 8½ light-years away, had an actual shift of 0°26' during this period of approximately 4,500 years (the actual shift is computed without taking into account the shift owing to the change in the obliquity of the ecliptic).

17 On account of the Earth's bulge at the equator, the circumference of the Earth at the equator, which is 24,901½ miles (40,075 km), is a little more than the circumference measured around the poles, which is 2 x 12,430 = 24,860 miles (40,008 km).

location corresponds to the meridian. Here it is conceivable that the location is not exact (to the mile or kilometer) but actually extends over a certain range, in which case the question is: What is the range? It would seem from applying method (A) that the above indication offers an approximate range (about 69 miles [111 km]) to the north and the same distance to the south). However, as we shall see from considering method (B), this is not at all an accurate conclusion.

To return to the above results applying methods (A) and (B) to the earthly projection of the star Aldebaran in relation to the city of Vienna, it was deduced by applying method (A) that the projection of Aldebaran lies about 100 miles (161 km) to the south of Vienna, whereas using method (B) the current projection lies less than seven miles (just over 11 km) south of the city. How may this be interpreted? In order to arrive at an interpretation, it is helpful to consider briefly the history of Vienna.

First, though, let us consider the symbolic significance of the alignment of Vienna with the star Aldebaran, which is the central star in the sign/constellation of Taurus. According to Greek mythology, Europe (*Europa*) is connected with Taurus. *Europa* was a daughter of King Agenor of Tyre. One day, while she played at Sidon's sea shore, Zeus, who was strongly attracted to the beautiful girl, appeared to her from the waves of the Mediterranean Sea in the shape of a magnificent white bull. Fascinated by the extraordinary creature, *Europa* mounted the bull's back. Instantly the bull plunged into the sea and eloped with her to the island of Crete, where Zeus had his way with her. From this union the first king of Crete, *Minos*, was born, and the bull was set in the heavens as the sign/constellation of Taurus.

The research of Astrogeographia outlined above confirms Greek mythology, since the earthly projection of Taurus coincides by and large with Europe. Moreover, the earthly projection of the star Aldebaran at the center of the Bull (15° Taurus) coincides with the city of Vienna, which for centuries was the center of the European Hapsburg empire. Now, with the expansion of the European Union to include a number of East European countries, Vienna is once again at (or near) the center of Europe. Already with the collapse of the iron curtain in 1989—coincidentally the year in which the last ruling

Hapsburg passed away—Vienna acquired a new sense of purpose as a gateway city to Central and Eastern Europe.

Already several hundred years before Christ, Celtic settlements existed in the area. Then around AD 9 the Roman army established Vindobona, a military camp located right in the center of what later became the city of Vienna. The first recorded mention of Vienna as a city dates from the year 1137. At that time it was ruled by the Babenberg dukes, a dynasty from Bavaria, Germany. Later, under the Hapsburgs—the dynasty founded by the German king Rudolf I of Hapsburg (1218-1291)—Vienna became a bishopric and the Hapsburgs became archdukes. Through a succession of politically motivated marriages the Hapsburg dynasty acquired a vast empire, and Vienna became their principal seat when the Hapsburg Emperor Ferdinand I (1503-1564) moved his court to the city in 1533, shortly after Suleiman the Magnificent and his marauding Turks (about 100,000 of them) had besieged the city in 1529. The Ottoman Turks returned to besiege the city again in 1683 with a 140,000-strong army. After being driven back by the united forces of some 65,000 Polish and German soldiers under the leadership of the Polish king, Vienna was largely rebuilt—in the baroque style that greets present-day visitors to the city. A highpoint for Vienna was attained during the reign of the Hapsburg Emperor Franz Josef I (1830-1916) and his wife the Empress Elisabeth (1837-1898), known as “Sisi.” From 1848 on, under Franz Josef’s rule, and particularly from 1867 on, as head of the newly formed Austro-Hungarian monarchy, the city attracted a large number of emigrants and the emperor carried through a number of impressive structural developments that gave the city its present façade. During that time Vienna became famous for its coffee houses and its free-spirited social and creative ideas, often originating at gatherings of writers, philosophers, and artists that took place at the various coffee houses.

Most significant is that Vienna came to be known as the *city of music.* As early as the twelfth and thirteenth centuries—at the Viennese court of the Babenberg dukes—numerous *Minnesinger* met and sang their songs of courtly love lyricism. Under the Hapsburgs, who were generally great music lovers, music played an important role at the imperial court. Opera, Baroque, religious, classical, romantic, entertainment (waltz), and modern music all flourished in the city of music, which gave birth to classical music through the triad: Joseph Haydn (1732–1809), Wolfgang Amadeus Mozart (1756–1791), and Ludwig van Beethoven (1770–1827). In addition to these three, the great composers of Vienna include Christoph Willibald Gluck, Franz Schubert, Anton Bruckner, Johannes Brahms, Hugo Wolf, Gustav Mahler, Arnold Schönberg, Anton von Webern, Alban Berg, and the central figures in the Strauss dynasty—Johann Strauss senior and Johann Strauss junior –who led the triumphant march of the Viennese waltz. In light of the correspondence between Vienna and Aldebaran, clearly Aldebaran's influence is highly musical!

> Vienna, the city of music.... Many homes and other sites recall the great musicians who lived and created their works in this city. Some of these buildings house commemorative museums, lovingly cared for by the Historischen Museum of the city of Vienna as well as by private associations. There are several archives and libraries in which precious manuscripts and mementos are kept.... The music of these great masters has remained immortal, as witnessed by the rich musical life of the city which remains a great attraction for visitors, who can enjoy the wide variety of concerts, operas, operettas, and musicals featuring star performers. Vienna was not only a musical capital in the past: it still is today.[18]

From the perspective of Astrogeographia, the ascent of Vienna as the "showpiece" of European culture and the center of the Hapsburg empire is reflected in the proximity of the *current projection* of Aldebaran to the center of the city—this projection being now less than seven miles (just over 11 km) south of the city center. Although the projection of Aldebaran according to method (A) lies some 100 miles (161 km) to the south of Vienna, the northward shift of the historical projection—using method (B)—ever closer and closer to the city was mirrored in the gradual ascent of Vienna to become the metropolis at the center of the vast Hapsburg empire stretching across Europe. Now, of course, it is no longer the Hapsburg empire but the great union of European states known as the European Union, stretching all the way

18 Spies and Nemeth, *Vienna: the City of Music*, p. 96.

to the Black Sea, which has its (approximate) geographical center in the city of Vienna. The identification of Europe with *Europa* in Greek mythology, depicted riding on a magnificent bull, is an imaginative picture expressing the reality in Astrogeographia of the projection of the sign/constellation of Taurus upon the Earth precisely in the region of Europe, with the star Aldebaran (15° Taurus) at the center of this sign/constellation being projected onto Vienna at the center (or "ideal center") of Europe.

Vienna is one of the most cultured cities on the planet, and this has to do with the "royal star" Aldebaran.[19] The influence of Aldebaran is to promote culture not just through "law and order" but in particular through the arts, especially music. Listening to the works of the triad of composers who gave birth to classical music—Haydn, Mozart, and Beethoven—one can gain a sense of the extraordinary beauty and richness of Aldebaran's influence on earthly culture and civilization. However, this ripe fruit of culture would not have been possible without human *creativity*, and is therefore an expression of *co-creation* between human beings and that which flows in as *inspiration* from above. Inspiration, creativity, and culture (especially the performing arts, and above all music) and are thus keywords in characterizing Aldebaran's influence, which everyone who goes to Vienna and participates in the rich palette of cultural offerings there can experience firsthand.

Of course, Aldebaran is not the only star to inspire human beings in a creative way. A cultural life like that of Vienna exists also in other cities of the world. Yet it was in Vienna that the inspiration underlying the creative outpouring of many of the great composers flowed. Classical music—Viennese classic—began there and has since spread around the world. Naturally, music is not the only gift of Aldebaran. There is also the gift of the *power of the word*. It was this inspired strength of the spoken word that made John F. Kennedy such an

19 Aldebaran is one of the four "royal stars" spoken of by Zarathustra/Zoroaster; see Powell, *Christian Hermetic Astrology*, pp. 16–21. Aldebaran, the thirteenth brightest star in the night sky, has a rose-red tint and is usually described as *rosy* or *pale reddish-orange*. It is 65 light-years away and has a luminosity 425 times that of our Sun. It is a fair-sized giant star with a diameter about 44 times that of our Sun.

inspiring figure as president of the United States. Kennedy was born with the Sun (14°15' Taurus) in conjunction with Aldebaran (15°03' Taurus).

In a subsequent volume we shall consider the application of Astrogeographia to the horoscopes of human beings, and we shall discover a whole world revealing the interplay between the stars above and the unfolding of human destiny on the Earth.

From this example of the correspondence between Vienna and Aldebaran something can be seen of the relationship between the projection found using method (A), and the historical projection, found using method (B)—the current projection being the historical projection for AD 2000. In light of this example it is clear that the historical projection is important, if one is to gain an understanding—from a contemporary perspective—of the correspondences between stars and earthly locations according to Astrogeographia. The expression "current projection" means the historical projection at the present time. As pointed out already, method (A) gives an accurate value of a star's projection in longitude, but it is not accurate with respect to the star's latitude,[20] whereas method (B) is accurate in determining a star's projection onto the Earth for any historical date both in longitude and latitude—i.e., method (B) determines a star's historical projection for any given date. Therefore method (B) is to be preferred and is the method that is used in the computer program described in appendix 1 (available online at astrogeographia.org) for computing astrogeographical projections. In the next chapter further illuminating correspondences between stars and places on the globe will be explored, and from now on it is only method (B)—applying the equation of declination—that is used.

20 There is also the question as to what is the meaning of method (A). Here with David Bowden's response to this question: I think that method (A) is the "archetypal future projection," which will apply in the future when the axial tilt of the Earth returns to zero—i.e., the equator will be in same plane as the ecliptic, so that the two stellar coordinates will become identical: declination = sidereal latitude. Then method (A) will hold, but it will then be the same as method (B).

Chapter 7
Orion on Earth

Through the application of Astrogeographia a remarkable deepening of understanding for the qualities of geographical locations is made possible. At the same time an extraordinary insight into the nature of individual fixed stars is opened up. This has emerged from the four examples that we have considered so far:

Alnitak	Giza (in particular, the Great Pyramid)
Alnilam	Alexandria
Mintaka	El Alamein
Aldebaran	Vienna

Let us now continue with this exploration. Having considered the three stars in Orion's belt, how does the earthly projection of other stars in this constellation appear? In fact, how does the projection of Orion onto the world map look? The constellation of Orion is mapped out by the stars Betelgeuse (right shoulder) and Bellatrix (left shoulder), by Meissa (Orion's head), Saiph (right knee), and Rigel (left foot). Let us consider the earthly projection of these stars mapping out the figure of Orion—using method (B) to find their *current or historical projection.*

Beginning with Bellatrix: this star is a blue-white giant star with a diameter about six times that of our Sun, at a distance of about 250 light-years, and with a luminosity, including its ultraviolet wavelengths, about 6400 times that of our Sun.[1] It is expected to evolve into an orange giant within a few million years. The current longitude

1 Bellatrix is known as "the female warrior" or "Amazon star." As we shall see below, this name is of great significance.

of Bellatrix is 26°12' Taurus; current declination 6°21' north. Since 26°12' is 3°39' west of the longitude of Alnitak (29°51' Taurus), the earthly projection of Bellatrix is 3°39' west of the longitude of Giza (31E08)—i.e., 27E29 is the geographical meridian of the projection of Bellatrix. Applying the "equation of declination," adding 6°21' to Jerusalem's latitude (31N47), yields a latitude of 38N08 for the current earthly projection of Bellatrix. Looking at a map, the coordinates 38N08, 27E29 of this current earthly projection are remarkably close to the ancient city of Ephesus (37N55, 27E19), the difference amounting to 0°13' in latitude and 0°10' in longitude.[2]

After having found the projection of Anitak to coincide with the Great Pyramid, one of the seven wonders of the ancient world, and then to find the projection of Alnilam to coincide with Alexandria, where the Pharos Lighthouse, also one of the seven wonders of the ancient world, was located, then to find that the projection of a third star from the constellation of Orion, Bellatrix, coincided with Ephesus, where the Temple of Artemis, also one of the seven wonders of the ancient world, was located, I realized that the method of Astrogeographia is something true and authentic. These three more-or-less exact alignments would be otherwise unthinkable. In each case, however, it is a matter of the current projection, rather than the historical projection, which leads me to consider that we are living in a very special time. Without going into detail concerning this, as we shall see later in this chapter (see also figure 4 in chapter 10), when we come to consider the Betelgeuse meridian, which runs through Jerusalem, this meridian is also aligned with the Pole Star, Polaris, at its northern end and with the point opposite to the projection of the apparent Ecliptic North Pole—this point being the portal to Shambhala, the heart of the Earth—at its southern end. Considering the current proximity of the celestial pole to Polaris, thus aligning with the Betelgeuse-Jerusalem axis, leads to the conclusion that we are in a time when these cosmic mysteries relating to Mother Earth are to be revealed.

Ephesus in Asia Minor (now on the west coast of Turkey) was colonized by the Greeks and was famous for the great temple of Artemis,

2 0°13' amounts to a distance of 15 miles (24 km) and 0°10' amounts to a distance of 11½ miles (18½ km).

one of the seven wonders of the ancient world, along with the Great Pyramid at Giza and the Pharos lighthouse at Alexandria. Thus, three of the locations of the seven wonders of the ancient world coincide closely with the earthly projections of three of Orion's stars: Bellatrix, Alnitak, and Alnilam. Whereas the latter location (Alexandria) was renowned for its library as a place of learning, the other two places (Giza and Ephesus) were *mystery centers*. At the Great Pyramid rites of death and ascension were cultivated. At Ephesus the mysteries there centered around conception and birth—the incarnation of the soul under the aegis of the Great Mother (Artemis of Ephesus).

According to the Greek historian Herodotus, it was the daughters of Ares, the Amazons, who originally founded the mystery center at Ephesus.[3] Herodotus relates that the Amazons were female horse-riding warriors from the region between Scythia and the Pontus. In battle with the Greeks they escaped to Ephesus and founded a cult of the Great Mother goddess (Cybele) there. The first idol was a painted wooden figure, called the *Xoanon*, which they found in the alluvial deposits of the estuary of the River Cayster that flows out into the Aegean Sea there at Ephesus. (According to another account the Xoanon was a black meteorite that had fallen from heaven.) The Amazons rejoiced at the divine protection that had saved them and they set up the image under an oak tree and danced their war dance to the sounds of the syrinx (shepherds' flute), as told by the third-century-BC Greek poet Callimachus in his "Hymn to Artemis" based on a lost poem by Pindar:

> Amazons, lovers of battle, set up a wooden image under an oak, in seaside Ephesus, and Hippo [Queen of the Amazons, usually called Queen Hippolyta] offered a holy sacrifice to you. Around the oak they danced you a war dance, Queen Oupis [one of Artemis' names], first with shields and then a wide circle dance, the shrill pipes joined in lithe song to keep time. The echo of the music leapt to Sardis and the Berekynthian song, their feet clicked quickly, the quivers rattled. Afterward around that wooden image, wide foundations were built. Dawn sees nothing richer or more divine.[4]

3 Herodotus, *The Histories* I.4, pp. 73–74.

4 Tr. Jean Alvares, words in [ ] added by RP; http://www.chss.montclair.edu/classics/hymnart.html.

The memory of the war dance of the Amazons lived on for more than one thousand years in the dance of the warrior youths (Curetes, attendants of Artemis), who—like the Corybantes (priests of Cybele)—danced in a frenzy at the spring festival dedicated to Artemis, each clashing their sword and shield loudly so as to prevent the birth cry of Artemis from being heard. The remarkable thing is that Bellatrix is called the "Amazon star" or the "Female Warrior"[5] as if to remind us of the association between this star and the cult founded at Ephesus by the Amazons, which led to the building of the great temple of Artemis—concerning which, according to the hymn of Callimachus, there was "nothing richer or more divine" under the Sun. This striking coincidence (the naming of Bellatrix as the "Amazon star"), and many others like it, suffice to underscore the truth of Astrogeographia. Moreover, there are far-reaching implications underlying this basic truth. In the case of the correspondence of Ephesus to the "Amazon star" Bellatrix, it is apparent that the stellar inspiration streaming down from this star "called" or "summoned" the Amazons to the geographical location of the place where later the temple of Artemis and the great city of Ephesus were to be built. A seed was planted with the arrival of these warrior females at this location through their institution of the cult of Oupis—later to become the cult of Artemis of Ephesus. How did the Great Mother goddess (Oupis of the Amazons, otherwise known as Cybele) acquire the name Artemis?

Before focusing upon this question, let us consider the implications of the stellar correspondence with geographical locations more closely, taking the correspondence between Ephesus and Bellatrix as an example. As indicated in the previous chapter, in connection with the correspondence between Vienna and Aldebaran, it is a matter of *co-creation*—in that case between the people (primarily the creative geniuses) of Vienna and the influence streaming down from Aldebaran. It is the same in the case of Ephesus and Bellatrix: that which arose in Ephesus was a co-creation between inspiration from above and human beings below. The first stage was the "calling" of the Amazons to Ephesus. Then, around the year 1087 BC Androklos, an Athenian prince, arrived there accompanied by a group of Greek

5 Hinckley Allen, *Star Names*, p. 313.

colonists. They were adherents of the cult of the Greek goddess of the Moon (Artemis) and after settling at Ephesus their cult of this goddess adopted elements from that of the ancient Anatolian (Phrygian) goddess Cybele introduced to the region by the Amazons whom, however, they called Oupis. In due course of time oriental characteristics associated with the Great Mother goddess cult of Cybele became transferred to the Greek goddess Artemis. She became transformed from the light-footed virgin huntress/goddess of the Moon to a Mother goddess—Artemis of Ephesus—and in the transition she became milder and more beneficent. Artemis of Ephesus is thus a blend of the Greek goddess Artemis and the Anatolian (Phyrgian) Great Mother goddess Cybele. She is referred to in the Acts of the Apostles by a silversmith named Demetrius, who spoke out against the missionary activity of St. Paul in Ephesus:

> This Paul has persuaded and turned away a considerable company of people...and there is danger...that the temple of the great goddess Artemis may count for nothing, and that she may even be deposed from her magnificence, she whom all Asia and the world worship." When they heard this they were enraged, and cried out, "Great is Artemis of Ephesus!."... And when the town clerk had quieted the crowd, he said, "Men of Ephesus, what man is there who does not know that the city of the Ephesians is temple keeper of the great Artemis, and of the sacred stone that fell from the sky? (Acts 19:26–35)

The stone might refer to a meteorite that hit the Earth at the location of Ephesus. However, in another translation, that of the Jerusalem Bible, since the meaning of the Greek is unclear, the last part of this passage is translated as follows:

> Citizens of Ephesus! Is there anybody alive who does not know that the city of the Ephesians is the guardian of the temple of great Diana and of her statue that fell from heaven? (Acts 19:35)

Diana is the Roman name for the Greek goddess Artemis. From the two translations it is unclear whether it was a statue or a stone that fell from the heavens. In Callimachus' "Hymn to Artemis" quoted above, it was a statue that the Amazons found when they arrived in Ephesus. It was this statue that was the reason, subsequently, for the Greeks to build the temple of Artemis, to provide a sanctuary for the statue.

What the Greek colonists led by Androklos found when they arrived in Ephesus was the statue of the goddess set up at a Cretan-style altar, a flat altar beneath a sacred tree, the oak of the Amazons, surrounded by a simple wall to create an asylum. Just as this place was an asylum for the Amazons in their battle with the Greeks, so it was always—down through the centuries of existence of the Artemision (temple of Artemis and precincts of the temple)—a place of refuge for the wounded and persecuted seeking the motherly protection of the goddess. Evidently some of the Amazons had remained in Ephesus and had married native people there, since Androklos then drove them away when he arrived. Thus began the Greek period of Ephesus.

Already early on the influence of the great goddess of Ephesus was widespread. She was the helper of all, in all situations of life, and was sought out by people from far and wide. The Artemision, comprising the precincts of the temple and the temple itself, built to house the sacred statue of Artemis, was one of the most significant places of pilgrimage in the ancient world, renowned as a place of healing, refuge, and protection. The temple of Artemis celebrated the feminine principle of fertility and the ever-recurring return of cycles of life.

Five temples in succession were erected there at different periods of time, each one grander and more magnificent than the preceding one. It was the fifth one (though according to some sources it was not the fifth but the fourth one) which ensured its place among the seven wonders of the world. Already the fourth one was the largest structure of its kind in ancient Greece. The fourth one took around one hundred years to complete. (It was begun around 546 BC and was completed around 450 BC.) It was made entirely of marble and was 377 feet (115 m) long and 180 feet (55 m) wide, with a total of 127 columns of great height—the top of the building was almost 90 feet (27 m) tall. The lengthy period of construction had to do not only with the grandeur and magnificence of the temple but also with the wealth of sculptural work that was executed in the temple and on the columns, with reliefs around the top and around the base sockets.

One can imagine what an extraordinary sight the temple of Artemis presented to visitors arriving by boat at the ancient harbor, beholding the west end of this magnificent temple supported by eight mighty columns facing out to the Aegean Sea, each column exquisitely carved with notable events from Greek history.

Within the temple, behind a curtain in the inner sanctuary, stood the great wooden statue of Artemis—supposedly the same statue that the Amazons had revered here—standing at the same place where it had stood originally. With her lower arms extended forward invitingly, wearing the signs of the zodiac like a broad necklace around her neck (indicating her cosmic nature), and with three rows of breasts (the bestower of life on all living beings), her robe was divided into geometrical zones. Various representations of the animal kingdom were etched into the fields making up the various zones—in the lower half: bees, bulls, winged beings, dogs, and apelike creatures; in the upper part: lions, griffins, bulls, and sphinxes. The first priestess of Artemis was supposedly the Amazon Ephesia, and the cult statue was referred to as "Artemis Ephesia." It was only at the great festivals, to which thousands of people came from far and wide, that Artemis Ephesia was carried out from her sanctuary, borne along at the processions in her honor.

Otherwise it was only her initiates and priests and priestesses and those neophytes deemed worthy of initiation, according to their spiritual maturity, who were allowed to be in the presence of Artemis Ephesia in her temple, where initiation into her mysteries took place. The essence of this initiation was that through an inner identification with the goddess the neophyte was elevated to an experience of the process of the soul's incarnation into a physical body, descending from cosmic realms, upon whom the gifts of the planets are bestowed: the gift of speech from Mars, the gift of movement from Mercury, the gift of wisdom from Jupiter, etc.[6]

In Ephesus it was the mysteries of birth and incarnation, in the pyramids of Egypt the mysteries of death and excarnation, which were at the center of the initiation rites practiced there. Bearing in mind the correspondence with Bellatrix (Ephesus) and Alnitak (the Great Pyramid), a

6 Steiner, *The Easter Festival in the Evolution of the Mysteries*, pp. 55–57.

polarity between the influences of Bellatrix and Alnitak emerges. Each star thus manifests itself in a unique way which, however, is dependent upon human beings who are receptive to that which a star is able to unfold of its spiritual gifts. This always depends upon human individuals, and may take centuries to unfold, as in Ephesus, beginning with the Amazons and continuing until the Virgin Mary came to Ephesus three years after Christ's ascension.[7]

During the centuries of the unfolding of the mysteries of Artemis of Ephesus, there was a highpoint reached during the period of the fourth temple, when Heraclitus, Cratylus, and Pythagoras (among others) were initiated there. The fourth temple was destroyed by arson when a young man named Herostratus, who sought to attain fame for all posterity by this terrible deed, set fire to the Artemision. This was in the year 356 BC, when Alexander the Great was born. The people of Ephesus set themselves to the task of rebuilding the temple—outwardly even more magnificent than the fourth temple—earning it a place among the seven wonders of the world. However, the inner spirit of the Artemis mysteries had been deeply affected by the event of the burning of the temple. From this point in time onward a decline set in, a decline in the inner life and vitality of the Artemis mysteries, which had ebbed away to a large extent by the time that the Virgin Mary came to Ephesus. Her arrival signified a refinement and a kind of completion to these dying mysteries which, through her, were then able to live on in a new way.

She was accompanied to Ephesus by the Apostle John, who built a small house for her on the hill south of the Artemision, about four miles (6½ km) from the temple of Artemis. There she lived for the last few years of her life, which culminated with a great mystery: her ascent (assumption) to heaven. That this mystery took place at (near to) Ephesus was significant as a counterpart to the mysteries of birth that had been celebrated there down through the centuries. The Virgin Mary revealed the mystery of death and ascension, there in Ephesus—i.e., she lived through there the essential content of the mystery that had been cultivated in the initiation rites of the priests and pharaohs in Egypt. Mary became the new "Female Warrior" showing

7 Powell, *Chronicle of the Living Christ*, pp. 134–136.

the way through the mystery of death and thus added something to the ancient mystery tradition inspired by Bellatrix and cultivated in Ephesus under the aegis of Artemis, the Great Mother.

Those who visit the ruins of the ancient city of Ephesus, which ranks as one of the most splendid architectural sites in the world (however, only one column remains standing of the temple of Artemis), should take the opportunity to visit the house of Mary, which was rediscovered in 1891 on the basis of Anne Catherine Emmerich's vision of the house and her exact description of its location.[8] The house was reconstructed according to the vision she had and is known as the Shrine of Our Lady of the Assumption. There is a statue of Mary in this shrine which—although not to be compared in any way with the great statue of Artemis—nevertheless welcomes each person from far and wide, as Artemis Ephesia once did. Through this statue of the Virgin Mary in the Shrine of Our Lady of the Assumption, the Divine Feminine is honored now in a metamorphosed form, differently than was the case during the many centuries from the time when the Amazons arrived in Ephesus until the Artemision was forced to close through the edict of the Emperor Theodosius the Great in the year AD 391. Through the statue of Mary in her shrine close to Ephesus something lives on of the ancient mystery of Artemis, making a visit to this shrine an unforgettable experience.

It is interesting to consider that Mary is generally depicted as the Madonna with the child, celebrating the mystery of birth. However, in Ephesus, a place where the mystery of birth was celebrated at the Artemision, with her assumption into heaven Mary lived through the mystery of death on the highest level. In contrast, in the region of the Great Pyramid, where the mystery of death was the central content of the rites enacted there, on account of the flight to Egypt Mary came with the child and lived in that region—at Matarea (present day Al-Matariya, near Cairo)[9]—as the bearer of the new birth mysteries.

A further aspect of the refinement of the ancient mystery tradition at Ephesus—that, in any case, was dying out—is the contribution of John the Evangelist, who wrote the Gospel of St. John there

8 Ibid. p. 135.

9 Ibid. p. 83.

at a very advanced age (almost one hundred years of age).[10] This is the Gospel that most approaches the Divine Feminine. Through this Gospel, John took up the Logos mystery that was first put forward by Heraclitus of Ephesus around 500 BC, and he also took up the mystery of the Divine Feminine (the Sophia mystery)—the latter implicitly rather than explicitly.[11] In his own unique and profound style, John contributed to the furthering of the Artemis mysteries, but in a completely new sense, without connecting onto these mysteries at all in any external way, other than living near the Artemision and thus imbibing the spiritual atmosphere of the temple of Artemis. Obviously there is much more that could be said regarding the mystery of John and Mary in Ephesus. Here it is a matter of indicating connections, which those who are interested can investigate further as much as possible.

These considerations regarding the correspondence between Ephesus and Bellatrix are based on the *current projection* of Bellatrix. It remains now to consider the location of the historical projection of this star according to method (B). Let us take the date 1500 BC as a possible date for the arrival of the Amazons in Ephesus. Where was the projection of Bellatrix for that date? To answer this question, we shall apply method (B)—the method of declination—described in the previous chapter. Our task here is greatly simplified by David Bowden's computer program ASTROGEO (see Astrosophy at sophiafoundation.org), with which it is easy to compute the historical projections of stars using method (B) for dates from 2950 BC to AD 2950.

First, though, let us consider the longitude of Bellatrix in 1500 BC. It was 26°09' Taurus. Since the longitude of Ephesus is 27E19, which is 3°49' west of the longitude of the Great Pyramid (31E08), and since 31E08 equates with 29°51' Taurus, subtracting 3°49' we arrive at 26°02' Taurus as the geodetic equivalent of the longitude of Ephesus. Here, therefore, there is a difference of 0°07' between the projection of Bellatrix (epoch 1500 BC) and the geodetic

10 Concerning the Apostle John and John the Evangelist in Ephesus, see Tidball and Powell, *Jesus, Lazarus, and the Messiah*, chapters 11, 12.

11 Scott, "Sophia and the Johannine Jesus"; in *Journal for the Study of the New Testament,* Supplement Series 71.

equivalent of the longitude of Ephesus, amounting to a distance of 8 miles (13 km).[12]

Applying the ASTROGEO program, developed according to method (B), we find from the latitude of the star at the date in question (the latitude of Bellatrix in 1500 BC was 17S16) that the declination of Bellatrix at that date was -3°40'59" and that, correspondingly, 28N06 was the projected geographical latitude of the star. In this example 28N06 is 9°49' south from the latitude of Ephesus, which is 37N55—i.e., the projected earthly location of Bellatrix in 1500 BC was about 680 miles (1,094 km) south of the actual location of Ephesus.[13]

Having considered the left shoulder of Orion—marked by the star Bellatrix whose current earthly projection coincides closely with the ancient city of Ephesus—let us now turn to Orion's right shoulder, marked by the star Betelgeuse. Whereas all the other stars in Orion appear white or bluish-white in color, Betelgeuse is an irregularly pulsating red supergiant that appears reddish-orange in color. Because of its pulsation, it is difficult to determine the exact distance of Betelgeuse from our solar system. Its distance is thought to be 643 light-years away but with a degree of uncertainty, so that it could be anywhere between about 500 and 800 light-years away. It is a red supergiant, meaning that its physical size is gigantic in comparison to that of our Sun and measured to be some 1,180 times larger! Its luminosity, which cannot be specified exactly without knowing its distance precisely, is estimated—including its infrared emission—to vary between 90,000 and 150,000 that of our Sun, thus qualifying it as a megastar (luminosity more than 10,000 times that of our Sun). Only about 13% of the star's radiant energy is emitted in the form of visible light, with most of its radiation occurring in the infrared. If human eyes were sensitive to radiation of all wavelengths, Betelgeuse would

12 This difference of 0°07' is less than the corresponding difference found for the current projection, which was shown above to be 0°10' in longitude.

13 This difference informs us that it is the meridian that is important, and that the influence of a star extends along the meridian—in this case with the meridian running through Ephesus. The historical projection (28N06, 27E25) of Bellatrix in 1500 BC was in the Egyptian desert, near Bawiti, about 236 miles (380 km) southwest of Cairo.

appear as the brightest star in the night sky. In terms of stellar evolution, it is—even though it is a red star (generally considered to be "old" stars, far advanced along their evolutionary path)—only about ten million years of age. As the most luminous star in the constellation of Orion, and being a red supergiant, it is an extremely significant star. Its current longitude is 4°01' Gemini and its current latitude is 16S02. Since 4°01' Gemini is 4°10' east of 29°51' Taurus, the geodetic equivalent to 4°01' Gemini is found by adding 4°10' to the longitude of the Great Pyramid (31E08), resulting in a longitude of 35E18, which is very close to Jerusalem's longitude (35E13).

As mentioned in chapter 4, according to Anne Catherine Emmerich the first human beings to incarnate on the Earth (Adam and Eve in the Biblical tradition) lived on the Mount of Olives in the region that later became the city of Jerusalem. She describes that the city was founded by Melchizedek, King of Salem, and that Abraham received the sacrament of bread and wine from Melchizedek in the Valley of Jehoshaphat (also called the Kidron Valley) that runs east of the old city of Jerusalem and separates it from the Mount of Olives.[14] The founding of the city of Jerusalem can thus be dated to the time of Melchizedek, a contemporary of Abraham, who lived—according to conventional dating—around 1950 BC.[15] At that time the longitude of Betelgeuse was 3°56' Gemini and its latitude was 16S34. The geodetic equivalent of 3°56' Gemini is found by adding 4°05' to the longitude of the Great Pyramid (31E08), resulting in a longitude of 35E13, which is precisely the longitude of Jerusalem. In terms of geodetic equivalents, therefore, Jerusalem lies exactly on the geodetic equivalent of the star Betelgeuse. It should also be mentioned that, since in 1950 BC the longitude of the Pole Star, Polaris, was also 3°56' Gemini, Jerusalem is also exactly on the same meridian as the geodetic equivalent of the star Polaris. And now that Polaris is the Pole Star, this meridian is of great importance, also in relation to Jerusalem.

---

14 Emmerich, "Blick auf Melchisedek"; in Brentano, *Sämtliche Werke und Briefe, vol. 26*, pp. 104–108.

15 Genge, "Versuch einer Abraham-Datierung"; *In Memoriam Eckhard Unger: Beiträge zu Geschichte, Kultur und Religion des alten Orients*, p. 94.

While continuing to focus on the correspondence between Jerusalem and Betelgeuse, it is also remarkable to consider, as pointed out in chapter 10, that the Jerusalem meridian (35E13), when followed southward, runs through the opposite point on the Earth's globe (35E13, 65S30) to the apparent North Pole of the Ecliptic. This point lies just off the coast of Antarctica (chapter 10, figure 4). As discussed in chapter 10, the projection of this point in the region of Antarctica can be understood as the archetypal root chakra (life pole) of the planet. And just as in the human being the root chakra is the portal to the heart of the Earth, known as Shambhala in esoteric teaching, so the Jerusalem meridian runs through the Earth's root chakra and is thus connected directly with Shambhala, the golden realm of life at the heart of the Earth. Against this background we can understand the significance of Christ's descent down to Shambhala after his death on the cross at Golgotha, Jerusalem—how this location was ideally suited to this tremendous event of Christ's descent to unite with the heart of the Earth, the deeper significance of which has remained veiled until now.[16]

Using the ASTROGEO program to find the historical projection of Betelgeuse in 1950 BC, given that the latitude of Betelgeuse in 1950 BC was 16S34, we find that its declination on that date was -2°28'29" and that, correspondingly, 29N18 was the projected geographical latitude of the star. In this example 29N18 is 2°29' south from the latitude of Jerusalem, which is 31N47—i.e., the projected earthly location of Betelgeuse in 1950 BC was about 171 miles (275 km) south of the actual location of Jerusalem.[17]

16 Concerning Shambhala and the significance of Christ's descent to unite with the heart of the Earth, see Powell, *Cultivating Inner Radiance and the Body of Immortality*, pp. 26–28, 39–44, 73, 86–95, 138, 146–149, 156–157, 171–174, 201.

17 This difference informs us again that it is the meridian that is important, and that the influence of a star extends along the meridian—in this case with the meridian running through Jerusalem. The historical projection (29N18, 35E14) of Betelgeuse at the time of Abraham in 1950 BC was about 20 miles (32 km) south-east of the ancient coastal city of Aqaba in the far south of present-day Jordan, inhabited since about 4000 BC. As shown in the table at the end of this chapter, Betelgeuse was last at its original, archetypal projection in 4439 BC, at which point in time it was at the midpoint of its declination journey along the 47° of its meridian (longitude

To summarize, the historical projection of Betelgeuse for the epoch 1950 BC is 29N18; 35E14.

The *current projection* (epoch AD 2000) is 39N11; 35E18, since—as referred to above—the geodetic equivalent to 4°01' Gemini (the current longitude of Betelgeuse) is 35E18 and, further, the current declination of Betelgeuse is +7°24' which, added to the latitude of Jerusalem (31N47) equates with 39N11.

The current projection of Betelgeuse, while still lying more or less on the same meridian as Jerusalem, is on a parallel of latitude 7°21' north of Jerusalem, coinciding fairly closely with Bogazliyan in Turkey (39N13; 35E17). In fact, the current projection of Betelgeuse (39N11; 35E18) coincides almost exactly with Bogazliyan, which in turn is close to Bogazkale (40N02; 34E37) known earlier as Hattusha, the capital of the ancient Hittite empire. (Bogazkale is now known also as Boghazköy.) The Hittites flourished during the second millennium BC, ruling over the "Land of Hatti" in Cappadocia from about 1900 BC on, their empire subsequently extending across the region of modern Turkey, northern Syria, and beyond. They had rich iron deposits which they mined and traded with the Assyrians, and also used to forge weapons. The Hittites were a warrior people and were noted for their ferocity.

> Unlike some of their neighbors, the Hittites were not cruel. They were, however, excellent strategists, tacticians, and warriors. They were superb horsemen, inventors of the most formidable war machine of their time—the light, two-wheeled battle chariot.... The two-wheeled Hittite war chariots were feared throughout Asia Minor.[18]

Little was known about the Hittites until about 10,000 clay tablets were discovered in 1906 at the archeological site at Bogazkale located about 130 miles (210 km) east of Ankara. This discovery of

---

projection) onto the Earth. (When a star is at mid-declination, it returns to its archetypal projection.) In the case of Betelgeuse, the archetypal projection is 16N24, 35E13—i.e., directly on the Jerusalem meridian, but 15½° south of Jerusalem—i.e., some 1,070 miles (1,720 km) south of Jerusalem—in Sudan about 195 miles (314 km) north-east of Khartoum.

18 From http://www.saudiaramcoworld.com/issue/196108/the.people.that.history.forgot.

the Hittite royal archives—clay tablets of Hittite hieroglyph inscriptions—led to the identification of this archeological site as the capital Hattusha of the Hittite empire. Thus, the extensive archeological site at Bogazkale is the location of the ancient city of Hattusha, with its great temple—dedicated to the Storm god Teshub, Lord of the Land of Hatti (Teshub was head of the Hittite pantheon) and the Sun goddess of Arinna—that was built under King Hattusili III (ruled 1275–1250 BC), which was the city's holiest shrine. Two blocks of Hittite hieroglyph inscriptions were also found near the village of Çalapverdi at Bogazliyan, indicating that here too the Hittites had some kind of center or settlement at this spot coinciding with the earthly projection of Betelgeuse.

At its height, the Hittite empire extended to Mesopotamia, Syria and Palestine. The Hittites dominated Mesopotamia from the time they sacked Babylon about 1595 BC until around 1193 BC. From about 1300 to 1200 BC the Hittites waged war against Egypt, which was disastrous for them, and shortly after their civilization began to disintegrate, although some Hittite cities and regions continued to thrive until they were conquered, probably by the Assyrians—the last surviving until 717 BC. The Hittite empire was greatest in the period 1595 to 1193 BC when they dominated Mesopotamia. After their conquest of Babylon they adopted the laws, religion, and literature of the Old Babylonians. Patriarchal and highly agricultural, their primary activity was trading—especially with the people around the Mediterranean. As great traders, they spread Mesopotamian ideas and culture far and wide.

Of special interest to our theme is the mention of two of King David's generals as Hittites: Ahimelech (I Samuel 26:6) and Uriah (II Samuel 11:3). David had the latter deliberately slain in battle on account of his desire for his wife Bathsheba, who David then took as his own wife. She became the mother of his son, the later King Solomon, who—in turn—had Hittite wives (I Kings 11:7) and who traded with the king of the Hittites (II Chronicles 1:17). This was during the Neo-Hittite period that lasted until 717 BC, after the time (1193 BC) when the Hittite empire had begun to disintegrate. What is revealed through this contact between the Hittites and

Jerusalem is an active exchange along the Betelgeuse meridian running down from the region of the Hittite capital Hattusha through the city of Jerusalem.

Let us now contrast the right (Betelgeuse) and left (Bellatrix) shoulders of Orion. The left shoulder, to which Ephesus corresponds, is feminine in nature, as we have seen in our consideration of the temple of Artemis at Ephesus. The right shoulder, to which Jerusalem—and also Hattusha—corresponds, is masculine. This is reflected in the Hittite culture, where the king was the supreme ruler and at the same time military commander, judicial authority, and high priest. "Betelgeuse portended fortune, martial honors, wealth, and other kingly attributes."[19] These characteristics of Betelgeuse were evidently extended to become applied to the whole constellation of Orion, since the martial connotations pertaining to this red supergiant marking the shoulder of the Giant—this being the meaning of *Gibbor* in the ancient Hebrew for Orion, also called "the mighty Hunter before the Lord"[20]—recur again and again in classical descriptions of Orion.

In this connection it is interesting to consider that the Hittite king was the "right-hand man" or earthly deputy of the Storm god, and that there is some resemblance between Orion the Hunter and the Hittite Storm god Teshub, who was head of the Hittite pantheon. Teshub's symbol was the bull, and the constellation of Orion extends beneath the zodiacal constellations of Gemini (the Twins) and Taurus (the Bull), with Betelgeuse located beneath the Twins (4° Gemini). Similar to depictions of Orion, Teshub is shown bearing a club, and he was a god of battle and victory. His mother was the Sun goddess of Arinna, who helped him to return from his journey to the underworld by opening the gates of the Dark Earth to allow him to pass through them. (Normally in Hittite mythology whatever enters into the underworld perishes there and does not return.) Teshub's descent to the depths echoes Hesiod's words referring to Orion's pursuit of the seven maidens (the Pleiades): "Strong Orion chases to the

19 Allen, *Star Names*, p. 311.

20 Ibid. p. 309.

deep the seven virgin stars."[21] Orion's descent into the depths is also related—albeit in a different context—in classical Greek mythology. There it is related that Orion had boasted about his prowess as a hunter, saying that he would eventually rid the Earth of all wild animals. As a precaution, to ensure that he would not actually do this, the Earth goddess Gaia sent a deadly scorpion that stung the mighty hunter in his foot—in some accounts killing him. The starry heavens graphically illustrate this myth: when Scorpio (the Scorpion) rises in the east, Orion sets in the west, descending into the underworld. Predating the mythology of the Greeks, as Richard Dibon-Smith points out, is that of the Hittites: "The mythic tales of Orion go as far back as the Hittites."[22]

Most striking is the relationship between Teshub as the Hittite Storm god and Orion, whose "stormy character appeared in early Hindu and perhaps even in earlier Euphratean days, and is seen everywhere among classical writers."[23] Thus Hesiod, around 650 BC, wrote of the rising of the constellation of Orion:

> Then the winds war aloud,
> And veil the ocean with a sable cloud:
> Then round the bark, already haul'd on shore,
> Lay stones, to fix her when the tempests roar.[24]

Also, Milton wrote in *Paradise Lost*, "When with fierce winds Orion arm'd.... "[25] In the ancient Hindu system of nakshatras (twenty-eight lunar mansions), Betelgeuse was associated with the fourth nakshatra, Ardra, ruled by the Vedic Storm god Rudra. And according to Rudolf Steiner:

> "The Lord God [Yahweh Elohim] ...breathed into his nostrils the breath of life and man became a living being" (Genesis 2:7). Yahweh is an Air/Wind God, the One who storms in the Wind. He

21 Ibid. p. 305.

22 Dibon-Smith, *The Constellations*, p. 201.

23 Ibid. p. 306.

24 Ibid.

25 Ibid.

> is the God the human being breathes in. The breathing process is not merely something physical but is also a spiritual process. It has to become something holy for us.[26]

Much later, historically, the Turks—from the same region as the Hittites—were greatly feared in Europe on account of their warring nature. Recalling the correspondence drawn in the previous chapter between Europe (Europa) and Taurus the Bull, whose central star is Aldebaran (15° Taurus), and contemplating the club of Orion raised in the direction of the constellation of the Bull, can one perhaps see here an earthly reflection: the image of the Turks who twice besieged Vienna (corresponding to Aldebaran, the Bull's eye), and who spread terror, oppression, and destruction across much of Eastern Europe, corresponding to the part of the constellation of the Bull located between 15° and 30° Taurus, including the Bull's horns, toward which the club of Orion is raised? Modern Turkey, of course, is not the Turkey of Suleiman the Magnificent (1494–1566), and has evolved considerably since those times, to the point of now being considered as a possible member of the European Union. Just as there was an evolution in Ephesus from the warring Amazons to the Virgin Mary—"full of grace" (Luke 1:28)—so there has been an evolution in Turkey from the time of the Hittites to modern Turkey.

Now let us consider the Betelgeuse meridian that runs south from Turkey directly through Jerusalem. As remarked upon in the discussion of megastars in chapter 6, these most luminous stars have been found to be extremely powerful *all the way along their meridians.*[27] Thus the influence of Betelgeuse as a megastar extends far beyond the region of its earthly projection. Above all, Jerusalem seems to be the "city of Betelgeuse" in terms of the spiritual impulse flowing along this meridian. In particular, the building of the great temple of Solomon—like the construction of the Great Pyramid at Giza in relation to

26 Steiner, *Aus den Inhalten der esoterischen Stunden* (in English as *Esoteric Lessons, 1904–1909: From the Esoteric School, vol. 1*), p. 222.

27 As we shall see, according to the research of Astrogeographia the meridians of all stars are important. However, it seems they are particularly important for megastars.

Alnitak, and the building of the temple of Artemis at Ephesus in relation to Bellatrix—was an inspiration connected with the influence of Betelgeuse flowing along its geodetic equivalent, the earthly meridian through Jerusalem.

In order to see more clearly the connections here—between Betelgeuse and the building of Solomon's temple—let us again consider the star's historical projection onto the Earth's globe. All that is necessary to find the *historical projection* is to utilize the "equation of declination" for the historical date in question, using the star's declination for that date—and this is a simple matter using the ASTROGEO program. As an example let us now utilize ASTROGEO for Betelgeuse for the historical date of the building of the temple of Solomon. First, though, we should consider the historical background to the event of the building of this great temple.

As referred to earlier, according to the visions of Anne Catherine Emmerich,[28] the city of Jerusalem was founded by Melchizedek, King of Salem, who helped to prepare Abraham for his mission. Some conventional sources refer to Abraham as having lived around 1950 BC,[29] although there is much controversy surrounding the dating of Abraham's life. The date 1950 BC has symbolic significance, since it denotes the start of the Age of Aries the Ram, the precise date being 1946 BC.[30] Abraham, whose name could be interpreted as "father of the people of the ram" (*Ab* meaning "father"), introduced the sacrifice of the ram on Mt. Moriah, where later the Temple of Solomon was built (Genesis 22:1–14).

If 1950 BC is accepted as an early date in Abraham's life, or perhaps even the date of his birth, it would at first sight appear

---

28 The reader may justifiably ask: Why should her visions be regarded as reliable? An answer to this question is given in Powell, *Chronicle of the Living Christ*, p. 455, where it is shown on the basis of a statistical analysis of the dates (in the Hebrew calendar) that she gave of events in the life of Christ, that the probability of these dates being found by chance is one in 435 billion. Another confirmation of the accuracy of her visions is the discovery of the house of the Virgin Mary in Ephesus on the basis of her vision and precise description of the location of this dwelling.

29 Genge, "Versuch einer Abraham-Datierung," p. 94.

30 Powell, *Hermetic Astrology*, vol. I: *Astrology and Reincarnation*, p. 63.

to fit with David Rohl's chronology.[31] Rohl dates the sojourn of the Israelites in Egypt to have begun around the year 1662 BC and states that the "period from Abraham's descent to Jacob's arrival in the Land of Geshom was 215 years."[32] This would place Abraham's descent into Canaan around 1877 BC—at the age of about 73 if he was born around 1950 BC—and in fact the Bible says that "Abram was 75 years old when he departed from Haran" (Genesis 12:4). However, there is a problem with this dating, since Jacob was Abraham's grandson who, according to Rohl, "died in 1645 BC."[33] If Jacob and his sons really did arrive in Egypt around 1662 BC, a more realistic dating of Abraham's life would be to locate his biography somewhere during the eighteenth century BC. Nevertheless the date 1950 BC, as remarked upon already, does have a *symbolic significance* for Abraham as the progenitor of a new people whose mission clearly had to do with the Age of Aries (the Ram), in contrast to the Egyptians and Babylonians whose missions were more associated with the Age of Taurus (the Bull).

There were many stages of preparation for the building of the temple of Solomon, one of the most important being the exodus of the Israelites from Egypt under the leadership of Moses. Rohl dates the exodus to about 1447 BC. According to I Kings 6:1 there were 480 years from the exodus to the founding of the temple of Jerusalem in the fourth year of the reign of King Solomon. If this biblical indication is reliable, and if 1447 BC or thereabouts really was the date of the exodus, the temple was founded in Solomon's fourth regnal years around 968 BC. Moreover, according to I Kings 6:38 it took seven years to build and thus—if we accept the foregoing assumptions—it was completed around 961 BC.

Let us consider the *historical projection* of the star Betelgeuse during the one thousand year period from the start of the Age of Aries in 1946 BC (as a possible date for Melchizedek as the founder of the city of Jerusalem) to the laying of the foundation stone of the temple of Solomon in about 968 BC. The declination of Betelgeuse in 1946 BC

31 Rohl, *A Test of Time.*

32 Ibid. p. 401.

33 Ibid. p. 433.

was 2°27' south and in 968 BC it was 1°33' north. Further, in 1371 BC the declination of Betelgeuse was 0°, and applying the "equation of declination" at this date—i.e., adding 0° to the latitude of Jerusalem, its historical projection latitude in 1371 BC was 31N47 (latitude of Jerusalem) and its geodetic equivalent longitude was 35E13 (longitude of Jerusalem). So, as discussed in chapter 8, including a graphic display, the *historical projection* of Betelgeuse was focused exactly on Jerusalem in 1371 BC and was very close to the city throughout the crucial time after the exodus up to the founding of the temple in the fourth year of Solomon's reign. Including the period from 1946 BC (start of the Age of Aries), the historical projection of Betelgeuse was within 2½° of Jerusalem (south of the city) and moved northward along the meridian directly across the city in 1371 BC and continued northward, yet was still only just over 1½° north of the city at the time of the founding of the temple of Solomon.

In light of Astrogeographia the historical projection of the star Betelgeuse coincided exactly with the city of Jerusalem in 1371 BC and was still only about 1½° away (in latitude) by the time of the founding of the temple of Solomon in about 968 BC. Further, during the whole one-thousand-year period the geodetic meridian equivalent to Betelgeuse coincided exactly with the meridian running through Jerusalem—i.e., there was no difference (to within 0°01' with respect to longitude) between Betelgeuse's projected meridian and the earthly meridian running through Jerusalem. It may be concluded, therefore, that the period leading up to the founding of the temple and also the building of the great temple there in Jerusalem was under the inspiration of the megastar Betelgeuse. That is, on an inspirational level Solomon's temple was associated with the influence of Betelgeuse, just as the Great Pyramid was an inspiration connected with Alnitak, and the temple of Artemis of Ephesus with Bellatrix.

In the case of Betelgeuse we have seen that the current projection is 7°21' north of Jerusalem, a value coinciding closely with the town of Bogazliyan in Turkey. In contrast, the historical projection of Betelgeuse in 1950 BC was 2°29' south of Jerusalem. In the example of projecting the stars of the constellation of Orion onto the globe, one sees that the current projection of Betelgeuse is in Anatolia,

Eastern Turkey, close to the ancient Hittite capital Hattusha (modern Bogazkale, also known as Boghazköy), and that the current projection of Bellatrix is across on the western side of Turkey close to the ancient city of Ephesus (modern Selçuk), that Alnitak coincides with Giza, Alnilam is close to Alexandria, and Mintaka is over the Mediterranean Sea, north of El Alamein.

Each star moves up (north) and down (south) along its projected longitudinal meridian, which extends over a distance of 47° on the surface of the Earth. The midpoint of this longitudinal meridian, which the star's projection crosses twice in 12,960 years, can be thought of as the *return of a star to its original position at the time the birth horoscope of the Earth took place.* This original position (midpoint of the longitudinal meridian) is referred to as the *archetypal projection.* This position of a star's projection onto the globe can be viewed as delineating the "organ" (by way of analogy with the meridians in Chinese medicine) and the meridians as the "energy flow" proceeding north and south from the geographical location of this projection. Following this analogy further (and this is simplified by using the SINEWAVE computer program), one is able to follow the flow of energy along a meridian as it is manifesting itself in a *particularly focused way* during the course of time. Thus, whereas the current projection of Betelgeuse is located in Anatolia, Turkey, the historical projection indicating the *primary flow of energy* along the Betelgeuse meridian was traversing Jerusalem during the years preceding and up to the founding of the temple of Solomon.

The temple of Solomon was not just Solomon's achievement. It was the result of a combined effort on the part of many—not least, on the part of Hiram of Tyre, who was the master builder of the temple. Solomon, out of his great wisdom, drew up the plan of the temple. Yet it was Hiram who executed the plan. Moreover, many of those who went before Solomon helped to prepare the way, especially his father, King David. It was, after all, David who had the idea to construct a house for God but who "could not build a house for the name of the Lord his God because of the warfare with which his enemies surrounded him" (I Kings 5:3). The task of erecting a "house for Yahweh" thus devolved to David's son Solomon. It was, however, the achievements of King David in successfully doing battle with his enemies that created the peaceful circumstances needed for this great project. In Solomon's own words: "The Lord my God has given me rest on every side; there is neither adversary nor misfortune" (I Kings 5:4).

The martial quality of Betelgeuse that was noted earlier in relation to the Hittites evidently also helped King David, who seems to have embodied this quality associated with this star. In fact, there is the deeper question as to Yahweh's relationship to Betelgeuse and—beyond Betelgeuse, as the star marking the "right shoulder" or "right arm"—to the whole constellation of Orion.

In the Book of Job, in Job's eulogy to the Lord, he refers to Him as the one "who seals up the stars, who stretched out the heavens... who made the Bear and Orion, the Pleiades and... who does great things beyond understanding" (Job 9:9). Then the Lord answered Job, "Can you bind the sweet influences of the Pleiades or loose the cords of Orion?" (Job 38:1,31).[34] Here Yahweh's great power is revealed, for not only did he create Orion but also—apparently—bound him with cords. What does this refer to? This is addressed in the following quote by Richard Hinckley Allen:

> Later on the Jews called Orion Gibbor, the Giant, considered as Nimrod bound to the sky for rebellion against Jehovah [Yahweh], whence perhaps came the Bands or Bonds of Orion, which some say should be Cords or a Girdle; but the conception of Nimrod as "the mighty Hunter before the Lord," at least in the ordinary sense of the word, is erroneous, for the original, according to universal Eastern tradition, signifies a Lurking Enemy, or a Hunter of men rather than of beasts.[35]

What Allen is referring to here is the account of Nimrod by the Jewish historian Josephus, who described Nimrod as a tyrant and as

34 In the authorized version (King James) of the Bible the Hebrew word is translated as "sweet influences," but as the Hebrew expression used here is not clear, it is translated in the revised version as "cluster" and in the revised standard version as "chains."

35 Allen, *Star Names*, p. 309.

the builder of the Tower of Babel.[36] Josephus was drawing upon extra-biblical sources, as all that the Bible says is that Nimrod, who was the great-grandson of Noah, "was the first on Earth to be a mighty man. He was a mighty hunter before the Lord...The beginning of his kingdom was Babel...." (Genesis 10:9–10).

In this discussion what has to be borne in mind is that the Jews, because they had separated themselves from the star-worshipping Babylonians and Egyptians, in general had a negative attitude toward the stars. One exception is Job, whose book stands apart from all other works of the Bible, in that the stars—for example, the Bear, Orion, the Pleiades—are mentioned explicitly.[37] In fact, they are spoken of in a way that extols them as signs in the heavens of God's majesty. This difference in attitude indicates that Job lived *before* Abraham. It is customary to identify Job as Jobab, descended (sixth generation) from Shem (Genesis 10:29). Abraham (tenth generation) was also one of Shem's descendants (Genesis 11:10–26). (Shem was the father of the Semites.) Thus, if the biblical record is accurate, Job and Abraham were both descendants of Shem, and Job lived four generations prior to Abraham.

Job was clearly not opposed to the ancient religion of the stars, in contrast to the descendants of Abraham. For Job the stars were a revelation of God, whose splendor shone forth from the starry heavens. Job wrote down what he heard from the divine voice that addressed him concerning the stars. He wrote about the "bands of Orion," which need not be interpreted as chains. They could just as well signify the invisible bonds of attraction linking the stars making up the constellation of Orion, as will be discussed later.

A much truer conception of Orion, than the one quoted above by Allen, is offered by Frances Rolleston, whose research in the field of etymology concerning the ancient names of the constellations is a treasure-trove:

> Orion, the splendid, coming as light, the most brilliant and striking constellation in the starry heavens, has been claimed by the

36 Josephus, *Antiquities of the Jews* I:4.

37 The prophet Amos also referred to, "He who made the Pleiades and Orion..." (Amos 5:8). This is undoubtedly a quote from Job.

> pride of man, from Nimrod, the first of those mighty hunters whose prey was their fellow-man, to Napoleon.... Meanwhile the starry emblem of the Mighty One, "who was, and is, and is to come," looks down in dazzling and undiminished luster on their mouldering dust. Long before Nimrod had founded the first worldly monarchy of bloodshed and oppression...this heavenly memorial of prophecy had been consecrated to the glory of a King who shall rule in righteousness, whose kingdom shall have no end. The names annexed to the constellation—the mighty one, the prince, the ruler—no doubt suggested the original assumption of it.... No ancient appellation has any more trace of Nimrod than of Napoleon.... Before Nimrod was a sovereign, "the host of heaven" had been perverted from their original destination of "declaring the glory of God."... In the book of Job mention is twice made of Chesil, translated and generally considered to be the constellation of Orion.... It always, however, is attributed to Orion; and in its radical meaning of *bound together* well applies to the nebulae so remarkable in this constellation, stars bound together by the all-pervading law of gravitation.... Those ancients knew that these white clouds of light in the far depths of space were *assembled* orbs, *bound together* by the universal law of the universal Lord.... Orion "coming forth as light." The victory over the serpent, and the wounded foot, equally indicate him in ancient mythology. The Greeks degraded Orion into a mere hunter, yet gave him divine parentage, and preserved the tradition of the wound in the heel from a venomous creature, which aids in identifying the Mighty One here figured with the promise of the Redeemer who should come "traveling in the greatness of His strength."[38]

Orion as the Mighty One is not to be confused with a human being such as Nimrod just because the Bible refers to him as "the mighty hunter before the Lord." As Rolleston indicates, the Mighty One is still shining down from the starry heavens while Nimrod has long disappeared, leaving behind nothing more than "mouldering dust." The prophet Isaiah points in a quite different direction than Nimrod. He points toward the Lord, Yahweh: "I am the Lord thy Saviour and

38 Rolleston, *Mazzaroth*, part II, pp. 30–31.

thy Redeemer, the Mighty One of Jacob" (Isaiah 60:16). He points toward the Messiah: "For there has been a child born to us; there has been a son given to us; and the princely rule will come to be upon his shoulder. And his name will be called Wonderful, Counselor, Mighty God, Eternal Father, Prince of Peace" (Isaiah 9:6).[39] And in the book of Genesis: "Yet his bow abode in strength, and the arms of his hands were made strong by the hands of the Mighty One of Jacob (by the name of the Shepherd, the Rod of Israel)" (Genesis 49:24). These (and similar) passages in the Bible could just as well be related to Orion the Mighty One as could the passage concerning Nimrod as "the mighty hunter before the Lord."

The fact that later some Israelites did draw this connection between Orion and Nimrod, interpreting the passage from Job in the same way as in the above quotation from Allen, is indicative of their attitude toward the star-worshipping Egyptians who held Orion in such high esteem, seeing it as the abode of their god Osiris. It was their way of distancing themselves from the Egyptians under whose yoke they had lived for so many years. This is how it is possible to view the derogatory perspective of (some) Israelites in contrast to the elevated perspective of Orion held by the Egyptians.

According to the research presented in this book, ancient Israel and Egypt had much in common, both lying within the domain of the projection of Orion onto the globe. It is against this background that the many contacts between the two lands can be viewed. This began with Abraham's journey to Egypt. The Bible reports that Abraham went to Egypt on account of a severe famine in the land of Canaan (Genesis 12:10–20). Then there was the sojourn of the Israelites in Egypt from the time of Jacob to the time of Moses. Later, "Solomon made a marriage alliance with Pharaoh King of Egypt; he took Pharaoh's daughter, and brought her into the city of David" (I Kings 3:1). Much later, there was the flight to Egypt of Mary and Joseph with the child Jesus.

In light of Astrogeographia there was an ongoing relationship between ancient Israel and Egypt, which was an expression of what they have in common—both coming under the influence of the constellation of Orion. This relationship meant that despite the

39 *El Gibbor* is the Hebrew expression used here for Mighty God.

manifest differences between their religious practices and orientation, there was a common core—and this has to do with finding a relationship with Orion "the Mighty One," "He who comes forth as light."[40] This core, which is most apparent in connection with Moses, has to do with preparation for the coming of the Messiah. It is clear, in the case of ancient Israel, that the mission of the Israelites was to prepare for the coming of the Messiah, who in the work of Joseph A. Seiss is brought into connection with Orion. "Christ was born of a woman, as some accounts allege of Orion; and he was at the same time the peculiar gift of the Deity to our world, as alleged by other accounts of this hero of the constellations."[41] Yet it is not quite so immediately obvious that the Egyptians also, in their own way, prepared for the coming of the Messiah. How may this be understood?

The religion of ancient Egypt is highly complex, with a multitude of gods, many of them of a local nature worshipped solely at one town or cult center but not elsewhere. All this changed—or appeared in a new light—with the introduction of the cult and worship of Osiris into Egypt, who was undoubtedly "the single most important Egyptian deity."[42]

Osiris became the most revered god in Egypt—and even beyond the confines of Egypt—in the millennia preceding the advent of Christianity. Orion was the abode of Osiris for the Egyptians. Hence the great importance of this constellation to them. The orientation of the Great Pyramid toward Alnitak, and the mirroring of the architectural layout of the three pyramids (Cheops, Chephren, Mycerinos) on Earth of the three stars in the belt of Orion is a testimony to the religion of Osiris as the central cult of the pharaohs.

> The religious literature of all the great periods of Egyptian history is filled with allusions to incidents connected with the life, death, and resurrection of Osiris, the god and judge of the Egyptian dead; and from first to last the authors of religious

40 Rolleston, *Mazzaroth*, part II, pp. 30–31.

41 Seiss, *The Gospel in the Stars*, p. 105.

42 Wallis Budge, *Osiris and the Egyptian Resurrection*, p. 1.

> texts took it for granted that their readers were well acquainted with such incidents in all their details. In no text do we find any connected history of the god, and nowhere are stated in detail the reasons why he assumed his exalted position as the judge of souls, or why, for about four thousand years, he remained the great type and symbol of the Resurrection. No funerary inscription exists, however early, in which evidence cannot be found proving that the deceased had set his hope of immortality in Osiris, and at no time in Egypt's long history do we find that the position of Osiris was usurped by any other god. On the contrary, it is Osiris who is made to usurp the attributes and powers of other gods, and in tracing his history... we shall find that the importance of the cult of this god grew in proportion to the growth of the power and wealth of Egypt, and that finally its influence filled both the national and private life of her inhabitants, from the Mediterranean Sea to the Sixth Cataract at Shablûkah. The fame of Osiris extended to the nations around, and it is to the hands of foreigners that we are indebted for connected, though short, narratives of his history.[43]

Against this background it is evident that world consciousness was being prepared for the *death and resurrection* of Christ by the Egyptian cult of Osiris. The orientation of the Great Pyramid toward Alnitak in the belt of Orion—the image of a man pointing up toward this star—speaks of the goal of the pharaoh at his death to journey to the abode of Osiris and to become one with Osiris. This cult of death and resurrection was a preparation for the death and resurrection of Christ, as can be seen from the following consideration.

Christ died on Friday, April 3, AD 33 and the resurrection took place "on the third day," on Sunday, April 5. Forty days later—on Thursday, May 14, AD 33—the ascension took place. Ten days after the ascension, on Sunday, May 24, AD 33—there was the event of Pentecost.[44] During this 10-day period between May 14 and May 24, AD 33 the Sun traversed the constellation of Orion! That is, the Sun moved from 23° Taurus to 2½° Gemini. This is the longitudinal

43 Ibid.

44 Powell, *Chronicle of the Living Christ*, pp. 175–178 lists all the dates and includes the horoscopes of these events in the life of Christ.

range of the central human figure depicted by the main stars in the constellation of Orion in the sidereal zodiac, extending from Rigel (22° Taurus) marking the left knee or foot to Betelgeuse (4° Gemini) marking the right shoulder of Orion—bearing in mind, of course, that Orion is located well below the zodiac. However, the stellar meridians running through the two brightest stars (Rigel and Betelgeuse) of Orion intersect the ecliptic through the range indicated—the last 8° of Taurus and the first 4° of Gemini.[45] This extraordinary fact, having to do with the Sun's location between Ascension and Pentecost, is a confirmation that the Egyptian cult of the death and resurrection of Osiris may be seen as preparation for the ascension of Christ.

Also Bullinger in his classic work *The Witness of the Stars* draws a relationship between Christ and Orion.

> Orion was anciently spelt Oarion, from the Hebrew root, which means *light*.... Orion is the most brilliant of all the constellations.... Thus beautifully is set forth the brilliancy and glory of that *light* which shall break forth when the moment comes for it to be said, "Arise, shine, for thy light is come." The picture presents us with "the Light of the world." His left foot is significantly placed upon the head of the enemy. He is girded with a glorious girdle, studded with three brilliant stars; and upon this girdle is hung a sharp sword. Its handle proves that this mighty Prince is come forth in a new character. He is again proved to be "the Lamb that was slain," for the hilt of this sword is in the form of the head and body of a lamb. In his right hand he lifts on high his mighty club.... This is "the glory of God" which the heavens constantly declare (Psalms 29:1). They tell of that blessed time when the whole Earth shall be filled with His glory (Numbers 14:21; Isaiah 11:9); when "the glory of the LORD shall be revealed, and all flesh shall see it together" (Isaiah 40:5), as all see now the beauty of Orion's glory.[46]

45 From the *Astrofire* star catalog it emerges that the full longitudinal extent of Orion, when the stars west of Rigel and east of Betelgeuse are included, is from 17° Taurus to 9½° Gemini.

46 Bullinger, *The Witness of the Stars*, pp. 126–128.

The Greek depiction of Orion with a club in his right hand differs from the Egyptian portrayal of Osiris in connection with the constellation of Orion. Usually Osiris-Orion is shown together with Isis-Sirius. When we look up to Orion in the heavens, the three stars in Orion's belt point toward Sirius, so that Sirius—the brightest star in the heavens—clearly belongs together with Orion. The Egyptians saw Sirius as the abode of Isis, who is nearly always shown alongside Osiris, just as astronomically Sirius is seen at the right side of Orion (from our perspective to the left of Orion). In the early depictions usually the body of Osiris is facing toward Isis and his head away from her, but this was often reversed in the later depictions—for example, "the depiction of Orion in the Seti I A and Seti I C families, even though here his body is turned away from Sothis [Sirius] while his head is turned toward her."[47]

Osiris-Orion is generally depicted holding a scepter in his right hand and an *ankh* in his left hand. (The *ankh*, the Egyptian symbol for life, is similar to a cross except that the upper part of the cross is replaced by a circle or oval.) The scepter in the right hand symbolizing the "good shepherd" and the *ankh* in the left hand symbolizing the "bread of life" are very different from the ancient Greek symbols of the raised club of Orion in his right hand and the skin of a slain lion over his left arm.

The reference in the Egyptian texts is usually to the "upper arm" holding the *ankh* and the "lower arm" holding the scepter, each arm marked by a star—the right arm (somewhat lowered) holding the scepter, being marked by the star Betelgeuse, and the left arm (raised) holding the *ankh*, being marked by the star Bellatrix.[48] Against the background of Astrogeographia, the right arm (Betelgeuse) found its expression on Earth in the temple of Solomon, located in the city of David the shepherd! On the other hand, the left arm (Bellatrix) manifested on the terrestrial globe in the temple of Artemis at Ephesus—Artemis being the Great Mother, the Mother of everything living

47 Neugebauer and Parker, *Egyptian Astronomical Texts, volume III*, p. 113.

48 This is by way of deduction as there is no explicit reference in the Egyptian texts to the names of the stars marking the "*upper arm*" and the "*lower arm*." However, it is a fairly obvious deduction.

(Genesis 3:20), for whom the *ankh* (denoting life) is a fitting symbol. The Great Pyramid itself—or rather the three pyramids of Giza—mark the girdle of the Messiah, recalling the words: "Righteousness shall be the girdle of His loins, and faithfulness shall be the girdle of His reins" (Isaiah 11:5).

It can be seen that the "Orion mystery" is much greater than it would appear at first sight. Without equating Orion with Osiris, Rudolf Steiner does identify Osiris as a pre-incarnatory form of Christ, whom he calls the *Cosmic Word* (Greek: *Logos*). He also relates how Moses was initiated into the Egyptian mysteries of Osiris and *took them with him* on the exodus from Egypt, so that from this point in time onward Isis—the bride of Osiris—was referred to as the *Mourning Widow*:

> Those who went through this initiation and came back into the physical world had a serious but resigned world outlook. They knew her, Holy Isis, but they felt themselves as "Sons of the Widow." And the point of time between the old initiation, wherein one was able to experience the birth of Osiris in those ancient Egyptian mysteries, and that wherein one met only the mute, mourning Isis and could become a "Son of the Widow" in the Egyptian mysteries; the point of time that separates these two phases of the Egyptian Initiation—when was it? It was the time in which Moses lived. For the destiny of Egypt was fulfilled in such a way that not only was Moses initiated into the mysteries of Egypt, but he took them with him. When he led his people out of Egypt he took with him the part of the Egyptian initiation that added the Osiris initiation to the mourning Isis, as she later became. Such was the transition from the Egyptian civilization to that of the Old Testament. Truly, Moses had carried away the secret of Osiris, the secret of the Cosmic Word! "I AM the I AM," ["*Ehiyeh asher Ehiyeh*"]. So was the Egyptian Mystery carried over to the ancient Hebrew Mystery.
>
> Let us enter the tragic mood of one about to be initiated during the Egyptian epoch. We transpose ourselves into this mood and find that it originated from experiences that the aspirant could express only by saying inwardly: "Formerly, when I entered the spiritual worlds, I found Osiris permeating cosmic space with

> the Creative Word and its meaning, which represent the ground-forces of all being and development. Now the Word has become mute and silent. The God who was called Osiris has forsaken these realms. He is preparing to penetrate into other regions; he has descended into the Earth-region in order to enter human souls."
>
> The Being who had been known spiritually to human souls in earlier days first became manifest in physical life when Moses heard in the physical world the Voice that in earlier ages had been heard only in the spiritual worlds *"Ehiyeh asher Ehiyeh!"*—"I AM the I AM, Who was, and is, and will be." And then this being, who, as the Creative Word, had gradually become lost to the experience of the candidate for initiation, transferred his life into the Earth region so that he could gradually come to life again in the souls of earthly human beings and, in this new life, rising to ever higher and higher glory, would consist in the further development of the Earth, even to the end of the Earth evolution.[49]

If these words of Rudolf Steiner are taken seriously, they signify that the ancient Egyptians and the Israelites—both under the domain or "jurisdiction" of Orion—were preparing for the incarnation of the Cosmic Word, and that Moses was the key figure here, who "transposed" the Osiris mysteries into the religion of ancient Israel. This raises the question as to the relationship between Yahweh and Osiris–Christ. The following statement by Rudolf Steiner offers a starting point for consideration of this question: "Humanity had now to be given time to experience the advent of Christ who had formerly made Himself manifest to Moses upon Mount Sinai. Jehovah [Yahweh] was the same being as Christ, though wearing another form."[50]

This statement is an astonishing one, considering that Yahweh—written YHWH in Hebrew—is translated throughout the Old Testament as "the Lord." Although it needs to be borne in mind that the name Yahweh was introduced by Moses:

> Then Moses said to God, "If I come to the people of Israel and say to them, 'The God of your fathers has sent me to you,' and they ask me, 'what is his name?' What shall I say to them?" God said to

49 Steiner, *The Mysteries of the East and of Christianity*, pp. 52, 57–58.

50 Steiner, *The East in the light of the West*, p. 214.

> Moses, "I AM the I AM" [Ehiyeh asher Ehiyeh] And he said, "Say this to the people of Israel, 'I AM has sent me to you.'" God also said to Moses, "Say this to the people of Israel, 'Yahweh [YHWH], the God of your fathers, the God of Abraham, the God of Isaac, and the God of Jacob has sent me to you: this is my name for ever, and thus I am to be remembered throughout all generations....'" (Exodus 3:13–15).

Prior to Moses, God had been known as "Elohim" (plural) as in "Let *us* make man in *our* image..." (Genesis 1:26) or "El Shaddai" as in "I am God Almighty..." (Genesis 17:1), when God appeared to Abraham and also when God appeared to Jacob, "I am God Almighty...." (Genesis 35:11). Thus to Abraham, Isaac, and Jacob, God appeared as El Shaddai, and it was to Moses that He made Himself known by His name Yahweh (YHWH): "And God said to Moses, 'I am *Yahweh.* I appeared to Abraham, to Isaac, and to Jacob, as *El Shaddai*, but by my name *Yahweh* I did not make myself known to them'" (Exodus 6:2–3). Moses, on account of his initiation into the Egyptian mysteries, had a new experience of the Divine, which was his experience of Osiris–Christ, who revealed Himself as "I AM the I AM" and who communicated His name as Yahweh.

However, it would be misleading to simply equate Yahweh with Osiris–Christ. Again referring to Steiner:

> In the course of great happenings in the cosmos this sublime Being drew ever nearer to the Earth-sphere. His approach could be perceived more and more distinctly by clairvoyance, and was unmistakable when in the flame of lightning on Mount Sinai the revelations came to Moses, the great forerunner of Christ Jesus. What did these revelations to Moses signify? They signified that the Christ Being, while approaching the Earth, was revealing Himself—in reflection to begin with—as if in a mirror-image. Let us consider, in its spiritual aspect, the process in evidence at every full Moon. When we consider the full Moon we see the rays of the Sun in reflection. It is sunlight that streams toward us, only we call it moonlight because we see it reflected by the Moon. What Being did Moses behold in the burning bush and in

> the fire on Sinai? He beheld the Christ! But just as the sunlight is not seen directly but reflected from the Moon, so did Moses see the Christ in reflection. And as we call the sunlight "moonlight" when we see it reflected from the Moon, Christ was called at that time, Jahve [Yahweh] or Jehovah. Jahve [Yahweh] or Jehovah is the reflection of the Christ before He Himself appeared on Earth. Christ announced Himself thus indirectly to a humanity as yet unable to behold Him in his immediate reality, just as the sunlight manifests itself through the rays of the moon in the otherwise dark night of full Moon. Jahve [Yahweh] or Jehovah is the Christ—but seen as *reflected light* not directly.[51]

Astonishing though they are, Steiner's insights help to shed light on the "Orion mystery." With the help of these insights, it emerges that the ancient Egyptians and the Israelites were devoted to the same God under different names: the Egyptians to Osiris, who is identified as a pre-incarnatory form of Christ, and the Israelites to Yahweh, who was a kind of reflection of this pre-incarnatory form of Christ. The Israelites were the *chosen people*, the race chosen to provide the physical vessel for this Divine incarnation.

If we take Steiner's insights seriously, many questions are raised, one of them being: How does Isis fit into this, the bride of Osiris, who was "left behind" when Moses took the Osiris mysteries with him? Given the association for the Egyptians of Isis with the star Sirius, it is possible to approach this question through Astrogeographia, once the earthly projection of Sirius is located, as we shall see later.

Now, however, it remains to consider the earthly projection of the other principal stars in the constellation of Orion—for example, Meissa, marking the head of Orion. Meissa, meaning "shining" or "white spot," is a double star at the center of a huge surrounding ring of gas called the *Meissa ring*. It is a blue, young, hot, and massive star, about twenty-eight times the mass of the Sun and about ten times larger—a giant star, some 1,100 light-years away and—including ultraviolet wavelengths—over 63,000 times more luminous than our Sun. Where is the projection of the star Meissa located?

51 Steiner, *The Gospel of St. Luke* (available now as *According to Luke: The Gospel of Compassion and Love Revealed*), pp. 133–134.

Using the ASTROGEO program let us see where the current projection of Meissa is located—at present Meissa's latitude is 13S22 and longitude is 28°58' Taurus. According to ASTROGEO the projection of Meissa (epoch: AD 2000) is 41N43; 30E10, which is located in the Black Sea, 75 miles (120 km) northeast of Istanbul, the ancient Constantinople (formerly Byzantium) at 41N02; 28E57. Against this background it is possible to understand why the Emperor Constantine the Great (fourth century AD) chose the location of Byzantium to be the capital of his world empire—intended to bridge East and West—this area corresponding to the region of the head of Orion. (The name Byzantium was then changed to Constantinople in honor of the Emperor Constantine the Great in AD 330 and the city was dedicated to the Virgin Mary.)

Tracking the *historical projection* of Meissa, in AD 57 the star's declination was 6N21, added to Jerusalem's latitude (31N47), yields 38N08 on the "Meissa meridian" (longitude 30E10), closely coinciding with the ancient city of Apamea (38N05; 30E09) in Phrygia (Dinar in modern Turkey). It was the foremost Phrygian city—and, moreover, one of the greatest cities in the whole of Asia Minor—a great trading center commanding the Maeander road. Apamea was founded by Antiochus Soter around 270 BC and its rise to prominence as a great trading center began after the Mithridatic wars (88-63 BC) between Rome and Mithridates, king of Pontus. Not long after the founding of Constantinople, trade routes were directed away from Apamea to this great capital, and Apamea rapidly declined in significance. From this example, however, it can be seen how the historical projection of Meissa passed from about 1° south of Apamea at the founding of the city around 270 BC to almost 1° north of Apamea at the time of the founding of Constantinople in AD 330, from which time Apamea went into decline.

From ASTROGEO, the projection of Meissa at the time of the founding of Constantinople in AD 330 was 30E10; 38N55, some 170 miles (273 km) south and somewhat east of the city. However, Meissa was on a trajectory north toward the Black Sea, which the historical projection reached around AD 1453, when the Turks conquered Constantinople and changed its name to Istanbul. It can be hypothesized that Constantinople/Istanbul was a "substitute" for the actual earthly geographical location of Meissa's earthly projection which at that time was 1°12' eastward of the city—just as the earthly projection of Mintaka lies in the Mediterranean Sea and yet El Alamein lies on the Mediterranean coast at the place where the Mintaka meridian meets the coast. In the case of Constantinople, however, it does not lie on the Meissa meridian but 1°12' to the west—i.e., 83 miles (133½ km) west thereof. At any rate, the location of Constantinople/Istanbul receives from the general region of influence of Orion's head (and more especially in that area as a kind of "substitute" for Meissa's earthly projection).

As with the great monuments associated with the earthly projections of other stars in the constellation of Orion, so the great church Hagia Sophia, erected in Constantinople in the years AD 532–537, can be seen in connection with the head of Orion in the region marked by Meissa. The original church, built on the site of a pagan temple, was consecrated by the Emperor Constantius, son of Constantine, in AD 360 and was known then as the Great Church, being the largest of its time. In AD 404 the church was destroyed by angry crowds rebelling against the decision of the Emperor Arcadius to send Archbishop John Chrysostom into exile. The church was rebuilt by the Emperor Theodosius II in AD 415 and by about AD 430 came to be known as *Hagia Sophia* ("Holy Wisdom"). The new church was destroyed by a rioting mob in AD 532 at the time of the Nika revolt, which brought much death and destruction with it. The Emperor Justinian conceived of a grand church bigger than any other ever built. The new Hagia Sophia was constructed between 532 and 537 as a vast domed basilica. It is an architectural wonder, considered as the "mother church" of all Eastern Christians of the Byzantine liturgical tradition—both Orthodox and Greek Catholic.

The most impressive architectural feature of Hagia Sophia is the vast dome supported by four massive piers, with four arches swinging across. The dome is pierced by forty single-arched windows, enabling beams of light to stream through and illuminate the interior, creating an impression of infinite space. Bearing in mind the correspondence with the head of Orion, the vast dome can be thought of in relation to the interior of the domed form of the head—reaching up to the starry heavens. Historical sources refer to the great number of clerics appointed to the service of the most holy Great Church of Constantinople: 80 priests, 150 deacons, 40 deaconesses, 60 subdeacons, 160 readers, 25 chanters, and 75 doorkeepers—a total of 590 people assigned to serve in Hagia Sophia.

The cathedral suffered a major blow in the year 1204 through the rapacious pillaging of the crusaders led by Enrico Dandolo, the aged, almost blind, Doge of Venice. Dandolo's deed was financially motivated when he led the crusaders of the Fourth Crusade from Venice to Constantinople, instead of to Egypt and Jerusalem to liberate the Holy Land from the Muslims. He had promised the European barons to provide the necessary supplies for the crusaders, who converged on Venice from various European lands (mainly France and Germany), for the enormous sum of 85,000 silver marks and in exchange for sharing the conquered territories. He saw the capture and pillage of Constantinople as a way in which the money owed to Venice by the crusaders could be paid. In the wake of the conquest of the city by the crusaders, Hagia Sophia was looted of its art treasures, which were—for the most part—carried off to Venice. Having achieved his goal, Dandolo, around ninety years old, died in Constantinople in June 1205, leaving the bulwark of eastern Christendom severely weakened.

A century and a half later, the Turks with an army of 80,000 were able to capture the imperial city, despite the valiant defense put up by an army of some 7,000 Greek soldiers. On May 29, 1453, the Ottoman Turkish Sultan Mehmet the Conqueror entered Constantinople and rode to Hagia Sophia. Amazed at the beauty of the cathedral, he decided to convert it into his imperial mosque. It remained a mosque until the fall of the Ottoman empire in 1918, and in 1935 the Turkish government secularized the building, converting it into a museum and restoring the original mosaics that had been plastered over by the Muslims when they had made it into a mosque.

With the fall of Constantinople and the desecration of Hagia Sophia in 1453, the Ottoman Turks proceeded to conquer the Christian peoples of the Balkans. One after another, Greeks, Bulgarians,

Macedonians, Serbs, Montenegrins, Croats, Slovenes, Romanians, and Hungarians came under the yoke of oppression, leaving Russia the only free Orthodox land. Twice in the following centuries, in 1529 and 1683, the Turks appeared at the gates of Vienna, only to be turned back miraculously, so that the march of Islam into the heart of western Christendom was stopped.

Bearing in mind the relationship of Europe (*Europa*) to Taurus, with its central star Aldebaran (15° Taurus) mirrored on Earth in the city of Vienna, and recalling the image of mighty Orion with raised club threatening in the direction of Taurus, and seeing the head and upper part of Orion mirrored on Earth in Turkey, it can be seen how through Astrogeographia a cosmic image or background emerges in relation to events taking place on the Earth. A modern example of this was referred to in the Introduction: the Muslim protest—to a certain extent violent and militant—that erupted in February 2006, when Mars entered Taurus and approached the Pleiades (mirrored on Earth off the west coast of Denmark), the protest arising as a consequence of the publication in a Danish newspaper of cartoons of the Prophet Muhammad.

However, before further exploring the background to historical events in the light of Astrogeographia, it still remains to complete the picture with regard to the projection of the remaining stars of Orion onto the Earth—in particular: Rigel, Saiph, and the Orion nebula (M 42).

First, Rigel: the "Left Leg of the Giant" (marking either the knee or foot of Orion, according to different depictions) is a blue supergiant star whose diameter is about 74 times that of our Sun.[52] Rigel is a "young" star just reaching the "prime of life" in terms of the time span of a star. Both Rigel and Betelgeuse are megastars, with a luminosity of 10,000 or more, whereby Rigel's luminosity, including the ultraviolet wavelengths, is about 117,000 times that of our Sun, making it one of the most powerful stars in our cosmos (using the word *cosmos* to indicate the local part of our galaxy). According to the Hipparcos catalog, Rigel is at a distance of 860 light-years, but with a margin of error, meaning

52 Rigel is accompanied by a small bluish companion star, Rigel B, visible with a good telescope.

that its distance could be anywhere between 700 and 900 light-years. After Sirius, Canopus, Alpha Centauri, Arcturus, Vega, and Capella, Rigel is the seventh brightest star in the night sky—according to *apparent* brightness rather than *intrinsic* brightness (luminosity).

Rigel (22° Taurus) and Betelgeuse (4° Gemini) determine—by and large—the longitudinal extent of Orion's influence. I say "by and large" because Orion's actual longitudinal extent is from 17° Taurus to 9½° Gemini.[53] However, in terms of the appearance of the human figure sketched out by the stars of this magnificent constellation, Betelgeuse (right shoulder) and Rigel (left knee or foot)—as the two brightest stars in this constellation—strikingly indicate the breadth of the figure of Orion, at least with respect to the main features of this figure. As mentioned earlier in this chapter, the ascension of Christ began when the Sun was at 23° Taurus, in longitudinal conjunction with Rigel, whereby the Sun's exact conjunction with Rigel was on the day before the ascension. And the end of the ten-day period between ascension (May 14 AD 33) and Pentecost (May 24 AD 33) came as the Sun was at 2½° Gemini, just 1½° from exact conjunction with Betelgeuse. In a certain respect Rigel could be called the "ascension star." As already noted, that the Sun traversed this area of the zodiac above Orion, between Rigel and Betelgeuse, during the ten-day period from the ascension to Pentecost, is a remarkable sign that the ancient Egyptian cult of Osiris, centered around the death and ascension of Osiris-Orion, was a prophetic religion pointing to the coming of Christ, in particular to the death and ascension of Christ.

Rigel as the star of the ascension indicates the remarkable nature of this megastar. It could be said that the event of the ascension was one that integrated spirit and matter, denoting a beginning of the future reintegration of Heaven and Earth. Christ came to the Earth, and in the hours following his death on the cross descended into the underworld, thus fulfilling what he had prophesied in having referred earlier to the *sign of Jonah*. "For as Jonah was three days and three nights in the belly of the whale, so will the Son of man be three days

---

53 According to the *Astrofire* star catalog, Orion extends from 17°11' Taurus to 9°36' Gemini.

and three nights in the heart of the Earth" (Matthew 12:40). Christ descended into the heart of Mother Earth (Mother = *Mater* in Latin, from the same root as the word *matter*) in order to implant seeds of redemption there, and then forty days later began his ascent to the Father, returning to the realm of pure spirit. In this sense the ascension was an act of integration of spirit and matter, the beginning of the reintegration of Heaven and Earth. As will emerge below, Rigel has to do not only with the mysteries of the heights but also with the mysteries of the depths.

In terms of Astrogeographia, let us now investigate the location of the earthly projection of Rigel. Without going into all the computational details, using ASTROGEO Rigel's historical projection for 2495 BC, when the Great Pyramid was under construction, was 8N37, 23E15 and its *current projection* for AD 2000 is 23N35, 23E17.[54] During the time span from 2495 BC to AD 2000 the latitude of the *historical projection* of Rigel increased from 8N37 to 23N35, ascending the Rigel meridian from the Central African Republic through Western Sudan and Chad into Libya. Rigel's current projection is located in the Cufra oasis (Al Kufrah) in Southern Libya, relatively close to the town Al Jawf (24N09, 23E19).

The Cufra oasis played a role in the Western Desert Campaign of World War II. Prior to that war, Cufra was an important trade route for various nomadic desert peoples, including the Senussi, who at one point made the oasis their capital. When the Italians captured Cufra in 1931, the Senussi appealed to the French for help. During World War II the Italians used Cufra as an airbase. However, at the Battle of Kufra on March 1, 1941, French forces successfully took the oasis, when Italian resistance crumbled in face of the French onslaught.

Unlike Alnitak (Great Pyramid at Giza), Alnilam (Pharos lighthouse of Alexandria), Bellatrix (temple of Artemis of Ephesus), Meissa (Hagia Sophia in Constantinople), and Betelgeuse (temple of Solomon in Jerusalem), there is no monumental building at the site of Rigel's projection upon the Earth. However, there are two mystery centers on the Rigel meridian. At the first mystery site (of the two) there was

54 Thus the geodetic equivalent to the Rigel meridian (23E15 in 2495 BC) is currently 23E17.

an enormous temple complex—at Eleusis (38N02, 23E33), some 12½ miles (20½ km) west of Athens. Here stood the great mystery center dedicated to the Earth Mother Demeter and her daughter Persephone, a center to which—during its heyday at the time of classical Athens—thousands of people came to participate in the mystery rituals enacted in the celebration of the cult of Demeter.

Eleusis is 14° north of the current projection of Rigel, corresponding to a distance of 967 miles (1556 km). It was, alongside the temple of Artemis of Ephesus, the most famous (and perhaps the most important in terms of the effect it had by way of those, such as Plato, who were initiated there) mystery center of the ancient world. Just as the temple of Artemis of Ephesus, corresponding to Bellatrix, was "seeded" from a star on the *left side* (marking the left shoulder) of Orion, so the mystery center of Demeter at Eleusis was "seeded" from a star (Rigel, marking the left knee or foot) on the *left side* of Orion—the left side being the *feminine* side. Both mystery centers celebrated the Divine Feminine. In contrast, the temple of Solomon, "seeded" from the star Betelgeuse, marking the right shoulder of Orion, was clearly masculine in nature, built as the "house of Yahweh."

Whereas the Demeter cult at Eleusis was concerned with the mysteries of the depths, the other mystery center on the Rigel meridian is a mystery center of "ascension to the heights." This second mystery center is one that currently exists, although not on a permanent basis. It reconstitutes itself for a few weeks in August each year in the Rila Mountains, south of Sofia, the capital of Bulgaria. Sofia (42N40, 23E18), which is on the Rigel meridian, is where the Master Peter Deunov (1864–1944) founded the White Brotherhood School in 1922 as the Bulgarian branch of the Great White Brotherhood. In 1927 he founded Izgrev ("Sunrise") on the outskirts of Sofia as a center for the School which, however, when the communists took over Bulgaria in 1944/1945 was discontinued—this was the point in time when Peter Deunov died (he retired from the physical world on December 27, 1944). In 1929 he started yearly summer camps of the White Brotherhood School. The summer camp takes place each year in August, the climax being the three-day period August 19–21. The camp is located at approximately 8,200 feet (2,500 m) above sea level in the area of the Seven Rila Lakes, just north of the Rila National Park comprising some 74,000 acres (30,000 hectares) of mountains and meadows surrounding the Rila Monastery that was founded in the tenth century by St. John of Rila. The highest mountain in the Rila chain is Moussala, which is around 9,600 feet (2,925 m) tall.

Peter Deunov spoke of the special nature of the Seven Rila Lakes:

> Thousands of years ago the Sentient Beings knew that we would go to the Seven Lakes in the Rila Mountains and they prepared them for us.... The oldest occult [spiritual] School is situated within the Rila Mountains.... Knowledge is stored in the Rila Mountains. The cultures of Egypt and India originated from the Rila Mountains.[55]

In these words a connection is drawn between Egypt, the land mirroring Orion, and the Rila Mountains. In light of Astrogeographia, the connecting link is the Rigel meridian, which passes through the Rila Seven Lakes (42N12, 23E18) and also through Sofia (42N40, 23E18), which is 32 miles (52 km) further to the north. Rigel, as a megastar, the star of Christ's ascension, exerts a powerful influence along its meridian. The spiritual school of Peter Deunov that meets each year in the month of August in the Rila Mountains could be described as a "school of ascension," reaching up to the heights,[56] just as the ancient mystery center of Demeter at Eleusis reached down to the depths.

Obviously much more could be said about both—the ancient mystery center of Demeter at Eleusis, and the modern mystery center in the Rila Mountains—and any reader who so wishes can follow up on these indications. Here it is important to emphasize that these two mystery centers are an expression of the "seeding" of mysteries on

55 Boev and Nikolov, *The Wellspring of Good*, pp. 222–223.

56 It was on purpose that Peter Deunov went with his students up into the mountains to teach there. He spoke of the mountain peaks as "spiritual antennae": "The high peaks are dynamic centers. They represent a reservoir of power which will be utilized in the future. The mountain peaks are connected with the Earth's internal forces and the cosmic forces, as well"—ibid. p. 221.

Earth from the star Rigel, which is concerned with the integration of the mysteries of the heights and the mysteries of the depths.

Now let us consider the star Saiph, whose name comes from the Arabic for "Sword of the Giant." This name, however, is inaccurate for Saiph, which marks the right knee of Orion rather than the region of Orion's sword. A blue-white supergiant, Saiph is the sixth brightest star in the constellation of Orion. At a distance of 720 light-years, it is at a distance comparable with that of Rigel. However, in terms of its intrinsic brightness, Saiph has a luminosity much less than that of Rigel—Saiph's luminosity, including ultraviolet wavelengths, being 65,000 times that of our Sun.

The historical projection of Saiph for the year 2495 BC equates with 10N11; 32E52 and for the year AD 2000 with 22N07; 32E52. During the period from 2495 BC to AD 2000 the historical projection increased from 10N11 to 22N07, moving up the Saiph meridian from the Upper Nile area in Southern Sudan all the way through Sudan, passing east of Khartoum (15N33; 32E32) and finally crossing the border of Sudan into Egypt, this border being located on the parallel 22° north of the equator. The current projection lies in Egypt just across the border with Sudan. Whether or not there was anything located at this place in earlier times is not known, but now (and, as far as is known, throughout the historical period of Egypt) there is nothing at this site. Interestingly, it is more or less on the same parallel as the Abu Simbel temple (22N19; 31E38), which is located some 83 miles (133½ km) to the west and is famous for its four colossal statues of Ramses II cut into the cliff face there.

Following the Saiph meridian northward, it passes through Philae (24N02; 32E59), an island south of Aswan with a most beautiful temple complex, the main temple dedicated to the goddess Isis. To save the Philae temple complex from destruction by water as a consequence of the construction of the Aswan dam, the temples were carefully dismantled and reconstructed—as a "carbon copy" of Philae—on the nearby island of Agilkia. The Philae temple complex was started relatively late—under the Ptolemies (post 332 BC)—and finished during the time of the Roman rule of Egypt. However, the Egyptian name for it meant "Island of the Time of Ra," which implies that it was a cult site of considerable antiquity, although no ancient ruins have been found there which would confirm this—the earliest ruins dating from the time of the Pharaohs Nectanebo I and II (404–343 BC). Philae became famous in Greek and Roman antiquity above all as the cult center of Isis. It was the last cult center to continue to practice the ancient Egyptian religion, until it was closed in AD 550 by the Emperor Justinian, resulting in the temple of Isis being converted to a Christian church and the Egyptian priests being driven away, so that knowledge of Egyptian hieroglyphs and religious practice was lost.

Philae lies on the Saiph meridian, some 132 miles (213 km) north of the current projection of this star, which radiated along its meridian to "seed" the Isis cult center on the island. This star, marking the right knee of Orion, is thus—like Bellatrix (temple of Artemis of Ephesus) and Rigel (cult center of Demeter at Eleusis)—associated with the mysteries of the Divine Feminine, as is confirmed by following the Saiph meridian further.

Following this meridian further northward, it crosses through Egypt, across the island of Cyprus in the Mediterranean Sea. As with the island of Philae, where the cult of the Egyptian goddess Isis flourished, so on the island of Cyprus the cult of the Greek goddess Aphrodite thrived.

> Muse, tell me the deeds of golden Aphrodite the Cyprian, who stirs up secret passion in the gods and subdues the tribes of mortal men and birds that fly in the air and all the many creatures that the dry land rears, and all the seas. (Homeric Hymn to Aphrodite)

The Greek poets Homer (eighth century BC) and Hesiod (seventh century BC) both associated the Greek goddess of love and beauty, Aphrodite, with Cyprus. In addition to Homer's hymns to Aphrodite ("golden Aphrodite the Cyprian" and "laughter-loving Aphrodite... left sweet-smelling Cyprus"—from the Second Homeric Hymn to Aphrodite), Hesiod portrayed the miraculous birth of the goddess from the sea foam off the coast of Cyprus. According to local tradition on the island, she came ashore at the cove on the southwest coast, where there is "Aphrodite's rock," *Petra tou Romiou* (34N39; 32E41), aligned closely with the Saiph meridian. Not far from this site was the famous temple of Aphrodite dating from the twelfth century BC and in use continuously until her cult was outlawed by the Emperor Theodosius I in AD 391. The ruins of the temple of Aphrodite are near Kouklia village (34N42; 32E34), also close to the Saiph meridian.

It seems that the temple of Aphrodite on Cyprus, like the temple of Isis on Philae, was "seeded" by the star Saiph. It should be noted that there was on Philae also a temple of Hathor, the Egyptian goddess corresponding to the Greek Aphrodite. Not only Isis and Hathor but also other Egyptian goddesses—Mut, Neith, Nekhbet, and Sekhmet—were worshiped on Philae. However, it was a time of great popularity of the goddess Isis and pilgrims came to her island of Philae from throughout the Mediterranean, so that worship of all the other Egyptian goddesses was subsumed into the cult of Isis. In fact, on Philae Isis and Hathor were seen as essentially one and the same.

Following the Saiph meridian further north into Turkey, it crosses one of the oldest cities in the world, Catal Hüyük (37N36; 32E54), dated to around 7000 BC or even earlier—the largest and most well-developed Neolithic site found hitherto.[57] The site was discovered in 1958 and many female figurines were found there, apparently representing a female deity—a corpulent Mother goddess. One from about 6000 BC, now in the Archeological Museum of Ankara, depicts the corpulent and fertile Mother goddess in the process of giving birth while seated on her throne, which has two handrests in the form of lion's heads. This brings an association with the later Phrygian goddess Cybele (known to the Greeks as Rhea), with whom lions are related in an aggressive but tamed manner.

As discussed in the earlier section (in this chapter) on Bellatrix, Cybele was the forerunner of Artemis of Ephesus, who represents a gentler, nobler version of Cybele. Worship of the Mother goddess Cybele was at the heart of Phrygian culture. Interestingly, Ankara (39N55; 32E52), the modern capital of Turkey, in the middle of Anatolia where the Phrygian culture flourished, lies exactly on the Saiph meridian. In light of Astrogeographia the Cybele cult, with its predecessor cult of the Mother goddess at Catal Hüyük, was also "seeded" from the star Saiph.

---

57 Settegast, *Plato Prehistorian*, pp. 162–208.

Lastly, let us turn our attention to the beautiful Orion nebula (M42) in the middle of the constellation, directly beneath the belt of Orion, more or less below Alnilam, the middle star of the three marking the belt. The Orion nebula marks the middle of the sword of Orion, hanging down from the belt. M42 is a spectacular sight, described by the astronomer William Herschel, back in 1789 (eight years after he had discovered the planet Uranus), as "an unformed fiery mist, the chaotic material of future suns."[58] The Orion nebula is part of a giant cloud of interstellar matter, estimated to be about twenty-four light-years in diameter. Within this cloud of gas and dust are young stars that have recently formed or are still in the process of formation. Within M42 is a cluster of newly formed stars called the *Trapezium cluster* (multiple star Theta Orionis). The Orion nebula, located at a distance of about 1,344 light-years, and the stars of the Trapezium cluster, still further away, are reckoned to be only about 300,000 years old, which is *very young* in terms of the age of stars.

M42's historical projection in 2495 BC was 13N38; 29E34, and its current projection in AD 2000 is 26N23; 29E27. The historical projection of the Orion nebula traveled northward along the M42 meridian from 13N38 in 2495 BC to 26N23 in AD 2000.

Remarkably, though, there is nothing striking to be found at the place of the current projection and also not along the M42 meridian. This was a strange thing to discover, considering the spectacular sight of the Orion nebula in the heavens. This discovery, however, is very significant. It tells us it is the stars themselves—and only when they have reached a certain age or maturity—that are "effective" on Earth in the sense of Astrogeographia. It would appear that a cloud (dust and gas) formation such as M42 or very young newly formed stars such as those comprising the Trapezium cluster, while offering a breathtaking sight in the heavens, do not transmit an impulse toward the Earth in the same way that older, more mature stars do.

For those readers who wish to consult a map, the current projection of the Orion nebula is located in the middle of the Egyptian desert about 150 miles (240 km) west of the town of Sohag on the

58 From http://www.seds.org/messier/m/m042.html.

Nile. Following the M42 meridian south and north, nothing striking is to be found. Of course, as M42 is south of Alnilam, whose current projection coincides closely with Alexandria, the geodetic equivalent of M42 (28°16' Taurus—geodetic equivalent: 29E28) is not far from that of Alnilam (28°43' Taurus—geodetic equivalent: 30E00). Following Alnilam's meridian north, it crosses the ancient town of Myra (36N17; 29E58), now known as Demre in modern Turkey. The Greeks who lived at Myra worshipped Artemis Eleutheria,[59] who was the protective goddess of the town—and also the goddess Athena was worshiped there: again indicative of the "seeding" of the Divine Feminine from yet another star in Orion, Alnilam. Myra is most famous as the town where St. Nicholas of Myra (the archetype of Father Christmas) was bishop in the fourth century AD. He died in Myra around the year 350.[60]

Following Alnilam's meridian further north, it crosses the ancient town (third millennium BC) of Kotyaeum, the city of the goddess Kotys, which is now known in modern Turkey as Kütahya (39N25; 29E56). Kotys was a Thracian goddess whose worship entailed much revelry, including midnight orgies. The Greek poet Aeschylus spoke of "adorable Kotys."[61] Again an ancient goddess worship, perhaps "seeded" from the star Alnilam.

In the north of Turkey the Alnilam meridian crosses the ancient town of Nicomedia, modern Izmit (40N47; 29E55), exactly on the geodetic equivalent of Alexandria (31N13; 29E55), but 9½° further north, corresponding to a distance of 660 miles (1,063 km). The ancient city was the capital of Bithynia at the time of King Zipoetas (third century BC). Nicomedia was rededicated by the son of King Zipoetas, Nicomedes I of Bithynia, in 264 BC. It was always

59 *Eleutheria* means "freedom" and Artemis Eleutheria was a form of the ancient Mother goddess Cybele, depicted with many breasts (like Artemis of Ephesus).

60 It is interesting to think of Father Christmas in connection with Alnilam. As mentioned already, the archetype for Father Christmas was St. Nicholas of Myra, who is the most popular saint in the Eastern Orthodox Church. The stories of his charitable acts took on legendary dimensions and one such act earned him the reputation of delivering gifts during the night.

61 From http://www.theoi.com/Thrakios/Kotys.html.

a significant city in this part of Asia Minor. However, it was shattered by a great earthquake on August 24 AD 358 and suffered further severe damage on account of the raging fire that swept through the city in the wake of the earthquake, after which the city was rebuilt, but on a smaller scale. A major earthquake struck again 1,641 years later on August 17, 1999, causing widespread damage in Izmit and resulting in the loss of about 17,000 lives, around 1,400 in Izmit itself, and the remainder in the surrounding region.

The ancient city housed several temples including one dedicated to the Phrygian goddess Cybele and another to the Egyptian goddess Isis. The temple of Isis was demolished by fire shortly after Pliny the Younger was appointed governor by the Emperor Trajan of the province of Bithynia around AD 112. Pliny reported to Trajan how, after the fire, worshipers thronged to the temples in Nicomedia to participate in the sacred rites there.[62]

From looking at the geodetic equivalent of Alnilam it can be seen that goddess worship thrived at various towns along this meridian: Myra, Kotyaeum, and Nicomedia—and, of course, in (and near) Alexandria. Isis was the mistress of the sea and patron of sailors. As such, she was the harbor goddess of Alexandria. Moreover, worship of Isis continued at the Iseum, temple of Isis, situated at Menouthis, about 15 miles (24 km) northeast of Alexandria, until the Iseum was closed in AD 414 by Bishop Cyril of Alexandria. Even after the closure of the Iseum, the cult of Isis continued at a secret Isis sanctuary at Menouthis until AD 486, when the sanctuary was destroyed by a pillaging mob of Christians who had been incited by the Patriarch of Alexandria. The temple of Isis was an important religious center in ancient Egypt to which thousands of pilgrims came from all over the ancient world. Menouthis (31N22; 30E04), on the Alnilam meridian, is thought to have been a suburb of the city of Canopus which, together with the nearby Egyptian city of Herakleion, thrived on commerce entering the Nile from the Mediterranean. However, a sudden, mysterious catastrophe plunged the two cities into the water some time around the middle

62 Pliny the Younger, *Letters* X.25 ff. http://www.fordham.edu/halsall/ancient/pliny-trajan1.html.

of the eighth century AD. Underwater archeological investigation at the site in the Mediterranean off the coast of Abu Qir (Aboukir) bay has revealed well-preserved houses, temples dedicated to Isis, Serapis, and Osiris, walls, a harbor, and large statues of the gods—all reflecting the wealth of the community from these ancient cities: Canopus (with Menouthis) and Herakleion,[63] that existed long before Alexander the Great founded Alexandria in 332 BC.

The underwater archeological survey that led to the discovery of the two submerged cities was announced in the year 2000. The cities are thought to go back possibly to about 1500 BC. On June 3, 2000 a large headless statue of Isis, dating from the fourth century BC, was recovered from the submerged temple of Isis in Menouthis, and has found a place in the new museum attached to the modern Library of Alexandria. A second huge statue of Isis—complete with head—which was also rescued from the waters of the submerged city, found in three pieces but now beautifully restored, is a new masterpiece now on display at the Egyptian museum in Cairo. In the words of Lucius Apuleius, one of the last great pagan philosophers, from his vision of Isis that he recorded in his work *The Golden Ass*, written around AD 200:

> Then by little and little I seemed to see the whole figure of her body, mounting out of the sea and standing before me, wherefore I purpose to describe her divine semblance, if the poverty of my human speech will suffer me, or her divine power give me eloquence thereto.

63 Herakleion was named after the classical hero Hercules (Heracles). Regarding the naming of Canopus and Menouthis: In Greek mythology Canopus was the helmsman of Menelaus, king of Sparta, who stopped in Herakleion during his return from Troy with his wife Helen. Canopus was bitten by a viper and died. He and his wife Menouthis were immortalized by having the cities named after them. It is said that the great astronomer Ptolemy made his observations from the terraced walls of the temple of Serapis in the city of Canopus. Interestingly, the star Canopus in the constellation of the Ship Argo marked the rudder on the side of the stern of the ship. Sirius and Canopus are the two brightest stars in the heavens, according to apparent brightness. Just as Sirius was seen by the Egyptians as the *star of Isis*, so Canopus was seen as the *star of Osiris*—see Allen, *Star Names*, pp. 67–72.

> First she had a great abundance of hair, dispersed and scattered about her neck, on the crown of her head she bare many garlands interlaced with flowers, in the middle of her forehead was a compass in fashion of a glass, or resembling the light of the Moon, in one of her hands she bore serpents, in the other, blades of corn, her vestment was of fine silk yielding divers colors, sometime yellow, sometime rosy, sometime flamy, and sometime (which troubled my spirit sore) dark and obscure, covered with a black robe in manner of a shield, and pleated in most subtle fashion at the skirts of her garments, the welts appeared comely, whereas here and there the stars glimpsed, and in the middle of them was placed the Moon, which shone like a flame of fire, round about the robe was a coronet or garland made with flowers and fruits.
>
> In her right hand she had a timbrell of brass, which gave a pleasant sound, in her left hand she bare a cup of gold, out of the mouth whereof the serpent Aspis lifted up his head, with a swelling throat, her perfumed feet were covered with shoes interlaced and wrought with victorious palm. Thus the divine shape breathing out the pleasant spice of fertile Arabia, disdained not with her divine voice to utter these words unto me: Behold Lucius I am come, thy weeping and prayers hath moved me to succour thee.
>
> I am she that is the natural mother of all things, mistress and governess of all the Elements, the initial progeny of worlds, chief of powers divine, Queen of heaven, the principal of the Gods celestial, the light of the goddesses. At my will the planets of the air, the wholesome winds of the seas, and the silences of hell be disposed.[64]

As mentioned earlier, there seems to be an identity between the Christian-Jewish *Sophia* and the Egyptian *Isis*. The Jews accounted for a significant proportion of the population of Alexandria. Philo of Alexandria (13 BC–AD 45), a Jewish philosopher and theologian, was a significant member of the Jewish community there, and in his works he describes the universe as the Son (Logos), whose Father is Yahweh and whose Mother is Sophia.[65] Philo, in his teaching concerning Sophia, elaborated on the Old Testament Books of Wisdom (such

64 Lucius Apuleius, *Metamorphoses or The Golden Ass*—Adlington's translation from the Latin (1566); see http://www.big.com.au/fallen/almagest.html.

65 Schipflinger, *Sophia Maria*, p. 41.

as Proverbs), in which Sophia is referred to, and yet he also drew upon Greek philosophy, particularly Stoicism, so as to develop an understanding of Sophia going beyond that of the Jewish tradition. Essentially, Sophia is Divine Wisdom, and since all learning is ideally an expression of wisdom, it transpires that not only was Isis the harbor goddess of Alexandria but also that—implicitly, as Sophia, Divine Wisdom—she was patron of the Library of Alexandria. Moreover, the notion of Sophia as the World Soul, which was developed in Alexandria, found its way into Neoplatonism and became transmitted to other parts of the ancient world.

It thus emerges that the Alnilam meridian has a deep connection with Isis-Sophia, whose mysteries were evidently "seeded" from this star. Like the other two stars in the belt of Orion—Alnitak and Mintaka—Alnilam has to do with Sophia. As discussed in chapter 4, the first cathedral erected on Russian soil, that of Holy Sophia in Novgorod (31E16), lies on the Alnitak meridian (31E08). And as mentioned earlier in this chapter, the great cathedral of Hagia Sophia in Constantinople, present day Istanbul (28E57), lies close to the Mintaka meridian (28E52). In this sense, both Alnitak and Mintaka also have a connection to Sophia, like Alnilam.

To be able to summarize the findings of Astrogeographia relating to the projection of Orion on Earth, it is important to have an understanding of the nature of the constellation of Orion, which in turn enables us to grasp the words of Hermes to Asclepius quoted earlier:

> Egypt is an image of heaven.... Even more than that, if the whole truth be told, our land is the temple of the entire cosmos.
> *Corpus Hermeticum*, "Asclepius" (3:29)

It cannot have been meant *literally* that Egypt is the "*temple of the entire cosmos*." However, since it is the reflection of the constellation of Orion on Earth—at least, of a significant part of Orion, from the belt downward—this has deeper cosmological implications which can be grasped against the background of the findings of modern astronomy concerning the structure of the Milky Way galaxy. In the light of Astrogeographia, the stars of Orion "seeded" various temples and mystery centers dedicated to the Divine Feminine, the exception being the star Betelgeuse marking Orion's right shoulder. For Betelgeuse "seeded" the temple of Solomon, which was dedicated to Yahweh as his "house." Interestingly, Betelgeuse is a unique star in the constellation of Orion. It is red and therefore has a different emanation, while all the other stars are blue or blue-white. The distance of Betelgeuse (634 light-years) is comparable to that of the other stars in Orion that we have been considering: (Saiph, 720 light-years; Rigel, 860 light-years; Bellatrix, 250 light-years; Mintaka, 900 light-years; Alnilam, 1,300 light-years; Alnitak, 736 light-years; Meissa, 1,100 light-years; Orion nebula, 1,344 light-years).

Some of these stars in Orion—for example, Alnitak, Alnilam, and Mintaka, comprising Orion's belt—belong to the *Orion OB1 association*, which for astronomers is a great assembly of hot, blue or blue-white massive stars of the spectral types O and B,[66] a loosely organized system not held together gravitationally but comprising stars born from the Orion cloud, which is a vast interstellar cloud of gas and dust centered approximately around the Orion nebula (M42). Betelgeuse does not belong to the Orion association. And it is of a quite different spectral type (M). Meissa, marking the head of Orion, while being of the spectral type O, might only belong to the Orion association in an extended sense. For Meissa is at the center of a faint, almost circular, large nebulous cloud, which may or may not be attached to the main cloud of the Orion association beneath it. The central position of the Orion nebula (M42) is highlighted as the birthplace of new stars entering into the Orion association. As we have seen though, while of significance as the "womb" or "creative source" within Orion, M42 does not play a role, in light of Astrogeographia, in the "seeding"

66 Here with a brief description of the spectral types O and B and also M, which is the spectral type of the star Betelgeuse:

O: blue; high temperature (33,000°K or greater); large mass; high luminosity; lines of ionized helium, nitrogen, oxygen, in addition to hydrogen. Examples: Zeta (ζ) Puppis, Lambda (λ) Orionis, Zeta (ζ) Orionis.

B: blue or blue-white, sometimes called "Orion stars"; temperature 10,000°K to 33,000°K; large mass; high luminosity; strong helium lines. Examples: Rigel, Spica, Algol A.

M: red stars; temperature less than 3700°K; many M-type variables show bright hydrogen lines; rich spectra showing many strong metallic lines with wide bands produced by titanium oxide. Examples: Betelgeuse, Antares.

of mysteries of the Divine Feminine on the Earth. It is obviously of enormous significance *within* the constellation of Orion, but evidently does not play such a role *outside* of the constellation—at least, not yet.

Lastly, the following table gives the archetypal projections (AP) of the main stars in Orion, together with the years when the latitudes of these stars last matched their archetypal latitude projections—i.e., when the star's projection was again as it was when the *thema mundi*, the birth horoscope of the Earth, took place.

Star	Year of last time	AP geographic latitude	geographic longitude
Meissa	4070 BC	18N53	30E12
Betelgeuse	4439 BC	16N24	35E13
Bellatrix	3867 BC	15N48	27E26
Alnitak	4138 BC	08N06	31E08
Alnilam	4048 BC	08N49	29E54
Mintaka	3967 BC	09N41	28E48
Saiph	4263 BC	01N11	32E50
Rigel	3557 BC	02N59	23E12

From the map of Sudan, showing the geographical locations of these archetypal projections, Orion was originally imprinted upon Sudan (North and South Sudan), with legs/feet extending into Uganda (Saiph) and the Democratic Republic of Congo (Rigel) (see map).

With its first historical mention, the region that later became known as Sudan was referred to as the Kingdom of Kush. Because of precession, the projection of Orion gradually shifted northward across Egypt, and more and more Egypt came to have a dominating significance influence over the Kingdom of Kush. Egyptian culture and religion became increasingly important in the region. It is interesting to consider this development in relation to the shift of Orion's projection northward across Egypt. In this connection we may also recall, as pointed out earlier in this chapter, that when Meissa's historical projection on its northward trajectory reached the Black Sea (approximately the latitude of Constantinople) around AD 1453, the Turks conquered Constantinople and changed its name to Istanbul.

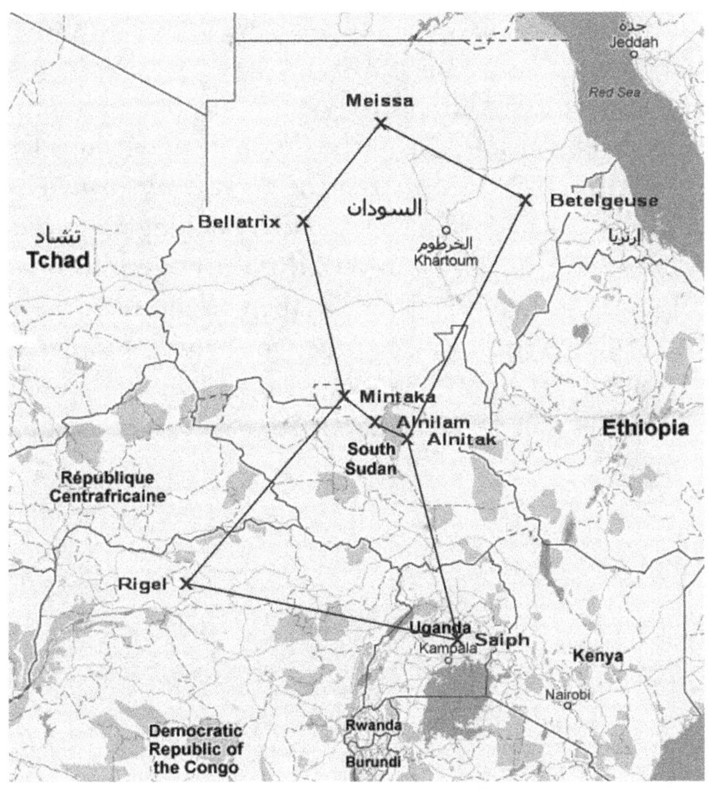

Map of Sudan

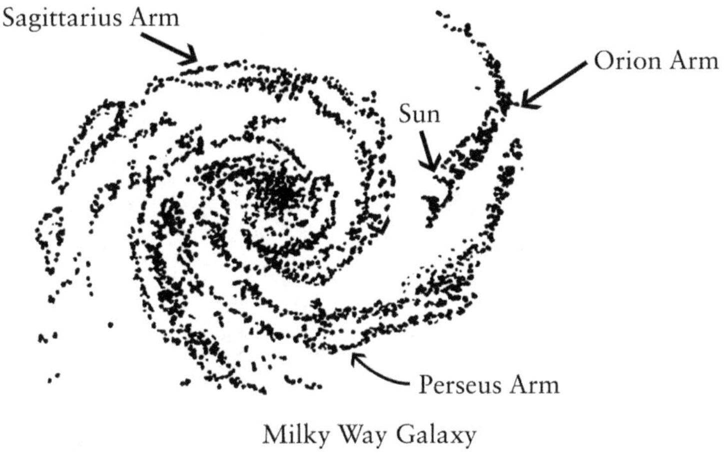

The Galactic Center with the Spiral Arms of the Milky Way

The Orion mystery is vast, and what we are able to touch upon here is only scratching the surface of this mystery. As we can see from the figure on page 173, our solar system is located within the Milky Way galaxy on the inside edge of the *Orion arm*, which is located in turn between the *Perseus arm* and the *Sagittarius arm*. The Orion arm is thus our "local part" of the galaxy. Looking up to the constellation of Orion, we are gazing toward the heart of our local arm, and perhaps the Orion nebula (M42) can be considered to be the very center of the Orion arm. In using the word *cosmos* to describe this local part of our galaxy,[67] the Orion arm, it is in this sense that the words of Hermes can be understood: "our land is the temple of the entire cosmos."

67 *Cosmos* for the Greeks denoted the entire visible, sense-perceptible world. Translated into the modern world, *cosmos* could be taken to denote the entire world visible to the naked eye (without telescopes, etc.).

Chapter 8

Mapping Astrogeographia for the Whole Earth

This chapter draws together many individual stars with their places on the Earth, as well as many constellations with their regions on the Earth. It then shows how to construct from these an Astrogeographia map connecting the starry heavens with the whole Earth.

Figure 1: The beautiful, domed Hagia Sophia in Istanbul mirrors Meissa in the head of Orion. It was built under the orders of the Byzantine Emperor Justinian, who on its completion in AD 537 *was said to have remarked: "Solomon, I have surpassed thee."*

The Sidereal Zodiac and the Twelve Zodiac Reference Points on the Ecliptic

The sidereal zodiac consists of the twelve zodiac constellations, each 30° wide. The observed path of the Sun through the constellations is called the ecliptic and this defines 0° sidereal latitude. The zodiac belt spans the band of sidereal latitude from 8° south to 8° north of the ecliptic, thereby including the twelve constellations (see figure 2). The initial points of the constellations are Aries (0AR00), Taurus (0TA00), Gemini (0GE00) and so on. These can be taken as twelve zodiac reference points on the ecliptic.

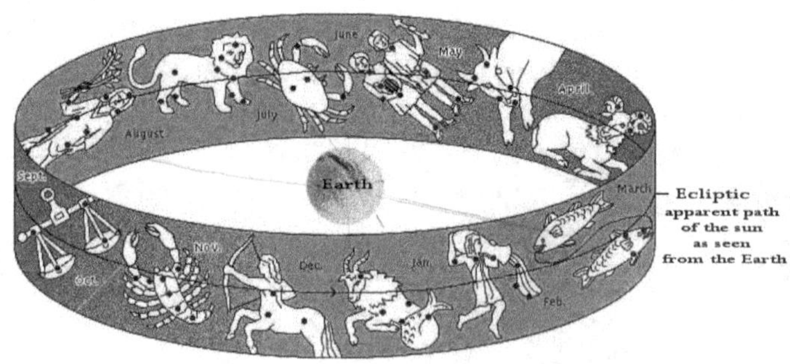

Figure 2: The zodiac belt spans the band of sidereal latitude from 8° south to 8° north of the ecliptic, thus including the twelve constellations.

A Simple Astrogeographia Map Based on the Twelve Reference Points

A simple Astrogeographia map can be constructed from the twelve zodiac reference points by applying the equations of latitude and longitude (see later in this chapter) to their stellar coordinates. The geographic points thus obtained are listed in table 1. They are also shown plotted on a flat map of the Earth in figure 3, with the constellations labelled AR (Aries), TA (Taurus), GE (Gemini) and so on. Figures 4, 5 and 6 show planetary views of an alternative three-dimensional Astrogeographia map of the Earth. In these

sidereal latitude	sidereal longitude	geographic latitude	geographic longitude
0N00	0AR00	41N22	28W48
0N00	0TA00	50N44	1E12
0N00	0GE00	55N07	31E12
0N00	0CN00	52N57	61E12
0N00	0LE00	45N03	91E12
0N00	0VI00	33N52	121E12
0N00	0LI00	22N12	151E12
0N00	0SC00	12N50	178W48
0N00	0SG00	8N27	148W48
0N00	0CP00	10N36	118W48
0N00	0AQ00	18N30	88W48
0N00	0PI00	29N41	58W48

Table 1: The twelve reference points on the ecliptic and their geographic projections (AD 2000)

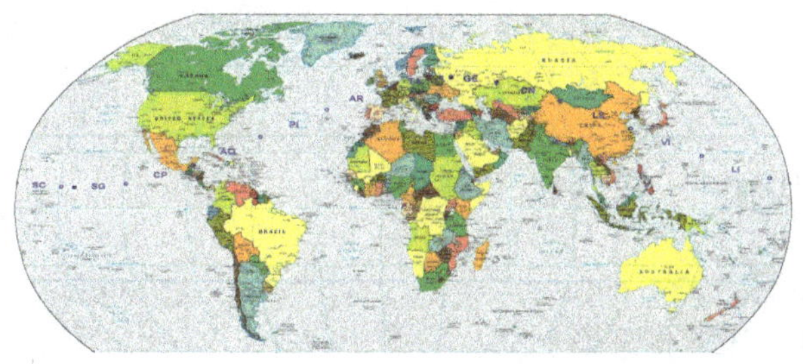

Figure 3: A simple Astrogeographia map showing ecliptic and the twelve zodiac constellations (AD 2000)

maps, the projected ecliptic appears as a white circle on the surface of the Earth.

In the flat map of figure 3, the projected ecliptic appears to be a kind of "wave" on the surface of the Earth. The three-dimensional views in figures 4, 5 and 6 reveal, however, that its true form is a circle embedded in the surface of the Earth. This circle is actually a "small circle" of the Earth because its plane does not pass through the center of the Earth. By way of contrast, a "great circle" of the Earth has a plane that passes through the center of the Earth, e.g., the equator. In figure 5, the white circle of the projected ecliptic is seen tilted toward the yellow latitude circle through Jerusalem (31N47) at an angle equal to the Earth's axial tilt of 23.5°. This means that the angle between the projected ecliptic and the Earth's equator is also 23.5°, because the Jerusalem latitude circle is parallel to the equator.

The most northerly point of the projected ecliptic is at (55N13, 36E28), about 56 miles (90 km) southwest of Moscow (see figure 4). This corresponds in the stars to the AD 2000 summer solstice point on the ecliptic at 5GE16 (see table 2). Similarly the most southerly point is at (8N20, 143W32), about 1,300 miles (2,090 km) southeast of Hawaii (see figure 6). This corresponds to the AD 2000 winter solstice point on the ecliptic at sidereal 5SG16. These two extreme latitude points are shown as filled dots in figures 4 and 6, about 6° to the east of the 30E00 and 150W00 meridians respectively.

The points on the ecliptic which are mid-latitude between these maximum and minimum points are the vernal equinox (5PI16) projecting to (31N47, 53W32), about 665 miles (1,070 km) east of the Bermudas; and the autumnal equinox (5VI16) projecting to (31N47, 126E28), in the middle of the East China Sea. These are the two points of intersection of the projected ecliptic with the 31N47 latitude line through Jerusalem (see figure 5).

point on the ecliptic	sidereal latitude	sidereal longitude	geographic latitude	geographic longitude	projecting to
vernal equinox	0N00	5PI16	31N47	53W32	665 miles (1,070 km) E of Bermudas
summer solstice	0N00	5GE16	55N13	36E28	56 miles (90 km) SW of Moscow
autumnal equinox	0N00	5VI16	31N47	126E28	middle of the East China Sea
winter solstice	0N00	5SG16	8N20	143W32	1,300 miles (2,090 km) SE of Hawaii

Table 2: The four cardinal points on the ecliptic and their geographic projections (AD 2000)

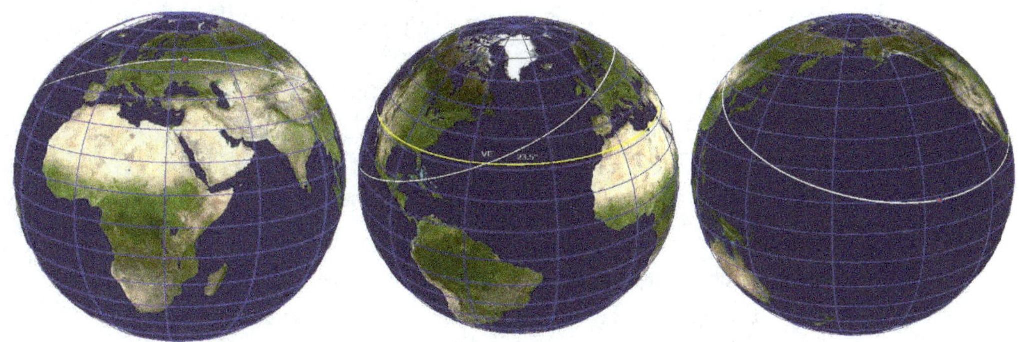

Figure 4 (left): Planetary view from above Europe and Africa showing most northerly point of the projected ecliptic (filled dot on the white circle), about 56 miles (90 km) southwest of Moscow.

Figure 5 (center): Planetary view from above the Atlantic Ocean showing the vernal equinox (VE) and the 23.5° angle between the projected ecliptic (white circle) and the 31N47 latitude line through Jerusalem (yellow circle).

Figure 6 (right): Planetary view from above the Pacific Ocean showing the most southerly point of the projected ecliptic, the filled dot on the white circle, about 1,300 miles (2,090 km) southeast of Hawaii.

The origin of the sidereal zodiac (0AR00, 0N00) projects to geographic (41N22, 28W48). This is close to Fayal Island, one of the main administrative centers of the Azores in the Atlantic Ocean.

The flat and three-dimensional maps in figures 3 to 6 have been constructed specifically for the star declinations of AD 2000. However an Astrogeographia map can be constructed for any year by basing the calculations for the equations of latitude and longitude (see appendix 1) on the observed declinations of the stars for that given year. When these equations are calculated in a stepped sequence over the 25,920-year precession cycle, a picture emerges of the living, breathing relationship between the heavens and the Earth:

- The equation of longitude shows that the movement of the star's projection during the whole 25,920-year precession cycle remains fixed on a particular geographic longitude meridian, apart from very small east–west shifts in this meridian due to the proper motion of stars. These shifts are typically 0.1° over thousands of years.

- The projection of each star is found to be moving over the surface of the Earth alternately north and south in a slow oscillating manner, 23½° north and 23½° south of a mid-latitude point. The equation of latitude shows that these large north and south movements are a result of the cyclical variation in declination of all stars, which arises in turn because declination is observed from a precessing Earth.
- The speed of the north and south movement over the surface of the Earth during the 25,920-year cycle varies according to the momentary distance of the projected star from its mid-latitude point. As an example see figure 7, which is the AD 2000 map of the ecliptic.
- The longer the arrow, the faster the projected star is moving. Maximum speed is reached when the projected star is aligned over its mid-latitude point, which is the intersection of the projected ecliptic with the 31N47 latitude line through Jerusalem. Minimum (zero) speed is reached when the projected star reverses its direction of movement, as it passes through its most northerly point (55N13), or through its most southerly point (8N20).
- The directions of the arrows show that in AD 2000, the stars on the half-ecliptic over America, the Atlantic Ocean, and Europe are currently moving upward on their fixed-longitude meridians. At the same time, the stars on the half-ecliptic over Asia and the western Pacific Ocean are currently moving downward on their fixed longitude meridians.

Figure 7: Every star moves alternately north and south on its fixed longitude meridian. The longer the arrow, the faster the star is moving. (AD 2000 map of the ecliptic)

As a result of the gentle rocking back and forth of the Earth in its precession, the position of the summer solstice point is observed to move all the way around the ecliptic, traversing the zodiac constellations in reverse order (see figure 8). This moving summer solstice point is always the most northerly point on the projected ecliptic (see table 2). Consequently as the summer solstice point moves around the ecliptic, the most northerly point of the projected ecliptic also moves. It rotates all the way around the Earth in a westward direction once every 25,920 years and at a constant latitude of 55N13 during this time. The westward direction corresponds to the fact that the summer solstice traverses the zodiac constellations in reverse order.

In fact, the projected ecliptic rotates as a whole in this same constant latitude way, westward all the way around the Earth every 25,920 years. To understand how the projected ecliptic is rotating as a whole around the Earth, consider the following:

- As the observed position of the summer solstice point moves around the ecliptic, it continues to come into alignment with new stars on the ecliptic. At the moment of its alignment with a given star, the angle between that star and the celestial equator (i.e., the star's declination) will be at its maximum (figure 8). From the equation of latitude, the star on the ecliptic with maximum declination corresponds to the most northerly point of the projected ecliptic.
- As the summer solstice point moves right around the ecliptic it comes into progressive alignment with a circle of stars having a full 360° sweep of sidereal longitude. By the equation of longitude, this causes the most northerly point of the projected ecliptic to rotate through a full 360° sweep of geographic longitude. As stated above, this is all the way around the Earth in a westward direction, which corresponds to the movement of the summer solstice in reverse order through the zodiac constellations.
- It is important to note in the above that the stars, as *fixed points in the heavens*, cannot themselves when projected rotate around the Earth, because as described above they remain during the whole precession cycle fixed on their particular geographic longitude meridian, apart from very small shifts

in this meridian due to the proper motion of stars. Rather it is a *moving point in the heavens*, (the moving summer solstice point) which moves right around the ecliptic, and under conditions that result in it always projecting to the most northerly point on the projected ecliptic.

- It is the projection of this *moving point in the heavens* that is found to be rotating around the Earth.
- The observed positions of the vernal equinox, winter solstice and autumnal equinox likewise move around the ecliptic in the same constant latitude way as the summer solstice.

To get a clearer picture of this rotation of the projected ecliptic as a whole around the Earth, a 30° part rotation is shown in figure 9. "G" marks the most northerly point on the ecliptic occurring in 160 BC at (55N13, 66E28), just north of Kazakhstan. This is the projection of sidereal 5CN16 on the ecliptic. "E" marks the same northerly point 2,160 years later in AD 2000 at (55N13, 36E28), southwest of Moscow. This is the projection of sidereal 5GE16 on the ecliptic. The movement in geographic longitude from "G" to "E" = 66E28 - 36E28 = 30° westward.

From the descriptions above, it is possible to see how the Astrogeographia map changes from year to year in a living way. This is

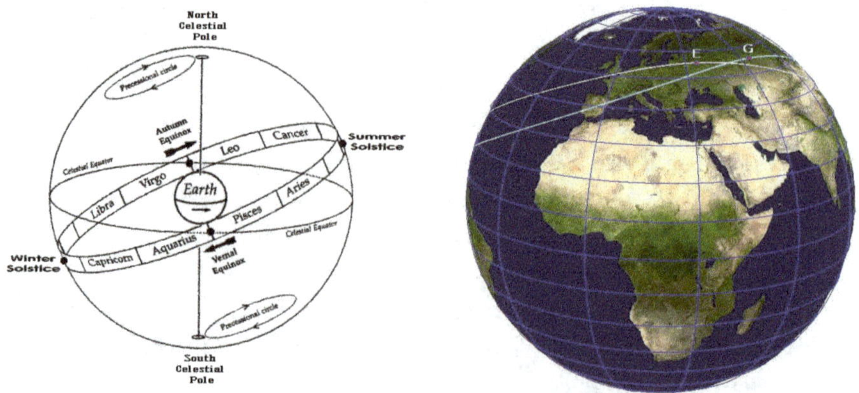

Figure 8 (left): The vernal equinox Sun is observed as a moving point on the ecliptic. It moves progressively backward through the stars of the ecliptic, traversing the zodiac constellations in reverse order over 25,920 years.

Figure 9 (right): 30° of rotation of the projected ecliptic (compare with Figure 4). "G" = most northerly point on the ecliptic in 160 BC, "E" = same point 2,160 years later in AD 2000.

because the Earth itself precesses or breathes within the sphere of the stars. If the Earth's present precession cycle of 25,920 years resulted from the departure of the Moon from the Earth during the Lemurian period (see the section later in this chapter "The vernal equinox meridian and the birth horoscope of the world"), then a deeper meaning is indicated for these living changes in the Astrogeographia map over time.

Each Constellation Projects onto Its Unique Region of the Earth

The Astrogeographia map in figure 3 shows that the projection of the constellation of Aries covers a geographic region 30° wide in longitude, stretching from the Azores (28W48) to slightly east of the Greenwich meridian (1E12), marked approximately by Dover in South East England. This region covers nearly the whole of Britain, exactly as Ptolemy had described it in his Tetrabiblos[1] of AD 150. In this foundational work, he states that Aries "has familiarity with" and "appears to exert sympathy on" the country of Britain (see chapter 5). Thus Ptolemy's description provides a clear confirmation of this initial finding of Astrogeographia.

In Ptolemy's *Geographia,*[2] he constructed maps of the then known world in which he was the first to use a scale that was something like our modern longitude and latitude. His longitude had 180 of his "degrees" covering what was, in his time, the whole of the known world. He gave a list of 8,000 cities and other localities and specified their locations in terms of his "longitudes" and "latitudes."[3] His original maps have not survived, but reconstructions were made in later centuries from the coordinates in his text—e.g., the fifteenth-century reconstruction in figure 10. At the bottom of this map we see that the longitude scale has a 0° origin in the far west near the Canary Islands and stretches from there across to the far east and China at 180°. It is interesting that the longitude origin of Ptolemy's map is to the west of Europe in the Atlantic. Also that the first three steps on his longitude grid (i.e., one twelfth of the total longitude steps) are seen covering the region of Britain.

1 See Ptolemy, *Tetrabiblos* II, 3, pp. 157–161.

2 See Ptolemy, *Geography*.

3 See Evans, *History and Practice of Ancient Astronomy*, p. 102.

Figure 10: Map of the "known world," reconstructed from Ptolemy's longitude & latitude coordinates

These observations possibly indicate that Ptolemy's map was actually an Astrogeographia map, i.e., with three grid steps for each of the twelve zodiac constellations beginning at 0° Aries. The twelve classical gods of the winds appear equally spaced around the edge of this map indicating the raying in of influences from the twelve directions of space, again a possible allusion to the zodiac.

Returning to the Astrogeographia map in figure 3, it is seen that the constellation of Leo projects in geographic longitude over China, Cancer over India, Gemini over Persia, and Taurus over Egypt. The equation of longitude shows that the 30° wide constellations remain stably connected over long periods of time with these 30° wide regions of the Earth. It is interesting that these correspondences are exactly as described by Rudolf Steiner for the influences of the zodiac constellations during the Atlantean and post-Atlantean cultural ages.[4] Specifically, the final age of Atlantis with its migration to Central Asia (western China) was under the influence of the constellation of Leo. After this, followed the first post-Atlantean cultural age of India (7227 BC to 5067 BC), which was under the influence of the constellation of Cancer. Then came the second cultural age of Persia (5067 BC to 2907 BC) under the influence of the constellation of Gemini. And finally, the third cultural age of Egypt (2907 BC to 747 BC) under the influence of the constellation of Taurus. Additionally the map in figure 3 shows the constellation of Capricorn projecting in geographic longitude over a major part of North America. As described by Rudolf Steiner, the future seventh (and last) cultural age of post-Atlantis (AD 5734 to AD 7894) will be centred on America and under the influence of the constellation of Capricorn. Thus the findings of Astrogeographia again receive clear confirmation, this time from the insights of Rudolf Steiner concerning the cultural ages of evolution.

The complete Astrogeographia Map of 82 constellations

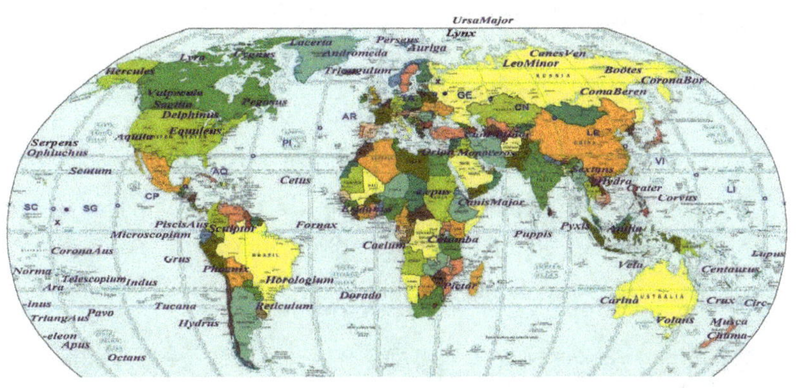

Figure 11: Astrogeographia map of 82 constellations (AD 2000)
(see larger version of map on page 298)

To construct an Astrogeographia map of the full heavens, the projections of the non-zodiacal (outside of the zodiac belt) constellations

4 Rudolf Steiner describes the first three post-Atlantean cultural ages as India, Persia and Egypt. These were under the signs of Cancer, Gemini and Taurus respectively. See Rudolf Steiner, *Ancient Myths*, pp. 51-58.

are added to the map of the 12 zodiac constellations in figure 3. The equations of latitude and longitude are applied to the stellar coordinates of the center of each of the 70 non-zodiacal constellations. In this way a complete Astrogeographia map of 82 constellations emerges (see figure 11).

When this complete map is studied in detail, many remarkable geographic correspondences can be found both for individual stars and for whole constellations. Some of these correspondences are tabulated below, including those described in other chapters of the book. Tables 3 and 4 show longitude alignment correspondences. Tables 5 and 6 show simultaneous longitude and latitude alignment correspondences.

Constellation	Longitude Alignment with
Aries	Britain, Spain, Africa (west), Iceland, Greenland (east)
Taurus	Europe, Africa (central), Russia (west)
Gemini	Iran (Persia), Iraq, Africa (east), Saudi Arabia, Syria, Turkey, Russia
Cancer	India, Pakistan, Afghanistan, Kazakhstan, Russia
Leo	China, Southeast Asia, Australia (west), Mongolia, Siberia
Virgo	Japan, Korea, Australia (central), Philippines, New Guinea, Siberia
Libra	New Zealand, Australia (east), Siberia
Scorpio	Alaska (west), Hawaii
Sagittarius	U.S. & Canada (west), Alaska (east)
Capricorn	U.S. & Canada (central), Mexico
Aquarius	U.S. & Canada (east), Central America, Caribbean, South America (west)
Pisces	South America (east), Greenland

Table 3: Longitude alignments for the zodiac constellations

Constellation	Star	Longitude Alignment with
Orion	Rigel (Beta Orionis)	Seven Rila Lakes, Bulgaria
	Saiph (Kappa Orionis)	Temple of Isis at Philae near Aswan, Egypt
	Mintaka (Delta Orionis)	El Alamein, Egypt
Canis Major	Sirius (Alpha Canis Majoris)	Persia (present day Iran), Yemen, Kazakhstan, Russia
Ursa Major	7 prominent stars of Ursa Major, associated with the Seven Holy Rishis of ancient India	India & China

Table 4: Longitude alignments for some specific stars

The Great Bear (Ursa Major) appears longitudinally aligned over India and western China. Its seven prominent stars have been associated since antiquity with the Seven Holy Rishis. These were the founders of the ancient Indian culture and their teachings were recorded in the Vedas.

Figure 12: Temple of Isis (island of Philae) is longitudinally aligned with the star Saiph in the Orion constellation.

Constellation	Geographic Region	Star	Bayer Designation	Geographic Location
Aries	Britain, Spain	Botein	Delta Arietis	Glastonbury, England
Taurus	Europe, Russia (west)	Aldebaran	Alpha Tauri	Vienna, Austria
		Pleiades	Messier object M45	west coast of Denmark
		El Nath	Beta Tauri	St Petersburg, Russia
Orion	Egypt, Israel, Turkey	Meissa (Head of Orion)	Lambda Orionis	Istanbul, Turkey
		Betelgeuse (1371 BC)	Alpha Orionis	Temple of Solomon, Israel
		Betelgeuse (AD 2085)	Alpha Orionis	Hattusha, ancient Turkey
		Bellatrix	Gamma Orionis	Ephesus, ancient Turkey
		Alnitak	Zeta Orionis	Pyramid of Giza, Egypt
		Alnilam	Epsilon Orionis	Alexandria, Egypt
Aquila	U.S. (west)	Altair	Alpha Aquilae	Salt Lake City, U.S.
Pegasus	U.S. & Canada (east)	Baham (Head of Pegasus)	Theta Pegasi	Washington DC, U.S.
Capricorn	Mexico	Lambda Capricorn	Lambda Capricorni	Chichen Itza, Mexico
Phoenix	Peru, Bolivia, Chile	Epsilon Phoenix	Epsilon Phoenicis	Machu Picchu, Peru

Table 5: Simultaneous longitude and latitude alignments for some specific stars

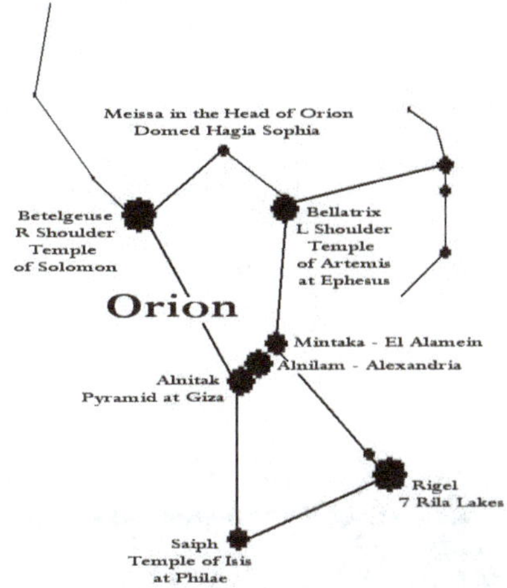

Figure 13: Orion, heavenly appearance of Osiris, archetype of the human being, projects over the region of the Middle East.

Figure 14: Machu Picchu in Peru is aligned with the epsilon star in the constellation of Phoenix.

Constellation	Longitude and Latitude Alignment with
Southern Cross (Crux) and the Southern Pointers	Australia & New Zealand
Hercules	Alaska

Table 6: Simultaneous longitude and latitude alignments for some non-zodiac constellations

Figure 15: Southern Cross (Crux) constellation and the Southern Pointers project to Australia and New Zealand

The Indian Ocean, Lemuria and the Legend of the Golden Fleece

The constellations Carina, Vela, Puppis and Pyxis (see figure 16) appear in the Astrogeographia map around the northern and eastern edges of the Indian Ocean, which is the former site of the ancient continent of Lemuria.[5] Carina, Vela, and Puppis were originally listed in Ptolemy's 48 classical constellations as one very large constellation called the 'Argo Navis' (see figure 17). For the ancients, this constellation was the Argo, the mythical ship in which Jason and the Argonauts sailed on their heroic journey to fetch the Golden

5 Certain islands to the South of Asia and the North of Australia are evidences of the metamorphosed remains of old Lemuria. See Steiner, *Esoteric Cosmology*, p. 91.

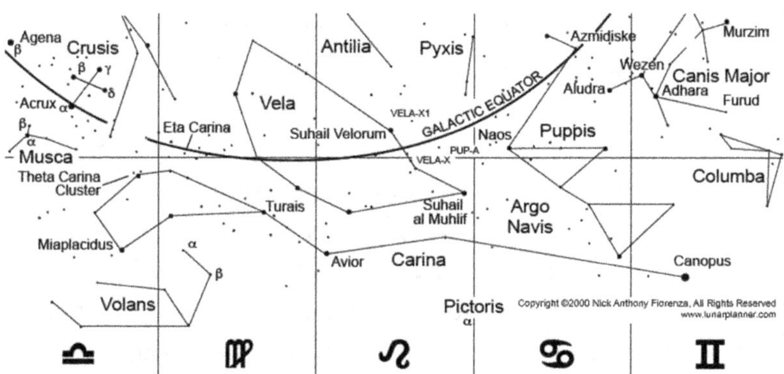

Figure 16: Argo Navis: Carina, Vela, Puppis and Pyxis constellations (Fiorenza Star Map)

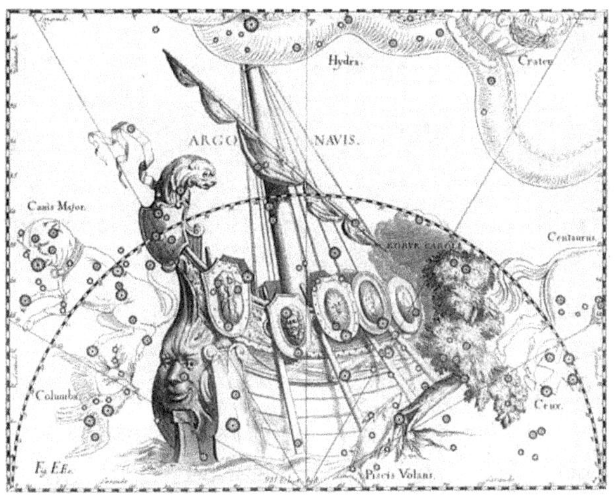

Figure 17: Argo Navis constellation. The large star at the base of the prow is Canopus (Carina constellation)

Fleece of the Sacred Ram from Colchis in Georgia. This constellation was however so large that in 1752 it was considered unwieldy and subdivided into three smaller constellations by the French astronomer Nicolas Louis de Lacaille. These he named Carina (the Argo's keel or hull), Vela (the Argo's sails) and Puppis (the Argo's poop deck). To complete the picture, the constellation Pyxis was already considered since antiquity to be the Argo's mast.

The Golden Fleece is described by Rudolf Steiner as a prototype for the transformation or purification of the astral body, firstly into sentient soul[6] and then into spirit self. It is a living symbol of our original golden radiant astral body at the time when it was still undimmed by the approaching egotism of humanity. Thus the voyage of Jason was in order to regain something infinitely precious to humanity, the lost innocence of the human soul. For the full recovery of the Golden Fleece on into the future, humanity will have to overcome terrible forces. In the story of the voyage of the Argonauts, its rescue from the claws of the dragon that is guarding it only becomes possible when the wisdom of humanity's self-developed consciousness (represented in the myth by Medea, the daughter of King Aietes of Colchis) comes to the aid of Jason with its magic power, lulling the dragon to sleep.

The astral body began to form on ancient Moon[7] and developed further during the Lemurian period of Earth evolution. As Lemuria was centred on the Indian Ocean, it is a remarkable finding for Astrogeographia that the four constellations of the Argo ship project onto the regions around the edge of the Indian Ocean. Further development of the astral body occurred during the third post-Atlantean cultural age of Egypt (a furthering of ancient Moon and Lemuria). The special task of the Egyptian age was to begin the transformation of the astral body into sentient soul. Rudolf Steiner remarked that the voyage of the Argonauts was "an actual historical voyage" that took place at the same time as the Trojan War.[8] This is the time of transition from the sentient soul age of Egypt under the sign of the Bull, to the fourth cultural age of Greece, under the sign of the Lamb, or Ram. This new age brought with it the approach of the Christ Being to the Earth, hence the unique task of evolution at this stage of transition.

---

6 See Steiner, *Christianity as Mystical Fact*, pp. 74–76. See also his *Egyptian Myths and Mysteries*, pp. 150–151.

7 Rudolf Steiner describes the first four stages of planetary development of the Earth as ancient Saturn, ancient Sun, ancient Moon and our present stage called Earth. See Steiner, *Occult Science, an Outline*, pp. 110ff.

8 Steiner, *Egyptian Myths and Mysteries*, p. 72.

Placed into this wider context of the cultural ages, we see how the voyage to retrieve the Golden Fleece during the classical Greek period is a prefiguring of the search for the Grail during the Middle Ages and on into modern times, a living symbol of modern Christian initiation. The fruits of this search will manifest in the sixth cultural age following our own present age, an age that will be centred on Russia and be under the guidance of the Sophia Being. Its task will be the further transformation of the astral body from sentient soul into spirit self.

The Atlantic Ocean, Atlantis and the Legend of Perseus and Andromeda

In the Astrogeographia map, the projection of the constellation Cetus the sea monster appears at the very center of the Atlantic Ocean, the former site of the ancient continent of Atlantis. The constellations Perseus and Andromeda also appear around the northern edge of the Atlantic Ocean.

Perseus was the Greek hero who married Andromeda after first rescuing her from the sea monster Cetus. Cetus had been sent by Poseidon in retribution for Queen Cassiopeia declaring herself more beautiful than the sea nymphs. Andromeda was the daughter of Cepheus and Cassiopeia, mythical king and queen of Ethiopia. After her death, Andromeda was placed by Athena amongst the constellations in the northern sky, near those of Perseus, Cepheus and Cassiopeia. As seen in figures 11 and 18, these four constellations are all at far northern latitudes and close together within the sidereal longitudes of Aries and Taurus.

In The Sophia Teachings[9] by Robert Powell, Perseus is described as representing the new and progressive faculty of intelligence; and Andromeda is the human soul at risk from Cetus, the sea monster from the depths—the atavistic force of the will, a remnant from Atlantis. At the very moment when Andromeda was bound to a rock and about to be devoured by Cetus, Perseus makes use of his newly developing intelligence and holds up the head of Medusa (the ancient power of clairvoyance) to the sea monster, thus turning it to stone.

9 Powell, *The Sophia Teachings, Emergence of the Divine Feminine in Our Time*, pp. 27–29.

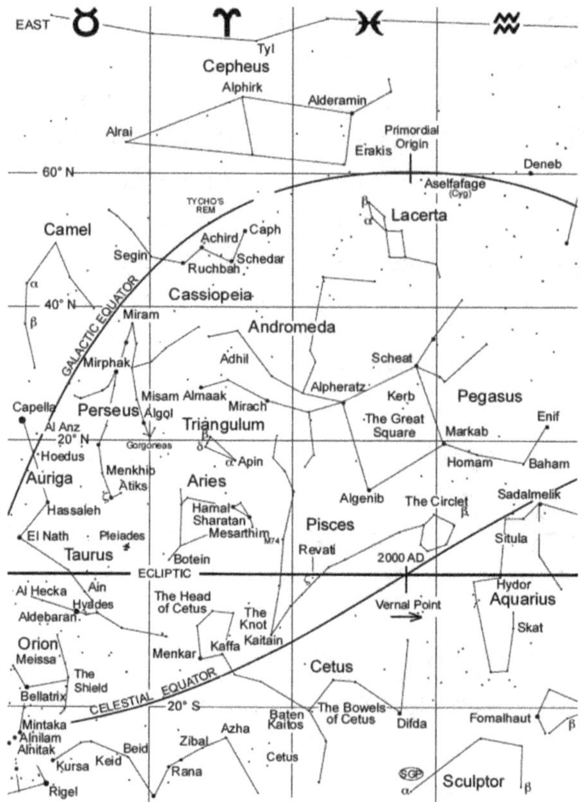

Figure 18: Perseus, Andromeda, Cepheus, Cassiopeia, Cetus and Pegasus constellations (Fiorenza Star Map)

Some versions of the mythology describe Perseus as the ancestor of the Persian peoples, who are a part of post-Atlantean evolution. The heroic deeds of Perseus can be seen as preparing for the task of post-Atlantis, which was (and still is) the development and transformation of thinking. In this context, it is interesting to note that in later legends Perseus was depicted as the rider of Pegasus the winged horse, a picture of human thinking taking flight and reaching the heights of spiritualized thinking. In relation to the task of the development of thinking, it is also interesting that the map of archetypal projections of the stars (see figure 27) shows Perseus and Andromeda projecting archetypically over the region of Europe. In chapter 10, the Externsteine in Europe are described as the planetary Jupiter chakra, which can be seen as an archangelic center for the light of thinking, related to the task of the

European peoples to work at the development of thinking. With the legends of Perseus and Andromeda, it is again a remarkable finding of Astrogeographia that all six of the constellations mentioned in them project to the region of the Atlantic Ocean, the former site of Atlantis.

The Astrogeographia Equations of Latitude and Longitude

Rudolf Steiner has stated in the Astronomy lectures,

> According to the Ptolemaic concept—for example, out there is the blue sphere, and on it a point (figure X)—we should have to think of a polar point in the center of the Earth. Every point of the sphere would have its reflected point in the Earth's center.
>
> The stars, in effect, would be here (figure Y). So that in thinking of the sphere concentrated in the center of the Earth, we should have to think of it in the following way: The pole of this star is here, of this one here, and so on (figure Y). We come then, to a complete mirroring of what is outside, in the interior of the Earth. Picturing this in regard to each individual planet, we have say Jupiter, and then a "polar Jupiter" within the Earth. We come to something, which works outward from within the Earth in the way that Jupiter works in the Earth's environment. We arrive at a mirroring (in reality it is the opposite way round), but I will now describe it like this: a mirroring of what is outside the Earth into the interior of the Earth.[10]

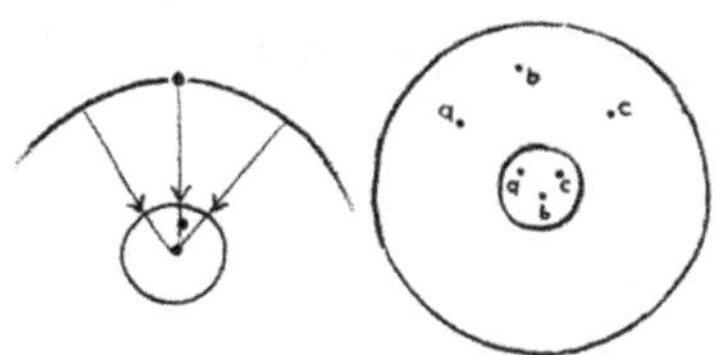

Figure X *Figure Y*

The basic idea of Astrogeographia, that there is a relationship between the stars and particular locations on Earth, was known to Ptolemy in AD 150 and was probably also known to the ancient Babylonians. The description given above by Rudolf Steiner of the

10 Steiner, *The Relationship of the Diverse Branches of Natural Science to Astronomy,* lect. 10., p. 117.

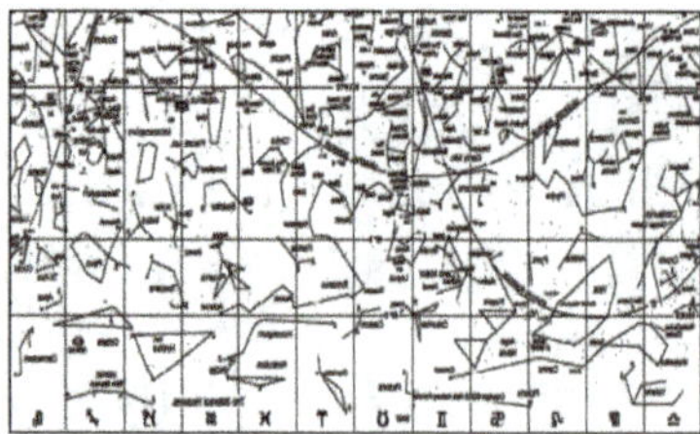
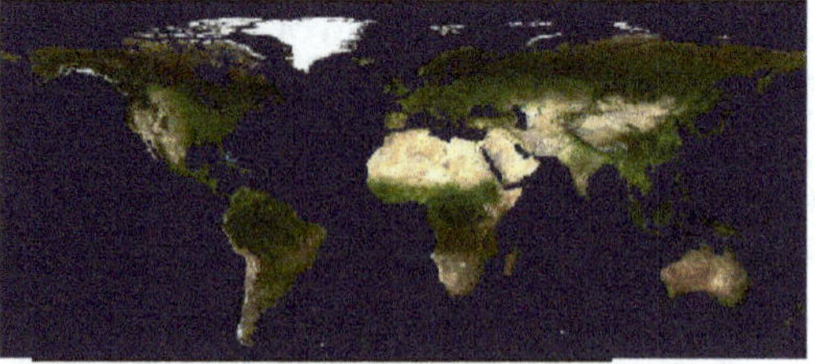

Figure 19A: Mercator's map of the stars (Fiorenza)
Figure 19B. Mercator's map of the Earth

mirroring of each star outside the Earth to a specific point within the Earth provides the essential geometric idea needed to place the new science of Astrogeographia on a clear foundation. From this description a line can be imagined for each star—a line which joins the star to the center of the Earth. This line also passes through the star's mirror point inside the Earth and most importantly it passes through the Earth's surface at a particular location. In this way, each star is uniquely corresponded with its place on Earth.

It could at first be thought that a single such correspondence between a star and its place on Earth would be enough to solve for a complete map of all the stars and their corresponding locations on Earth. Take for example the correspondence of the star Alnitak with Giza in Egypt. A transparent map of the stars could be overlaid on a map of the Earth and positioned by sliding it in latitude and longitude until Alnitak is lined up over Giza (see figures 19A, 19B, 19C). This composite map could then be searched to see if it contained any new stellar-terrestrial correspondences. Although this approach is a good starting point for conceptualizing the basic idea of Astrogeographia, it has not in practice led to any new findings of interest.

An alternative approach is to work with two independent alignments: a separate latitude alignment (or its equivalent in stellar coordinates, declination), as well as a separate longitude alignment. This second approach has been found to lead to numerous new correspondences and insights concerning the relationships between the stars and the Earth. As a result, this approach is the one adopted as the basis for the Astrogeographia model in this book. The separate declination and longitude alignments are described in detail below as the first and second reference alignments for Astrogeographia.

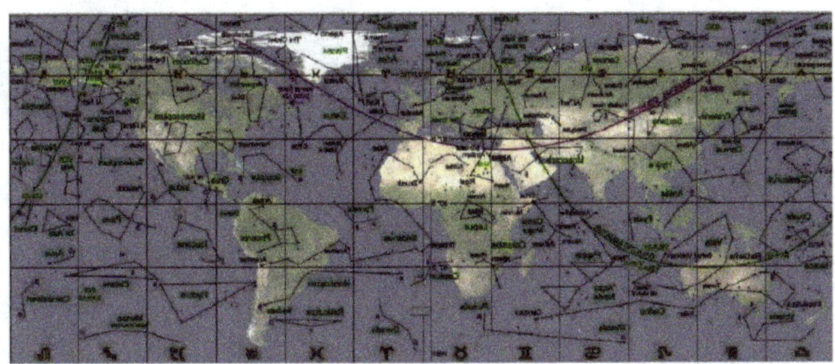

Figure 19C: Map A overlaid on map B—
Alnitak in the Orion constellation is lined up over Giza.

First and Second Astrogeographia Reference Alignments

The first Astrogeographia reference alignment aligns the 0° declination stars so that they are always directly over the 31N47 latitude line passing through Jerusalem. The basis of this alignment is the identification of Jerusalem with "the Middle of the Earth" (see chapter 9).

The second Astrogeographia reference alignment aligns the star Alnitak so that it is always directly over the 31E08 longitude meridian passing through the Great Pyramid of Giza. Because of the difference in sidereal longitude between Alnitak and Betelgeuse, this means that the star Betelgeuse will be always directly over the 35E13 longitude meridian, which passes through Jerusalem. See figures 22 to 24 for these alignments.

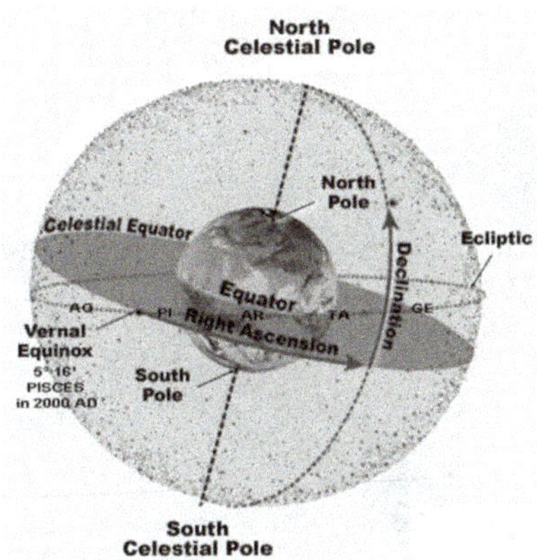

Figure 20: The 0° declination stars are those on the Celestial Equator, which is the projection of the Earth's equator outward onto the sphere of the stars.

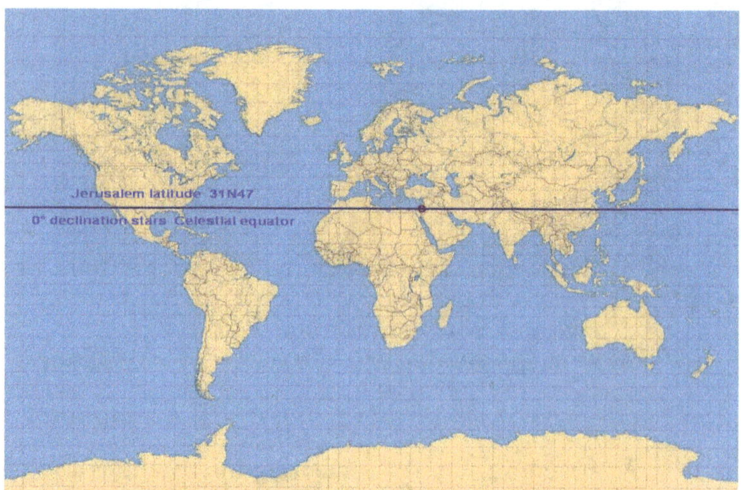

Figure 21: The first Astrogeographia reference alignment aligns the 0° declination stars directly over the 31N47 latitude line through Jerusalem—the Jerusalem horizontal axis.

Figure 22: The second Astrogeographia reference alignment aligns the star Alnitak directly over the 31E08 longitude meridian passing through the Great Pyramid of Giza.

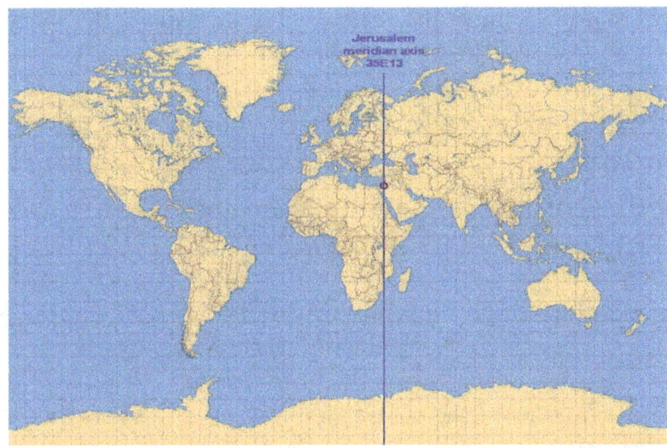

Figure 23: The Jerusalem vertical axis is the 35E13 longitude meridian—the projection of the star Betelgeuse.

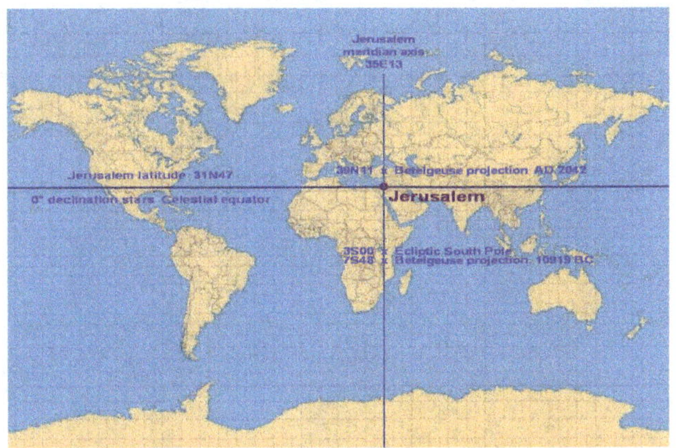

Figure 24: The central importance of Jerusalem for Astrogeographia is indicated here by the exact meeting point of its significant horizontal and vertical axes.

Astrogeographia equations of latitude and longitude

The equation of latitude is obtained from the first reference alignment:

geographicLatitude(Place) = declination(Star) + 31.77844°

Jerusalem, taken as Golgotha, is identified with "the Middle of the Earth" (see chapter 9). Golgotha is traditionally located at the Church of the Holy Sepulchre (latitude 31.77844°, longitude 35.22975°).

The equation of longitude is obtained from the first reference alignment:

geographicLongitude(Place) = siderealLongitude(Star)—
siderealLongitude(Alnitak) + 31.13436°

The sidereal longitude of Alnitak is close to constant at 59.93333°. Its variation about this value is 0.07° over the period 3000 BC to AD 3000, being due entirely to the proper motion of the star. So the equation of longitude can also be stated as:

geographicLongitude(Place) = siderealLongitude(Star)—
28.79897° (to within 0.1% accuracy)

From this equation it can be seen that 0° Aries projects to the 28W48 geographic meridian—i.e., 28.8° west of the 0° Greenwich meridian. The origin of the sidereal zodiac (0AR00, 0N00) projects to geographic (41N22, 28W48). This is close to Fayal Island, one of the main administrative centers of the Azores in the Atlantic Ocean. The 28W48 meridian also passes through the east coast of Greenland (see figure 25).

Figure 25: Origin of the sidereal zodiac 0° Aries is close to Fayal Island in the Azores on the 28W48 longitude meridian. This meridian also passes through the east coast of Greenland.

The Meridian Influence of a Star in Relation to Its Historical Projection

The primary influence of a star is called its meridian influence (see stellar meridians in chapter 9). This influence acts along its entire geographic meridian, at all times. An example of this meridian influence is with the star Betelgeuse, which had meridian influence on Hattusha in Turkey, the seat of the fourteenth century BC Hittite empire. At a later time in 968 BC, Betelgeuse had meridian influence on Solomon's building of the Temple in Jerusalem. Both of these locations are on the same 35E13 meridian, which coincides with the longitude projection of the star Betelgeuse (see figure 23). Another example is the meridian influence of Sirius, the brightest star in the night sky, on the region of ancient Persia and the work of Zarathustra there from about 6000 BC, in relation to the post-Atlantean cultural age of Persia, of which Zarathustra was the founder. Rudolf Steiner referred to Zarathustra as the founder of the Persian cultural epoch in the age of Gemini, some eight thousand years ago, and he described Sirius as the "heart of Jesus–Zarathustra."[11]

Owing to the precession of the Earth, there is in every year a unique location on a star's longitude meridian where its meridian influence becomes especially heightened. At this place the star comes into simultaneous latitude and longitude alignment. This is called the star's historical projection for that given year. The increase in the star's influence at this location results from the resonance effect of the two simultaneous alignments. Over the 25,920-year precession cycle, the historical projection of a star moves alternately north and south on the star's meridian (see the next section). A heightened resonance effect relating to Aldebaran's movement northward along its meridian is exemplified by its simultaneous latitude and longitude alignment with Northern Africa in 2450 BC (the time of the building of the Great Pyramid in Egypt); with southern Italy in 135 BC (the time of the Romans' First Servile War occasioned by the revolt of slaves in Sicily); and with Vienna since the mid-eighteenth century, when this city became a great cultural center for the arts, sciences, and music.

Latitude Journey of a Star over the Precession Cycle and the Sinewave Formulas

As an overall picture, a star's projection onto the Earth moves alternately north and south on its longitude meridian, as a result of the Earth's precession. From the equation of longitude, a star's projected longitude varies only slightly over thousands of years, typically

11 Words of Rudolf Steiner recorded in Rudolf Steiner, *The Birth of a New Agriculture: Koberwitz 1924*, p. 89.

less than 0.1°, corresponding to 6.9 miles (11.1 km) on the surface of the Earth. This slight variation is due to the proper motion of the particular star, but also to that of the star Alnitak, because it too is involved in the calculation of the equation of longitude. The proper motion of all stars is very small even over thousands of years, so the projected longitude remains remarkably constant.

In contrast, the projected latitude of a star varies markedly on the surface of the Earth, as a result of the Earth gently rocking back and forth on its axis over the 25,920-year precession cycle. This has the effect that the observed declination position of the star varies by + and - the axial tilt of the Earth, or between 23.5° north and 23.5° south of a certain mid-declination point. Mid-declination (or the midpoint of the star's declination journey) occurs when the star is in longitude alignment with the vernal point (e.g., with 5PI16 in AD 2000). This movement of the observed position of a star in the heavens over a 25,920-year precession cycle is called its declination journey.

From the equation of latitude, the projected geographic latitude of a star directly follows its declination, so that it too increases and decreases about a certain mid-latitude point by the same 23.5° north and 23.5° south. This movement of the star's projected position on the surface of the Earth over a 25,920-year precession cycle is called its latitude journey. Geographic mid-latitude occurs simultaneously with mid-declination of the star—i.e., when the star is in longitude alignment with the vernal point on the ecliptic (5PI16 in AD 2000). Mid-latitude occurs for a second time in the cycle when the star is in longitude alignment with the autumnal point on the ecliptic (5VI16 in AD 2000). Maximum geographic latitude occurs when the star is in longitude alignment with the summer solstice point (5GE16 in AD 2000); and minimum geographic latitude when the star is in longitude alignment with the winter solstice point (5SG16 in AD 2000). The latitude journey of all stars returns to its starting point and begins anew at the completion of a precession cycle.

To visualize this latitude journey of a star, imagine a line drawn from a particular star to the center of the Earth. It will intersect the surface of the Earth at a certain latitude. The effect of the three-dimensional precessional rocking back and forth of the Earth is that this intersection point will move alternately north and south on its longitude meridian in such a way that a sine wave movement in latitude results.

The maximum variation in latitude on either side of the mid-latitude point is the amplitude of the sine wave. This is equal to the axial tilt angle of the Earth, about 23.5°. The total geographic latitude movement for a star is thus twice the axial tilt of the Earth, or 2 x 23.5° = 47°. This is equal to a distance of 3,245 miles (5,222 km) on the surface of the Earth—about half the distance between the North Pole and the equator.

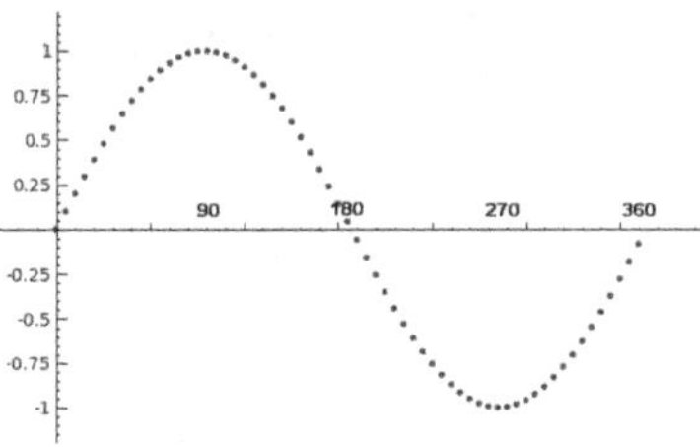

Figure 26: Movement of latitude in a sine wave is slower near the peak and valley, and faster near the middle of the wave.

The movement in latitude is slowest near both the peak and valley of the wave, and fastest near the middle part of the wave. This can be seen by observing the variation in the gradient of a sine wave function graph over a full cycle (see figure 26). Thus the historical projection of a star moves with greatest speed when at its mid-declination, and with slowest (zero) speed when at its furthest north or furthest south. Compare this with the 2,000-year unequal timeline steps in figure 31 showing the movement of Alnitak's projection across Africa.

In a certain year (call this $year_0$) the mid-declination is reached. This occurs when the vernal point comes into longitude alignment with the star:

sidereal longitude of the star at mid-declination =
sidereal longitude of the vernal point = $(220.78029 - year_0)/72$

This is based on October 11 AD 220 (near the time of Ptolemy) as the date when the vernal equinox Sun aligned with the First Point of

Aries, i.e., 0° Aries. With a knowledge of a star's sidereal longitude and declination in any given year (call these sidereal $Longitude_1$ and $declination_1$ in $year_1$).

The mid-declination angle, the mid-declination year in which it occurs, as well as the geographic latitude for any given year of the precession cycle can be calculated from the sine wave formulas below:

$$\text{mid-declination angle} = \text{declination}_1 - 23.49167° \times \sin(\text{year}_1/72 - \text{year}_0/72)$$

$$\text{mid-declination year} = \text{year}_0 = 220.78029 - 72 \times \text{siderealLongitude}_1$$

$$\text{geographicLatitude(year)} = \text{mid-declination} + 23.49167° \times \sin(\text{year}/72 - \text{year}_0/72) + 31.77844°$$

Thus the sine wave formulas provide a very convenient and straightforward way to track the movement of a star over the millennia. Starting with the declination and sidereal longitude of a star in any given year, a once-only calculation is made for the mid-declination angle and also for the year in which this occurs ($year_0$). Then the formulas are set up and ready for use. The declination journey and the latitude journey of the star can now be easily calculated over a very wide range of years of interest. The range of years is not limited to 25,920 years, because the formulas automatically extend into adjacent precession cycles.

In the next section, the concept of the "vernal equinox meridian" is developed as it arises in relation to the mid-declination of a star. The projection of a star at its mid-declination is called its archetypal projection, which is beyond the stream of time. The projection at any other time is called its historical projection, and this occurs within the stream of time.

The Vernal Equinox Meridian and the Birth Horoscope of the World

In any given year, there is only one geographic meridian that is longitudinally aligned with the vernal equinox Sun in that year, and this is called the VE meridian (vernal equinox meridian). Its geographic longitude in any given year can be calculated from the

Figure 27: Map of archetypal projections of the stars—the birth horoscope of the world (see larger version on page 299)

equation of latitude by setting the sidereal longitude(star) = sidereal longitude(VE):

geographic longitude of the VE meridian = sidereal longitude(VE) -28.79897°—e.g., in AD 2000: sidereal longitude(VE) = 5PI16 = -24.73333°
VE meridian = -24.73333° - 28.79897° = -53.53230 = geographic 53W32

The concept of the VE meridian is a vital key for understanding the birth horoscope of the world. In any given year, all geographical latitude locations along the VE meridian return momentarily to full alignment with their star of birth, as at the moment of the birth horoscope of the world. This is because all stars on the VE meridian pass simultaneously through their mid-declination positions in that year.

Thus the historic projection of all stars on the VE meridian is momentarily lifted out of time into its archetypal projection. Expressed in another way, the VE meridian in any given year is a picture of the archetypal projections of all of its stars. As the observed position of the vernal equinox precesses around the ecliptic over the 25,920 year cycle, the VE meridian sweeps in longitude right around the globe, and a whole series of such pictures arises. This series can be assembled into a composite map that shows the archetypal projections for the whole globe. In this way, the birth horoscope of the world can be built up (see figure 27). Each place on Earth celebrates a return to its birth horoscope star twice every 25,920 years. The first occurs when the meridian of the given place aligns with the vernal equinox. The second occurs when it aligns with the autumnal equinox.

The map of the birth horoscope of the world can be visualized by rotating the axis of the Earth until its axial tilt is 0°. The equator now aligns with the ecliptic plane, so that the precession of the Earth is no longer a part of earthly existence. Every place on Earth is in constant latitude and longitude alignment with the star of its birth, as at the moment of the birth horoscope of the world. The declination of stars no longer continuously changes because there is no longer any precession. Instead the declination of each star is identical with its sidereal latitude. Because the sidereal latitude of stars changes only slightly over the millennia owing to their very small proper motion, so every place on Earth now remains in close permanent latitude and longitude alignment with the star of its birth.[12]

From an astrogeographical perspective, this whole picture points strongly to the birth horoscope of the world being imprinted onto the Earth when its axial tilt was 0°—i.e., at a time before the departure of the Moon from the Earth. This would have been a time before the seasons as we know them. This is hinted at in the Italian expression *primavera*—literally "the first spring," in particular in relation to Botticelli's well-known painting. From this point of view, the departure of the Moon is the main cause of the Earth's present axial tilt. Since that time, the effect of the axial tilt of the Earth has been for every place to return to full alignment with the star of its birth twice every 25,920 years—a kind of cosmic breathing process. In spiritual science the departure of the Moon is described as having occurred

12 Over long periods of hundreds of thousands of years, for some stars their proper motion could amount to something significant, possibly even changing the shapes of the constellations. Without an advanced computer program to investigate this astronomically, this aspect of Astrogeographia has not yet been explored—yet we do see the importance of investigating this when we have an appropriate computer program to do so. Therefore we have proceeded under the assumption that the proper motion of stars does not amount to anything of significance in terms of the magnitude of the shifting of the positions of the stars in latitude and longitude and in relation to one another. This assumption certainly holds for the historical period that has been the main focus of our attention, since the shapes of the constellations are more or less the same now as they were for the Sumerians seven thousand years ago.

during the third epoch of the Earth, called Lemuria.[13] Also described is how the Moon, after first drawing nearer to the Earth, will fully reunite with it in about five to six thousand years from now.[14] This can be understood as a result of human consciousness having become more closely aligned with the cosmic consciousness, and thus bringing about a realignment of the Earth's equator with the ecliptic plane. Even wider vistas of human evolution are possible, such as a realignment of the ecliptic plane with the galactic plane, occurring in some far future time when human beings are ready for this.

Study 1: The Latitude Movement of Betelgeuse over 12,960 Years

The projection of the star Betelgeuse in the Orion constellation over the years 10919 BC to AD 2042 (a half precession cycle of 12,960 years) can be calculated using the equations of latitude and longitude and also the sine wave formulas. In this way it is possible to follow Betelgeuse's latitude journey northward across the continent of Africa, the Middle East and as far as central Turkey. We see how the declination movement of Betelgeuse is reflected in its projection onto the Earth—a living picture in time. Although this is a study of the projection of one particular star, namely Betelgeuse, what is seen here is exemplary for every star.

The overview of the complete latitude journey over these 12,960 years is shown in figure 28. The archetypal projection of Betelgeuse is at mid-latitude (16N24, 35E13), in eastern Sudan. The historical projection of this occurs in the year 4439 BC, which means that in 4439 BC a particular location in eastern Sudan celebrated a return to the star of its birth, Betelgeuse. This place has at all times a unique archetypal relationship with the star Betelgeuse. This return

13 Rudolf Steiner describes five ages of the Earth so far: the Polarean, Hyperborean, Lemurian, Atlantean, and post-Atlantean—this being the present age. See Steiner, *Cosmic Memory*, pp. 69–135.

14 Events in Lemuria become transformed or fulfilled in the present post-Atlantean age. So the departure of the Moon that was necessary for human evolution at that time will be paralleled by its reuniting with the Earth toward the end of the present age. See Steiner, *Materialism and the Task of Anthroposophy*, p. 263.

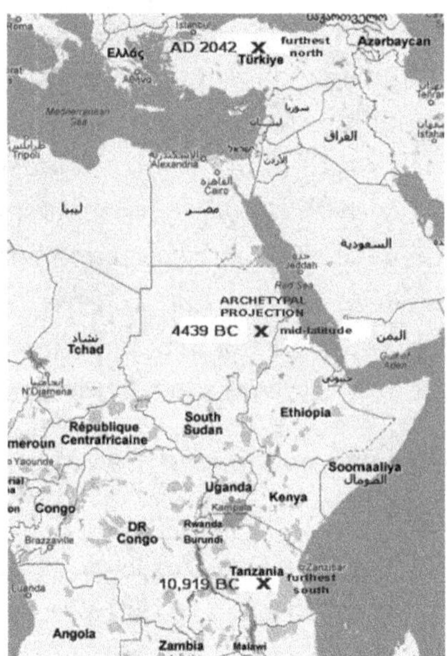

Figure 28: Overview of the complete latitude journey of Betelgeuse over 12,960 years. Its archetypal projection is at mid-latitude (16N24, 35E13), in eastern Sudan. Its historical projection is furthest south in 10919 BC *and furthest north in* AD *2042.*

was to the same alignment that occurred at the moment of the birth horoscope of the world. Earlier in Betelgeuse's journey in 10919 BC, it was at its furthest south (7S48, 35E13), in central Tanzania. In AD 2042, it will reach its furthest north (39N11, 35E13), in central Turkey.

By zooming in on the years 2950 BC to AD 2950, a more detailed study of 5,900 years of the 12,960-year journey can be made. The geographic points thus obtained were then plotted onto a map of the Middle East (see figure 30). The data obtained in this more detailed study reveals that the projected longitude of Betelgeuse remains steady over the 5,900-year period, varying either side of its average 35E13 longitude meridian by less than 0.1°. This slight variation is due to the proper motion of Betelgeuse and also to that of the star Alnitak, because it too is involved in the equation of longitude calculations. In terms of distance on the surface of the Earth the projection of Betelgeuse remains within a few miles (km) of the 35E13 longitude meridian.

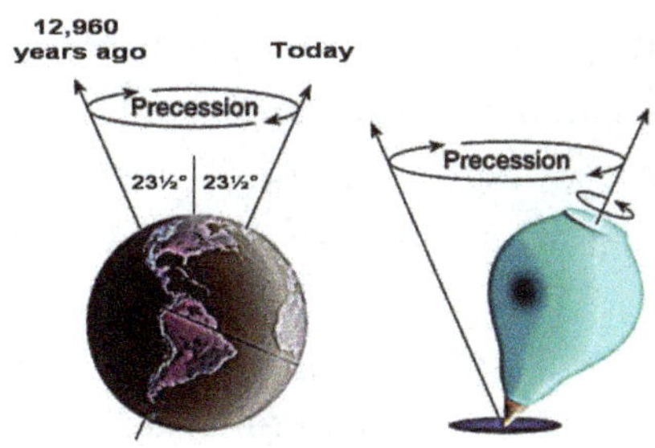

Figure 29: Luni-solar component of precession gives rise to the picture of the Earth as a spinning top.

In contrast, the projected latitude of Betelgeuse does not show the same kind of steady picture as seen above for the projected longitude. The declination of every star varies considerably over time mainly because the observation of a star's position is made from a precessing Earth. For example, consulting an ephemeris shows that the declination of Betelgeuse increased by 16° over the years 2950 BC to AD 2950. Consequently the projected latitude (exactly tracking this declination) also shows a 16° northerly movement over this period. This is about one third of the total 47° (= 2 x 23.5°) north-south movement that occurs during a full precession cycle.

The variation in declination of a star results mainly from the luni-solar component of precession of the Earth. This is the main component of precession and is what gives rise to the picture of the Earth as a spinning top (see figure 29). Other smaller sources of variation in the declination over the millennia are: the planetary components of precession; slight changes in the Earth's axial tilt due to the 41,000-year Milankovitch cycle; nutation of the Earth's axis due to the Moon's orbital plane being tilted at about 5° to the ecliptic; movements occurring within the Earth; and slight changes in the sidereal latitude and longitude of the star due to its proper motion. This proper motion for stars of the Milky Way (most stars) arises in turn from the galactic rotation of the Milky Way. The magnitude of this proper motion depends on where the star is located within its local spiral arm, in relation to the galactic center.

The variation in declination of any given star over a 25,920-year precession cycle can be modeled with a mathematical sine wave law (see the sine wave formulas section in this chapter). With this model, the declination moves alternately 23.5° north and 23.5° south of Betelgeuse's mid-declination point of -15.38451°. Projecting this sine wave movement in declination onto the Earth gives a similar sine wave movement in geographic latitude, alternately 23.5° north and 23.5° south of Betelgeuse's mid-latitude point of (16N24, 35E13), which is in eastern Sudan. The 16° increase in declination over this 5,900-year study is thus only a part of the total 47° variation in declination over the whole sine wave.

The map of this 5,900-year study begins in 2950 BC with Betelgeuse's projected latitude approximately level with Aswan in Egypt (see figure 30). Moving north it reaches a point within 1.8 miles (3 km) of the site of Solomon's Temple in 1371 BC. In AD 33, it is just below the southern coast of Turkey. Continuing further north and noticeably slowing, it will reach its most northerly point in AD 2042 near Hattusha (modern Bogazkale) in central Turkey. This was the center of the Hittite kingdom, which rose to its height in the fourteenth century BC. From this most northerly point the Betelgeuse projection turns to move south again, very slowly at first and then it arrives at a location slightly west of Kayseri in central Turkey in AD 2950, which marks the end point of this study period. Kayseri is the site of ancient Caesarea in Cappadocia. Notice how in passing northward in approximately 1,000-year steps through 2950 BC, 2000 BC, 1000 BC, AD 33, AD 1000 and AD 2042, the projections grow closer together on the map, indicating a progressive slowing down of the speed of movement. In AD 2042, this slows to zero speed as the projection of Betelgeuse reaches its most northerly point, at which it turns to move south again, slowly at first and then progressively gaining speed.

A study like this one for Betelgeuse can be made for any star. Such studies show how the influence of a star works most strongly at one particular historical location, a location which moves north and south on the star's meridian over time. However, there is one particular location on the Earth, which has a unique archetypal

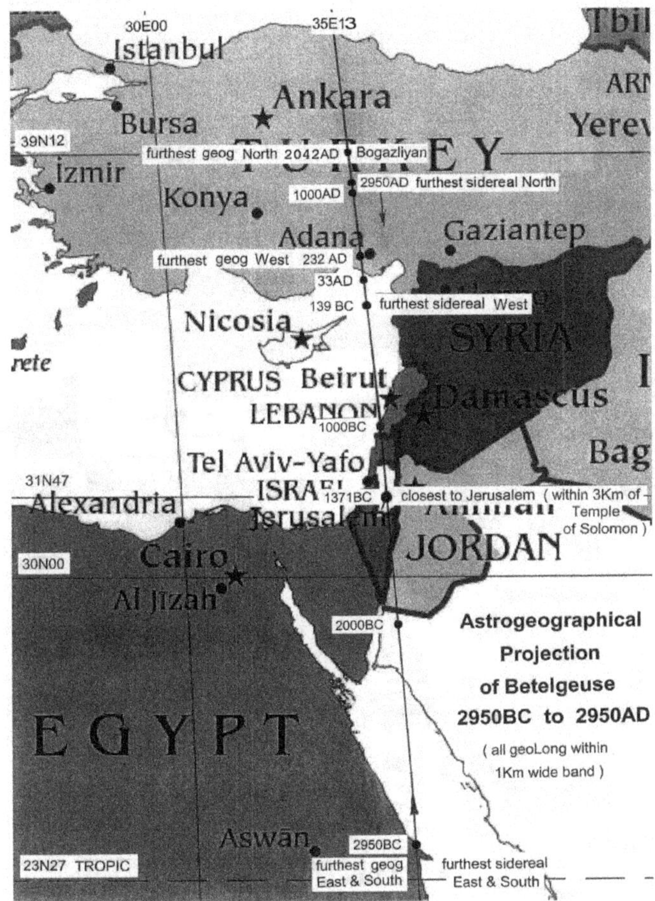

Figure 30: Detailed study of the moving projection of Betelgeuse over 5,900 years from 2950 BC to AD 2950

relationship that holds with the given star for all times. This is because it is the star of that location's birth. From these pictures we begin to experience Astrogeographia as a living picture in time, one which is characterized by a fixed aspect in space for geographic longitude and a moving aspect in time for geographic latitude. Such astrogeographical studies provide definite confirmation of the essential truth of the sidereal zodiac. Namely, that if one accepts even a single correspondence between a particular star in the heavens and a certain place on Earth (e.g., between the star Alnitak and

Giza in Egypt), then this can only remain a stable correspondence over time if the stellar coordinates used to locate the star's position in the heavens also remain stable over time. This can only be so if the star's coordinates have as their framework the stars themselves. Thus the sidereal zodiac is the essential tool which makes it possible for Astrogeographia to reveal stable spatial relationships between the starry heavens and the Earth, relationships that endure in a living way over the millennia.

Study 2: The Latitude Movement of Alnitak over 12,960 Years

The sine wave formulas can be applied to calculate and draw the timeline for the historical projection of Alnitak as it moves up the continent of Africa over a half precession cycle from 10574 BC to AD 2386.

The results of the calculations for particular years of interest in the 12960 half precession cycle are shown in table 7, with the corresponding timeline projection across the continent of Africa shown in figure 31.

Figure 31: Alnitak's projection traces out a non-linear timeline on the 31E08 meridian of Africa. The 2,000-year steps show slower movement near the top and bottom, and faster near the middle.

YEAR	DECLINATION	GEOGRAPHIC LATITUDE	ALNITAK
AD 2386	-1.8°	29N56	• closest to Giza, within 3.7 miles (6 km) • most northerly point, turns to move south again • vernal equinox Sun enters Aquarius in AD 2376
AD 33	-5.6°	26N13	• vicinity of Thebes (Luxor)
2450 BC	-16.2°	15N34	• building of the Great Pyramid of Giza • 3 miles (150 km) W of Khartoum, Sudan
2907 BC	-18.7°	13N07	• beginning of Egyptian cultural age (beginning of Kali Yuga was 3102 BC) • 186 miles (300 km) S of Khartoum, Sudan
5067 BC	-30.8°	0N57	• beginning of the Persian cultural age • source of Nile (White Nile meets Lake Victoria)
7227 BC	-41½°	9S44	• beginning of the Indian cultural age • Northern Zambia
10574 BC	-48.8°	17S03	• most southerly point, turned to move north • the "First Time" of the ancient Egyptians (about 3300 years before the end of Atlantis) • 62 miles (100 km) N of Harare, Zimbabwe • vernal equinox Sun enters Leo in 10,764 BC

Table 7: Historical projection of Alnitak; timeline as it moves up the 31E08 Nilotic meridian of Africa

Why Was the Great Pyramid Built at Giza?

No satisfying answer to this question seems to come from either archaeology or archaeoastronomy. If it is only a matter of the Pyramid's shafts being aligned to certain stars, then the Pyramid does not need to be located at Giza for this. To shed some light on this unanswered riddle we can consider the declination journey of Alnitak as described in the previous section. According to most researchers the Great Pyramid was built around 2450 BC. Much earlier in 10574 BC (during the last millennia of Atlantis) Alnitak had, on its declination journey, reached its most southerly declination of -48.8°. This journey was a result of the precessional movement of the Earth. It then turned to move north again, and has since been rising upward on the 31E08 meridian of Africa.

The beginning of the rising of Alnitak in 10574 BC can be taken as what the ancient Egyptians called The First Time. It was then that Orion, a constellation of great significance for them, was at its lowest point in the southern sky, and seen for only a few hours each night. From The First Time onward, the precession of the equinoxes has gradually carried Orion (Osiris) and his consort Sirius (Isis) higher and higher in the sky—in effect a return and resurrection of Osiris. The ancient Egyptians oriented themselves toward the south as the direction of Upper Egypt and the source of the Nile. And the south was also the direction from which they observed Orion and Sirius ascending in the sky over the centuries. Later in the Egyptian cultural age, the resurrection of Osiris was experienced in the annual cycle as well, as the much awaited heliacal dawn rising (rebirth) of Orion and Sirius from their 70-day annual absence (death) in the night sky. The ancient Egyptians greatly welcomed this yearly return as the sign of the imminent flooding of the Nile and the return of abundant life.

The carrying of Orion and Sirius higher in the sky by the precessional movement of the Earth continues into modern times, and is yet to culminate in its full return in AD 2386. It is then that Alnitak will reach its most northerly point in the sky, with a declination of -1.8°. From an astrogeographical perspective, it is remarkable that as the northward journey of Orion and Sirius comes to its end in AD 2386, the projection of Alnitak simultaneously comes into closest alignment with the Great Pyramid, within 3.1 miles (5 km), after a journey of 3,245 miles (5222 km). This occurrence in AD 2386 is very close to AD 2375, when the vernal equinox Sun leaves the constellation of Pisces and enters the constellation of Aquarius, marking the beginning of the astronomical age of Aquarius (see figure 32). Perhaps these coincidences can bring some new understanding to the riddle of why the Great Pyramid was built at Giza. The riddle could be rephrased as to why the Pyramid was built exactly where the projection of Alnitak comes into full latitude and longitude alignment with it, and just at the time of the beginning of the astronomical age Aquarius.[15]

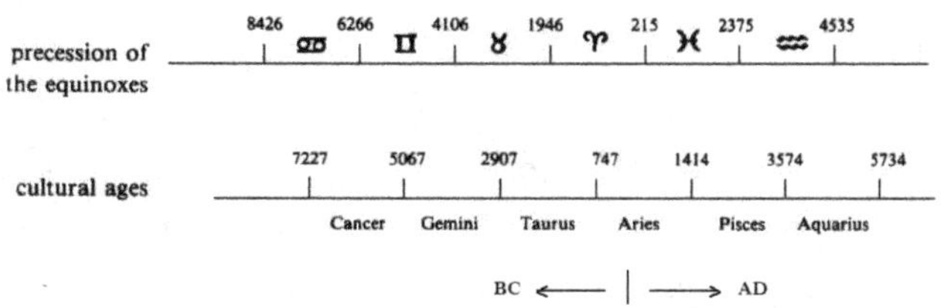

Figure 32: The astronomical ages based on the precession of the equinoxes. The cultural ages follow 1,199 years later.

Rudolf Steiner described how events that occurred during the Egyptian cultural age of Taurus[16] reappear transformed as their fruit or fulfillment[17] in our own cultural age of Pisces. One hypothesis for this riddle could thus be that the Pyramid was built to convey a message (as fruit of the Egyptian age) across the millennia to the humanity of AD 2386 in the cultural age of Pisces. This message will proclaim to Piscean humanity that with the full return of Orion and Sirius to their most northerly points in the sky, the great evolutionary work of the Egyptian age of transforming the astral body into sentient soul has come to a certain fulfillment (see the section on the "legend of the Golden Fleece" in this chapter). Then following the entry of the vernal equinox Sun into Aquarius there will be a period of 1,199 years, which is needed for the seed of a new spiritual impulse to come into cultural flourishing. After this gestation period will come the Russian cultural age of Aquarius under the guidance of Sophia. It is during

15 See Powell, *Hermetic Astrology*, vol.1, p. 63.

16 Rudolf Steiner describes the first five cultural ages of post-Atlantis: India, Persia, Egypt, Greece-Rome, and Europe as under the signs of Cancer, Gemini, Taurus, Aries and Pisces respectively. See Steiner, *Ancient Myths*, pp. 80–87.

17 See Steiner, *Egyptian Myths and Mysteries*, pp. 13–14, 20. "Glancing at the immediate implications of our theme, we see a large domain. We see the gigantic Pyramids, the enigmatic Sphinx. The souls that belonged to the ancient Indians were also incarnated in Egypt and are again incarnated today. If we follow our general line of thought into detail, we will discover two phenomena that show us how, in superearthly connections, there are mysterious threads between the Egyptian culture and that of today."

this age that the evolutionary work begun by the Egyptians will continue with the further transformation of sentient soul into spirit self.

A related riddle regarding the Great Pyramid is the question of why it was built next to the Sphinx, which according to some researchers predates it by at least 6,000 years. The Sphinx is the largest monolithic sculpture in the world and has a lion's body and a human head. One hypothesis for this is that the Sphinx was built close to 10586 BC when the vernal equinox Sun had just entered the constellation of Leo the Lion. This time was very close to "The First Time" of the ancient Egyptians (10574 BC) mentioned above, when Orion and Sirius began rising from their lowest point in the night sky. Thus the picture arises of the building of the Lion-Sphinx in 10586 BC at the beginning of the astronomical age of Leo to commemorate The First Time. And then the later building of the Great Pyramid next to the Sphinx in 2450 BC to prefigure what could be called "The Last Time." This will be the time of AD 2386 near the beginning of the astronomical age of Aquarius (as described above), when Alnitak comes into full alignment with the Great Pyramid and, at the same time, Orion and Sirius rise to their most northerly points in the sky. Then will be proclaimed from the heights the fruit and fulfillment of the great evolutionary work of the Egyptian age.

Chapter 9

Astrogeographia: Further Reflections

The Earth as an Autonomous Organism

Most astrologers work with a twofold system: the ecliptic system of the zodiac for the positions of the planets, and an Earth system for the houses. The house system is an example of the saying "as above, so below," in that the twelve houses of the house system correspond to the twelve signs of the zodiac. Not many astrologers dispute the validity of this principle, even though the two systems are quite different from one another. Why is this?

It is a matter of grasping "organisms" great and small, and that each organism is organized according to its own principles. For our solar system, as an organism, the movements of the planets are viewed against the background of the twelve constellations of the zodiac. Once one has grasped that not only the twelve constellations of the zodiac but also all the constellations above and below the zodiac also weave into the ecliptic—this is the principle of "meridians"—then the whole night sky appears as an organism. For example, on June 19/20 the Sun is at 4° Gemini aligned with Betelgeuse some 16° south of the ecliptic and simultaneously with Polaris some 66° north of the ecliptic. (For a visual representation of this, see the Star Map created by Nick Fiorenza, reproduced on pages 296–297.)[1] Both Betelgeuse and Polaris are conjoined with the Sun at this time, each sending their influences through the 4° Gemini meridian to the Sun. Later in this

1 For a discussion of the Polaris–Betelgeuse meridian, see Powell and Dann, *The Astrological Revolution*, p. 161; for the star map created by Nick Anthony Fiorenza, see the figure reproduced on pages 296–297. See also http://www.lunarplanner.com/ArgoNavisPublications/SiderealHeavensGiclee/index.html.

chapter, connecting onto the foundation laid in chapter 6, the theme of the significance of the celestial meridians is developed in detail, offering evidence of this principle at work in practice. The entire celestial sphere is revealed as a great organism into which our solar system is embedded. For our solar system, the key as to how our solar system interacts with this great organism is the ecliptic, which is a "heart axis" running through the center, as indicated in the Fiorenza Star Map. From outside of our solar system, the ecliptic does not mean much—for example, if one's standpoint were to be on a planet orbiting around the star Alpha Centauri. However, from the Earth's standpoint within our solar system, the ecliptic is the heart axis.

When we turn our attention to the Earth as an organism, there is the question as to how our Earth interacts with the greater organism of the solar system? The Earth is an autonomous organism, albeit very much bound up with the rest of the solar system. The house systems in astrology reflect this autonomy. They are not simply projections from the ecliptic system onto the Earth. The house systems depend upon the rotation of the Earth, and there are various ways of arriving at a twelvefold division with respect to this rotation.

For astronomy, the equatorial coordinate system discussed in chapter 1 is an Earth-based system that is useful for determining the relationship of planets, stars, and other celestial bodies to the Earth. The equatorial system of declination and right ascension is mirrored on the Earth in geographical coordinates of latitude and longitude and, as pointed out in chapter 1, this mirroring underlies the "equation of declination" used in Astrogeographia for determining the projection of stars onto the earthly globe. The coordinate system of latitude and longitude is the Earth's own frame of reference as an autonomous organism. Just as in astrology the principle of "as above, so below" is applied in the relationship between the ecliptic based system of the zodiac ("above") and the Earth based system of the houses ("below"), so Astrogeographia is based upon "as above, so below" in terms of a correspondence between the ecliptic system and the equatorial system expressed in geographical latitude and longitude. The longitudes are equivalent to the ecliptic longitudes—understood as meridians—referred to above, and the latitudes are equivalent to ecliptic latitudes. It is simply a question as to where to start in the application of this correspondence?

The Center of the World

As mentioned at the start of chapter 1 of this book, Astrogeographia is based on Rudolf Steiner's indication in the *Astronomy Course* that the stars of the celestial sphere are mirrored in the earthly sphere. The question is: How are they mirrored? In the valuable work of Dennis Klocek, as discussed in chapter 5, he has come up with an answer to this question. Essentially, he identifies the projection of the ecliptic with the equator, and he determined the 0° Aries (sidereal) starting point to lie 23° west of the Greenwich meridian. For his work with weather patterns, this correspondence seems to fit very well. As a comparison, we include here our empirical research employing the 0° Aries (sidereal) starting point used in Astrogeographia. In Astrogeographia the 0° Aries (sidereal) starting point is located 28°48' west of the Greenwich meridian, in the region of the Azores, a shift of 5°48' further west than in the system of Dennis Klocek, which is a relatively small difference. The key to understanding this shift is the exact alignment of the star Alnitak with the meridian running through the Great Pyramid. When Alnitak is aligned with the Great Pyramid, the zero point of the projection of the sidereal zodiac onto the Earth is specified to lie 28°48' west of the Greenwich meridian. Alnitak currently lies on the meridian of 29°56' sidereal Taurus—rounded to 30° Taurus/0° Gemini in terms of whole degrees.[2]

While both Dennis Klocek's system and that of Astrogeographia are equatorial in principle, with sidereal longitudes and latitudes superimposed upon geographical longitudes and latitudes, there is, however, a major difference between the system of Dennis Klocek and that of Astrogeographia, in that for Astrogeographia the projection of the ecliptic is not identified with the equator as 0° latitude, but the

2 See appendix 2 (at astrogeographia.org) for empirical research comparing the system of Dennis Klocek with the system of Astrogeographia, where empirical findings are presented. The question raised by these findings is whether, when it comes to weather prediction, a higher degree of precision is made possible by refining the location of the 0° Aries (sidereal) meridian through shifting it 5°48' farther west?

latitude of Jerusalem (31N47) is considered as 0° latitude. What is the background to this?

A key to understanding this shift of 31°47' to the north—from the equator to Jerusalem—is Rudolf Steiner's indication that Jerusalem (or Palestine) is the center of the world. He did not say this explicitly, but it is implicit in various statements. For example, Rudolf Steiner indicated on many occasions that Golgotha (Jerusalem) is associated with a great mystery that is of central importance for humanity and the whole world. Against this background it could be interpreted, spiritually understood, that Israel—more specifically Golgotha—is the heart of the world. Based upon Rudolf Steiner's indications concerning the centrality for the world of Israel, a group of German anthroposophists (Andreas Suchantke, Hans-Ulrich Schmutz, Wolfgang Schad, Wolfgang Fackler) have written a book entitled *Israel, Middle of the World* in which they elaborate on Steiner's indications from various points of view.[3] Once the east–west axis through Jerusalem has been set to line up with 0° latitude astrogeographically and, simultaneously, Alnitak is aligned longitudinally with the Great Pyramid, a series of remarkable alignments between earthly locations and stars emerges, as shown by the various correspondences between stars and places discussed in this book.

Regarding the centrality of Jerusalem:

> The Temple Mount in the Old City of Jerusalem measures today approximately forty-five acres in extent. The present-day platform area of the Temple Mount lies topographically just below the peak of a Jerusalem ridge system known as Mount Moriah. This is the site David purchased from a Jebusite named Ornan late in his reign. King David prepared the area in order build a permanent House of God to replace the Tabernacle of Moses which accompanied the Jews after their Exodus from Egypt to the Promised Land. David had the plans drawn up for a building whose dimensions were twice those of the Tabernacle, and he amassed great quantities of building materials: stone, cedar, and much gold and silver. However, it was his son Solomon

3 Suchantke et al., *Mitte der Erde.*

> who actually built the First Jewish temple (1 Chronicles 22:14–15, 28:11–20). The ridge system where the Temple Mount is now located is believed by many reputable sources to be the site where Abraham was told to sacrifice Isaac (Genesis 22:1-2). While Solomon built the First Temple about three thousand years ago, Abraham's visit to Mt. Moriah was about a thousand years earlier. According to Rabbinical sources both the First and Second Temples were built on the same foundations, at the same location somewhere on the Temple Mount. The site had to be consecrated ground that had not been previously used for tombs and that was not a previous pagan worship site ("high place"). The innermost sanctuary of the Temple, the Holy of Holies, or *Kodesh Hakodeshim*, where the Ark of the Covenant was placed, *marked the exact center of the world*.[4]

In this connection, star wisdom researcher David Tresemer discovered an important finding from his study of the life of Christ. He found that major events in Christ's life—indeed, the most significant events—occurred on the east–west axis through Jerusalem: the baptism of Jesus in the River Jordan near the village of Ono, the "Palm Sunday" entrance of Jesus Christ into Jerusalem through the Golden Gate, the Mystery of Golgotha, and the ascension of Christ from the Mount of Olives forty days after his resurrection.[5] And, moreover, the Temple Mount (Mount Moriah), thought by some to be the original location of Solomon's Temple, as well as being the place, according to tradition, of the sacrifice of Isaac by Abraham, also lies exactly on this same east–west axis. This east–west axis running from Ono through Jerusalem—or, more specifically, through the Mount of Olives, Mount Moriah and Mount Calvary—emerges

4 "On The Location of the First and Second Temples in Jerusalem" by Lambert Dolphin and Michael Kollen, http://www.templemount.org/theories.html.

5 David Tresemer in a manuscript (written as an adventure story): http://www.DavidAndLilaTresemer.com. "Palm Sunday" is placed in quotation marks, since the triumphant entry of Jesus into Jerusalem, which is celebrated each year on Palm Sunday, took place historically on Thursday, March 19, AD 33, two weeks prior to the Last Supper on Thursday, April 2; see Powell, *Chronicle of the Living Christ*; also the website www.starwisdom.org.

here as a kind of *spiritual equator* in relation to the central events of the history of the Earth, both at the time of Christ and also before. There is even the legend that Adam and Eve lived on the Mount of Olives. As referred to in chapter 4, Anne Catherine Emmerich also indicates that Adam and Eve lived on the Mount of Olives. And in Anne Catherine Emmerich's *The Life of Jesus Christ*, vol. 4, after describing that the name Golgotha, which means "place of the skull," has to do with the fact that the skull of Adam was buried within the hill and that this is how the hill received the name Golgotha, Anne Catherine Emmerich says: "I saw that the cross of Jesus stood vertically above the skull of Adam, and I was told that this location is the middle of the earth."[6] (The expression "middle of the earth"—like the expression "center of the world"—is to be distinguished from "center of the earth." By "middle of the earth" is meant *the central location on the earth's surface.*) Anne Catherine Emmerich's indication of Golgotha as the middle of the earth is implicitly confirmed by Rudolf Steiner's research, who often referred to the central importance of Golgotha for the whole Earth. In any case, the difference between Golgotha and the Temple of Solomon, which (as stated) was considered by ancient rabbinical sources the center of the world, is one-third of a mile (500 m). Moreover, as indicated by David Tresemer, both these locations lie on the same east–west axis through Jerusalem.

From the foregoing, therefore, there is good reason for considering that there is a spiritual equator in addition to the Earth's physical equator and that this spiritual equator lies along the east–west axis running through Jerusalem—more specifically, through Golgotha—and that this spiritual equator may be understood to specify 0° latitude for Astrogeographia.

The Four Levels of the Earth

Just as the human being is fourfold, with different members at different levels, so also the Earth is a fourfold being. Within the limits of this book, it is not possible here to substantiate the following

6 From the original German of Emmerich, *Das bittere Leiden unseres Herrn Jesus Christi*, p. 221 (tr. by RP).

statements regarding the Earth as a fourfold being, because this would require a whole book in itself. However, the reader can regard the following as a series of hypotheses to be tested in relation to the four levels of the being of the Earth, even though these statements are presented here as self-evident facts.

There is the Earth's physical body, which embraces the entire physical world. Then there is the Earth's etheric (life) body, which extends up to the Moon's orbit around the Earth. Then there is the Earth's astral (soul) body, which extends up to the Sun. Over and above this is the Earth's "I," or self, which reaches up to the realm of the fixed stars. Astrogeographia is concerned with this fourth level—that of the Earth's "I." When Christ sacrificed himself on Golgotha, he united with the Earth's "I." The enactment of the Mystery of Golgotha on the east–west axis running through Jerusalem was the event at which the union of Christ with the Earth's "I" took place. In this sense this axis can be thought of as the Earth's spiritual equator and, correspondingly, there is a perception of the Earth's "I" from the vantage point of this spiritual equator that beholds the mirroring of the stars upon the Earth in a certain way, as described by Astrogeographia. Of course, it is not just the east–west axis which is significant, but also the north–south axis, the meridian running through Jerusalem, which—as indicated above—lies at 4° Gemini and runs northward through Polaris, the current pole star, and southward through Betelgeuse, now reckoned to be the most powerful star in the constellation of Orion, which was associated by the ancient Egyptians with Osiris who, as indicated earlier, was a pre-incarnatory manifestation of Christ. Regarding the Betelgeuse meridian which runs through Jerusalem, this meridian is not only aligned with the Pole Star, Polaris, at its northern end, but also with the opposite geographical point to the apparent Ecliptic North Pole—coinciding with Antarctica, the portal to Shambhala, the heart of the Earth—at its southern end (see figure 4, chapter 10). The specification of Jerusalem's meridian as 4° Gemini follows from the alignment of Alnitak, in the belt of Orion, with the Great Pyramid. These facts are foundational for Astrogeographia.

Astrogeographia Research Update

In October 2009 there took place an "astrogeographical journey" in Turkey. The journey followed two sides of a triangle. In the heavens the triangle is formed by the star in the head of Orion (Meissa) and the stars marking the right (Betelgeuse) and the left (Bellatrix) shoulders of Orion. On the Earth Istanbul corresponds approximately to Meissa, Hattusha corresponds approximately to Betelgeuse, and Ephesus corresponds more or less exactly with Bellatrix. Our journey took us from Istanbul to Hattusha, and then from Hattusha across Turkey to Ephesus, visiting many places in between. Herewith a report of this journey.

A JOURNEY IN TURKEY WITH ROBERT POWELL OCTOBER 1–11, 2009

Lacquanna Paul & Uberta Sebregondi

Our group of 35 people, travelling through central Anatolia in Turkey, on October 4 visited Hattusha, the ancient capital of the Hittites. There we discovered in the stones of the remains two cult chambers alongside one another in the great twin temple of the Hittites. The two most important deities of the Hittites were worshiped here at the twin temple, wherein the cult chamber dedicated to Teshub, the god of wind, storm, and the elements, stood side by side with the cult chamber dedicated to his consort Arinna, the Sun goddess.

Journeying on through Cappadocia, visiting many other remarkable sites on the way, we subsequently arrived at the site of the ancient city of Ephesus as the culmination of our tour of Turkey. Here, on the evening of October 9, Robert's first public lecture presenting his research into Astrogeographia took place. Bernt Rossiwall, who together with his wife Jane organized this tour of Turkey, introduced Astrogeographia as a "science for the future, just as Kepler's laws are nowadays the basis for calculating interplanetary space missions." The lecture was entitled "Ephesus: City of Artemis and the Virgin Mary—the Astrogeographical Significance of Ephesus" and was held at the Crisler Library in Ephesus.

Seen in light of the ancient hermetic axiom "as above, so below," Astrogeographia is a new science revealing the existence of a one-to-one correspondence between the celestial and terrestrial globes—i.e., between individual stars in the heavens and identifiable earthly geographical locations scattered around the globe, such that each star is mirrored at a specific place on the Earth. Astrogeographically it is theoretically possible to refer to any particular site—such as Ephesus—as being the place of the *earthly projection* of a certain star.

The basic hypothesis of Astrogeographia is that there is a mirroring on the Earth of the entire heavenly sphere, implying that particular places on the earthly globe correspond to particular stars in the heavens. But how may these places be identified in relation to the corresponding stars?

In his quest to answer this question, Robert described how his point of departure drew upon the research that had been first presented in 1988 by R. Bauval and A. Gilbert in their book *The Orion Mystery*. Bauval's central thesis presented in this book concerns a correspondence between the three pyramids of Giza and the three stars marking the belt of Orion. For Robert the primary correspondence that serves as the starting-point for Astrogeographia is that between the lower star in Orion's belt, Alnitak, and the great pyramid of Giza, as beautifully illustrated in an artist's sketch from page 209 of the 1994 edition of *The Orion Mystery*. The sketch portrays the Egyptian god Osiris in relation to the constellation of Orion, with the red supergiant star Betelgeuse marking his right shoulder and Bellatrix his left shoulder. In his right hand Osiris is holding a sceptre, and his left hand is extended out toward the star Aldebaran marking the Bull's eye in the constellation of Taurus.

Robert's research developed further from this starting-point of a correspondence between Alnitak and Giza. His further research resulted in discovering—through computation—that the projection of the central star in Orion's belt, Alnilam, closely corresponds to Alexandria in Egypt, and further that the projection of the star marking Orion's left shoulder, Bellatrix, corresponds to Ephesus. The discovery that prominent stars in the constellation of Orion are mirrored on Earth at these ancient mystery sites lends support to the

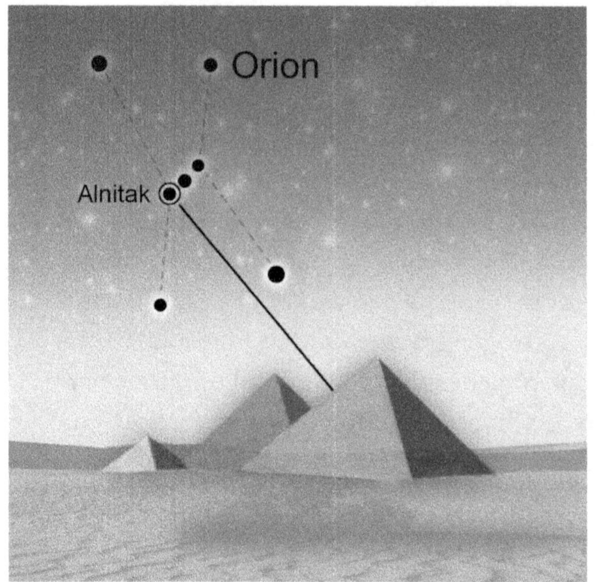

The great pyramid, temple of Osiris, aligned with Orion, the constellation of Osiris

basic principle of Astrogeographia. For these three spiritual centers of antiquity—Giza, Alexandria, Ephesus—were indeed the locations of three of the Seven Wonders of the ancient world—i.e., the great pyramid of Giza, the Pharos lighthouse at the harbour of Alexandria, and the temple of Artemis at Ephesus.

Such correspondences point toward a direct connection between sacred places on Earth and the spiritual influences of the starry worlds, broadening and deepening our understanding of the cosmic dimension of humanity's spiritual history, and confirming the potential of Astrogeographia to make a valuable contribution toward a new understanding of the relationship between heaven and earth.

Moreover, the discovery of this one-to-one correspondence between these three ancient mystery centres and three of the most prominent stars in Orion opens the possibility through comprehending that which lived in these ancient mysteries, of gaining insight into the nature of the cosmic influences proceeding from these three stars—and, beyond this, through the further application of Astrogeographia to come to understand the influences proceeding from other stars as well, when seen in relation to the earthly locations corresponding to them. We see, for example, in the impulse toward cultivating the worship of the Mother Goddess that flourished at Ephesus, the particular quality of the star Bellatrix, known in earlier times as the "Amazon star." For, according to legend, it was the Amazon women who established the first temple at Ephesus—originally a small edifice which, however, was the forerunner of the great temple of Artemis, later identified as one of the Seven Wonders of the ancient world. In light of Astrogeographia, something of the stellar influence of Bellatrix evidently attracted the legendary tribe of Amazon women to Ephesus to settle there and to start a new cult center dedicated to the Mother Goddess, who later became known as Artemis of Ephesus. And the name "Amazon star"—how else can this mysterious designation for Bellatrix be explained? From that which lived in this mystery of the great temple dedicated to Artemis of Ephesus, the quality of the Mother Goddess was evidently an influence connected with and proceeding from the star Bellatrix. This influence continued there on into the Christian era. Thus, when the temple of Artemis went more and more into decline, particularly around the start of the Christian era, the Virgin Mary, accompanied by the Apostle John, came from Jerusalem to live in Ephesus—from AD 36 to 44. As Theodora Jenny-Kappers states in her book *Muttergöttin und Gottesmutter in Ephesus: Von Artemis zu Maria* ("Mother Goddess and Mother of God in Ephesus: From Artemis to Mary"), where she refers to the time of transition from Artemis worship to devotion to the Virgin Mary:

> Artemis was merely a symbol.... Then a successor emerged as a reality in physical form: Mary, the Christian "Mother of God." It is impossible to say to what extent the ancient cult of the motherly-virginal Artemis of Ephesus lived on again in the devotion to Mary, but certainly Mary in Ephesus took over Artemis' role to a great extent, especially after the Church council of the year AD 431 when Mary was declared to be the "Mother of God," the "Bearer of God."

A further research finding of Astrogeographia indicated by Robert is that the archetypal projection of the red supergiant star marking the right shoulder of Orion, Betelgeuse, falls close to

Hattusha. Against this background, it emerges that the influence proceeding from Betelgeuse was the cosmic source of inspiration for the great twin temple of Teshub, the wind god, and Arinna, the Sun goddess, that we visited at Hatthusha. Robert also indicated that astrogeographically Jerusalem falls longitudinally more or less on the same meridian as Hatthusha and hence on the same cosmic meridian as Betelgeuse—and, moreover, that at the time of the building of the temple of Solomon in the tenth century BC, the historical projection of Betelgeuse was directly over Jerusalem. The historical projection of a star shifts over long periods of time north and south along the same longitudinal meridian, half the time north of the archetypal projection and half the time south of it—the terrestrial location of the archetypal projection being the midpoint of the north–south movement of the historical projection along the meridian. The shifting historical projection has to do with the changing relationship between the celestial globe and the terrestrial globe due to the precession of the equinoxes. Returning to the example of Betelgeuse, the red supergiant star marking the right shoulder of Orion, the current projection of this powerful star falls close to Hatthusha, and the historical projection in 1371 BC, shortly before the time of the building of the temple of Solomon, was directly aligned with Jerusalem.

Yet another finding of Astrogeographia of significance for our tour of Turkey is that the earthly projection of the main star marking Orion's head, Meissa, is located in proximity to Istanbul, the ancient city of Constantinople, chosen by the Emperor Constantine the Great to be the new capital of the vast Roman empire. In AD 330 Constantine transferred the imperial residence from Rome to the new capital, which he called the "New Rome." Subsequently, in the sixth century AD, the Emperor Justinian accomplished between 532 and 537 the building of the great domed basilica of the Hagia Sophia there, at that time the largest cathedral in Christendom. The remarkable domed structure of Hagia Sophia was seen as a new World Wonder, outdoing even the temple of Solomon. Just as the temple of Artemis at Ephesus can be seen—astrogeographically—in connection with the star Bellatrix, Hagia Sophia in Constantinople/Istanbul can be seen in relation to the inspiring cosmic influence proceeding from the star Meissa in the head of Orion. *Sophia* is the Greek word for "Wisdom," and the connection of Meissa to Divine Wisdom is revealed in the majestic architectural structure of Hagia Sophia, the domed shape reminding us of the domed structure of the head. At the inauguration of the new basilica on December 27, 537, because of the majestic architectural structure and the extraordinarily rich and artistic interior decoration, Justinian exclaimed, "Solomon, I have outdone thee."

Our journey in Turkey started in Istanbul, where we visited Hagia Sophia, the magnificent architectural monument testifying to the cosmic influence of Meissa in the head of Orion. From Istanbul we flew to Ankara and travelled from there to Hattusha to visit the remains of the great twin temple of Teshub and Arinna, the cult center of the ancient Hittite empire, an earthly testimony to the stellar influence proceeding from the star Betelgeuse marking the right shoulder of Orion—bearing in mind also that the temple of Solomon at Jerusalem was another architectural monument testifying to the influence of Betelgeuse. After journeying through Cappadocia we came to Ephesus and visited the remains of the majestic temple of Artemis, that was an architectural manifestation on Earth of the influence stemming from Bellatrix, the star at the left shoulder of Orion. Thus our journey in Turkey mapped out a triangle on the Earth corresponding to the triangle of stars (Meissa–Betelgeuse–Bellatrix) marking the head and shoulders of Orion. This was perhaps the first group journey on Earth to consciously trace out a constellation—or, rather, part of a stellar constellation—according to the earthly projections of the stars comprising that constellation. Indeed, this was probably the world's first consciously planned astrogeographical journey!

The Tilt of the Earth's Axis: Two Alternatives

Following on from the above report, herewith are further reflections on the new science of Astrogeographia following the October 2009 "astrogeographical journey" in Turkey. As pointed out in chapter 7, in terms of the current projections, three of the seven wonders of the ancient world were located at sites corresponding to stars in Orion:

- the Great Pyramid at Giza corresponds exactly to Alnitak
- the Temple of Artemis at Ephesus corresponds fairly exactly to Bellatrix
- the Pharos Lighthouse at Alexandria corresponds approximately to Alnilam.

These three more-or-less exact alignments of three of the seven wonders of the ancient world with three prominent stars in the constellation of Orion would be unthinkable simply as a coincidence, thus lending support to the method of Astrogeographia as something true and authentic. Moreover, as discussed in chapter 6, the current projection of the first magnitude star Aldebaran at the center of Taurus aligns exactly with Vienna at the heart of Europe (recalling the relationship, according to Greek mythology, of Europa to the Bull). Moreover, the current projection of the first-magnitude star Altair in the constellation of the Eagle aligns exactly with Salt Lake City in Utah, the center of the Mormon religion (bearing in mind that the Eagle is traditionally associated with the mystic power of vision—think of John the Evangelist, whose symbol is the Eagle—and the Mormon religion is based on the visions of Joseph Smith).[7] And the current projection of the fourth-magnitude star Botein in the constellation of Aries aligns exactly with Glastonbury, England, the great mystical New Age center there, discussed in more detail at the end of chapter 10.

These half-a-dozen correspondences, which are mentioned here as examples (there are many more), hold true and are highly meaningful, as should be evident from the research findings presented so far in this book. As can be seen from the latter three of these six examples, it is a matter of expanding from Orion to the rest of the world, in order to discover the worldwide correspondences between the celestial globe and the earthly globe. In taking this step, certain assumptions need to be considered—and perhaps called into question—in

7 On June 8, 2010, I held a lecture in Salt Lake City entitled "Salt Lake City—A Cosmically Significant Location on Planet Earth," in which I spoke in detail about the building of the Mormon Temple in Salt Lake City as a (relatively) modern example of a building erected in response to stellar inspiration—in this case the inspiration streaming from the star Altair—drawing an analogy with the building in antiquity of the Temple of Artemis of Ephesus in response to the inspiration streaming from the star Bellatrix.

order to arrive at the truth. Any theory remains a hypothesis until it is proven to be true.

In this book the implicit point of departure is the *thema mundi* (horoscope of the birth of the world)—i.e., that at a certain moment in time in the far-distant past an imprint took place of the celestial sphere into the earthly sphere, rather like the imprint of the celestial sphere into the human brain at the moment of a person's birth. Alternatively, in view of the perspectives offered earlier in this chapter, it is also possible to view the Earth as an autonomous "I"—united with Christ—corresponding to the celestial sphere *by way of analogy* (rather than by way of projection). A parallel can be drawn here with the twelvefold house system in astrology, which corresponds *by way of analogy* with the twelvefold division of the zodiac—simply by virtue of the twelve houses, connected with the Earth's diurnal cycle, belonging to the autonomous system of the Earth's daily movement, being an analogous division of the daily cycle corresponding to the twelvefold division of the zodiacal constellations in the heavens.[8]

In Astrogeographia, it is helpful to consider "meridian lines" associated with stars. For example, Betelgeuse is located at 4° Gemini and, as already mentioned, the Betelgeuse meridian runs through Hattusha (40N02; 34E37), Jerusalem (31N47; 35E13), and the opposite geographical point (at 65S30; 35E13) to the apparent Ecliptic North Pole, as shown in chapter 10, figure 4. All stars having a longitude of 4° Gemini lie on the same meridian as Betelgeuse—one such star being the star Polaris. Even though Polaris (66° North) and Betelgeuse (16° South) lie some 82° apart, they share the same meridian. This means that their earthly projections according to Astrogeographia lie on the same earthly meridian, about 82° apart on that meridian.

Assuming that at a certain time in the distant past an imprint took place of the celestial sphere into the earthly sphere, if the inclination of the Earth's axis at the time of the *thema mundi* was 0° (let us call this Assumption 1), this means that the earthly meridians are identical with geographical longitudes. For example, Jerusalem (31N47; 35E13) lies on the Polaris-Betelgeuse meridian (4° Gemini) as also does Teriberka (69N10; 35E11) on the Barents Sea in the far north of Russia—Jerusalem

8 Powell, *History of the Houses.*

and Teriberka lying 37°23' apart latitudinally. Assumption 1 (Earth's axis at 0° inclination) is assumed to have been the case at some point in time in the far-distant past of the history of the Earth.

If, however, the *thema mundi* took place after the event known as "the Fall," which occurred during the phase of Earth evolution known as Ancient Lemuria, the inclination of the Earth's axis was then already 23½°, which is its current tilt. Let us now consider Assumption 2. Under Assumption 2 (Earth's axis at 23½° inclination), the projection of stellar meridians onto the Earth would be tilted by 23½° to the longitudinal axis. Taking Jerusalem as the starting point the projection of the 4° Gemini meridian through Jerusalem would run north from Jerusalem at an angle of 23½° to the Teriberka-Jerusalem longitudinal axis.

A question arises here as to whether Assumption 2 would provide a better fit between astrogeographical star projections and ancient sites on the Earth—for example, between Betelgeuse and Hattusha?

Let us recall that the fundamental premise of Astrogeographia is that there is a one-to-one correspondence between the celestial and terrestrial spheres. Under the hypothesis that continental drift figures into the imprint of the stars upon the Earth, one hypothesis that could be made is that Jerusalem was at 0° latitude at the time when the imprint (*thema mundi*) took place. Instead of this hypothesis (associated with Assumption 1), let us now consider an alternative hypothesis.

If one sphere, much larger, is placed around the outside of another, smaller sphere, this could be considered to replicate the celestial sphere around the terrestrial sphere. For the following, let us consider that continental drift has already taken place and that the Earth has approximately its present structure of oceans, seas, and continents. Imagine that the smaller sphere, the Earth, is then simply rotated within the larger sphere, representing the heavens, and that this rotation is suddenly frozen at the moment when Jerusalem is on the Betelgeuse meridian (4° Gemini). If the relationship between the two spheres is fixed at that time—considering the imprint (*thema mundi*) to have taken place at that moment—there is a well-defined one-to-one correspondence between every point on the celestial sphere and every location on the terrestrial globe. Under this hypothesis, associated with

Assumption 2, there is a linear projection between the celestial sphere and the earthly globe, whereas under the previous hypothesis (associated with Assumption 1), there is not a linear correspondence between every point on the celestial sphere and every location on the earthly globe. For example, as discussed below, earthly latitudes below about 32° south are excluded from the correspondence.

What are the practical implications of these alternative hypotheses? Let us take as an example the star Polaris and consider that we wish to find the astrogeographical projection of Polaris onto the earthly sphere. As indicated above, there are two alternative assumptions (Assumption 1 and Assumption 2) to be considered. In the case of Assumption 1, one would follow the projection of the Betelgeuse meridian (4° Gemini) due north from Jerusalem to arrive at an earthly projection of Betelgeuse somewhere in the location of Hattusha (40N02; 34E37). It would then be a matter of following this meridian north for a further 82° to find the earthly projection of Polaris. However, 82° further north from 40° North leads to a latitude more than 120° north, lying beyond the North Pole by more than 30°, which no longer corresponds to a terrestrial location. This kind of anomaly is considered below in the section on *Anomalies*.

The case of Assumption 2 is complicated because of the 23½° tilt. The principle is the same, though. One would follow the projection of the Betelgeuse meridian (4° Gemini) north from Jerusalem—at a tilt of 23½° west of due north—to arrive at the current earthly projection of Betelgeuse somewhere in the location of Hattusha (40N02; 34E37).

As indicated in chapter 7, there is a strong resonance between Betelgeuse and Hattusha in terms of the martial quality generally associated with Betelgeuse and the military prowess of the Hittites, whose center was the city of Hattusha. At this point in our considerations it would be important to see which Betelgeuse projection—that under Assumption 1 or that under Assumption 2—is closer to Hattusha. In terms of Assumption 2, it is a matter of following the meridians not due north or south, but with the meridians tilted 23½° west of due north.

David Bowden conducted a test to compare the two hypotheses based on Assumption 1 and Assumption 2. The result was clear: the due north meridian (Assumption 1) gives a much closer alignment with Hattusha than the tilted meridian (Assumption 2). The reason for conducting this test arose through an exchange with a much respected colleague who has consistently represented the view that the meridians ought to run 23½° NW–SE to be aligned with the ecliptic plane. As we have all been interested in these astrogeographical questions for so many years, we thought it important to test this hypothesis. We realize that this test of one instance of a correspondence between an earthly location and a star is not in any way conclusive and that further research is required into this question. However, we felt that it was important to present an example in order to indicate a methodology for testing Assumption 1 and Assumption 2.

Under Assumption 1, the minimum distance from Hattusha to the Betelgeuse meridian due north is 32½ miles (52½ km), with Hattusha west of the meridian. This occurs when the projection is at a latitude of 40°02' north and a longitude of 35°13' east (noting that the latitude of Hattusha is 40N02 and the longitude is 34E37). Under Assumption 2, the minimum distance from Hattusha to the Betelgeuse meridian running 23½ ° northwest is 196¾ miles (316½ km), with Hattusha east of the meridian. This occurs when the projection is at a latitude of 38°54' north and a longitude of 32°06' east (noting that the latitude of Hattusha is 40N02 and the longitude is 34E37).

Regarding the difference of 32½ miles (52½ km) of Hattusha (40N02; 34E37) from the place of projection of Betelgeuse (40N02; 35E13), this amounts to a difference astrogeographically of 0°36' (Assumption 1). Under the basic assumption of Astrogeographia (formulated, albeit implicitly, by Rudolf Steiner in his *Astronomy Course*), there is an exact location on the Earth corresponding to the star Betelgeuse. The determination of this exact location is discussed in appendix 1 (at astrogeographia.org). As described there, the mid-declination point of a star can be considered its original location according to Assumption 1. However, we also have to take account of the continually shifting relationship between the Earth and the celestial sphere because of precession, and this is what gives rise to the *historical projection* indicating the shift of a star's projection astrogeographically in the course of time along the north–south meridian running through the location of the archetypal projection (mid-declination point). Thanks to David Bowden's test, we can say with a high degree of certainty that with respect to the correspondence between Hattusha and Betelgeuse, which was found by looking at the current projection of Betelgeuse onto the Earth, it is the north–south meridian (Assumption 1) that is significant for Astrogeographia. This example demonstrates a methodology for further tests comparing the two hypotheses referred to above.

Proper Motion and the Precision of Projections

In addition to the mid-declination projection signifying the original projection of a star onto the Earth at the time of the birth horoscope of the Earth, the example discussed in chapter 7 of the building of the temple of Jerusalem around the time when the historical projection of Betelgeuse was close to Jerusalem exemplifies the importance of taking account also of the *historical projection* of a star, which moves up and down the astrogeographical meridian with the changing relationship between the Earth and the celestial sphere caused by precession. Yet the primary starting point of Astrogeographia is the one-to-one correspondence between the celestial and terrestrial spheres expressed in the mid-declination (original or archetypal) projections of stars on the Earth.

An interesting question arises in connection with the proper motion of stars, which in Astrogeographia needs to be taken into consideration. This is possibly a question that can never be satisfactorily resolved, because the proper motion of stars is so small. The question is: Does the projection move with the proper motion of the star? It would make sense if it does, but it is virtually impossible to establish whether or not this is so, since the shift in location of mid-declination (original or archetypal) projections is generally very small. Nevertheless, perhaps in relation to close stars—i.e., stars close to our Sun—such as Sirius, whose proper motion in latitude over 7,000 years is a little over 3° and in longitude over 7,000 years is a little more than 1½°, it might be possible to make a study of this question.

To return to the difference of 32½ miles (52½ km) of Hattusha from the location of Betelgeuse's current projection, from the figure it is evident that over a period of 7,000 years Betelgeuse's proper motion is only 11' in longitude. This is insufficient to explain the difference of 0°36' of Hattusha to the place of projection of Betelgeuse (under the assumption that the place of projection shifts with the proper motion). What can be said, however, is that a prominent star such as Betelgeuse—considering its projection onto the Earth—would have a certain sphere of influence upon the Earth. Even with just a one degree radius for this sphere of influence, Hattusha lies well within Betelgeuse's sphere of influence. In Astrogeographia, 1° = 69 miles (111 km). Thinking of this sphere of influence, the people who originally settled in the Hattusha area, later taken over by the Hittites to become the capital of the Hittite empire, perhaps chose the specific location of Hattusha (a) because it lies within the sphere of influence of the projection of Betelgeuse, and (b) because of topographical considerations. Obviously with any settlement of people, topographical considerations play a role. And this explains why ancient mystery sites need not necessarily have been located *exactly* at the place of a star's projection, but at any rate within the sphere of influence of the region associated with that star. The first settlement around Bogazkoy (Hattusha) took place in the sixth millennium BC, and so the area was settled long before the Hittites established themselves there.[9]

Apart from the foregoing discussion, there is another reason for discounting the hypothesis associated with Assumption 2 of a linear (i.e., tilted) projection of the celestial sphere onto the earthly globe, and that is the evidence provided by examples demonstrating that the north–south geographical meridians are a definite reality—something that was evidently known in antiquity. One such example is the geographical north–south *Nilotic meridian* which, as the name implies, approximately coincides with the River Nile and runs through the area of Giza, where the Great Pyramid and the Sphinx are located. In Astrogeographia, the Nilotic meridian coincides with the 0° Gemini meridian, rounded to the nearest degree. It is thus one of the *primary reference meridians* on the surface of the Earth. (See below for a discussion of the significance of the Nilotic meridian).

9 See http://en.wikipedia.org/wiki/Hattians and http://ancient-anatolia.blogspot.com/2006/09/hattians-first-civilization-in-anatolia.html.

Anomalies

There are still some anomalies to consider that arise in Astrogeographia by virtue of the displacement northward by 31°47' from the equator of the east–west axis through Jerusalem as the (spiritual) equator for the Earth's "I." From the foregoing considerations it is evident that Astrogeographia comprises an exploration of the relationship of the Earth's "I" (united with Christ since the Mystery of Golgotha) to the starry heavens and that the east–west axis through Jerusalem is the spiritual equator of the Earth. In this connection, an underlying hypothesis could be that the Jerusalem east–west axis coincided with the Earth's physical equator at the time when the birth of the Earth's "I" took place, and that subsequently a shift to the north of 31°47' took place with respect to this east–west axis.

Based on this hypothesis, in terms of correspondences of stars with earthly locations, the northern circumpolar stars would have been projected at that time[10] onto the Earth over regions to the far north, prior to the shift of land masses northward to their present locations. Further, it has to be recalled that the formation of the physical Earth only began during the Lemurian period, with the event of the Fall. What does all of this mean for Astrogeographia?

Let us consider a specific example, the seven stars comprising the Big Dipper: their astrogeographical coordinates (projected geographical longitudes and latitudes) are:

7 stars of the Big Dipper	Astrogeographical longitude	Astrogeographical latitude	mag.	light-years	luminosity
Benetnasch (Alkaid)	123E24	81N06	1.85	101	151
Mizar	112E10	86N43	2.06	78	64
Alioth	105E24	87N44	1.76	81	106
Megrez	97E31	88N49	3.31	81	26
Phad	96E56	85N28	2.43	84	62
Merak	85E54	88N10	2.36	79	60
Dubhe	81E39	93N32	1.80	124	236

10 That is, at the time of the birth of the Earth's "I."

Because of the northward shift by 31°47', the projection of these stars now lies in the far northern Arctic regions. In the case of Dubhe, as can be seen from the above table, an anomaly arises, since there is no location further north than 90° latitude. This is an anomaly like the one referred to already concerning the star Polaris, whose astrogeographical projection (more than 120° north) lies more than 30° north of the northernmost latitude of 90°. Nevertheless, the projection of Polaris and Dubhe are still realities for the Earth's "I" *in terms of their meridians*. In the case of Dubhe this is evident from the fact that Mt. Kailash (81E19, 31N04), one of the most sacred mountains on the Earth (see chapter 10), is more or less exactly on the Dubhe meridian, albeit 62½° further south than Dubhe's astrogeographical latitude. Mt. Kailash lies on the meridian line of influence of Dubhe and is thus associated astrogeographically with Dubhe, which is by far the most luminous of the seven stars of the Big Dipper. In light of Astrogeographia, Mt. Kailash can be regarded as an earthly "transmitter" of the cosmic influence of Dubhe. The same line of reasoning applies to all those northern circumpolar stars which, like Dubhe, have an astrogeographical latitude exceeding 90°. In the case of Polaris, as we have already seen, it lies on the same meridian as Jerusalem, regarded as the center of the world—obviously a very important meridian.

From the examples of Polaris and Dubhe, it is evident that even though there are anomalies with the northern circumpolar stars whose astrogeographical latitudes exceed 90°, these stars nevertheless exert a real influence along their meridians. The calculation underlying the computation of astrogeographical latitudes yields anomalous results, whereby certain stars show up with astrogeographical latitudes greater than 90°—something that is physically impossible. There is nevertheless a *spiritual influence* exerted by such stars along their lines of meridian, recalling that in the starry heavens a stellar influence is exerted by a star along its line of meridian regardless as to how far north or south it is from the ecliptic. It is the same with the astrogeographical meridians, according to the principle "as above, so below."

Against this background, it emerges that the astrogeographical meridians—and the same applies to the astrogeographical latitudes (as we have seen with the zero latitude running through Jerusalem)—are spiritual realities for the Earth's "I" and also for Christ's "I," since Christ united with the Earth's "I" at the Mystery of Golgotha. Together these astrogeographical meridians and parallels (latitudes) comprise a *spiritual grid* that is real for the "I" of the Earth. A comprehension of these meridians as a spiritual reality is a key to Astrogeographia and also to understanding the anomalies. It needs to be borne in mind that the earthly astrogeographical grid mirrors a heavenly grid comprising stellar meridians and parallels relative to the ecliptic. The meridians through the stars intersect the ecliptic and form a grid when seen together with the lines of latitude running parallel to the ecliptic. Stars having the same latitude north of the ecliptic are on the same parallel of latitude. And stars having the same latitude south of the ecliptic are also on the same parallel. Analogously, the earthly meridians in Astrogeographia intersect the Earth's spiritual equator, the east–west axis running through Jerusalem, which in Astrogeographia is the zero latitude, theoretically corresponding to the ecliptic in the heavens.[11] The

11 Theoretically, because—as may be seen from the figure of the projection of the ecliptic onto the earthly globe (see figures 3 and 11 in chapter 8)—the actual projection onto the two dimensional map of the earth forms a double wave curve whose path at the present time (AD 2000) runs close to Moscow, high above Jerusalem. Nevertheless, following the shifting projection back historically in connection with the precession of the equinoxes, there was a date historically when Jerusalem did lie on the projection of the ecliptic. This date is found by applying the equation: year 0 = 220.78029 – 72 x sidereal longitude. Since the sidereal longitude of Jerusalem is the same as that of the star Betelgeuse (4° Gemini), year 0 = 4388 BC. The year 4388 BC is close to the start of the Age of Taurus in 4106 BC. According to Anne Catherine Emmerich, Melchizedek (= Noah of Biblical tradition = the Manu of Hindu tradition) was the founder of Jerusalem (meaning "abode of peace"), and the earliest settlement there is traced back by archeologists to the fourth millennium BC, making it one of the oldest cities in the world. Perhaps we can picture the Manu originally founding the city around 4388 BC, toward the end of the Age of Gemini, in preparation for the following ages of Taurus and Aries—knowing the great significance of this location as the center of the world in a spiritual sense—that this would be a most important place in the history of humanity. This founding deed on the part of the Manu subsequently came to fulfillment with Christ's sacrifice on Golgotha in the Age of Aries signifying the *turning point* in the evolution of the Earth and humanity.

stellar meridians and parallels can best be grasped as a reality in the heavens by way of contemplating the Fiorenza Star Map, reproduced on pages 296–297.

The Fiorenza Star Map and the Significance of Stellar Meridians

In the Fiorenza Star Map (see pages 296–297), the ecliptic is the horizontal axis (0° latitude) through the middle of the twelve signs/constellations of the sidereal zodiac. It should be noted that the astronomical definition of the zodiacal belt extends 8° north and 8° south of the ecliptic. Above the central axis of the ecliptic/zodiacal belt are the constellations of the northern sky (N latitude) and below the ecliptic/zodiacal belt are the constellations of the southern sky (S latitude). The orientation of the figure is from the perspective of a viewer in the northern hemisphere, who sees the zodiacal constellations proceeding in a counterclockwise direction–from right to left: Gemini (♊), Cancer (♋), Leo (♌), Virgo (♍), Libra (♎), Scorpio (♏), Sagittarius (♐), Capricorn (♑), Aquarius (♒), Pisces (♓), Aries (♈), Taurus (♉). A southern hemisphere view necessitates turning the figure upside down, whereby the viewer beholds the constellations upside down and sees the zodiacal signs/constellations proceeding in a clockwise direction—from left to right. For ease of reference, the northern hemisphere perspective, as presented by the figure, is adopted in the following discussion.

The Sun is pictured moving through the signs of the sidereal zodiac from right to left, starting in the figure with the sign of Gemini. On June 19/20 the Sun comes into conjunction with the red supergiant Betelgeuse—a megastar (luminosity somewhere between 130,000 and 180,000).[12] Moreover, the sidereal longitude of Betelgeuse is 4° Gemini. As the Sun travels approximately one degree through the zodiac each day, and since the Sun enters Gemini on June 15/16, therefore it reaches 4° Gemini (conjunction with Betelgeuse) four days later,

12 The precise luminosity of Betelgeuse is difficult to ascertain, as it is a variable star that fluctuates in size and brightness. It is one of the largest stars known, with a diameter about 1,180 times that of our Sun, which would mean that, in the place of our Sun, it would extend in size between the orbits of Mars and Jupiter.

on June 19/20. Betelgeuse marks the right shoulder of the giant Orion and is a star associated with military might and prowess: "The star is indicative of great fortune, martial honors, and kingly attributes."[13] It is worth noting that Saturn was conjoined with Betelgeuse at the outbreak of World War I on August 1, 1914, and was again in conjunction with this red supergiant on D-Day (June 6, 1944), which was a decisive battle and turning point during World War II.[14]

Just one day after the Sun's conjunction with Betelgeuse at 4° Gemini, the summer solstice (winter solstice in the southern hemisphere) takes place—at the present time when the Sun is at 5° Gemini.

High above Betelgeuse is the Pole Star, Polaris, which lies on the same meridian (4° Gemini) as Betelgeuse. Thus, at the same time as the Sun crosses the Betelgeuse meridian, receiving the energy flow of Betelgeuse from "below" (Betelgeuse's latitude is 16° south), it is also crossing the Polaris meridian, receiving the energy flow of Polaris from "above" (Polaris's latitude is 66° north). The luminosity of Polaris is about 2,200 and this star is about 430 light-years away. Because of the simultaneous conjunction of the Sun with Betelgeuse and Polaris, both lying on the same meridian (4° Gemini), but 82° apart, it is a question of distinguishing the influences of these two stars in any given situation where 4° Gemini is involved in astrological considerations. For example, at the birth of Franklin D. Roosevelt on January 30, 1882, Mars was at 4° Gemini, in conjunction with Betelgeuse and Polaris. He was president of the United States for twelve years, and led the U.S. during a time of severe economic crisis, the Great Depression. During this time he was a kind of "Pole star" for the American people, leading them through the crisis. This would speak for the influence of Mars in conjunction with Polaris, toward which the Earth's axis is oriented. Although also the influence of Mars conjunct Betelgeuse, to

13 From http://www.constellationsofwords.com/stars/Betelgeuse.html.

14 This research finding relating to Saturn's conjunction with Betelgeuse indicates that it is not only the conjunction of the Sun with other suns/stars that is significant, but that also the conjunction of the planets with stars is important for astrology. Indeed, further research along these lines confirms Rudolf Steiner's statement that the conjunctions of planets with stars is fundamental to astrology; see Powell and Dann, *The Astrological Revolution*, pp. 158–163.

a lesser degree, was playing in as well, as is evident from the resolute fortitude demonstrated by the president in this difficult time. He also led the U.S. during World War II, which would seem to be more the influence of Mars in conjunction with Betelgeuse, whereby the influence of Mars in conjunction with Polaris also played in here, expressed through the president's firm quality of leadership. It is also interesting that when Jesus pronounced woe upon the Pharisees, on March 24 in the year 33, Mars was in conjunction with the Betelgeuse-Polaris meridian at 4° Gemini. This powerful speech (see Matthew 23:13–36) evidently had to do with Mars being conjunct Betelgeuse and Polaris, Mars being the planet of speech.

Another striking example of two prominent stars lying on the same meridian (more or less) are Spica (29° Virgo) and Arcturus (29½° Virgo). Their astrological influences are commingled by virtue of lying on the same stellar meridian. At the present time the Sun crosses the Spica meridian around October 17 and the Arcturus meridian half a day later. A further one-half of a day later the Sun enters Libra, where it was located at the baptism of Jesus in the River Jordan (0½° Libra). Indeed, in relation to the life of Jesus Christ, every step he took was "in accordance with the collective being of the whole universe," as indicated by Rudolf Steiner. Thus the life of Christ offers an archetype to help us understand the influences of Spica and Arcturus. For, on the day prior to the baptism in the Jordan, Jesus had a most significant conversation with the Virgin Mary.[15] The Sun (representing Christ) was conjunct Spica (representing the Virgin Mary). It is noteworthy that in ancient astrology Spica had to do with wise women priestesses: "Spica makes people become the interpreters of sacred things, high, supreme, honored and respected priests or philosophers or the inspired interpreters of some mysteries and, especially... in female genitures, it makes the natives priestesses of Demeter, who is the mother of the gods, or of Core or of Isis, as well as women who are the interpreters of sacred things or experts in mysteries or in initiation rites... and who are helped by the gods very much."[16]

15 Powell, *Chronicle of the Living Christ*, pp. 107–109.

16 From http://www.cieloeterra.it/eng/eng.testi.379/eng.379.html.

Spica, as it lies just 2° south of the ecliptic, is well within the zodiacal belt extending 8° above and below the ecliptic. On the other hand, Arcturus in the constellation of Boötes (the Ploughman) is located 31° north of the ecliptic. In the course of his conversation with the Virgin Mary, the inner decision was taken by Jesus to go to the place of baptism, to receive the baptism of John the Baptist. Here, in making this decision, evidently the influence of Arcturus began to make itself felt. Arcturus, thought of by the ancient Britons as the star of King Arthur,[17] can be seen as inspiring a heroic deed—that of Jesus offering himself up to Christ in a deed of sacrifice bringing hope for the future. It was John the Baptist who facilitated the deed of baptism, whereupon he proclaimed, "Behold the Lamb of God!" (John 1: 29). Perhaps this pronouncement by John can be seen as an earthly correspondence to the influence of Arcturus pouring down from above through the Sun?—an influence that is connected with joy,[18] in this case the joy of the coming of the Messiah, the Christ.

The Primary Phenomenon

Without going into too much detail, the primary phenomenon to be noted is that the Sun is influenced on its path along the ecliptic not only by stars *within* the zodiacal belt, but also by stars *above and below* the zodiacal belt. The primary phenomenon, since the Sun is a star among stars, is that the Sun is literally "in" a zodiacal constellation, its rays uniting with the rays of other Suns/stars within that constellation, when from the perspective of the Earth the Sun is located against the background of a particular zodiacal constellation. To illustrate this, let us consider again the sign/constellation of Gemini as an example.

Having entered Gemini on June 15/16, the Sun is "in" Gemini until it passes beyond the stars Castor (25½° Gemini) and Pollux (28½° Gemini) marking the heads of the Twins. The Sun enters Cancer on July 16/17 and is then "in" Cancer, uniting its rays with Suns/stars in

17 Tradition "links the name *Arthur* to *Arcturus*, the brightest star in the constellation Boötes"; http://en.wikipedia.org/wiki/King_Arthur.

18 Prehistoric navigators between the Polynesian islands referred to Arcturus as *Hōkūle'a,* the "Star of Joy"; http://en.wikipedia.org/wiki/Arcturus.

the starry region of Cancer. At the time when the Sun is "in" Gemini from mid-June to mid-July, it is also receiving influences from stars in the constellations above and below Gemini (see Fiorenza Star Map reproduction on pages 296–297): above—Ursa Minor (the Lesser Bear), Lynx (the Lynx), and Auriga (the Charioteer); below—Orion (the Giant), Monoceros (the Unicorn), Canis Major (the Greater Dog), Columba (the Dove), and the tip of the oar of Argo Navis (the Ship Argo) marked by the star Canopus.

Here, it is worth noting that the two brightest stars in the heavens—brightest in terms of their apparent magnitude, not in terms of luminosity—Sirius (19½° Gemini) and Canopus (20° Gemini), are also (more or less) on the same meridian, which at the present time the Sun crosses each year around July 6/7—Sirius being located 39½° south and Canopus 76° south of the ecliptic. As a matter of fact, two presidents of the United States—Calvin Coolidge (born July 4, 1872) and George W. Bush (born July 6, 1946) were each born with the Sun between 19½° Gemini and 20° Gemini, aligned with the Sirius-Canopus axis.

Clearly there is much research remaining to be done in terms of expanding consciousness toward a more galactic perspective embracing all the stars/constellations in the heavens. The foregoing is intended to draw attention to this primary phenomenon of the Sun's passage each year through the twelve zodiacal signs/constellations along the ecliptic, simultaneously receiving also from the extra-zodiacal constellations above and below the ecliptic.[19] Conscious recognition of this primary phenomenon is significant at this special time of humanity opening to galactic consciousness in connection with the year 2012.[20]

To grasp the stellar meridians in the heavens requires an expansion of consciousness from the Sun's path through the twelve

19 Paul and Powell, *Cosmic Dances of the Zodiac,* gives an overview of the ancient 36 extra-zodiacal constellations above and below the twelve zodiacal signs/constellations, where these 36 constellations according to ancient tradition correspond to the 36 decans (10° sectors of the zodiac, three to each sign of the sidereal zodiac).

20 Powell and Dann, *Christ and the Maya Calendar,* discusses the special significance of the times associated with the year 2012; see also Powell, "World Pentecost," *Journal for Star Wisdom* 2010, pp. 53–65, reproduced as appendix 3 in Powell, *Prophecy-Phenomena-Hope.*

zodiacal signs/constellations to include the entire celestial sphere—all the extra-zodiacal constellations above and below the zodiac—ultimately embracing all the stars of the entire galaxy. Then, for example, when the Sun is at 10½° Aquarius—clearly "in" the constellation of Aquarius—it is at the same time *in conjunction with Deneb*, the tail of the Swan (or head of the Northern Cross), 60° north of the ecliptic. Whereas the influence of Aquarius at that moment in time (presently: around February 24 each year) is obvious by virtue of the Sun blending with other Suns/stars in the constellation of Aquarius located at this degree, our Sun is also receiving the energy flow along the entire meridian running through 10½° Aquarius extending all the way up through Deneb and beyond to the north pole of the ecliptic and all the way down to the south pole of the ecliptic. Deneb is of special interest as a powerful megastar, some 250,000 times more luminous than our Sun. (Megastars are those stars whose luminosity exceeds 10,000.)

Contemplation of the significance of the megastars in the life of Christ—such as the Sun's conjunction with the megastar Deneb at the feeding of the 5,000 and the walking on the water, and all the other examples described in detail in chapter 5 of *The Astrological Revolution*—reveals the truth of the foregoing account concerning the essence of the stellar meridians in the heavens.[21] This truth is embedded in a meditation which serves to uplift the human spirit to the galactic level of existence—bearing in mind that the word *mega* means *great*: "Christ's Light from great stars streams into my heart" (from a meditation which Rudolf Steiner is said to have given to Ita Wegman). These words are a potent mantra serving as a powerful focus of orientation to the mysteries of the starry heavens, which are mirrored also on the Earth, as revealed by Astrogeographia.

Once the heavenly meridians are grasped, it is possible to comprehend—through Astrogeographia—that the earthly meridians (lines of geographical longitude) exactly mirror the stellar meridians in the heavens, and that this is a reality for the Earth's "I." Here it is important to bear in mind that—even though *projections* are referred to in Astrogeographia—it is actually a matter of *correspondences*, since

21 Powell and Dann, *The Astrological Revolution*, pp. 153–156.

the Earth is an autonomous organism within the greater organism of the solar system.

In other words, on the one hand the heavenly meridians are a reality for our solar system defined in relation to the ecliptic axis as the central axis (see Fiorenza Star Map on pages 296–297), and on the other hand the earthly meridians, which exactly correspond to the heavenly meridians, are a reality for the Earth's "I" defined in relation to the spiritual equator of the Earth, the east–west axis running through Jerusalem. There is a correspondence here between the greater organism of our solar system "above" and the smaller organism of the Earth "below." For our solar system it is a matter as to how our solar system is embedded in the greater reality of the surrounding stars. At one time the Earth's "I," existing on a higher plane of existence prior to the Fall, was deeply and more closely embedded in this greater reality. Then came the event of the Fall and the descent of the Earth's "I" to its present location at the heart of the Earth. The Christ, too, descended from a higher plane of existence and united with the Earth's "I."

The Earth's "I"—and subsequently Christ's "I"—carried over the memory of the greater reality of our solar system into the Earth's organism, where it lives as an earthly correspondence to the higher reality, a correspondence that finds expression in the Earth's spiritual grid that is the focus of Astrogeographia. The earthly reality of this grid is the system of geographical longitudes and latitudes. In astronomy the heavenly equivalent to the system of geographical longitudes and latitudes is the equatorial system of right ascension and declination. In Astrogeographia the equivalent is the spiritual grid of astrogeographical coordinates of sidereal longitudes and latitudes—for example, that Jerusalem's sidereal longitude is 4° Gemini and latitude is 0°.

The geographical longitude (35E13) of Jerusalem extends up and down—as an earthly meridian—mirroring the heavenly meridian of 4° Gemini on which Betelgeuse and Polaris are located. Mirrored on the Earth, the current (epoch: AD 2000) astrogeographical projection of Betelgeuse (35E18, 39N11) lies 7½° north of Jerusalem (31N47), in the region of Hattusha, the ancient capital of the Hittite Empire. Extending this meridian further to the north, the current astrogeographical projection of Polaris (35E02, 121N03) is not located physically upon the Earth. Nevertheless, it is a reality for the Earth's "I." The influence of Polaris, although astrogeographically so far north of the northernmost latitude, is still a spiritual reality for the Earth's "I," even though not corresponding to a physical location on the Earth.

Here the question arises regarding the astrogeographical correspondence between stars and locations to the far south, say in the Antarctic Circle? If the astrogeographical coordinates of a star are computed initially *by equating the Earth's spiritual equator with the physical equator*—as expressed in one hypothesis that might be considered to underlie Astrogeographia that this was the case at the birth of the Earth's "I"—and then, as a final step, the astrogeographical latitudes are shifted 31°47' to the north, this leaves a region around the Antarctic Circle without any *direct* astrogeographical correspondences to specific stars in the heavens. Nevertheless, the meridians are still a reality also here in the far southern region of the Earth. In other words, for the Earth's "I" the stellar meridians projected astrogeographically onto the Earth's globe extend all the way down to the Antarctic Circle, down to the South Pole.

Parallels of Latitude

Having discussed the significance of the meridians (longitudes) in Astrogeographia, there is still the question of the significance of the latitudes as the other component making up the spiritual grid of the stellar projections of stars onto the Earth. The geographical latitudes, indicated by stellar declinations, are obviously significant. This is discussed in chapter 3 in relation to the star Benetnasch:

If we consider one particular star—for example, Benatnasch or Benetnasch (also known as Alkaid), marking the tip of the tail of the Great Bear[22]—this star's current declination is 49°16' North of the celestial equator. Thus once every twenty-four hours it passes directly over all cities whose geographical latitude is around 49N16.

22 Benetnasch is the end star of the group of seven bright stars in the Great Bear—these seven stars being referred to as the Plough or the Dipper—and is used as a pointer star (together with the other two bright stars in the tail of the Great Bear) toward Arcturus, which is the second brightest star visible in the northern heavens (after Sirius).

It passes directly over Vancouver (latitude 49N16), British Columbia, on the west coast of Canada, and then crosses the Pacific Ocean on its passage from east to west. After traversing the Pacific it passes over Poronaysk (49N13) on the Sakhalin Island off the east coast of Russia, then Kukan (49N12) in the far east of mainland Russia, then Hailar (49N12) in China, Bayandun (49N12) in Mongolia, Katon-Karagaj (49N11) in Kazakhstan, Star'obelsk (49N16) in the Ukraine, Brno (49N12) in the Czech Republic, Saarbrücken (49N14) in Germany, Reims (49N15) in France. Then it traverses the Atlantic Ocean and crosses over Canada (not the United States, with the exception of Alaska and the Northwest Angle, since the 49th parallel divides Canada from the United States).[23] It passes directly over Lewisporte (49N15) on Newfoundland, then Hornepayne (49N13) in Ontario, Morris (49N21) in Manitoba, Warner (49N17) in Alberta, returning to cross directly over Vancouver (49N16) in British Columbia, completing its apparent daily circuit of the Earth.[24]

In the course of time, the declination of Benetnasch and the precession of the equinoxes are caused by the tilt in the Earth's axis. Correspondingly its daily passage around the globe, as beheld from the surface of the Earth, shifts correspondingly. In fact, it is the changing declination of stars during the precession cycle which gives rise to the shift of a star astrogeographically up and down its stellar meridian, as in the example of Betelgeuse, currently aligned with a location in the region of Hattusha, Turkey, and previously aligned with Jerusalem about 1371 BC (see chapter 8, figure 12). Obviously this is of great significance, a phenomenon that is traced astrogeographically

23 The term *49th parallel* is used as a popular term for the entire Canada–United States border. However, many of Canada's most populated regions are well south of the 49th parallel, including the two largest cities: Toronto (43N39) and Montreal (45N31) and the capital Ottawa (45N25)—as are the three Maritime provinces and parts of Vancouver Island. Similarly parts of the United States—Alaska and the Northwest Angle—are located north of the 49th parallel. Nevertheless, it is accurate to say that the 49th parallel of north latitude forms *part* of the international boundary between Canada and the United States from Manitoba to British Columbia on the Canadian side and from Minnesota to Washington on the U.S. side.

24 In reality, of course, it is the Earth's rotation once every twenty-four hours which gives the appearance that the stars move overhead from east to west making a circuit of the Earth during this period of time.

by determining stellar projections onto the Earth at different points in time—referred to as *historical projections.*

Another example is that of the Pleiades, where it emerges that astrogeographically the Pleiades' declinational transit of the Great Pyramid was *prior* to the building of the Great Pyramid around 2500 BC—it was around the beginning of Kali Yuga (3102 BC). Astrogeographically Alcyone, the brightest star of the Pleiades cluster, was transiting over the future location of the Great Pyramid when its declination was -1°48', which is the difference between the latitude of Jerusalem (31N47) and the latitude of the Great Pyramid (29N59). This took place around 3100 BC, about the time of the start of Kali Yuga. At that time the Great Pyramid of Pharaoh Cheops did not yet exist as a physical structure, although it is possible that some other structure—a forerunner to the Great Pyramid—existed there at that time. Evidently the location was a powerful place even before the Great Pyramid was there, because of the alignment of Giza with the meridian running through Alnitak. This relationship of the Pleiades to the place of subsequent location of the Great Pyramid, a relationship from the time of the start of Kali Yuga, is not along the meridian of Alcyone, but has to do with the declination of Alcyone at that time. At that time the astrogeographical projection of Alcyone (6E31, 29N59) coincided in latitude with the Great Pyramid (31E08, 29N59), but lay 24°37' to the west of the Great Pyramid. It remains to be seen whether further research into such alignments in declination are significant. An obvious name for the declination lines in Astrogeographia is *parallels.* Thus the astrogeographical grid is made up of meridians and parallels. The significance of the *meridians* is evident, and only further research will determine whether the *parallels* are also astrogeographically important, as would appear to be so in this example of the Pleiades. Obviously, though, there is not a case for emphasizing the parallels based on only a few examples.

The Nilotic meridian

Earlier in this chapter, reference was made to the geographical north–south Nilotic meridian in support of the reality of north–south meridians, as opposed to the hypothesis of meridians tilted at 23½°

because of the tilt of the ecliptic to the Earth's equator. The ancient Nilotic meridian is just one example of the reality of north–south meridians.[25] The following concerning the Nilotic meridian is from the book *Mystery of the White Lions* by Linda Tucker:

> Significantly, the course of the Nile follows a longitudinal line.... For the ancients this meridian represented 0°. That is, the line by which they began measuring longitude...Naturally, the ancient Egyptians would not have chosen Greenwich as their touchstone, but rather the Nilotic meridian...The fact that this very meridian is the prime meridian at the center of the earth's landmasses underlies the strategic nature of the ancients' identification of this specific line...From the Nile delta...with its pyramids and Sphinx...step by step, due south, until it reaches my special kingdom of lions...If the Giza plateau was a perfect star map on earth, and Timbavati was in perfect alignment with it, what is the significance of the White Lion's birthplace located precisely here on our globe?... Timbavati's furthermost corner extends out to a point which is in almost perfect alignment to the pyramids at the apex of the Nile Delta: 31°14' east.... Why should today's living lion legends align with the lion monument [the Sphinx] of ancient days?[26]

Here is a review by John Lash of Linda Tucker's book:

> Timbavati lies on a great meridian, a line running north–south, from pole to pole, but not just any great meridian. It occupies the Nilotic meridian (31 East longitude), which runs through the Giza plateau where, in times of undetermined antiquity, a massive stone lion was carved: the Sphinx. Tucker points out that the Nile is the only great river in the world that runs due north, and it does so in a straight line, corresponding to the geographical meridian. Southward into the depths of Africa, the meridian passes through Laetoli, Tanzania, and the ruins of Great Zimbabwe, a massive

25 Another example is the Chaco meridian of the ancient Pueblo people known as the Anasazi; see Lekson, *The Chaco Meridian*, which presents evidence that the Anasazi leaders reckoned by the stars and established centers along the 108th meridian, migrating north and south—the longitude of the primary center of the Anasazi at Chaco Canyon being 107°58' west—i.e., almost exactly 108° west of the Greenwich meridian.

26 Tucker, *Mystery of the White Lions*, pp. 253–256.

> megalithic site associated with lion lore. At its terminus, it reaches the Sterkfontein caves of South Africa, not far from where the white lions have appeared. The Nilotic meridian is connected with the most important sites of archeological discovery concerning the current theory of human evolution.
>
> Leotoli and the Olduvai Gorge where the primate skeleton called Lucy was discovered lie in the Rift Valley, a massive land-seam formed by seismic upheavals in the Earth's mantle. Following shamanic lore imparted to her by Credo Mutwa, Tucker suggests that the phenomenon of the white lions is deeply related with what we know, and have yet to learn, about the origins of our own species and our survival over the long term. She connects the Nilotic meridian with the Zulu legend of an underground stream corresponding to the Nile that runs all the way to the tip of Africa.[27]

The idea that the Nilotic meridian is the basic meridian of the Earth is not new. It was part of ancient geography:

> The frame of ancient geography was based on the assumption that the Nile is the basic meridian of the inhabited Earth. The Nile begins from two lakes at the Equator and can be conceived of as ending at 30°, 31°, or 31°30'N, all highly significant latitudes. The Nile is closely identified with the Milky Way which, in its ideal position, goes from the extreme south to the extreme north, arching over the earth. The Milky Way is the Nile of the Sky or the Nile is the Milky Way of the Earth.[28]

This introduces the idea, also referred to by Robert Bauval in *The Orion Mystery*, that the River Nile on Earth reflects the Milky Way in

27 John Lash, http://www.metahistory.org/reading/reviews/whitelions.php.

28 From http://www.metrum.org/mapping/cosmol.htm; note that the latitude of 31°30' referred to here is very close to the latitude of Jerusalem (31°47'), which would fit the idea put forward of a mythological River Oceanus flowing from west to east, intersecting the Nile at an angle of 90°. The conception from Greek mythology was that the River Oceanus had its source in the Garden of the Hesperides in the extreme west—corresponding to the Garden of Eden in the Bible. Ancient geographers were unsure about the latitude of River Oceanus, which some said flowed along the equator intersecting the Nile at its source, but which—as in the above quote—was thought by some to flow latitudinally more in the region of the Nile delta, for which reason the latitudes 30°, 31°, and 31°30' are mentioned.

the heavens. In terms of Astrogeographia this is to be understood symbolically rather than as an actual astrogeographical correspondence. The important point is that for Astrogeographia the heavenly correspondence to the Nilotic meridian is the meridian running through the star Alnitak (0° Gemini–rounded value). How does this relate to the previous finding that the *center of the world*—Golgotha—lies on the Betelgeuse meridian at 4° Gemini?

Looking up to the Milky Way we behold a band of stars several degrees wide—in places ten or more degrees wide—that intersects the ecliptic approximately between 0° Gemini and 10° Gemini on the one side and between 0° Sagittarius and 10° Sagittarius on the opposite side of the ecliptic. The galactic equator, running through the center of the Milky Way, intersects the ecliptic at the respective midpoints of the Milky Way band: at 5° Gemini and 5° Sagittarius. However, the sidereal longitude of the galactic center, because it is 5½° south of the ecliptic, is located at 2° Sagittarius, and the galactic anticenter, 5½° north, has a sidereal longitude of 2° Gemini. The two figures on

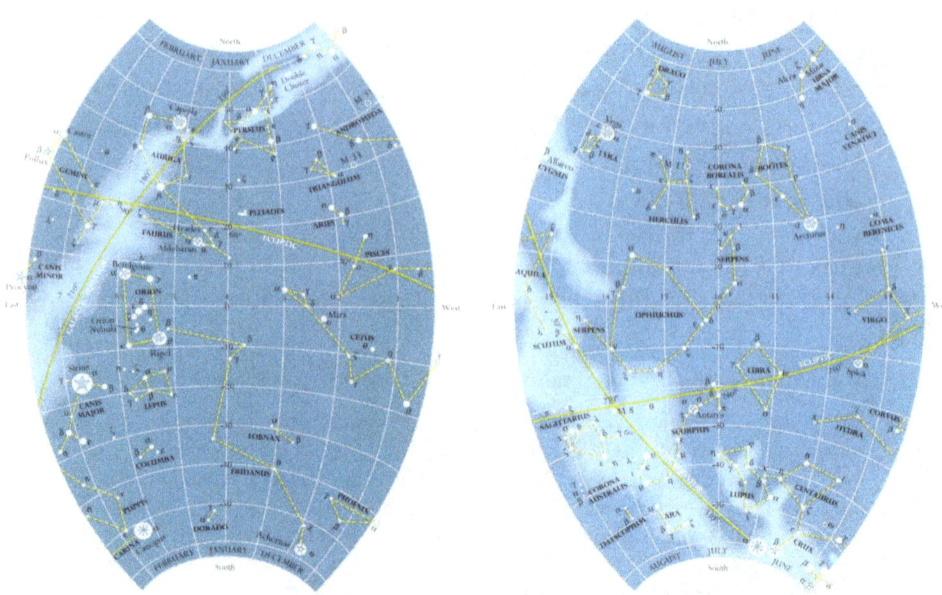

Galactic equator, Taurus–Gemini (left);
Galactic equator, Scorpio–Sagittarius (right)

page 252 depict 1) the arc of the celestial equator passing through the starry region between Taurus and Gemini, corresponding to the start of the sidereal sign of Gemini, and 2) the arc of the celestial equator passing through the starry region between Scorpio and Sagittarius, corresponding to the early degrees of the sidereal sign of Sagittarius.[29]

The Nilotic meridian is a clear example supporting the reality of north–south meridians on the Earth, corresponding to stellar meridians in the heavens. It is evidently aligned with the celestial meridian passing via the star Alnitak, in turn aligned with the earthly meridian running through the Sphinx and the Great Pyramid. Alnitak's meridian is currently at 29TA56 having shifted from 29TA51 at the time of the building of the Great Pyramid around 2500 BC. This shift is on account of Alnitak's proper motion. If the future proper motion of this star is taken into account, the Alnitak meridian will lie exactly at 0° Gemini in about 3,500 years' time. Based on this, the range between 0° Gemini and 4° Gemini (Betelgeuse meridian, coinciding with Jerusalem) is very important, centered in the heavens around the sidereal location of the galaxy's anticenter (2° Gemini)—opposite the galactic center at 2° Sagittarius—and on Earth signifying astrogeographically the region extending from the Great Pyramid to Jerusalem. Also, Mt. Sinai lies in this region close to the 3° Gemini meridian. Interestingly, the event of Moses receiving the ten commandments on Mt. Sinai is considered to be the Old Testament precursor of the event of Pentecost recorded in the New Testament. The Sun actually crossed the 3° Gemini meridian running through Mt. Sinai on the historical day of the event of Pentecost (May 24 AD 33). In order to understand this, let us recall that the galactic center is at 2° Sagittarius, signifying, when the Earth (viewed heliocentrically) is conjunct the galactic center, that the Sun is at 2° Gemini in conjunction with the galactic anticenter. At the historical event of Pentecost the Sun was at 2° Gemini.[30] At the same time, the Earth—as seen from the perspective of the Sun—was in conjunction with the galactic center at 2° Sagittarius.

29 These two figures are from Jim Kaler's STARS website, http://stars.astro.illinois.edu/sow/cm3.html and http://stars.astro.illinois.edu/sow/cm5.html.

30 Powell, *Chronicle of the Living Christ*, p. 161.

Regarding Golgotha as the spiritual center of the world, the entire area marked by Jerusalem (Golgotha), Mt. Sinai, and the Great Pyramid (a *man-made mountain* as an antenna for the cosmic energy of Alnitak), can be considered to delineate the Earth's *heart chakra*—hence the great significance of this area for Astrogeographia.

Chapter 10
Earth Chakras

The Imprint of the Stars upon the Earth

So far in this book we have been considering the relationship of the earthly globe to the celestial sphere comprising multitudes of stars, looking at how the stars in the heavens are mirrored on the Earth at various locations, as indicated in Rudolf Steiner's words, "*we can conceive of the active heavenly sphere mirrored in the Earth*" quoted at the start of chapter 1 of this book and as described mathematically in the appendix (astrogeographia.org). Elsewhere Rudolf Steiner said:

> The continents upon the Earth are held in place from without by the starry constellations. When the constellations change, the continents change, also. On the old maps and atlases these relationships between starry constellations and configurations on the Earth's surface were correctly shown, including also the constellations of the zodiac.[31]

What we believe to be the correct depiction of the projection of the zodiacal constellations—in particular, of the ecliptic running through the middle of the zodiacal constellations—is shown in chapter 8, mapped out by David Bowden.

What we have not approached so far is the question as to whether or not only the stars but also the planets might be mirrored upon the Earth. This is the main theme in this chapter. Like the theme of the rest of this book concerning the projection of the stars upon the earthly globe, the theme of this chapter—the relationship of the planets to the earthly globe—is a vast one, which we can only briefly

31 Steiner, *Faculty Meetings with Rudolf Steiner,* vol. 2 (1922–1924), CW 300c, "Questions and Answers," April 25, 1923 (tr. amended by RP after comparing with the German original).

depict here in outline. We ask the reader to bear with us in this sketch, in the understanding that it deserves a much more profound treatment than we are able to give it here.

In chapter 3 it was made clear that, while the relationship of the stars and planets to the Earth are continually changing each hour of the day on account of the Earth's rotation, in Astrogeographia we are interested in the *archetypal relationship* of the heavens to the Earth. And to express what is meant by "archetypal relationship" an analogy was drawn with the horoscope at a person's birth.

> If one were to photograph a person's brain at the moment of birth and then photograph also the heavens lying exactly over the person's birthplace, this latter picture would be of exactly the same appearance as that of the human brain. As certain centers were arranged in the latter, so would the stars be in the photograph of the heavens. The human being has within himself a picture of the heavens, and every person has a different one, according to whether he was born in this place or that, and at this or that time. This is one indication that the human being is born from out of the whole cosmos.[1]

The analogy for the Earth to the birth horoscope of an individual is the *thema mundi*, the birth horoscope of the Earth, when at some time in the early history of the Earth an imprint of the starry heavens upon the Earth took place. It is this imprint that is the focus of Astrogeographia. The question now is whether there is also an archetypal relationship of the planets to the Earth? That there is such a relationship is expressly stated by Rudolf Steiner. After saying in relation to the stars, "We come, then, to a complete mirroring of what is outside in the interior of the Earth," he says that the same holds also for the planets:

> Picturing this in regard to each individual planet, we have, say Jupiter, and then a "polar Jupiter" within the Earth. We come to something that works outward from within the Earth in the way that Jupiter works in the Earth's environment. We arrive at a mirroring (in reality it is the opposite way round), but I will now

1 Steiner, *The Spiritual Guidance of the Individual and Humanity*, p. 63.

describe it like this: a mirroring of what is outside the Earth into the interior of the Earth.[2]

In addition, another of his indications, which we shall come to below, alludes implicitly to an archetypal relationship of the planets to various continents of the Earth.

The Seven Planets, the Seven Continents, and the Seven Earth Chakras

There are seven classical planets—Sun (Sunday), Moon (Monday), Mars (Tuesday), Mercury (Wednesday), Jupiter (Thursday), Venus (Friday), Saturn (Saturday)—according to which the seven days of the week are named, and there are seven continents. It is thus worth considering whether there is a correspondence between the seven continents and the seven classical planets. Even though, in the quote from Rudolf Steiner at the start of this chapter, he indicates that there is a correspondence between the continents and the starry constellations—this being also the core theme of Astrogeographia—the question is whether, over and above this correspondence to the constellations, there is, in addition, also an archetypal relationship between the continents and the seven planets? If there is, we could ask the further question as to whether there is a specific location upon each continent that is the central focus of the in-streaming planetary impulses? Such locations would be special "power points" or "planetary chakras" upon the Earth; and this brings us to the main theme of this chapter.

The terminology for describing the chakras in this chapter is tabulated below.[3] This tabulation is based upon indications given by Rudolf Steiner:[4]

2 Steiner, "The Relationship of the Diverse Branches of Natural Science to Astronomy," lecture 10 January 10, 1921(CW 323), *Das Verhältnis der verschiedenen naturwissenschatlichen Gebiete zur Astronomie* ("The Astronomy Course").

3 See Paul and Powell, *Cosmic Dances of the Planets*, pp. 179–183.

4 Although Rudolf Steiner indicated not only the approximate locations (larynx, heart, etc.) and the planetary correspondences but also, albeit

Lotus	Chakra	Planet	Color
8-petal	crown	Saturn	violet
2-petal	third eye	Jupiter	blue
16-petal	larynx	Mars	green
12-petal	heart	Sun	yellow
10-petal	solar plexus	Mercury	orange
6-petal	sacral	Venus	red
4-petal	root	Moon	peach blossom

In 1967, Robert Coon described in his book *Earth Chakras*[5] the basic principle of one major Earth chakra on each continent, with the exception of Antarctica. We begin our study of the planetary Earth chakras first by quoting from Robert Coon from the opening chapter to his book *Earth Chakras*:

> Geography teaches us about the continents, oceans, mountains, and rivers of the world. Geology studies stone formations—the skeleton of the Earth. These sciences investigate the more material aspects of the planetary body. The study of Earth chakras is more akin to acupuncture in that we are exploring the more subtle energy structures of the Earth. Earth chakras are like bodily organs that are vital to the health of the world, and to all living beings dependent upon the various environments provided by the world. Each chakra serves a different function, which is twofold:
>
> 1. To maintain the overall global health.
> 2. To transmit and receive energy encoded with information.
>
> There is one great Earth chakra located on each continent.

He gives permanent (fixed) map locations for six of the major chakras and a temporary (moving) location for the Third Eye chakra

indirectly (in artistic form), the colors of the lotus flowers in his 1923 sketch "The Human Being in Relation to the Planets," he did not specify either in this sketch or elsewhere the number of petals belonging to the lotus flower located in the region of the crown. See the discussion in the previous reference as to why this lotus flower (crown chakra) is indicated to have eight petals.

5 See Coon, *Earth Chakras*, p. 3.

(see table below), indicating that the current location of this mobile chakra coincides with the place of the heart chakra. He weaves the Earth chakras within a wider context of 156 sacred sites across the planet. This number he derives from 52 "inspirational earth chakras,"[6] multiplied by three since each of these 52 earth chakras, he says, "generates a related structural and a related creative gate." He also pointed to a system of spinner wheels and gates for the Earth, that become progressively activated into the future, in 19-year cycles. He says that he received his inspiration for the sacred geography of the Earth from the prophet Elijah.

Chakra	Continent (Country)	Place
seventh chakra (crown)	Asia (Tibet/China)	Mount Kailas
sixth chakra (third eye) [moving]	Europe (England)	Glastonbury and Shaftesbury
fifth chakra (throat) [larynx]	Asia-Africa (Israel/Palestine-Egypt)	Great Pyramid, Mount Sinai, and Mount of Olives
fourth chakra (heart)	Europe (England)	Glastonbury and Shaftesbury
third chakra (solar plexus)	Australia (Northern Territory)	Uluru and Kata Tjuta
second chakra (sexual area) [sacral]	South America (Bolivia-Peru)	Island of the Sun, Lake Titicaca
first chakra (base of spine) [root]	North America (California)	Mount Shasta

Table of Robert Coon's identification of seven Earth chakras on seven continents[7]

With Robert Coon's basic idea of one chakra on each continent as a starting point, we proceed in this chapter to construct a map of the planetary chakras of the Earth, based on the insights of spiritual science given by Rudolf Steiner—in particular his description of the influences of the planets upon the Earth. In this way we find an

6 Ibid., p. 95.

7 Ibid., pp. 6–16.

assignment of seven planetary chakras to locations on the surface of the Earth—still, however, adhering to the principle of one chakra on each continent, with the exception of Antarctica. We derive our basic insight from Rudolf Steiner's indications given in his lectures *The Mission of Folk Souls*,[8] In the sixth lecture he connects the influence of Mercury with Africa, that of Venus with Southeast Asia, that of Mars with "the broad region of Asia" of the Mongolian peoples (this includes not just Mongolia but also China, Tibet, and other parts of Asia), that of Jupiter with Europe, and that of Saturn with America, whereby it is clear from the context that he means North America. Then in the twelfth lecture of *The Mission of Folk Souls* he is more specific about the key location of a place in Germany as "the point on the continent of Europe from which once the greatest impulses rayed out in all directions." We believe that with these words Rudolf Steiner identified the *Jupiter chakra* of the Earth as the Externsteine. In this lecture it is clear that he meant the Externsteine by his reference to this point lying between "the cities of Detmold and Paderborn," since the ancient site of the Externsteine does in fact lie between Detmold and Paderborn and there is no other noteworthy ancient site between these two cities in Germany. His description of this location as being "the point on the continent of Europe from which once the greatest impulses rayed out in all directions" fits what can be thought of as the planetary chakra of Europe—the place of in-streaming cosmic forces for the spiritual evolution of Europe.

Having—with Rudolf Steiner's help—identified the Jupiter chakra—i.e., the "third eye" chakra, with the Externsteine on the continent of Europe, the task remains to find the locations of the other planetary chakras on the other continents of the Earth. The seven main continents are: Asia, Africa, North America, South America, Antarctica, Europe, and Oceania, comprising the region of Australia, New Zealand, New Guinea, and neighboring islands (now collectively known as Australasia)—although often simply "Australia" is named as the seventh continent in this list, instead of Oceania.[9]

8 Steiner, *The Mission of Folk Souls*.

9 There are widely diverging views as to how Oceania is defined. Oceania was originally conceived as the lands of the Pacific Ocean, stretching

Leaving Antarctica out of consideration reduces this to six continents. However, Rudolf Steiner considered Southeast Asia separately from the rest of Asia, bringing the number back to seven. Southeast Asia he correlated with Venus, and the rest of Asia—at least, that part of Asia comprising the natural habitat of the "Mongolian peoples"—he brought into connection with Mars. Thus, just as we looked for the Jupiter chakra in Europe, so our search for the Venus chakra is in Southeast Asia, the Mars chakra in Asia, and the Saturn chakra in North America. However, as will be elucidated in our discussion concerning the location of the Sun and Mercury chakras, there is a question—bearing in mind that Africa is correlated with Mercury by Rudolf Steiner—about the position on the globe of the Mercury chakra.

Now let us move forward for a discussion regarding the corresponding resonances of the Sun, Mercury, Venus, and the Moon, with the continents of the Earth. Regarding the Sun chakra: contemplating the Earth as a whole, on numerous occasions Rudolf Steiner referred to the central significance of the location of Golgotha/Jerusalem for the entire Earth. Here Christ's sacrifice took place, which signified on a spiritual level the transition from a descending to an ascending phase of evolution for the Earth and humanity. Astrogeographia connects onto the fundamental significance of Golgotha/Jerusalem and, as discussed in earlier chapters of this book—especially in chapter 9—Jerusalem is identified as the location on the Earth's surface that can be regarded as the spiritual center of the Earth—i.e., the heart chakra, corresponding to the Sun. In terms of continents, Jerusalem lies in Asia, but is very close to Africa, and is not far from the southernmost reaches of Europe. However, as discussed in chapter 9, Golgotha,

---

from the Straits of Malacca to the coast of the Americas. It comprised four regions: *Polynesia*, *Micronesia*, *Malaysia* (now called the Malay Archipelago), and *Melanesia* (now called Australasia). Geopolitically Oceania includes Australia and the nations of the Pacific from Papua New Guinea east, but not Indonesian New Guinea or Malaysia. Sometimes Oceania is defined as a continent comprising Australia and nearby islands. This definition is sometimes extended to include Micronesia, Polynesia, and every island in between, where New Zealand is considered to belong to Polynesia. The widest definition of Oceania includes the entire region between continental Asia and the Americas.

Mount Sinai, and the Great Pyramid are all spiritually connected with one another, which indicates something of the great outreach of this heart chakra of the Earth.[10]

Taking this into consideration, the Earth's heart chakra is very much linked with the continent of Africa. In fact, Africa looks like a heart! And just as the location of the heart chakra in the human being is not identical to the physical heart, but is nevertheless intimately linked to it, so Golgotha/Jerusalem can be considered as the heart chakra, which is intimately linked to the "physical heart" of the Earth—Africa. As the Sun is the center of our solar system, and as the heart chakra, corresponding to the Sun, is the spiritual center of the human being, so Golgotha/ Jerusalem is the spiritual center of the Earth—on account of Christ's sacrifice there, bestowing upon the Earth and humanity the central transforming impulse for the spiritual evolution of the world. And long before the city of Jerusalem existed at this location—in fact, from the time of the *thema mundi*, the birth horoscope of the Earth—on a spiritual level this place was the center of the world, as was recognized later in the Rabbinic tradition discussed in chapter 9: "The innermost sanctuary of the Temple [of Solomon], the Holy of Holies, or *Kodesh Hakodeshim*, where the Ark of the Covenant was placed, *marked the exact center of the world*."

Apart from identifying Africa's chakra, the heart chakra, with Golgotha (Earth's Sun chakra) and Europe's chakra, the "third eye," with the location of the Externsteine (Earth's Jupiter chakra), we are in agreement with Robert Coon's pinpointing of the locations of four of the other five Earth chakras. However, based on Steiner's research connecting the planets with regions of the Earth, we come to a different correspondence of the chakras to these locations. This is to be expected, because we are looking from a cosmic perspective (*Earth's planetary chakras*), whereas Robert Coon is focused upon *Earth chakras*. We are indebted to Robert Coon for his work in identifying the locations of the Earth chakras, which has served as a starting point for our research. Our work approaches this subject from a

10 For Robert Coon, as indicated in the above table, the great expanse covered by the Great Pyramid, Mount Sinai, and the Mount of Olives comprises the throat (larynx) chakra of the Earth.

cosmic perspective, in order to identify the positions of the planetary chakras upon the Earth. We respect Robert Coon's research and are grateful for his pioneering work in this field, and we believe that in this vast field of inquiry there is room for different perspectives.

Beginning with Robert Coon's identification of Mount Shasta as the Earth chakra on the continent of North America, given the association, according to Steiner, of North America with the planet Saturn, we see Mount Shasta as the Saturn chakra of the Earth—i.e., the crown chakra. Proceeding from West to East across the northern hemisphere, North America corresponds to Saturn, Europe to Jupiter, and Asia to Mars. Having identified Mount Shasta as the Earth's Saturn chakra and the Externsteine as the Earth's Jupiter chakra, it is a matter now of finding the Earth chakra on the continent of Asia that corresponds to Mars. According to Robert Coon, the Earth chakra of Asia is Mount Kailash in the Gangdisê Mountains (part of the Transhimalaya) in Tibet—regarded as THE sacred mountain in Buddhism, Hinduism, Jainism, and the Bon religion, a branch of Tibetan Vajrayaha. The Earth's Mars chakra is thus Mount Kailash. Summarizing our findings so far:

Planet	Chakra	Continent	Place/Planetary Chakra
Saturn	Crown	North America	Mount Shasta
Jupiter	Third Eye	Europe	Externsteine
Mars	Larynx	Asia	Mount Kailash
Sun	Heart	Asia-Africa	Golgotha/Jerusalem

Whereas these four places belong to the Northern Hemisphere, the other three locations of Earth chakras belong to the Southern Hemisphere. Given that Africa is already accounted for in terms of the Earth's heart chakra at Golgotha being the chakra corresponding to the "heart continent" of Africa, what are the remaining three continents and where are their corresponding chakras? In light of Rudolf Steiner's indication referred to above, it is Mercury that is the planet of Africa in terms of the people indigenous to that continent. Before considering a continent other than Africa in relation to Mercury, let us look further at the question of Africa's relationship to the Sun.

As a starting point, it is well-known that Africa is the world's main source of gold, the precious metal corresponding to the Sun. Already from the time of the building of the Great Pyramid, around 2500 BC, during the reign of Pharaoh Khufu (Cheops) of the Fourth Dynasty in Egypt, gold is recorded as having been brought from the "land of Punt"—a trading partner for the ancient Egyptians known for producing and exporting gold. The exact location of Punt remains a mystery. Most researchers now say that Punt was located in the region of the Horn of Africa, where today Northern Somalia, Eritrea, Djibouti, and Sudan (Red Sea coast) are located. In the fifteenth century BC it is recorded that Queen Hatchepsut traded gold from Nubia for myrrh and other goods from the land of Punt. Later, around 1000 BC, agricultural communities south of the Sahara began to resort to gold production for part of the year, and from that time onward transported the gold across the Sahara to trade it for goods. The Phoenician city-state of Carthage (814-146 BC), located in North Africa on the Gulf of Tunis on the Mediterranean coast, was renowned for its gold, which probably came from the Sub-Saharan region. After the destruction of Carthage, regular trade across the Sahara broke down. Around AD 100 the camel was introduced from Arabia into North Africa by the Romans, making trans-Saharan trade possible again. It is known that from around AD 400 onward camels were regularly transporting gold across the Sahara from West Africa, which for the ensuing eleven hundred years became the world's most important supplier of gold. The Ghana Empire, located in what is now southeastern Mauritania and Western Mali, obtained much of its gold from the Bambuk and Boure goldfields in Sudan. The Ghana Empire was superseded in the thirteen century by the Islamic Mali Empire, which flourished above all through its gold trade. It contained three immense gold mines within its borders, unlike the Ghana Empire, which was only a transit point for gold. Mali was the source of almost half the world's gold—exported from the goldfields of Bambuk, Boure, and Galam. Then, in 1868 gold was discovered in South Africa—since then the source of nearly 40% of all gold ever mined, and thought to be still home to an estimated 50% of the world's gold reserves. This brief history of Africa's relationship with gold, the metal of the Sun, lends support to the identification of Africa as the Sun (heart) continent on account of its gold reserves—gold being the metal corresponding to the Sun.

On another level, not forgetting that Steiner related the people of Africa to Mercury rather than to the Sun, as the Sun is universal, its influence cannot really be limited to one continent. However, it needs to be borne in mind that Steiner was focusing upon the indigenous people of Africa as the "Mercury race" and not so much upon the continent of Africa as such—and this applies also to the other correspondences between continents and planets referred to in this chapter. On a physical level, according to the "World Sunshine Map" the continent of Africa receives many more hours of bright sunshine during the year than any other continent of the Earth, and this could also be a reason for considering Africa as the "Sun continent" or the continent where the Sun's influence is greatest.[11] Apart from Africa's relationship to the physical Sun in terms of hours of bright sunshine, and to gold, the metal of the Sun, it is also the natural habitat of the lion; and as Linda Tucker shows convincingly in her book, the lion—especially the white lion—is a symbol both of the Sun and of the spirit of Africa.[12] Moreover, in astrology the heart corresponds to the constellation of Leo—i.e., to the lion, so again we see a correspondence here relating Africa to the heart—and also to the Sun, to which the heart (from another perspective) corresponds.[13]

Relating to the Earth as a living being mirroring in kind the planetary life of our solar system, the lungs are said to correspond to Mercury.[14] If Africa is the heart, where do we find the lungs of the Earth? Everyone knows that trees are the lungs of the Earth and that, in particular, the tropical rainforests are the greatest suppliers of life-giving oxygen on the planet. The Amazon represents over

11 See http://earth.rice.edu/mtpe/geo/geosphere/hot/energyfuture/Sunlight .html for the "World Sunshine Map."

12 Tucker, *Mystery of the White Lions*, pp. 253–256.

13 In astrology the Sun is said to be "at home" in Leo. In other words, there is a deep relationship between the Sun and Leo. And just as the heart corresponds to Leo in terms of its physical structure, on a soul/spiritual level it corresponds to the Sun.

14 For the correspondences of the organs with the planets, see Paul and Powell, *Cosmic Dances of the Planets*.

half of the Earth's remaining rainforests and supplies an estimated 20% of the planet's oxygen. This is one reason for considering South America, home of the Amazon basin, as the Mercury continent. If Africa is regarded as the Sun (heart) continent, South America can perhaps be identified as the Mercury (lungs) continent. There are various considerations that support this. For example, Mercury is thought of as the planet of movement—Steiner refers to "Mercury's swift-winged movement in our limbs"[15]—and considering the love of movement in South American countries, where an extraordinary number of dance forms have originated, the "Mercurial quality" of South America comes to expression in their penchant for dance.[16] Mercury (lungs) clearly also has to do with breathing, and during breathing the diaphragm contracts and flattens, producing an outward movement of the upper abdominal wall—the epigastric region (solar plexus or "pit of the stomach"), where Steiner locates the Mercury chakra.[17]

There is yet another consideration here, which emerges when we turn our attention to Cuzco, the capital of the Inca civilization and of the whole Tawantinsuyu (Peruvian) empire. According to the Incas the word *Qosqo* (their word for Cuzco) meant "navel of the world." We find here, in this expression, an allusion to a Mercury center. For the navel is related to the solar plexus (Mercury) chakra.[18] Robert Coon

---

15 Paul and Powell, *Cosmic Dances of the Planets.*

16 The people of Africa, too, have a great love of dance—in line with Steiner's identification of the indigenous African people as the "Mercury race." Further, many people of Black African descent came to Latin America, mainly to Brazil and the Caribbean, but also to Columbia and Venezuala, as part of the Atlantic slave trade.

17 Rudolf Steiner likens the Earth to a human being: "America appears like the breast"; see Steiner *Menschheitsentwickelung und Christus-Erkenntnis* ("Human Evolution and Knowledge of Christ" CW 100), p. 287. It is in line with these words of Steiner to relate the lungs to South America; see also Steiner, *Esoteric Develolpment*, lecture of March 16, 1905, p. 110, for Rudolf Steiner's location of the Mercury chakra in the "pit of the stomach" (German: *Magengrube*)—i.e., solar plexus.

18 The close relationship between the navel and the solar plexus (Mercury) chakra is evident in the Hindu tradition, where the location of the 10-petal lotus flower (Sanskrit: *Manipura*) is sometimes identified as the region of the navel and sometimes as the region of the solar plexus. A possible

identifies Lake Titicaca as the Earth chakra for the continent of South America, and in Inca mythology there is a link between Lake Titicaca and Cuzco. Manco Cápac was said to be the mythological founder of the Inca Dynasty in Peru and the Cuzco Dynasty at Cuzco. He was thought to have arisen from the depths of Lake Titicaca. If Lake Titicaca is the Earth's solar plexus (Mercury) chakra, Cuzco was evidently conceived of as the closely related "navel center of the world" and the Inca connected these two places in the personage of their legendary founder. Thus, Lake Titicaca is identified as the location of the Earth's Mercury chakra, closely linked with Cuzco as the "navel of the world."

In relation to identifying the location of the Earth's Venus chakra, it is helpful if we now turn to an important aspect of Robert Coon's research: that six of the seven Earth chakras all lie along one or the other of two great ley lines of the Earth, which he calls *ley arteries* and names the *Rainbow Serpent* (female) and the *Plumed Serpent* (male). The expression *ley arteries* is appropriate in terms of their overriding magnitude and significance in comparison with all other ley lines (energy lines) on our planet. Our own research confirms the validity of two principle ley arteries encircling the Earth and that six of the seven planetary chakras of the Earth are indeed located on these arteries—the only one not lying on one of the two lines being the Earth's Sun (heart) chakra at Golgotha/Jerusalem. However, the paths of the two ley arteries which David Bowden has mapped out mathematically (see below) differ slightly from the paths of the ley arteries indicated by Robert Coon.

Since Robert Coon in his work does not consider Southeast Asia to be a separate continent from Asia, he does not indicate that one of the seven Earth chakras is located in Southeast Asia. However, in his mapping of the paths of the Rainbow Serpent and the Plumed Serpent

---

solution to this conundrum comes through Rudolf Steiner's identification—see previous footnote—of the location of the 10-petal lotus flower as the region of the "pit of the stomach," which would seem to indicate the solar plexus (rather than the navel)—i.e., the epigastric region rather than the umbilical region. Given that the solar plexus is the location of the Mercury chakra, nonetheless in other traditions—for example, Daoist and Hindu traditions—the navel is of great significance. Thus, according to Ayurvedic medicine, the navel is an important energy center in the human body, with nearly 72,000 subtle nerves (*nadis*) converging in this area.

around the globe, he identifies two locations where these ley arteries meet and cross one another. One is Lake Titicaca, and the other is the island of Bali. The crossing point on Bali he calls "the World Purification Center," seeing it not as an Earth chakra but as a *sacred gate*—one of the *twelve foundation gates of the world.* He indicates that the sacred sites located on the island of Bali serve in the purification of the Earth's blood. This is exactly the function of the kidneys in the human being, to help in the purification of the blood, removing toxic materials from the body. Just as the heart is the organ corresponding to the Sun, and the lungs are the organ corresponding to Mercury, so the kidneys are the organ corresponding to Venus.[19] Further research led us to the identification of the highest mountain on Bali, Mount Agung, as the location of the Earth's Venus chakra. The Balinese believe that Mount Agung is a mystical mountain, which they think of as a replica of the mythical Mount Meru, the sacred mountain in Hindu and Buddhist cosmology, considered to be the center of the universe. Moreover, the most important, largest, and holiest Hindu temple on Bali, *Purah Besakih* (the Mother temple of Besakih), is located high on the slopes of Mount Agung. According to our research, it is here on this volcanic mountain that the Earth's Venus chakra is located.

Now, in coming to the task of mapping the flow of the two great ley arteries, we looked for the crossing points of these two circles around the globe connecting the locations of the Earth's planetary chakras. Focusing first upon the crossing point in the Asia/Southeast Asia region against the background of our cosmic perspective (complementary to Robert Coon's Earth-based perspective), the crossing point we found is not on the island of Bali, but interestingly coincides more or less exactly with Mount Kailash (within 32 miles, or 51½ km), the Earth's Mars (larynx) chakra, which, as described in chapter 9, lies on the Dubhe meridian—Dubhe being the most luminous of the seven stars comprising the Big Dipper—even though Mount Kailash astrogeographically is not aligned directly with any prominent star. We found that the other crossing point, located in the Andean highlands in Peru, South America, lies some 854 miles (1,374 km) northwest of Lake

19 For the correspondences of the organs with the planets, see Paul and Powell, *Cosmic Dances of the Planets.*

Titicaca, the Earth's Mercury (solar plexus) chakra,[20] about 8,900 feet (2,700 m.) above sea level. Like Mount Kailash, the Andean crossing point is not aligned directly with any prominent star. However, it is on the meridian of a very powerful star, since it lies close to the Deneb meridian—Deneb having a luminosity of about 250,000, listed as the thirty-second most luminous star in our galaxy.[21]

The Andean crossing point is just 20 miles (32 km) southeast of Kuntur Wasi ("House of the Condor"), the name given to ruins of a religious center with complex architecture and stone sculptures at the headwaters of the Jequetepeque River. Kuntur Wasi is thought to have been constructed around 1000 to 700 BC and was occupied until around 50 BC. This was the time of the Chavin civilization in ancient Peru, and lithosculptures found at Kuntur Wasi are similar to the Chavin style. The crossing point of the two great ley arteries is also 19 miles (30½ km) southwest of Cajamarca, the city remembered as the place where the Inca empire came to an end when the Spanish conquistadors captured and murdered the Incan emperor Atahualpa there.

Also very close, just 56½ miles (91 km) southwest of the Andean crossing point, lying on the western outskirts of the Peruvian city of Trujillo on the Pacific coast, is the World Heritage archeological site of Chan Chan, the largest pre-Columbian city in South America—some 500 acres (2 km^2),[22] with many pre-Columbian palaces. The vast adobe city of Chan Chan on the Pacific coast, which was a triangular city surrounded by walls 50 to 60 feet (15–18 m) high, was built by the Chimú around AD 850 and lasted until its conquest by the Inca Empire in AD 1470. It was the imperial capital of the Chimú until it was conquered by the Incas in the fifteenth century. It is estimated that around 30,000 people lived in the city of Chan Chan, sometimes

20 It is also interesting that the Andean crossing point lies some 578½ miles (931 km) northwest of Machu Picchu, the great Inca ceremonial center in the Cuzco region,

21 See Powell and Dann, *The Astrological Revolution*, chap. 5, concerning the extraordinary significance of the megastar Deneb in the constellation of the Swan.

22 Trujillo is the third largest city in Peru and is known as the *culture capital of Peru* and the *city of eternal spring*. It is an economic hub in Northern Peru, a Mercurial function, recalling that for the Greeks Hermes/Mercury was patron of merchants and commerce.

called the City of the Moon because they worshipped the Moon there. In terms of size and complexity, it has been compared with Teotihuacan in Mexico and with some of the ancient cities of Egypt. Also very interesting is the somewhat older archeological site of the Sun and Moon temples six miles (9½ km) from Chan Chan, on the southeastern outskirts of Trujillo. This complex is dominated by two huge adobe brick buildings: an artificial platform called the Temple of the Moon, and one-quarter of a mile (400 m) away the Pyramid of the Sun, the largest pre-Columbian structure in Peru. This step pyramid, towering 135 feet (41 m.) above the surroundings, is the tallest adobe structure of the Americas. This major archaeological site was built at the time of the Moche culture (AD 100–800)—perhaps out of a sense of those ancient peoples for this crossing point of two great ley arteries carrying the male solar (Plumed Serpent) and female lunar (Rainbow Serpent) energies.[23]

The balancing of the Sun and Moon energies—manifested by the great Pyramid of the Sun and the Temple of the Moon, near Trujillo, perhaps as an expression of the meeting of the Plumed Serpent and the Rainbow Serpent nearby in the highlands—is an activity of Mercury, the planet closest to the Sun. In the words of Rudolf Steiner:

> I hold the Sun within me—
> As King he leads me into the world;
> I hold the Moon within me—
> She preserves my form;
> I hold Mercury within me—
> He holds Sun and Moon together.[24]

23 This is an example of what is referred to earlier in this book that often a site connected with a power spot is built not at the actual power spot but, for practical reasons, some distance from the power spot. In this case the practical reasons are obvious: the coastal area is much more hospitable than the Andean highlands. Hence the city of Chan Chan and the nearby ceremonial site with the Pyramid of the Sun and the Temple of the Moon were located on the Pacific coast rather than up in the highlands where the actual crossing point of the two great ley arteries is located.

24 Kirchner-Bockholt and Kirchner-Bockholt, *Rudolf Steiner's Mission and Ita Wegman*, p. 113.

This "holding Sun and Moon together" comes to expression at Lake Titicaca, where there is the Island of the Sun and the Island of the Moon, thus indicating a close resonance between the Earth's Mercury chakra, Lake Titicaca, and the Andean crossing point of the two great ley arteries with the nearby Pyramid of the Sun and the Temple of the Moon on the outskirts of present-day Trujillo.

It now remains to determine the location of the Earth's Moon chakra. As mentioned already, leaving Antarctica out of consideration, the remaining continent is Oceania, often simply identified with Australia. According to Robert Coon, the Earth chakra on this continent is Uluru, formerly known to non-Aborigines as Ayers Rock, a large sandstone formation in the center of Australia, which is also a World Heritage site. It is the second largest monolith in the world (after Mount Augustus, also in Australia). Uluru is sacred to the Aborigines and is important in their creation mythology. Archeological research shows that the Uluru area has been inhabited by human beings for at least 10,000 years, and some sources maintain that the Aborigines have been there for at least 20,000 years. Uluru, with its distinctive color, glowing red at dawn and sunset, is one of Australia's most recognizable national landmarks. Our research indicates that Uluru is indeed the location of the Earth's Moon chakra, lying on the great ley artery (red line in the map below) running through the Externsteine, Mount Kailash, Mount Agung, and Uluru. The other great ley artery (blue line in the map below) runs through Lake Titicaca, Mount Shasta, and Mount Kailash. Golgotha/Jerusalem, as the Earth's Sun (heart) chakra, being of spiritual significance for the whole world, does not lie on either of the two great ley arteries mapped out below.

According to Rudolf Steiner, the region of Oceania was where the Moon was located before it separated out from the Earth.[25] As part of Oceania, Australia comes under the influence of the Moon—also in an evolutionary sense, since the Aborigines, comparing their culture with that of the Lemurians described by Steiner,[26] are evidently descendants from the ancient Lemurians, a culture associated with

25 See, for example, Rudolf Steiner's lectures to the workers, *From Crystals to Crocodiles*.

26 Steiner, *Cosmic Memory*, see chapter on the Lemurian Race.

the lunar influence as an echo of the Ancient Moon stage of evolution. Steiner described Lemuria as a continent very much influenced by the Moon that was located in the region between Australia and Africa, in the general region where now the Indian Ocean is located, which became submerged tens of thousands of years ago.[27] The Aborigines are thought to have inhabited Australia for some 50,000 years—supported by the archeological findings of human remains from Lake Mungo, Australia, dated to about 45,000 years ago—making the Aborigines the oldest continuous population outside of Africa.

Planet	Chakra	Continent	Place/Planetary Chakra
Saturn	Crown	North America	Mount Shasta
Jupiter	Third Eye	Europe	Externsteine
Mars	Larynx	Asia	Mount Kailash
Sun	Heart	Asia-Africa	Golgotha/Jerusalem
Mercury	Solar Plexus	South America	Lake Titicaca
Venus	Sacral	Southeast Asia	Mount Agung
Moon	Root	Australia/Oceania	Uluru

The above table offers a summary of our findings identifying the seven planetary chakras of the Earth, where the place of the Christ's resurrection—Golgotha, Jerusalem—is the heart or Sun chakra of the Earth. In Astrogeographia, the latitude of Golgotha corresponds to the alignment of the stars on the Celestial Equator, or 0° declination. The three upper chakras are identified with locations in the northern hemisphere: Mount Shasta, California, with the crown chakra; the Externsteine in Europe with the third eye chakra; and Mount Kailash, Tibet, with the larynx chakra. Conversely, the three lower chakras are identified with locations in the southern hemisphere: Lake Titicaca on the border of Peru and Bolivia with the solar plexus chakra; Mount Agung on the island of Bali with the sacral chakra; and Uluru, Australia, with the root chakra. The tabulation is depicted graphically in figure 1.

27 It is conceivable that prior to the destruction of Lemuria there were Lemurians who migrated to regions surrounding the Lemurian continent—to Africa and Australia, for example. In this case, there is a likelihood that Aborigines are descendants of the people who emigrated from Lemuria.

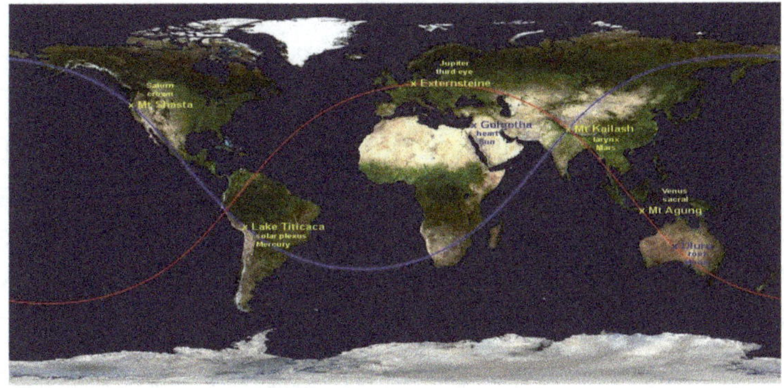

Figure 1: The seven chakras of the Earth

Figure 2: Planetary views of the red and blue chakra circles of the Earth

Mapping the Chakras of the Earth

In figures 1 and 2, the red and blue chakra circles are shown weaving back and forth between the upper chakras of the northern hemisphere and the lower chakras of the southern hemisphere. The red curve passes through Uluru, Mount Agung, Mount Kailash, and the Externsteine. The blue curve passes through Mount Kailash, Lake Titicaca, and Mount Shasta. As mentioned already, these two circles have a crossing point at Mount Kailash, a major cosmic creation center for Hindu mythology. And, as referred to above, the second crossing point is on the west coast of Peru near the site of the ancient pre-Columbian city of Chan Chan.

It is in line with Aboriginal mythology to identify the red and blue curves as *serpent paths*. For we find a reference in one of the Australian Aboriginal stories of a battle between two serpents, Kuniya and Liru, which took place at Uluru (the root or Moon chakra of the Earth). This vast battle signaled the end of an era—the era of the creative period of what the Aborigines call "the Dreamtime," being the "time before time," "the time of the creation of all things," the time when the spirit ancestors came to Earth and gave to the rocks, plants, animals and humans their present forms. In terms of Rudolf Steiner's cosmology, this can be seen as the transition time from the Ancient Moon stage of evolution to that of the present Earth. The activity of the spiritual hierarchies, in service of the creator, had during the earlier periods of world evolution—the periods known as Ancient Saturn, Ancient Sun and Ancient Moon—created and progressively developed in seed form the physical, etheric, and astral bodies of plants, animals, and human beings. At the transition to the present Earth, these seeds became manifest and finally evolved into the mineral, plant, animal, and human forms that we know today.

Robert Coon's account of his own findings of related curves weaving between north and south[28] is as follows: The red curve is the path of the Wonambi (Rainbow Serpent) as it left Uluru and travelled across the Pacific Ocean to South America. At the creation of Lake Titicaca it entered into the waters and submerged. On resurfacing, a second great serpent was with her, the birth of the male Plumed Serpent. This male serpent then turned to the northwest (direction of Mount Shasta) and began its own circling of the planet (blue curve), while the Rainbow Serpent continued on her way (red curve), crossing the Atlantic to Europe and finally returning via Asia to Uluru, thus completing the circuit.

Until now, the continent of Antarctica has been left out of consideration. According to paleogeography, there are links between Antarctica and Australia, which long ago are thought to have been part of the supercontinent of Gondwana. Pangaea, referred to in earlier chapters, described the Earth when all the landmasses were joined. It is believed that during the mid-Mesozoic era Pangaea separated into two supercontinents, Laurasia to the north and Gondwana to the south. Our research leads more specifically to the uncovering of a relationship between Antarctica and Uluru, the Earth's Moon (root) chakra.

28 See Coon, *The Rainbow Serpent and the Holy Grail*, pp. 102–104.

In order to elucidate this connection, we shall take as a starting point an indication by Rudolf Steiner connecting the North Pole of the Earth with the head. "The Earth is quite regular. Around the North Pole she appears so that we would find there an expression of the Earth's astral and etheric bodies. This one designates as the Earth's head. One designates Asia as the one hand and Europe together with Africa as the other hand. America appears as the breast, Australia, etc., as the extremities. This impresses itself into the cultures. The Earth's life proceeds from one pole, as astral consciousness rays out from the brain."[29] This very concise statement was not made during a lecture, but during the question and answer session after the lecture. Hence the brevity of this statement relating to a vast theme: the analogy of the Earth to a human being, which offers a new and interesting perspective, complementary to the perspective we have been developing hitherto in this chapter.

In line with Rudolf Steiner's statement we can say that the Earth's North Pole, connected with the head, has a relationship to the crown chakra—meaning the crown chakra in an archetypal sense rather than in the sense of the Earth's Saturn (crown) chakra, the location of which we identify with Mount Shasta. Further, we venture to say that this archetypal crown chakra of the Earth is not identical with the projection of the Celestial North Pole upon the Earth but with the location, according to Astrogeographia, of the point on the Earth's surface that appears to correspond to the Ecliptic North Pole—what may be called from the standpoint of Astrogeographia the "apparent Ecliptic North Pole." This point is not identical with the earthly projection of the actual Ecliptic North Pole, but is the heavenly point corresponding to the earthly location at which all the Astrogeographia meridians meet. This point lies in Eastern Alaska 145 miles (234 km) northeast of Fairbanks (see figure 3). Its coordinates are 66N34 and 144W47—in Astrogeographia this equates with the sidereal longitude of 4°01' Sagittarius and latitude 58N13. At the present time, this point lies within the sphere of influence of the constellation of Hercules.

Correspondingly, the exact opposite point on the Earth's surface—in the Southern Ocean at 66S34, 35E13—lies 98½° due south of Jerusalem,

29 Steiner, *Menschheitsentwickelung und Christus-Erkenntnis* ("Human Evolution and Knowledge of Christ"), p. 287.

on the Jerusalem meridian, about 170 miles (273½ km) north of the coast of Antarctica (see figure 4) and can be considered as part of Antarctica, considering that the continent of Antarctica is at least 5,400,000 square miles (14 million km.²) in size. This is a very special location for the whole organism of the Earth, as we shall see below.

In Astrogeographia, we are interested not only in the "apparent Ecliptic North Pole" but also in the "apparent Ecliptic South Pole" lying exactly opposite the apparent Ecliptic North Pole on the celestial sphere. The sidereal projection of the apparent Ecliptic South Pole equates with the sidereal longitude of 4°01' Gemini (opposite 4°01' Sagittarius) and latitude 58S13 (opposite 58N13). The projection of this celestial point (4°01' Gemini, 58S13) is located on the Earth at 3S00, 35E13. This identifies the location on the Earth's surface of the projection of the apparent Ecliptic South Pole, which belongs to Africa, near the equator (see figure 5). This point is in the Serengeti National Park (Ngorongoro Conservation Area) in Tanzania, across the border from Kenya, about 160 miles (257 km) southwest of Nairobi. This point is not to be confused with the the opposite point on the Earth's surface to the apparent Ecliptic North Pole, which is an important location on the Jerusalem meridian, between Jerusalem and Antarctica, whereby, as indicated below, Antarctica has a special significance for the whole organism of the Earth.

When Rudolf Steiner says, "The Earth's life proceeds from one pole," this can be understood as the Earth's life pole or archetypal root chakra connected with Antarctica, whereas the consciousness pole (in contrast to the life pole) is the one referred to above in Alaska (archetypal crown chakra of the Earth). Upon a visit to Uluru, the surprising and completely unexpected discovery was made that Uluru is energetically connected with the archetypal root chakra of the Earth and serves—as the Earth's Moon (root) chakra—to represent the Earth's archetypal root chakra for humanity, thereby receiving a continual influx of energy from that powerful life center (see figure 4) associated with Antarctica. Uluru, already potent as a power point in its own right, as everyone who visits this site can experience, is potentized even further by virtue of the influx of energy streaming from the Earth's archetypal root chakra. By the same token, the great power

Figure 3 (left): At the center of the projected ecliptic circle is the apparent Ecliptic North Pole (66N34, 144W47), about 145 miles (234 km) northeast of Fairbanks, Alaska.

Figure 4 (center): Opposite geographical point at 66S34, 35E13 to the apparent Ecliptic North Pole (above), about 170 miles (273½ km) north of the coast of Antarctica.

Figure 5 (right): The apparent Ecliptic South Pole is at (3S00, 35E13), on the Jerusalem meridian, in the Serengeti National Park, Tanzania, about 160 miles (257 km) southwest of Nairobi.

spot Mount Shasta, the Earth's Saturn (crown) chakra, is potentized by an influx of energy streaming from the Earth's archetypal crown chakra in Alaska (see figure 3), and serves—as the Earth's Saturn (crown) chakra—to represent the Earth's archetypal crown chakra for humanity, thereby receiving a continual influx of energy from that powerful consciousness center on the surface of the Earth.

Earth Chakra Creation Mythologies

It is perhaps not surprising that the locations of all seven chakras on the Earth's planetary chakras map are deeply connected with cosmic and local creation myths. At many of these locations the belief has long been held that their place is THE center of creation for the entire universe. This placing of one's self at the center of everything is a natural human tendency. For example, for millennia it was believed that the Earth is at the center of the universe—this was the geocentric ("Earth-centered") perspective that only became displaced in the sixteenth century, when the Polish astronomer Copernicus introduced the heliocentric ("Sun-centered") astronomical view. Another example is that of the English-German astronomer William Herschel, who in 1785 correctly deduced the disk shape of the Milky Way galaxy from star counts, but mistakenly assumed that our own Sun was very near the galactic center.

Five of the Earth's chakras (exceptions being the Externsteine and Uluru) are found located on tectonic plate boundaries. In relation to this, Rudolf Steiner describes how these tetrahedral boundaries allow warmth ether from the Sun to enter the Earth more than at other places:

> The Earth actually consists of four pieces flung out of cosmic space and joined together, four pieces which then form a tetrahedron, and along the edges there are still, as it were, places not tightly closed. At these leaky places it is possible for the cosmic heat (warmth ether) from the Sun to get into the Earth more than at other places.[30]

Another finding from our map of the locations of the Earth chakras is that during the age of European discovery, three of the countries of Europe formed a connection with the region of their corresponding southern hemisphere chakra. Thus Spain (Mercury) formed a connection with South America (Lake Titicaca being the Earth's Mercury chakra); Holland (Venus) with Indonesia (Mount Agung being the Earth's Venus chakra); and England (Moon) with Australia (Uluru being the Earth's Moon chakra)—see figure 5: Countries of Europe and their corresponding planets.

Planet	Country
Saturn	Poland
Jupiter	Germany
Mars	France
Sun	Italy
Mercury	Spain
Venus	Holland
Moon	England

Figure 5: Countries of Europe and their corresponding planets[31]

30 See Steiner, *The Evolution of the Earth and Man and Influence of the Stars*, p. 197.

31 See Powell, "The Vision of Europe" in *Shoreline Journal*, no 2, p. 32.

Mount Shasta in North America: Earth's Saturn chakra (crown)

Mount Shasta, located at the southern end of the Cascade mountain range, is 14,179 feet (4,322 m.) high. This mountain in Northern California has long been revered by Native American Indians who regard it as the center of creation. Historically various Native American Indian peoples—for example, the Shasta, Modoc, Achomawi, and Wintu—were located about the base of Mount Shasta. The Shasta believe that the Great Spirit first created the mountain by pushing down ice and snow through a hole from heaven, then using the mountain stepped onto the Earth. The Modoc teach that the Great Spirit lived on Mount Shasta after creation. His daughter fell from the mountain and was raised by grizzly bears and married one of their clan. Today, the tribes honor the mountain with rituals and sweat lodges and are actively involved with protecting the sacred springs on the mountain. Against the background of Steiner's relating the Native American Indians to Saturn, Mount Shasta, which also many non-Native America Indians recognize as a most significant power spot on the North American continent, appears as the Earth's Saturn (crown) chakra. As well as the Native American Indian legends, there are many people in recent times who have had profound spiritual experiences at Mount Shasta. That it is an extraordinary power spot on the Earth, a powerful chakra, would explain why there is such an unusual panoply of legends concerning this mountain. One of the best known more recent examples is that of Guy Warren Ballard who, writing under the pseudonym Godfré Ray King, stated in 1934 that he had an encounter with the "Ascended Master Saint Germain" on the slopes of Mount Shasta in 1930. According to him, Saint Germain is a great spiritual teacher who has attained such a level of balanced wisdom and harmony that he is able to manifest Divine Love. This and other similar accounts of experiences undergone at Mount Shasta lend support to the correspondence of Mount Shasta to the crown chakra, which in the human being is regarded as the portal to higher worlds of Divine Love.

The Externsteine in Europe: Earth's Jupiter Chakra (Third Eye)

The Externsteine is in the region of the Teutoburg Forest between Detmold and Paderborn in Northern Germany. It comprises a group of five sandstone fingers, or pillars, each about a hundred feet (30 m) high. To this day, there is controversy as to whether this was a pagan center of worship until the region was Christianized by Charlemagne in 772. Certain features of the Externsteine lend support to the notion that it was a pagan ceremonial site. For example, there are steps carved from the sandstone pillars that seem to lead nowhere. There is also a sarcophagus hewn from a large boulder, and there are caves that honeycomb the pillars, which could have served as ceremonial chambers. High on the central one of the five pillars there is a chapel hewn out of the rock and known as "Tower Rock," which perhaps was a pagan chapel at one time, as the rising midsummer Sun penetrates through a circular opening in an alcove—viewed from a niche in the opposite wall. One overhanging rock appears in the form of a man with his arms raised up, as if he were bound to the rock. Although a natural feature, it has been established that this was worked upon long ago with tools. Some maintain that it is a representation of Odin hanging on the World Tree. As referred to earlier in this chapter, the site of the Externsteine is described by Rudolf Steiner as a great spiritual center from which the most powerful inspirations radiated.[32] Among those Archangels who streamed their impulses into this center was Odin (*Wotan*), who was looked upon as the leading god of the Germanic people. Steiner describes how Odin and the other Archangels of Europe each went on their missions to the peoples of northern, central, and Western Europe, and thereby the various European peoples each underwent their unique development.

The third eye chakra, or two-petalled lotus (as seen on Michelangelo's sculpture of Moses, for example), is related to the development of thinking. The Externsteine can thus be seen as an archangelic center for *the light of thinking*, related to the task of the European peoples to work at the development of thinking.

32 See Steiner, *The Mission of the Individual Folk Souls*, p. 122.

Pondering these connections further: In the Edda creation myths, Odin and his two brothers Vili and Ve killed Ymir the Frost Giant and created the universe from his body. Connected with this mythology is the idea of the *Irminsul*—a sacred tree or pillar—which played an important role in Germanic mythology. It is generally believed that the Irminsul derives its name from Irmin, who, according to Steiner, was the divine "all father" of the Germanic tribes, and thus bears a relationship with the Germanic God Odin, whom the Germanic tribes considered their leading god, the same god as Wotan for the Anglo-Saxons. In the Germanic mythology, the World Ash, Yggdrasil, played an important role. According to Steiner,

> The human being in nine worlds is comparable to a tree, the ash...the World Ash called *Yggdrasil,* in which the world forces came together. The human being was depicted at the moment where one's "I" should become conscious, where the word *I* should resound from within. *Yggdrasil* means "I"-bearer; "I"-bearer is this tree. *Ygg* is "I," and *drasil* comes from the root word *bearer.*[33]

Yggr is also considered to be an ancient name for Odin (*Wotan*). The usual interpretation of *Yggdrasil* was that it was the yew or ash tree upon which Odin sacrificed himself, and which connected the nine worlds. For a time it was considered that a bent tree depicted on the Externsteine relief showing Christ being taken down from the cross represented a bent or fallen Irminsul. Today, however, it is generally accepted that there is no historical evidence linking the Externsteine relief to the Irminsul. Nevertheless, through Steiner's description, in which he links Odin with the Archangels who poured their inspiration into this Earth chakra, an inner correspondence with Christ's sacrifice on the cross, depicted on the relief, which gave birth to the true human "I," can be discerned. Since the third-eye chakra is the center where "I"-consciousness is expressed most strongly, there is a profound level of connection between this Jupiter center in the human being and the Jupiter chakra of the Earth.

33 Steiner, *Mythen und Sagen* ("Myths and Legends"; CW 101), p. 26.

Mount Kailash in the Himalayas: Earth's Mars Chakra (Larynx)

Until the year 1800, there was a great mystery for Western cartographers—the ancient and powerful belief that somewhere in Asia, between India and China, there stood a sacred mountain (an Asian Mount Olympus), a mountain of cosmic proportions called Mount Meru, considered the absolute central point of the universe, the birth place from which the entire universe springs. This mountain was said not only to be the axis of the universe, but also to have a mighty river flowing from its summit, falling into a lake and then dividing to form four of the great rivers of Asia. This holy mountain was revered by millions of Hindus, Buddhists, and Jains as the home of their gods. Then it became known that the myths and cosmologies of Hinduism, Buddhism, and the Jainism speak of Mount Kailash, located in the far west of Tibet, close to the border with India and Nepal, as the earthly manifestation of the mythical Mount Meru (see figure 6), and that at the foot of Mount Kailash was a vast lake and that Mount Kailash was indeed the source of four great rivers.

For Buddhists Mount Kailash is the *navel of the universe.* Made of black rock, the symmetrical peak has a distinctive diamond-like shape with four steep facades, and in fact the word *Kailasa* means "crystal" in Sanskrit. In Tibetan, Mount Kailash is called *Kang Rinpoche* (Precious Jewel of Snow). For Hindus, Mount Kailash is the throne of Lord Shiva, whose name means "The Auspicious One" and who is regarded as fulfilling various divine works—primarily the destroyer of evil, the transformer, and the revealer (a work of blessing). He is depicted holding in his left hand the *damaru,* representing the sacred sound *AUM* (pronounced "OM" by Hindus), from which all languages are formed, in particular Sanskrit. Here a connection of Mount Kailash with the Mars chakra (larynx) is evident, as the larynx is the source of speech, and the Divine Word (*AUM*) is said to be that from which "all things were created" (John 1:3). *Namah Shivaya*—"adoration to Shiva," preceded by the sacred word AUM—is the mantra ("*AUM Namah Shivaya*") recited in honor of Shiva in the Hindu religion. As another example of the connection of Mount Kailash with sacred sound, which is considered to emanate from this holy mountain eternally and unceasingly: Milarepa, the Buddhist spiritual leader, is said to have gone to Mount Kailash in 1093 and created the supreme mantra of Tibetan Buddhism—*OM Mani Padme Hum* (OM jewel in the lotus).[34] According to legend, the Buddhist Milarepa triumphed over the representative of the ancient Tibetan shamanistic faith, the Bon religion by riding upon the rays of the Sun to the top of Mount Kailash. To Milarepa are attributed these words concerning Mount Kailash: "There is no place more powerful for practice, more blessed, or more marvellous than this; may all pilgrims and practitioners be welcome!" Because of the sacredness of the mountain, it would be an act of sacrilege to endeavor to climb it. Apart from the legendary ascent to the summit by Milarepa, all others who have ventured to defy the taboo of climbing Mount Kailash have died in the process or had to discontinue their ascent of the 22,000-foot (6,700 m) peak. In the Bon faith, Mount Kailash is referred to as the nine-storied Swastika Mountain, the seat of all spiritual power. Bon believers consider Mount Kailash, and Lake Manasarovar at its foot, to be the foundation of their shamanistic religion—Lake Manasarovar, at 15,000 feet (4,557 m) above sea level, being the highest freshwater lake of the world. Since *manas* means "mind," or "consciousness," Lake Manasarovar is considered to be the "lake of consciousness" or the "lake of enlightenment."

Figure 6: Mount Meru Tibetan Buddhist Mandala

As if unconsciously following the clockwise and counterclockwise rotations of the petals of the lotus flowers (*chakras*), the *kora*, or meditative circumambulation, of Mount Kailash by pilgrims is made in a

34 Rudolf Steiner translated *Aoum mani padme hum* as "My 'I' is enclosed in the lotus blossom," signifying that the "I" is enclosed in the three sheaths of the physical, etheric, and astral bodies; *Esoteric Lessons 1913–1923*, p. 476.

clockwise direction by Hindus and Buddhists, and counterclockwise by followers of the Jain and Bon religions. The rugged path around Mount Kailash is 32 miles (52 km) long. Some hardy pilgrims make this path in just one day, but most take much longer. According to legend, pilgrims long ago supplicated Brahma for water on their pilgrimage, upon which he created on the south side of the mountain the huge and sacred Lake Manasarovar. It is said that one circumambulation of Mount Kailash wipes away all the sins (bad karma) of one's lifetime, and that then to bathe in the ice-cold waters of the lake brings salvation.

Golgotha/Jerusalem: Earth's Sun Chakra (Heart)

Much has already been said earlier in this book (chapters 4 and 9) concerning Golgotha/Jerusalem as the center of the world—this centrality being fundamental to the whole of Astrogeographia. Jerusalem is viewed in ancient Jewish tradition as the *axis mundi* (world axis, world pillar, center of the world). Given Rudolf Steiner's indication that the mysteries of the Hebrews brought the true authentic *geology* in relation to the Logos,[35] we are given to understand that there is a profound level of truth to the Jewish tradition concerning the centrality of Jerusalem. For example, the prophet Ezekiel spoke of Israel, and by extension Jerusalem, as the "center of the earth" (Ezekiel 38:12). The first-century Jewish historian Flavius Josephus, who wrote in Greek, referred to Jerusalem in the same manner (*Wars of the Jews* 3.3½). Further, Jewish tradition propounded that Mount Moriah, also known as the Temple Mount—so named as the mount upon which the Temple of Solomon was located—was the first part of God's creation, indeed, that it was the site of Adam's creation. However, according to the stigmatist and clairvoyant nun Anne Catherine Emmerich it was not Mount Moriah but the nearby Mount of Olives on the outskirts of Jerusalem, just half-a-mile (800 m) to the east: "It was here on the Mount of Olives that Adam and Eve, driven from Paradise, had first descended upon the inhospitable earth...."[36] This notion was

35 See Steiner, *Christ and the Spiritual World, and the Search for the Holy Grail*, lecture 4, Dec. 31, 1913, pp. 75–84.

36 Emmerich, *The Life of Jesus Christ*, p. 80.

complemented by the idea that Adam had also been *buried* at nearby Golgotha, just one-third of a mile (500 m) west of Mount Moriah. Golgotha means the "place of the skull"—i.e., the skull of Adam. Hence it is believed that Adam's skull lies interred beneath the Church of the Holy Sepulcher on what remains of the Mount of Golgotha.[37] Several centuries later, when Muslims laid claim to Jerusalem, they adopted similar ideas as to the importance of Jerusalem in the order of creation as part of their own justification for the religious significance of the site upon which they built the Dome of the Rock, that is located centrally on the Temple Mount.

In his study of the Temple of Solomon James Wasserman refers to the Foundation Stone—the name of the rock at the heart of the Dome of the Rock—as the location of the Holy of Holies in the Temple of Solomon, the holiest site in Judaism, which Jewish tradition views as the spiritual junction of heaven and Earth, and which Jews traditionally face while praying:

> The Temple was built upon the Foundation Stone of the World,[38] the Rock upon which Abraham was to have sacrificed Isaac.... The Foundation Stone is also believed to have been the location of the Garden of Eden where the first humans walked with God.... Before Eden, the Rock of Ages is said to have been the point of coalescence of that Ray of Light which burst forth from Heaven, traveling through Space, until it mysteriously transformed itself into Matter, creating the pinpoint of Substance upon which the three-dimensional world was born. The point grew, first to become the Rock upon Mount Moriah in Jerusalem, then expanding outward to create the Earth upon which we move today.... Adam and

37 The Mount of Olives lies one-half mile (800 m) east of Mount Moriah (Temple Mount), and Mount Golgotha (Church of the Holy Sepulcher) is one-third mile (500 m) west of Mount Moriah. By reconciling the various accounts, it is possible that Adam and Eve were born on Mount Moriah, lived on the Mount of Olives, and Adam died and was buried on Mount Golgotha.

38 Footnote inserted by RP: The Foundation Stone is the name of the rock at the heart of the Dome of the Rock constructed by Muslims upon Mount Moriah that was completed in AD 691 by order of the Caliph Abd al-Malik. Early Jewish writings assist in confirming that the Dome of the Rock is the site of the Holy of Holies (Solomon's Temple) and therefore the location of the Foundation Stone.

> Eve were...cast forth into the plane of material life.... Solomon built the physical Temple...on the mystical mountain of Moriah in Jerusalem.... Solomon's Temple served as the geographic spiritual center...for a thousand years.[39]

Moreover, Golgotha/Jerusalem as the place of the crucifixion and resurrection, is for Christianity the center of the second creation of the world, the birthplace of the second Adam, who is the risen Jesus Christ as the "first-born of the dead" (Revelation 1:5)—considered as the progenitor of a new and spiritual human race, just as Adam was the progenitor of the physical human race. Through the Risen One there is the possibility in the future of the coming into being of the New Jerusalem as the "heavenly city" of the spiritualized human race. "The old Jerusalem will become transformed into the spiritual New Jerusalem, which will be built from above down."[40] Correspondingly there will take place in relation to the individual development of the seven chakras the formation of a completely new chakra which will make possible a new kind of highly developed "*thinking of the heart*" as described by Rudolf Steiner.[41]

Further, Steiner drew attention to the relationship of Palestine as a whole—through Christ—to the Sun, whereby the culmination of Christ's activity was at Golgotha/Jerusalem:

> Whenever Christ is mentioned in the Gospel of Saint Mark, the Sun force is meant, which, in that epoch of human evolution, was especially active in Palestine. The Sun force could be seen at this or that time as Christ went from one place to another. We could just as well say that at that time, the spiritual force of the Sun, as though focused in one point, went from one place to another. The body of Jesus was the external sign that made the movements of the Sun force visible. The journeys Jesus made in Palestine were those of the Sun force come down to the Earth. If you trace his

---

39 Wasserman, "The Temple of Solomon," *Mind Body Spirit*, vol. 29, pp. 78–80; see also Wasserman, *The Temple of Solomon.*

40 Steiner, *The Book of Revelation and the Work of the Priest*, p. 139.

41 Steiner, *How to Know Higher Worlds*, p. 133; see also Steiner, *Anthroposophical Leading Thoughts*, p. 62, "Hearts are beginning to have thoughts."

steps on a map, you have a diagram of a cosmic event: the influence of the Sun force from the macrocosm on the land of Palestine.[42]

Lake Titicaca in South America: Earth's Mercury Chakra (Solar Plexus)

Lake Titicaca is a vast sacred lake that lies on the border between Peru and Bolivia—3,200 square miles ($8{,}300^2$ km) in size and up to 1,000 feet (305 m.) deep. Titicaca is one of the largest, highest, and deepest lakes in the world, and is renowned for its deep blue quality. According to Incan lore, it was from Lake Titicaca that Viracocha, the Incan god of creation, rose up to create the world. In the year 2000 an archaeological expedition discovered an ancient temple submerged in the depths of Lake Titicaca. The huge temple structure is estimated to be over 1,000 years old—perhaps even 1,500 years old. This temple can be considered a monument to the Earth's Mercury chakra.

According to Incan mythology, Viracocha commanded the Sun god Inti, the Moon goddess Mama Quilla, and the stars to arise, and then proceeded to create the first human beings, Manco Cápac and his sister and wife Mama Ocllo—the Incan "Adam and Eve." They were formed from stone and brought to life by Viracocha, who instructed them to go out and populate the world. In this sense, Lake Titicaca was thought to be the birthplace of the Incas, who believed that their spirits returned to their place of origin in the lake upon death. In addition to Lake Titicaca itself, several of the forty-one islands on the lake were considered holy. Especially important to the Incas was the largest one, the Island of the Sun,[43] which was said to be the home of the Sun god Inti. The highest point on the island is 13,441 feet (almost 5,000 m.) above sea level. The Incas also believed that the Island of the Moon was the home of the Moon goddess Mama Quilla, who was the sister and wife of Inti, the daughter of Viracocha, and the mother of Manco Cápac and Mama Ocllo. During Inca times, specially chosen women known as "Virgins of the Sun" were sent to the Island of the Moon and lived there as

42 Steiner, *Background to the Gospel of St Mark*, lecture 3, Dec. 12, 1910. (English tr. revised by RP after comparing with the German original.)

43 As indicated earlier in this chapter, Robert Coon identified the Island of the Sun as the precise location of the Earth chakra at Lake Titicaca.

nuns, where they performed ceremonies dedicated to the Sun. This is an example of the Mercurial quality of balancing the Sun and Moon energies that was referred to earlier in this chapter, where it was mentioned that the Island of the Sun and the Island of the Moon are pointers to Lake Titicaca's function as the Earth's Mercury chakra. This balancing quality is also evident on Amantani Island, where there were two pre-Incan temples on two different hills, one dedicated to Pachamama (Mother Earth) and the other honoring Pachatata (Father Earth), again indicating the balancing nature of Lake Titicaca as the Earth's Mercury chakra. According to the myth about the founding of the Inca peoples, the Sun god Inti instructed Manco Cápac and Mama Ocllo to emerge from the depths of Lake Titicaca and found the city of Cuzco. To do so, it is said that they travelled underground by means of caves. They are believed to have made this underground journey to a location some two hundred miles (320 km) northwest from Lake Titicaca, until reaching Cuzco where they established the first Inca dynasty, that of the kingdom of Cuzco. As referred to earlier, Cuzco was considered the *navel of the world*—the navel being closely linked with the Mercury chakra in the region of the solar plexus.

Mount Agung on Bali: Earth's Venus Chakra (Sacral Region, Lower Abdomen)

Reaching up 10,308 feet (3,142 m.), the top of Mount Agung is the highest point on Bali, located on the east side of the island. Like Mount Fuji, Mount Agung is an active stratovolcano—it last erupted in the year 1963 and the massive volcano is still active. It is considered to be the holiest mountain on Bali. This "mother mountain," which is so highly sacred to the Balinese, is central to their beliefs. They consider it to be the abode of the gods and the ancestors and also to be the place to which they return when they die. It is believed by Balinese Hindus, who make up over ninety percent of the population of Bali, to be a replica of Mount Meru, the central axis of the universe. One legend holds that the mountain is a fragment of Mount Meru brought to Bali by the first Hindus. For the Balinese Hindus, who practice a special blend of Hinduism, Buddhism, and ancestor worship, the largest and most important temple on Bali is *Pura Besakih* ("the

Mother Temple of Besakih"), the building of which began over one thousand years ago high on the slopes of Mount Agung at 3,610 feet (1,100 m). It is actually a vast complex of temples sprawling across the mountainside. One temple is dedicated to Brahma, another to Vishnu, another to Shiva, and there are nineteen further Hindu temples at this location, each with its own purpose and ceremonial season. This lends a strongly religious, devotional quality to the area, which can be associated with Venus, the planet of devotion. Almost every day village groups come to pray and collect holy water to take home for local temple ceremonies, or to pay their respects upon completion of the complicated cycle of rituals in Balinese Hinduism. Each temple in the complex has its own annual ceremony and approximately every tenth year the impressive *Panca Wali Krama*, a purification for the whole of Bali, draws almost everyone on the island to refresh their links to the gods. Not a day passes in the lives of every Balinese Hindu where not at least once a day he or she visits a local temple for a prayer in respect of the holy mountain and *Pura Besakih*, the mother temple—such is the sacred power of this great Earth chakra, the Venus planetary chakra. In mythology, Venus has a connection with both air and water—see, for example, Botticelli's famous painting of the birth of Venus.[44] This connection is also readily apparent with Mount Agung, which dominates the surrounding area and influences the climate, since the clouds come from the west and Agung takes their water. This creates a mysterious barrier in which the western side of the mountain is green and full of vegetation and the eastern side is dry and barren. Like the planet Venus, which is veiled by a dense cloud covering, Mount Agung is normally covered with clouds, which make it difficult to see the mountain's wondrous beauty. For Venus is the planet of beauty and harmony, love and devotion, and this devotional atmosphere is impressed upon the whole of Bali.

There are few societies in the world where religion plays such a role as it does on the Venus island of Bali. The extraordinary beauty

44 Paul and Powell, *Cosmic Dances of the Planets*; see the chapter on Venus for further details about the relationship of this planet to air and water, and see also the reproduction of Botticelli's famous painting of the birth of Venus.

and color that accompanies the ever-recurring rituals and offerings is a sign that the Balinese continually seek to harmonize the human world with the world of the gods. For them the human being should constantly endeavor to maintain the harmony of the whole, whereby rituals play an important role in this. They believe that it is only by adhering to the rules of the Balinese religion that balance between heaven and Earth can be maintained. Indeed, the Balinese religion is replete with rituals. In order to uphold the balance of the world, there are rituals for everything imaginable. The rituals consist primarily in calling upon the gods and the ancestors to descend from their abode where they dwell in the heavenly land above the sacred mountain of Mount Agung. The gods and ancestors are imagined to respond by coming down during temple festivals to be entertained with dances and also fed with offerings. The entreaties of the priests during the rituals hold the intention of calling down the gods and ancestors. Everyday life in Bali merges with social duties and religious obligations while their unique art reflects an integration of environment, religion, and the community to which the artist belongs. The organization of the villages, the cultivation of the land, and the creation of art are communal efforts motivated by the overriding impulse for beauty and harmony—the whole island being an expression of a "Venus culture."

Uluru in Australia: Earth's Moon Chakra (Root, Base of the Spine)

Listed as a World Heritage Site, Ayers Rock is usually known by its aboriginal name *Uluru*. It is sacred in the creation mythology of the Aborigines. Considered one of the wonders of the world, it is Australia's best-known natural feature. It is a large sandstone rock formation in central Australia, in the Northern Territory, 208 miles (335 km) southwest of Alice Springs. The summit of Uluru is 1,142 feet (348 m) above the surrounding plain and this vast rock is believed to extend at least seven times its height—another 1½ miles (2½ km)—down into the ground. It is a six-mile (9½ km) walk around its base. In the aboriginal culture there are many stories of the mythical past, which are the core of the ceremonial life of the Aborigines: the theme of their ritualistic songs, and the subject of their art. In such ways, the Aborigines of Uluru keep alive the ties that bind them so closely to the massive sandstone rock, the great monolith under whose shadow they were born.

For the Aborigines their identity is based partly on the birthplace and partly on the child's perceived character. Long family genealogies are not found in this society, but by giving each individual a personal dreaming, the community reaffirms its links to the past and constantly re-creates the ancestral world. It is believed that at death a person becomes his or her dreaming. That this will occur—for the Aborigines at this place in the heart of Australia—is ensured, they believe, by being buried at Uluru. In this belief the root chakra quality of Uluru can be seen—that is, being "rooted" at a particular location on the Earth: in this case Uluru. Also, the relationship with the Moon, which is the planet of dreams and dreaming, is evident. For the Aborigines, Uluru is inhabited by a great number of ancestral beings—the Moon being also the planet of genealogy, linking with the ancestral blood stream.

As mentioned above, Uluru is the scene in the Australian Aboriginal story of the vast battle between the two serpents Kuniya and Liru (the female non-venomous carpet snake and the male venomous snake), which signaled the end of an era—that of the creative period called by the Aborigines "the Dreamtime." This was the "time before time," "the time of the creation of all things," the time when the spirit ancestors came to Earth and gave to the rocks, plants, animals and humans their present forms. In terms of Rudolf Steiner's cosmology, this can be seen as the transition time from the Ancient Moon stage of evolution to the present Earth.

The stories of the Aboriginal Dreamtime describe how long ago the Earth was soft and had no form, and how the heroic deeds of the ancestral spirits during the Dreamtime created the features of the landscape that we see today. Thus the huge sandhill on which the battle was fought between Kuniya and Liru at the close of the Creation era was turned into the rock of Uluru. The Kuniya people themselves were changed into various features of this rock. The women seated in their camp became large boulders in Tjukiki Gorge, while their *piti* (wooden carrying dish) became a tall slab of rock at the head of the gorge. A rockhole represents their campfire and small grasses and bushes which grow in tufts in the gorge are their hairs. The sleeping Kuniya men turned into boulders which now lie motionless in the Sun on the plain beneath. The spears that the Liru men threw made indentations in the sand which are now seen as the pitted vertical cliff face on the northeast side of Uluru.

Throughout Australia, the Rainbow Serpent is a personification of fertility and rain. In 1926 a British anthropologist Professor Alfred Radcliffe-Brown coined the term "Rainbow Serpent" to describe the recurring myth of a snake of some enormous size living within the deepest waterholes, and described in the Aboriginal stories as descended from the larger being visible as the dark streak in the Milky Way.[45] Robert Coon adopted the term *Rainbow Serpent* to describe the great ley artery that runs through Uluru on its circuit around the globe. For the other ley artery he used the term *Plumed Serpent*, the name of the great deity of various Mesoamerican religions—the Feathered Serpent of the Olmecs, Quetzalcoatl of the Aztecs, and Kukulkan of the Maya.

Bearing in mind the deep truth of the words "as above, so below," relating to the principle of correspondences between the macrocosm ("great world") and the microcosm ("the little world" of the human being), it is interesting, in relation to the idea of two serpents encircling the globe, that Rudolf Steiner draws attention to two "snakes" within the human being:

> There is a symbol that one must enliven within oneself. This is the Staff of Mercury (see figure 7), the luminous staff with a black snake and a bright luminous shining snake. The snake is a symbol for the astral body. Every night the astral body sheds its skin; it throws off the used-up skin. The black snake is a symbol for this. Overnight it gets a new, shimmering skin, and this newly enlivened, beautiful, shining skin of the astral body is symbolized by

45 See Radcliffe-Brown, "The Rainbow-Serpent Myth of Australia," *Journal of the Royal Anthropological Institute of Great Britain and Ireland* (Volume 56, 1926), pp. 19–25.

the shining snake...this symbol, the Staff of Mercury, who is the "messenger of the gods."[46]

Figure 7: The Staff of Mercury

Applying the principle of correspondences, we believe that Robert Coon's insight into two great ley arteries encircling the Earth is a true one, which is mirrored in the human being in the Staff of Mercury described by Rudolf Steiner, and that this is of significance for the interconnections between the seven planetary chakras located on the seven continents of the Earth.

Readers will have noticed that we do not discuss the well-known power point Glastonbury in England, identified by Robert Coon as both the heart center and the temporary third-eye center of the world. What we found through Astrogeographia is that Glastonbury is indeed highly significant, as it is the location at which the star Botein in Aries, sometimes depicted marking the rear right hoof or flank of the Ram (but "the western one of the three in the tail" according to Ptolemy), is impressed upon the Earth. Botein is the fourth brightest star in Aries. In other words, there are three stars in Aries which are brighter than Botein—these being Hamal ("the star above the head of the Ram"), Sheratan ("the eastern star of the two in the horn"), and Mesartim ("the western star of the two in the horn"). Astrogeographically, Botein is the most important of these four stars, since the projection onto the globe of the other three is in the Northern Atlantic Ocean—that of Hamal is 292½ miles (470½ km) west of Knockfola on the northwest coast of Ireland, Sheratan is 458 miles (737 km) west of Limerick, and Mesartim is 514 miles (827 km) west of Cork. Hence Botein serves astrogeographically as the primary star of Aries in terms of the ordering of stars according to their apparent brightness, being the brightest star of Aries which is projected onto firm land rather than onto the Atlantic ocean. And since, according to Ptolemy and as confirmed by Astrogeographia, England as a whole is associated with Aries, Glastonbury assumes special significance for the whole

46 Steiner, *Esoteric Lessons 1904–1909*, p. 393.

of England and for the entire region falling under the influence of the constellation of the Ram.

Glastonbury, held sacred long before Christianity, was settled already in pre-Christian times by the Celts. According to legend, after Christ's crucifixion Joseph of Arimathea, in whose tomb (the Holy Sepulcher) the body of Christ was laid to rest, went on a mission and came to Glastonbury bearing the cup of the Holy Grail which had been used at the Last Supper and in which some of Christ's blood had been collected as it flowed down from his body on the cross. Legendary accounts relate that through Joseph of Arimathea, there were Celts in the Glastonbury region who converted to Christianity. Under the Celtic monks, a church is said to have been built at Glastonbury, which according to tradition became known as the "Holiest Earth of England," since it was acknowledged as the place where Christianity first came to England. Later, Arthurian legends associated King Arthur with Glastonbury, who supposedly was buried in a grave at the great abbey which grew there from the original church. During the twentieth century a New Age community has grown at Glastonbury, attracting many people with Neopagan beliefs. According to the research of Astrogeographia, Glastonbury is closely aligned with the star Botein, lying exactly on the Botein meridian. And on account of the steady movement northward along this meridian of the projection of Botein, since the beginning of the twentieth century, the projection of Botein onto the Earth coincides exactly with Glastonbury, giving grounds to associate the influence of this star with the tremendous growth of interest in Glastonbury as a spiritual center.

We conclude our study of the planetary Earth chakras by quoting from Rudolf Steiner, through whom we came to an understanding of the correspondence between each continent and the seven planets—here contemplating the centrality of Golgotha as the Sun chakra:

> With the event of Golgotha, when the blood flowed from the wounds of the great Redeemer, when the Cosmic Heart's blood penetrated the Earth and its forces poured down as far as its center, the Earth became illumined from within and light rayed outward into the surroundings...In the Temple of the human body is the Holy of Holies...Those who have an inkling of it receive from it

the power to purify themselves to such an extent that they can enter into this holiest place. Therein is the Holy Vessel that has been prepared throughout the ages as a container for the blood and life of Christ when the time for it arrives. When one has entered therein, one has found the way to the Holy of Holies in the great Temple of the Earth.... When one discovers oneself within one's innermost sanctuary, one will be allowed to enter in and there discover the Holy Grail.... One enters into the Mystery Center of one's own heart and a divine being emerges from this place and unites itself with the God outside, with the Being of Christ.... Because the human being is a twofold being, one is able to pour the Sun forces into the Earth and act as a connecting link between the Sun and the Earth.... It is the mission of every single human being and of the whole of humanity to fill themselves with the Christ Spirit and to recognize themselves as a center living in this Spirit, through which spiritual light, spiritual strength and spiritual warmth can flow into the Earth, thereby redeeming it and raising it aloft into spiritual realms.[47]

---

47 Steiner, *"Freemasonry" and Ritual Work*, pp. 429–430.

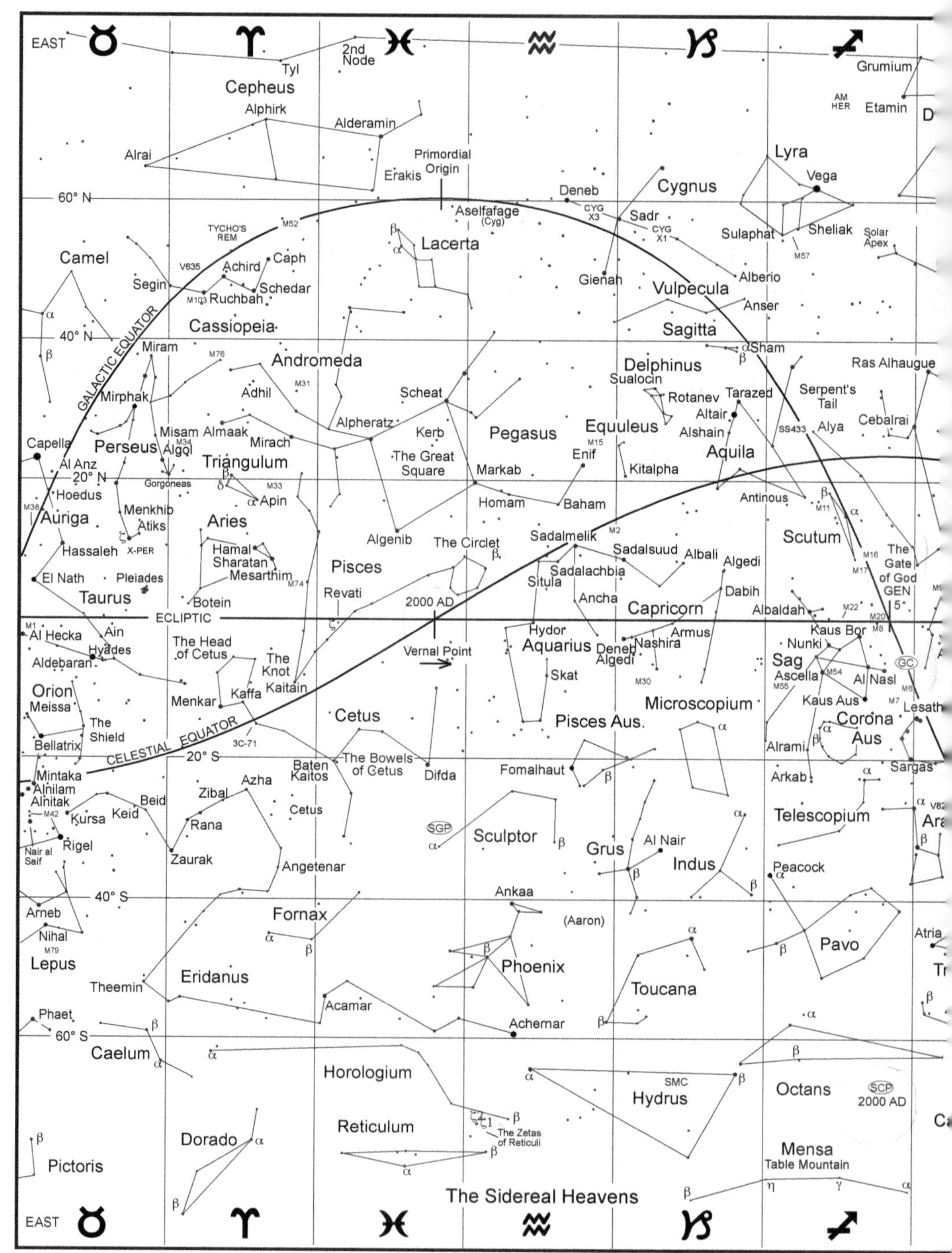
EAST
Cepheus
Alphirk
Alderamin
Alrai
Tyl
2nd Node
Primordial Origin
Erakis
Lacerta
Aselfafage (Cyg)
Deneb
Cygnus
Sadr
Lyra
Vega
Sulaphat
Sheliak
Grumium
Etamin
AM HER
Solar Apex
Camel
Segin
Achird
Caph
Schedar
Ruchbah
Cassiopeia
TYCHO'S REM
V635
M52
M103
Gienah
Vulpecula
Alberio
Anser
Sagitta
Sham
GALACTIC EQUATOR
Miram
Andromeda
M76
M31
Adhil
Mirphak
Perseus
Misam
Almaak
Algol
Mirach
M34
Capella
Al Anz
Triangulum
Gorgoneas
Hoedus
Auriga
Menkhib
Atiks
M38
M33
Apin
Aries
Hassaleh
X-PER
Hamal
Sharatan
Mesarthim
El Nath
Pleiades
Taurus
Botein
Scheat
Alpheratz
Kerb
The Great Square
Pegasus
Markab
Homam
Baham
Enif
M15
Equuleus
Kitalpha
Delphinus
Sualocin
Rotanev
Tarazed
Altair
Alshain
Aquila
Serpent's Tail
SS433
Alya
Cebalrai
Ras Alhaugue
Antinous
Scutum
M11
M16
M17
The Gate of God
GEN 5°
Algenib
The Circlet
Pisces
Revati
M74
Sadalmelik
M2
Sadalsuud
Albali
Algedi
Sadalachbia
Situla
Ancha
Dabih
Capricorn
Albaldah
M22
M20
M8
ECLIPTIC
2000 AD
Al Hecka
M1
Ain
Hyades
Aldebaran
The Head of Cetus
The Knot
Kaitain
Vernal Point
Hydor
Aquarius
Deneb Algedi
Nashira
Armus
Kaus Bor
Nunki
Sag
Ascella
M54
M55
Al Nasl
GC
M6
M7
Orion
Meissa
The Shield
Bellatrix
Menkar
Kaffa
Cetus
Skat
M30
Microscopium
Pisces Aus.
Kaus Aus
Lesath
Corona Aus
CELESTIAL EQUATOR
3C-71
Alrami
Sargas
20° S
Baten Kaitos
The Bowels of Cetus
Difda
Fomalhaut
Arkab
Mintaka
Alnilam
Alnitak
M42
Zibal
Azha
Beid
Kursa
Keid
Rana
Rigel
Nair al Saif
Zaurak
SGP
Sculptor
Grus
Al Nair
Indus
Telescopium
Peacock
Angetenar
40° S
Ankaa
Arneb
Nihal
M79
Lepus
Fornax
(Aaron)
Phoenix
Toucana
Pavo
Atria
Eridanus
Theemin
Acamar
Achernar
Phaet
60° S
Caelum
Horologium
Hydrus
SMC
Octans
SCP 2000 AD
Reticulum
The Zetas of Reticuli
Dorado
Pictoris
Mensa
Table Mountain
The Sidereal Heavens
60° N
40° N
20° N

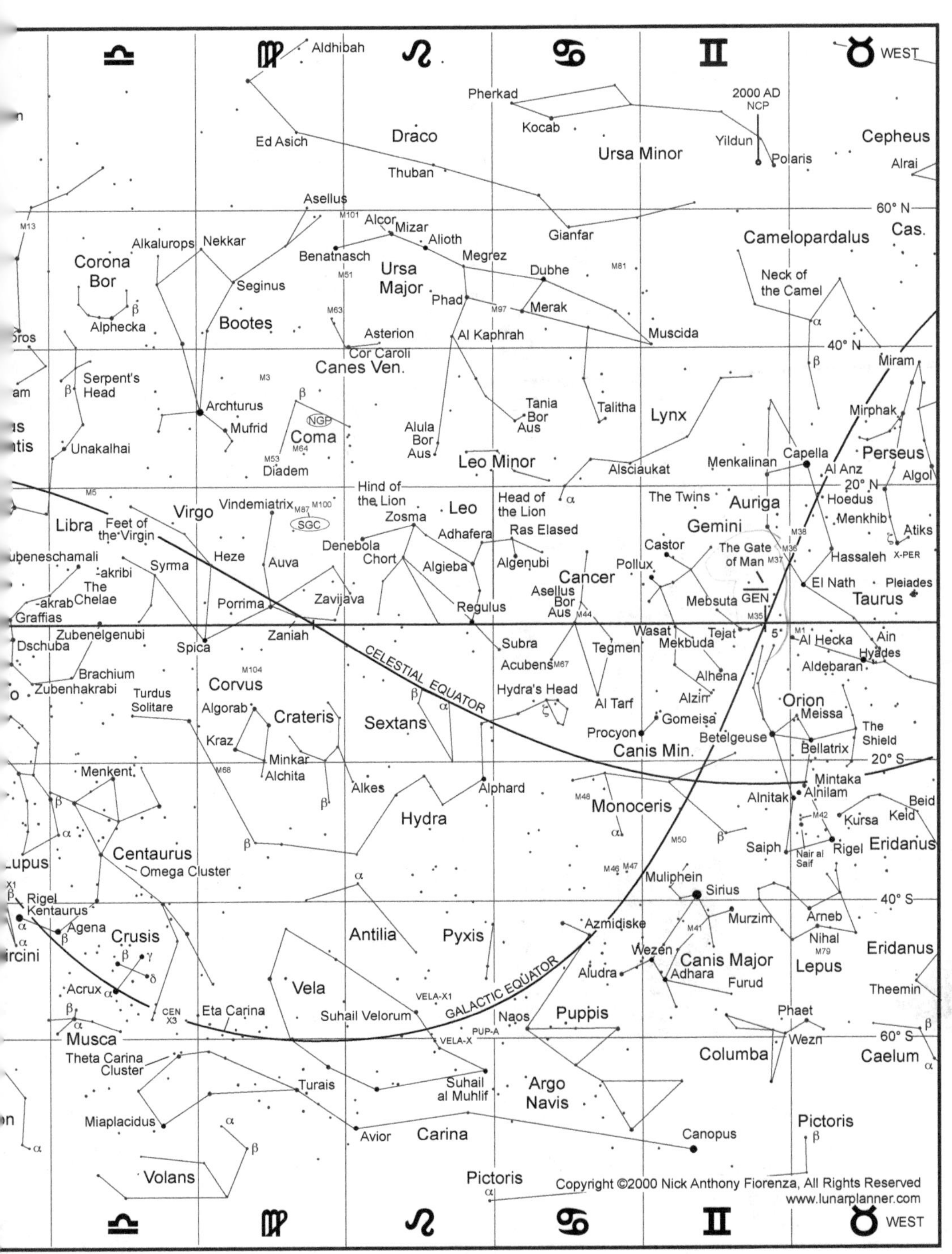

 See discussion on page 240

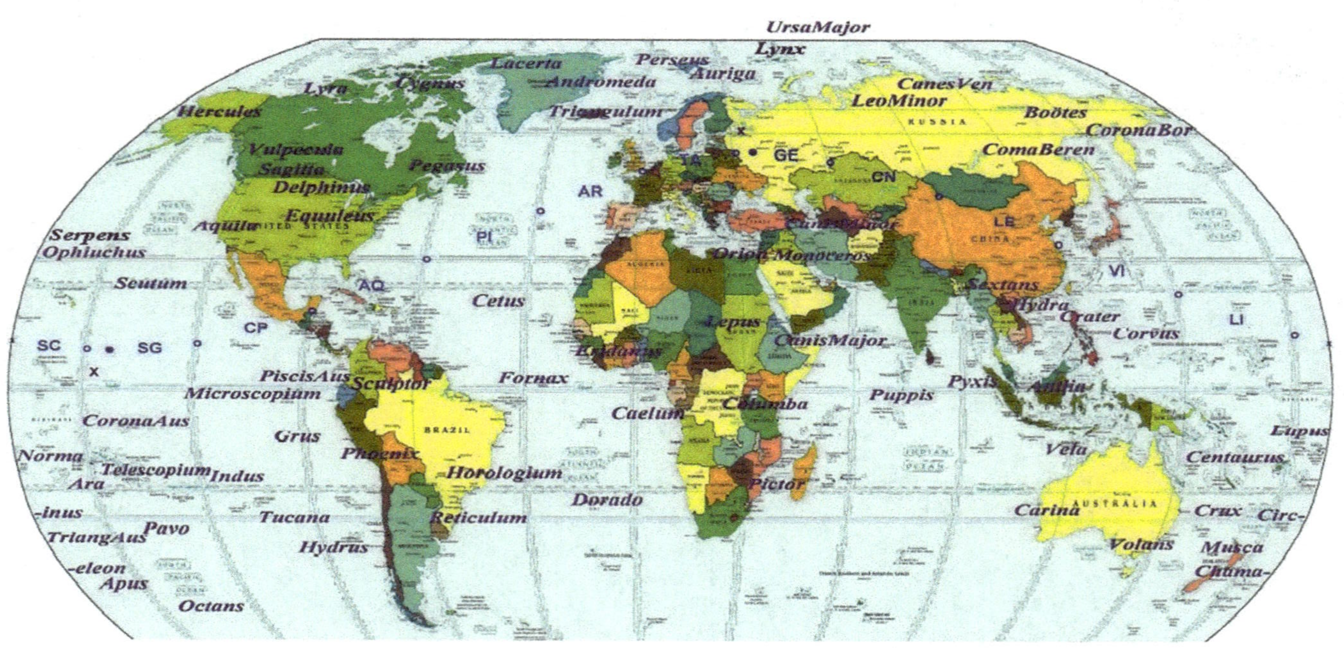

Astrogeographia map of 82 constellations (AD *2000); see page 185*

Map of *archetypal projections of the stars—the birth horoscope of the world;* *see page 205*

Bibliography

Works Cited:

Aaboe, Asger, and Abraham Sachs. "Two Lunar Texts of the Achaemenid Period from Babylon." *Centaurus* 14, 1969.

Akcam, Haluk. "Precession and the Obliquity of the Ecliptic." 2004. http://www.tenspheres.com/researches/precession.htm. Accessed 2006.

Allen, Richard Hinckley. *Star Names: Their Lore and Meaning.* New York: Dover, 1963.

Anonymous. *Meditations on the Tarot: A Journey into Christian Hermeticism* (tr., R. Powell). New York: Tarcher-Putnam, 2002.

Apuleius, Lucius. *Metamorphoses,* or *The Golden Ass.* (tr., W. Adlington), 1566; http://www.big.com.au/fallen/almagest.html; accessed 2006.

Bauval, Robert, and Adrian Gilbert. *The Orion Mystery.* London: William Heinemann/Mandarin Paperbacks/Arrow Books, 1994).

Boev, B. and B. Nikolov (eds.). *The Wellspring of Good: The Last Words of the Master Peter Deunov.* Walnut Creek, CA: Kibea, 2002.

Brentano, Clemens. *Sämtliche Werke und Briefe,* vol. 26: *Das bittere Leiden unsers Herrn Jesu Christi.* Stuttgart: Kohlhammer Verlag, 1980.

Bullinger, E.W. *The Witness of the Stars.* Grand Rapids, MI: Kregel Publications, 1967.

Callimachus."Hymn to Artemis." Tr. by Jean Alvarez. www.chss.montclair.edu/classics/HYMNART.HTML. Accessed 2006.

Cohen, I. B. "Isaac Newton." *Dictionary of Scientific Biography.* Edited by C. Gillespie. New York: Charles Scribner's Sons, 1970–1980.

Coon, Robert. *Earth Chakras.* Self published, 1967–2009.

———. *The Rainbow Serpent and the Holy Grail.* Self-published, 1998.

Copernicus, Nicholas. *On the Revolutions.* Translation and commentary by E. Roger. Baltimore, MD: John Hopkins University Press, 1992.

Dibon-Smith, Richard. *The Constellations.* Toronto: Clear Skies Publishing Company, 2002.

Dolphin, Lambert, and Michael Kollen. "On The Location of the First and Second Temples in Jerusalem." http://www.templemount.org/theories
.html. Accessed 2012.

Edwards, I. E. S. "The Air Channels of Cheops' Pyramid." *Studies in Honor of Dows Dunham.* Boston, MA: Museum of Fine Arts, 1981.

Emmerich, Anne Catherine. "Blick auf Melchisedek." in Clemens Brentano, *Sämtliche Werke und Briefe,* vol. 26: *Das bittere Leiden unsers Herrn Jesu Christi.* Stuttgart: Kohlhammer Verlag, 1980.

———. *Das bittere Leiden unseres Herrn Jesus Christi*. Stuttgart: Kohlhammer Verlag, 1983.

———. *The Life of Jesus Christ*. Rockford, IL: Tan Books, 2004.

Evans, James. *The History and Practice of Ancient Astronomy*. Oxford, UK: Oxford University Press, 1998.

Faulkner, R. O. *The Ancient Egyptian Pyramid Texts*. Oxford: Clarendon Press, 1910.

Gantenbrink, Rudolf. "The Lower Southern Shaft." http://www.cheops.org
/startpage/thefindings/thelowersouthshaft/lowersouth.htm. Accessed 2012.

Genge, Heinze. "Versuch einer Abraham-Datierung." *In Memoriam Eckhard Unger: Beiträge zu Geschichte, Kultur und Religion des alten Orients*. Baden-Baden, Germany: 1971.

Giessen, Juergen. *Obliquity Applet*. (2004); http://www.jgiesen.de /obliquity. Accessed 2006.

Herodotus. *The Histories* I.4. Tr. by A. de Sélincourt, revised by A.R. Burn. Hammondsworth, UK: Penguin, 1972.

Hunger, Hermann, and David Pingree. *Astral Sciences in Mesopotamia*. Leiden: Brill, 1999.

Josephus. *Antiquities of the Jews* I:4. Blacksburg, VA: Unabridged Books, 2011.

Karim, Ibrahim. *BioGeometry: Back to a Future for Mankind*. Cairo: BioGeometry Consulting, 2010.

Keats, Brian. www.astro-calendar.com; accessed 2012.

Keller, Hans-Ulrich. "Kippt die Erdachse?" *Kosmos Himmelsjahr 2000*. Stuttgart: Kosmos, 1999.

Kennedy, E. S. and David Pingree. *The Astrological History of Masha'allah*. Cambridge, MA: Harvard University Press, 1971.

Kepler, Johannes. *Harmonice Mundi* IV,11. Tr. by Max Caspar. *Weltharmonik* ("Harmony of the World"). Munich: Oldenbourg Verlag, 1997.

———. *Weltharmonik* ("Harmonies of the World.") Munich: Oldenbourg Verlag, 1997.

Kirchner-Bockholt, Margarete and Erich. *Rudolf Steiner's Mission and Ita Wegman*. London: Rudolf Steiner Press, 1977.

Klocek, Dennis. *Climate: Soul of the Earth*. Great Barrington, MA: SteinerBooks, 2010.

———. "Projective Fields in Astroclimatology"; in *The Cosmic Harbinger*. 2000.

———. *The Seer's Handbook: A Guide to Higher Perception*. Great Barrington, MA: SteinerBooks, 2005.

Koestler, Arthur. *The Sleepwalkers*. London: Penguin, 1973.

Kollerstrom, Nicholas. "On the Measurement of Celestial Longitude in Antiquity." *Optics and Astronomy*. Proceedings of the XXth

International Congress of History of Science, held July 20–26, 1997, in Liege. Vol. 12, edited by G. Simon and S. Débarbat. Brussels: 2001.

———. "The Star Zodiac of Antiquity." *Culture and Cosmos*, vol. 1. London: Garland Publishing, 1997.

Kugler, Franz Zavier. *Sternkunde und Sterndienst in Babel.* vol. 1. Münster: 1907.

Lash, John. http://www.metahistory.org/READING/reviews/WhiteLions.php; accessed 2012.

Lekson, Stephen. *The Chaco Meridian: Centers of Political Power in the Ancient Southwest.* Lanham, MD: AltaMira Press, 1999.

LePage, Victoria. *Shambhala.* Wheaton, IL: Quest Books, 1996.

MacKenzie, D. N. "Zoroastrian Astrology in the Bundahišn," *Bulletin of the School of Oriental and African Studies* 27. London: Cambridge University Press, 1964.

Manilius. *Astronomica.* I.895–909. Tr. by G. P. Goold. Cambridge, MA: Harvard University Press, 1977.

McRae, Chris, *The Geodetic World Map.* Tempe, AZ: American Federation of Astrologers, 1988.

Meyers Grosse Sternenatlas. Mannheim: Meyers Lexikonverlag, 2002.

Michelsen, Neil F. *The American Sidereal Ephemeris, 1976–2000* and *The American Sidereal Ephemeris, 2001–2025.* San Diego, CA: Astro Communications Services, 1981.

Milne, Courtney, *The Sacred Earth.* Saskatoon, Canada: Western Producer Prairie Books, 1991.

Naydler, Jeremy. *Temple of the Cosmos.* Rochester, NY: Inner Traditions, 1996.

Neugebauer, Otto. *A History of Ancient Mathematical Astronomy,* 3 vols. New York: Springer Verlag, 1975).

Neugebauer, Otto, and H. P. van Hoesen. "Greek Horoscopes." *Memoirs of the American Philosophical Society*, vol. 48. Philadelphia, 1987.

Neugebauer, Otto, and Richard A. Parker. *Egyptian Astronomical Texts, volume III: Decans, Planets, Constellations and Zodiacs.* Providence, RI: Brown University, 1969.

Paul, Lacquanna, and Robert Powell. *Cosmic Dances of the Planets.* San Rafael, CA: Sophia Foundation Press, 2006.

———. *Cosmic Dances of the Zodiac.* Palo Alto, CA: Sophia Foundation of North America, 2003.

Pingree, David. "Astronomy and Astrology in India and Iran." *Isis* 54, 1963.

———. *The Thousands of Abu Ma'shar.* London: Warburg Institute, 1968.

Pliny the Younger. *Letters* X.25 ff; http://www.fordham.edu/halsall/ancient
/pliny-trajan1.html; accessed 2012.

Pogacnik, Marko. *Sacred Geography: Geomancy: Co-creating the Earth Cosmos*. Great Barrington, MA: Lindisfarne Books, 2007.

Powell, Robert. *Christian Hermetic Astrology: The Star of the Magi and the Life of Christ*. Great Barrington, MA: Steiner Books, 1998.

———, (ed.). *Christian Star Calendar*. Palo Alto, CA: Sophia Foundation, annual journal (title since 2010: *Journal for Star Wisdom*).

———. *Chronicle of the Living Christ: The Life and Ministry of Jesus Christ: Foundations of Cosmic Christianity*. Great Barrington, MA: SteinerBooks, 1996.

———. *Cultivating Inner Radiance and the Body of Immortality: Awakening the Soul through Modern Etheric Movement*. Great Barrington, MA: SteinerBooks, 2012.

———. *Hermetic Astrology*, vol. I: *Astrology and Reincarnation*. San Rafael, CA: Sophia Foundation Press, 2007.

———. *History of the Houses*. San Diego, CA: Starcrafts/ACS Publishing, 1997.

———. *History of the Planets*. San Diego, CA: Starcrafts/ACS Publishing, 1989.

———. *History of the Zodiac*. San Rafael, CA: Sophia Academic Press, 2006.

———. (ed.), *Journal for Star Wisdom*. Great Barrington, MA: SteinerBooks/Lindisfarne Books, annual journal.

———. "Megastars." *General Introduction to the Christian Star Calendar*. Palo Alto, CA: Sophia Foundation of North America, 2003.

———. *Prophecy-Phenomena-Hope: The Real Meaning of 2012: Christ & the Maya Calendar—An Update*. Great Barrington, MA: SteinerBooks, 2011.

———. *The Sophia Teachings, Emergence of the Divine Feminine in Our Time*. Great Barrington MA: Lindisfarne Books, 2007.

———. "The Vision of Europe." *Shoreline Journal*, no. 2. Penmorfa, Gwynedd, Wales : Living Art & Science Trust, 1989.

———. *The Zodiac: A Historical Survey*. San Diego, CA: San Diego, CA: Starcrafts/ACS Publishing, 1984.

Powell, Robert, and Kevin Dann. *The Astrological Revolution: Unveiling the Science of the Stars as a Science of Reincarnation and Karma*. Great Barrington, MA: SteinerBooks, 2010.

———. *Christ & the Maya Calendar: 2012 and the Coming of the Antichrist*. Great Barrington, MA: SteinerBooks, 2009.

Powell, Robert, and Peter Treadgold. *Christian Star Calendar 2006*. Palo Alto, CA: Sophia Foundation, 2005.

———. *The Sidereal Zodiac*. Tempe, AZ: AFA, 1984.

Ptolemy. *Almagest*. Ed. and tr. by G. J. Toomer. Princeton, NJ: Princeton University Press, 1998.

———. *Geography*. Ed. and tr. by E. L. Stevenson. New York: Dover, 1991.

———. *Tetrabiblos*. Ed. and tr. by F. E. Robbins. London: Loeb Classical Library, 1980.

Radcliffe-Brown. Alfred, "The Rainbow-Serpent Myth of Australia," *Journal of the Royal Anthropological Institute of Great Britain and Ireland,* vol. 56, 1926.

Roach, John. "Why Does Earth's Magnetic Field Flip?", http://news.nationalgeographic.com/news/2004/09/0927. Accessed 2012.

Rochberg, Francesca. *Babylonian Horoscopes*. Philadelphia, PA: American Philosophical Society, 1998.

Rohl, David. *A Test of Time: The Bible—Myth to History*. London: Century/Random House, 1995.

Rolleston, Frances. *Mazzaroth*. York Beach, ME: Weiser, 2001.

Schipflinger, Thomas. *Sophia-Maria: A Holistic Vision of Creation*. York Beach, ME: Samuel Weiser, 1998.

Scott, Martin. "Sophia and the Johannine Jesus"; *Journal for the Study of the New Testament,* Supplement Series 71. Sheffield, UK: Sheffield Academic Press,1992.

Seiss, Joseph A. *The Gospel in the Stars: Or, Prímeval Astronomy*. Grand Rapids, MI: Kregel Publications, 1972.

Settegast, Mary. *Plato Prehistorian: 10,000 to 5,000 B.C.—Myth, Religion and Archaeology*. Cambridge, MA: Rotenberg Press, 1987 (current edition, Great Barrington, MA: Lindisfarne Books, 1990).

Spies, Hansjörg, and Carl Nemeth. *Vienna: the City of Music*. Graz, Austria: Bonechi Verlag Styria, 2001.

StarFire Three (William Bento, Robert Schiappacasse, and David Tresemer). *Signs In the Heavens: A Message For Our Time*. Hygiene, CO: SunShine Press, 2000.

Steiner, Rudolf. *According to Luke: The Gospel of Compassion and Love Revealed*. Great Barrington, MA: SteinerBooks, 2001.

———. *Ancient Myths*. (CW 180). Toronto: Steiner Book Center, 1971; in print as *Ancient Myths and the New Isis Mystery*. Hudson, NY: Anthroposophic Press, 1994.

———. *Anthroposophical Leading Thoughts* (CW 26). London: Rudolf Steiner Press, 1998.

———. *Aus den Inhalten der esoterischen Stunden, Gedächtnisaufzeichnungen von Teilnehmern. Band.1, 1904–1909* (CW 266/1). Dornach, Switzerland: Rudolf Steiner Verlag, 1995; English edition: *Esoteric Lessons, 1904–1909: From the Esoteric School,* vol. 1. Great Barrington, MA: SteinerBooks, 2007.

———. *Background to the Gospel of St. Mark* (CW 124). Hudson, NY: Anthroposophic Press, 1985.

———. *The Birth of a New Agriculture: Koberwitz 1924 and the Introduction of Biodynamics* (edited by Adalbert Graf von Keyserlingk). London: Temple Lodge Press, 1999.

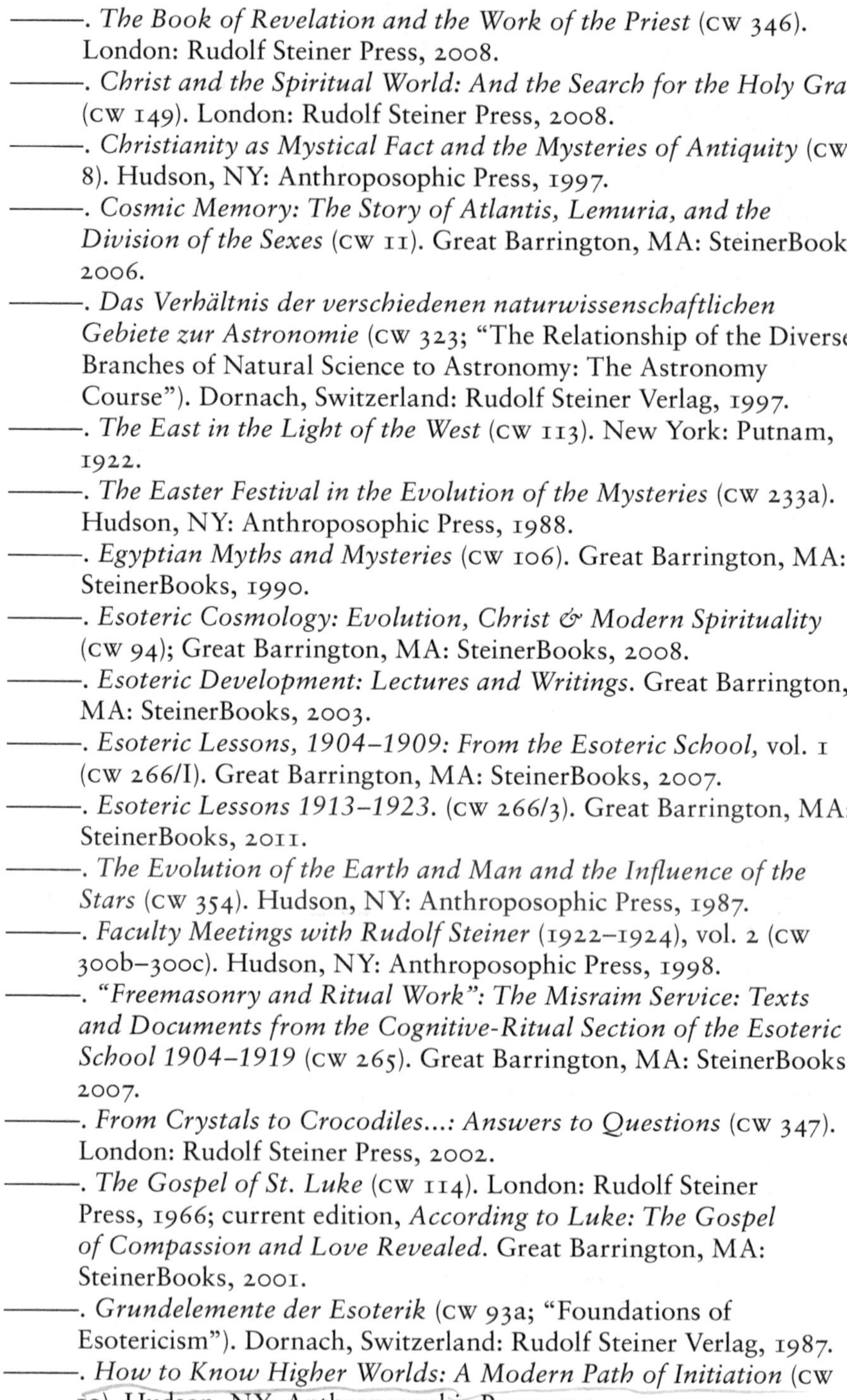

———. *The Book of Revelation and the Work of the Priest* (CW 346). London: Rudolf Steiner Press, 2008.

———. *Christ and the Spiritual World: And the Search for the Holy Grail* (CW 149). London: Rudolf Steiner Press, 2008.

———. *Christianity as Mystical Fact and the Mysteries of Antiquity* (CW 8). Hudson, NY: Anthroposophic Press, 1997.

———. *Cosmic Memory: The Story of Atlantis, Lemuria, and the Division of the Sexes* (CW 11). Great Barrington, MA: SteinerBooks, 2006.

———. *Das Verhältnis der verschiedenen naturwissenschaftlichen Gebiete zur Astronomie* (CW 323; "The Relationship of the Diverse Branches of Natural Science to Astronomy: The Astronomy Course"). Dornach, Switzerland: Rudolf Steiner Verlag, 1997.

———. *The East in the Light of the West* (CW 113). New York: Putnam, 1922.

———. *The Easter Festival in the Evolution of the Mysteries* (CW 233a). Hudson, NY: Anthroposophic Press, 1988.

———. *Egyptian Myths and Mysteries* (CW 106). Great Barrington, MA: SteinerBooks, 1990.

———. *Esoteric Cosmology: Evolution, Christ & Modern Spirituality* (CW 94); Great Barrington, MA: SteinerBooks, 2008.

———. *Esoteric Development: Lectures and Writings*. Great Barrington, MA: SteinerBooks, 2003.

———. *Esoteric Lessons, 1904–1909: From the Esoteric School,* vol. 1 (CW 266/I). Great Barrington, MA: SteinerBooks, 2007.

———. *Esoteric Lessons 1913–1923*. (CW 266/3). Great Barrington, MA: SteinerBooks, 2011.

———. *The Evolution of the Earth and Man and the Influence of the Stars* (CW 354). Hudson, NY: Anthroposophic Press, 1987.

———. *Faculty Meetings with Rudolf Steiner* (1922–1924), vol. 2 (CW 300b–300c). Hudson, NY: Anthroposophic Press, 1998.

———. *"Freemasonry and Ritual Work": The Misraim Service: Texts and Documents from the Cognitive-Ritual Section of the Esoteric School 1904–1919* (CW 265). Great Barrington, MA: SteinerBooks, 2007.

———. *From Crystals to Crocodiles...: Answers to Questions* (CW 347). London: Rudolf Steiner Press, 2002.

———. *The Gospel of St. Luke* (CW 114). London: Rudolf Steiner Press, 1966; current edition, *According to Luke: The Gospel of Compassion and Love Revealed*. Great Barrington, MA: SteinerBooks, 2001.

———. *Grundelemente der Esoterik* (CW 93a; "Foundations of Esotericism"). Dornach, Switzerland: Rudolf Steiner Verlag, 1987.

———. *How to Know Higher Worlds: A Modern Path of Initiation* (CW 10). Hudson, NY: Anthroposophic Press, 1994.

———. *Isis Mary Sophia: Her Mission and Ours*. Great Barrington, MA: SteinerBooks, 2003.

———. *Man: Hieroglyph of the Universe* (CW 201). London: Rudolf Steiner Press, 1972; current edition, *Mystery of the Universe: The Human Being, Model of Creation*. London: Rudolf Steiner Press, 2001.

———. *Materialism and the Task of Anthroposophy* (CW 204). Hudson, NY: Anthroposophic Press, 1987.

———. *Menschheitsentwickelung und Christus-Erkenntnis*. (CW 100; "Human Evolution and Knowledge of Christ"). Dornach, Switzerland: Rudolf Steiner Verlag, 2005.

———. *The Mission of Folk-Souls: In Relation to Teutonic Mythology* (CW 121). London: Rudolf Steiner Press, 2005.

———. *The Mysteries of the East and of Christianity*. London: Rudolf Steiner Press, 1972.

———. *Mythen und Sagen. Okkulte Zeichen und Symbole* (CW 101; "Myths and Legends: Occult Signs and Symbols"). Dornach, Switzerland: Rudolf Steiner Verlag, 1992.

———. *Occult Science, an Outline*. London, Rudolf Steiner Press, 2011.

———. *Rudolf Steiner on Astronomy* (CW 323). Redondo Beach, CA: Rudolf Steiner Research Foundation, 1989.

———. *The Spiritual Guidance of the Individual and Humanity*. Great Barrington, MA: Anthroposophic Press, 1992.

Suchantke, Andreas, et al. *Israel: Mitte der Erde* ("*Israel: Midpoint of the Earth*"). Stuttgart: Verlag Freies Geistesleben, 1988.

———. *Mitte der Erde: Israel und Palästina im Brennpunkt nature-und kulturgeschichtlicher Entwicklungen*. Stuttgart, Germany: Verlag Freiesgeistesleben, 1996.

Tester, Jim. *A History of Western Astrology*. New York: Ballantine Books, 1987.

The Times Atlas of the World. London: Times Books, 1983.

The Wellspring of Good: The Last Words of the Master Peter Deunov. Compiled by B. Boev and B. Nikolov. Walnut Creek, CA: Kibea Publishing/Evera Books, 2002.

Tidball, Charles, and Robert Powell. *Jesus, Lazarus, and the Messiah*. Great Barrington, MA: Steiner Books, 2005.

Treadgold, Peter. *Astrofire*. Computer program, distributed by the Sophia Foundation of North America. www.sophiafoundation.org.

Tucker, Linda. *Mystery of the White Lions*. Carlsbad, CA: Hay House, 2010.

Van der Waerden, B. L. *Science Awakening, vol. ii: The Birth of Astronomy*. Leyden: Noordhoff International Publishing, 1974.

Wallis Budge, E. A. *Osiris and the Egyptian Resurrection*. London: Dover, 1973.

Wasserman, James. "The Temple of Solomon." *Mind Body Spirit*, vol. 29. London: Watkins Books, 2012.

———. *The Temple of Solomon: From Ancient Israel to Secret Societies.* Rochester, VT: Inner Traditions, 2011.

Weidner, E. F. "Babylonische Hypsomatabilder." *Orientalistische Literatur-Zeitung* 22, 1919.

Websites Cited

http://ancient-anatolia.blogspot.com/2006/09/hattians-first-civilization-in-anatolia.html; accessed 2006.

http://earth.rice.edu/mtpe/geo/geosphere/hot/energyfuture/Sunlight.html; accessed 2012.

http://en.wikipedia.org/wiki/Arcturus; accessed 2012.

http://en.wikipedia.org/wiki/Hattians; accessed 2012.

http://en.wikipedia.org/wiki/King_Arthur; accessed 2012.

http://stars.astro.illinois.edu/sow/cm3.html; accessed 2012.

http://stars.astro.illinois.edu/sow/cm5.html; accessed 2012.

http://www.cieloeterra.it/eng/eng.testi.379/eng.379.html; accessed 2012.

http://www.constellationsofwords.com/stars/Betelgeuse.html; accessed 2012.

http://www.lunarplanner.com/ArgoNavisPublications/SiderealHeavensGiclee/index.html; accessed 2006.

http://www.metrum.org/mapping/cosmol.htm; accessed 2012.

http://www.saudiaramcoworld.com/issue/196108/the.people.that.history.forgot.htm; accessed 2012.

http://www.seds.org/messier/m/m042.html. Accessed 2006. http://messier.seds.org/m/m042.html; accessed 2012.

http://www.theoi.com/Thrakios/Kotys.html; accessed 2012.

Astrogeographia Website: A Resource for Further Study

Astrogeographia website: www.astrogeographia.org

- Appendix 1: Mathematical and Astronomical Basis of Astrogeographia: A full treatment of all calculations and equations in this book is given in this 32-page online appendix
- Appendix 2: Earth's Weather and Earthquakes in Relation to the Planets and Stars

Links to both appendices are at:

www.steinerbooks.org/detail.html?id=9781584201335

Also at www.astrogeographia.org and www.sophiafoundation.org

CD of Computer Programs for Astrogeographical Research

Full details are available at:

sophiafoundation.org/activities/star-wisdom
/astrogeo-and-sinewave-cds-available-for-purchase

The two programs, ASTROGEO and SINEWAVE, are intended to be used as Astrogeographia research tools in conjunction with the present book.

Finding the answers to Astrogeographia research questions is greatly facilitated by these programs. They can easily compute what otherwise must be done as numerous time-consuming hand calculations. Pictures begin to build and insights are gained from the programs' output. When more precise research is suggested, it can be verified by calculating star data with full accuracy from an ephemeris.

The two programs are available from the Sophia Foundation. Follow the links from the home page of the Sophia Foundation:

www.sophiafoundation.org > Astrosophy > Star Wisdom >
Astrogeo and Sinewave CDs available for purchase.

You may also order a CD of these programs by calling the Sophia Foundation administrative office directly at (415) 522-1150, or by sending e-mail to sophia@sophiafoundation.org.

Please note: the ASTROGEO and SINEWAVE programs work with any 32-bit Windows operating system, but they DO NOT work with 64-bit Windows systems.

ASTROGEO program calculates a star's projection onto the Earth, or the reverse calculation of finding which star corresponds to a given place on Earth. It is based on the Astrogeographia equations of latitude and longitude described in the book, and can calculate these equations for any year in the range from 2950 BC to AD 2950. Accuracy over the 5,900 years is about 0.5°, which corresponds to 35 miles (56 km) on the surface of the Earth.

SINEWAVE program calculates a star's declination journey and also its latitude journey on the surface of the Earth over and beyond the 25,920 years of the Earth's precession cycle. It is based on the sinewave formulas described in the book, which can be calculated for any year from 25000 BC (or earlier) to AD 25000. Accuracy is to within several degrees over the 50,000 years. One degree of error corresponds to approximately 69 miles (111 km) on the surface of the Earth. Improving on the accuracy of the results is easy with the *Astrofire* Astrosophy computer program by manually stepping adjacent to the years indicated by the SINEWAVE program output.

About the Authors

ROBERT POWELL, Ph.D., is an internationally known lecturer, author, eurythmist, and movement therapist. He is founder of the Choreocosmos School of Cosmic and Sacred Dance, and cofounder of the Sophia Foundation of North America. He received his doctorate for his thesis *The History of the Zodiac,* available as a book from Sophia Academic Press. His published works include *The Sophia Teachings,* a six-tape series (Sounds True Recordings), as well as *Elijah Come Again: A Prophet for Our Time; The Mystery, Biography, and Destiny of Mary Madgalene; Divine Sophia—Holy Wisdom; The Most Holy Trinosophia and the New Revelation of the Divine Feminine; Chronicle of the Living Christ; Christian Hermetic Astrology; The Christ Mystery; The Sign of the Son of Man in the Heavens; The Morning Meditation in Eurythmy;* and the yearly *Journal for Star Wisdom* (previously *Christian Star Calendar*). He translated the spiritual classic *Meditations on the Tarot* and co-translated Valentin Tomberg's *Lazarus, Come Forth!* Robert is also coauthor with Kevin Dann of *The Astrological Revolution: Unveiling the Science of the Stars as a Science of Reincarnation and Karma* and *Christ & the Maya Calendar: 2012 and the Coming of the Antichrist;* and coauthor with Lacquanna Paul of *Cosmic Dances of the Zodiac* and *Cosmic Dances of the Planets.* He teaches a gentle form of healing movement: the sacred dance of eurythmy, as well as the *Cosmic Dances of the Planets* and signs of the zodiac. Through the Sophia Grail Circle, Robert facilitates sacred celebrations dedicated to the Divine Feminine. He offers workshops in Europe, Australia, and North America, and with Karen Rivers, cofounder of the Sophia Foundation, leads pilgrimages to the world's sacred sites: Turkey, 1996; the Holy Land, 1997; France, 1998; Britain, 2000; Italy, 2002; Greece, 2004; Egypt, 2006; India, 2008; Turkey, 2009; the Grand Canyon, 2010; and South Africa, 2012. Visit www.sophiafoundation.org and www.astrogeographia.org.

DAVID BOWDEN is a teacher of phenomenological physics and projective geometry and has taught at Orana School for Rudolf Steiner Education in Canberra, and the Mount Barker Waldorf School in Adelaide, Australia. He originally trained in electronics and telecommunications and is currently a researcher and a teacher of projective geometry and the new Goethean physics.

CPSIA information can be obtained
at www.ICGtesting.com
Printed in the USA
FFHW010118081218
49712535-54139FF

9 781584 201335